WEBER'S™
COMPLETE
BARBECUE
BOOK

Step-by-step advice and over 150 delicious barbecue recipes

BY JAMIE PURVIANCE

PHOTOGRAPHY BY TIM TURNER

hamlyn

An Hachette UK Company
www.hachette.co.uk

First published in Great Britain in 2010 by
Hamlyn, a division of Octopus Publishing Group Ltd
Endeavour House
189 Shaftesbury Avenue
London WC2H 8JY
www.octopusbooks.co.uk

Weber, the kettle configuration, 🍖 , RapidFire, and the kettle silhouette are registered trademarks; Smokey Mountain Cooker is a trademark; all of Weber-Stephen Products Co., 200 East Daniels Road, Palatine, Illinois 60067 USA.

Diamond Crystal® is a registered trademark of Cargill Incorporated, Wayzata, Minnesota; Dr. Pepper® is a registered trademark of Dr. Pepper/Seven Up, Inc., Plano, Texas.

ISBN 978-0-600-62111-9

A CIP catalogue record for this book is available from the British Library

Printed and bound in Italy

10 9 8 7 6 5

www.weber.com®

www.sunset.com

acknowledgements

The idea for this book emerged from the agile publishing minds of Mike Kempster, Susan Maruyama and Christina Schroeder. With the help of Jim Childs and Bob Doyle, they outlined an ambitious project and honoured me with the job of tackling it. I am grateful to each of them for their confidence and support.

When it came down to managing all the words and pictures here, Marsha Capen was a thoughtful and remarkably hard-working editor. She always found a gracious way to herd the flock of pigeons involved in this creative process.

The sheer quantity of photographs required for this book would strike fear into the hearts of many photographers, but Tim Turner, who is a master of light and lens (and quite a good griller, too), thrived on the challenge. He was assisted by a particularly talented crew, which included food stylists Lynn Gagné, Nina Albazi and Christina Zerkis, as well as photo assistants Takamasa Ota, Christy Clow, David Garcia and Justin Lundquist.

There is another excellent reason why the meat in this book looks so irresistibly fabulous. Almost all of it came from Lobel's of New York (www.lobels.com). Evan, Stanley, Mark and David Lobel, along with David Richards and all their colleagues, maintain standards so high for meat quality and customer service that whenever I open a box with Lobel's on the label, I am always delighted.

For the recipes, I relied on a sharp team of culinary minds. Many thanks to April Cooper, who handled most of the testing and tweaking, and thank goodness for the many other barbecuers involved, too. I especially want to acknowledge Patty Ada, Emily Baird, Gary Bramley, Neal Corman, Jerry DiVecchio, Ryan Gardner, John Gerald Gleeson, Joyce Goldstein, Gary Hafer, Jay Harlow, Rita Held, Susan Hoss, Ellen Jackson, Elaine Johnson, Carolyn Jung, Alison Lewis, James McNair, Andrew Moore, Merrilee Olson, Jeff Parker, David Pazimo, Craig Priebe, Anne-marie Ramo, Justin Roche, Rick Rodgers, James Schend, David Shalleck and Bob and Coleen Simmons.

I love what Shum Prats and Elaine Chow did with the design of this book, managing to strike a gorgeous balance between clear instructions and imaginative aesthetics.

I want to thank Weber's Creative Services department for improving the look of every last page. Thank you, Becky LaBrum, for a very useful index.

For lots of good advice and generous support all along, I offer special thanks to Sherry Bale, Brooke Jones, Nancy Misch and Sydney Webber.

While working on this book, I referred to many other books for solid culinary information. I found the following ones very helpful: *The Complete Meat Cookbook*, by Bruce Aidells and Denis Kelly; *The Cook's Illustrated Guide to Grilling and Barbecue*, by the editors of *Cook's Illustrated*; *The New Food Lover's Companion*, by Sharon Tyler Herbst; *The Barbecue Bible*, by Steven Raichlen; and *How to Cook Meat*, by Chris Schlesinger and John Willoughby.

In the final weeks of production, I had impeccable editing help from Sarah Putman Clegg and Carolyn Jung.

This book took me out of town for many days and nights, away from my wife, Fran, and our children, Julia, James and Peter. I missed some family holidays and quite a few weekends with the people that matter most to me. I owe them a lot for remaining patient and supportive throughout the whole process.

Finally, I want to thank a few mentors who gave a great deal of themselves to me early in my culinary career, Antonia Allegra, Esther McManus and Becky and David Sinkler. With selfless generosity, each one of them set me on the right course and encouraged me to get going.

CONTENTS

INTRODUCTION

I wasn't born with a complete understanding and mastery of barbecue techniques. As a kid growing up in suburban America, I had to pick up the basics from my dad and other weekend barbecuers. Eventually, when it was my turn to barbecue, I had to imitate what I'd seen and I had to develop my own style by doing what so many other barbecuers do. I had to experiment. I had to wing it. Sometimes it worked, and other times...well, it did not.

To be honest, I didn't really learn to barbecue until I was about thirty years old. That's when I tackled the subject in a much more methodical way. Obsessed with good food and frustrated by the limitations of winging it, I enrolled at the Culinary Institute of America. There I immersed myself in a rigorous curriculum of the hows and whys of topics like meat butchering, food chemistry, sauce making and charcuterie. Under the supervision of demanding chefs, I learned serious science-based lessons like how heat affects the structure of meats and fats, how sauces are held together and how marinades can unravel proteins.

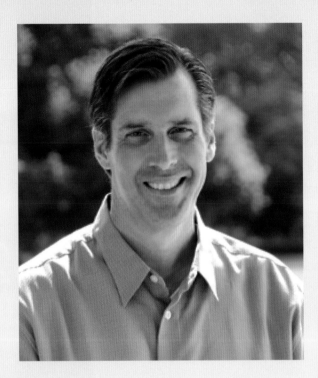

Since my graduation about fifteen years ago, I've focused my attention on how advanced culinary ideas relate to barbecuing. With the help of many experts at Weber, I've done extensive research on this particular way of cooking and I've written five books on the subject. Each book was an opportunity to learn more about what works on the barbecue and why some techniques work better than others. This book is a culmination of all the lessons I've learnt.

So what is the right way to barbecue? Well, first of all, there's not just one way to do it. It is not about absolute right and wrong when it comes to issues like gas versus charcoal, direct versus indirect heat, or barbecuing with the lid on or off. This book includes and embraces any way to barbecue – so long as it works. And what works best, I've learned, is paying attention to culinary details. There is a big difference between winging it and paying attention.

Let me share a couple of examples of what paying attention can do. The first deals with the reason why most steaks turn out beautifully when barbecued over direct high heat but most pork chops do not. Why should this be? High heat, of course, can char the surface of meat long before the centre is fully cooked. For a steak, that's a fine result, because you are left with a nicely caramelized outer crust and an interior that is dripping with rosy red juices. A pork chop is another matter. We don't like our pork chops raw in the middle, but if we barbecued most pork chops over direct high heat until the centres were properly cooked, the surfaces would be badly burned. That's why using medium heat is a better way to cook most pork chops. It allows the centres to reach an ideal degree of doneness without over-cooking the surfaces. Simple enough, right? But back in my early days, when I was winging it, I threw every kind of meat over the same high heat. That's one reason things did not always work out.

Successful barbecuing is about paying attention to details as basic and significant as salt.

A second example about the importance of paying attention deals with something quite fundamental: salt. Many of you might not give salt much thought, but did you know that, teaspoon for teaspoon, common table salt has about twice the sodium as some types of sea salt? So if you happened to use common table salt instead of the sea salt that I call for in almost every recipe in this book, I'm afraid your food will taste awfully salty (and a little metallic from calcium silicate found in common table salt). To take

this topic one step further, I suggest that you pay attention to which brand of sea salt you use. They are not all the same. I recommend Diamond Crystal® kosher salt (available from internet suppliers), because its salt crystals are hollow diamonds that dissolve easily on the surface of food, meaning the salt is less likely to fall off the food on the barbecue. On the other hand, there are sea salts on the market that are made of salt grains mixed with an anti-caking agent, which do not dissolve as well, and are high in sodium to boot. Read the labels carefully.

So, yes, culinary details matter. They explain why you would want to wrap barbecued ribs in foil during the final stages of cooking. They explain why you would grill fish fillets longer on the first side than the second. They explain why you would smoke a turkey with the breast side down.

That's why this book includes so many how-to photographs and explanatory captions and detailed recipes. The emphasis here is on paying close attention. It's about learning how and why certain methods work well, so you can move beyond the limits of winging it. Great taste lies in the details. Just pay attention and enjoy a new level of barbecuing success.

Jamie Purviance

BARBECUE BASICS

Barbecuing is so woven into the culture when the sun is shining that almost everyone has something to say about how to do it. All of us have had experiences that help us to be better barbecuers. I think what separates the master barbecuers from the beginners is really an understanding of the fundamentals. What follows here are the questions I hear again and again during my barbecuing classes. The answers make the biggest difference in anyone's ability to barbecue.

STARTING A CHARCOAL FIRE

Q: WHAT'S THE DIFFERENCE BETWEEN COOKING OVER A WOOD FIRE VERSUS A CHARCOAL FIRE? IS ONE BETTER THAN THE OTHER?

A: It's all about ease and time management. Barbecuing began over a wood fire, which imparts a wonderful flavour, but it has its drawbacks. A wood-log fire tends to create huge amounts of smoke and often requires waiting up to an hour or more for the flames to settle down and the embers to reach a manageable level of heat. Charcoal is essentially pre-burned wood, which means it reaches ideal barbecuing temperatures faster than wood and with much less smoke. It is made by slowly burning hardwood logs in an oxygen-deprived environment, like an underground pit or kiln. Over time, the water and resins are burned out of the logs, leaving behind big chunks of combustible carbon. These chunks are then broken into smaller lumps, hence the name lump charcoal. It's also known as 'charwood'.

Q: WHAT ABOUT BRIQUETTES? HOW ARE THEY DIFFERENT FROM LUMP CHARCOAL?

A: With many barbecuers, briquettes are more popular than lump charcoal. They are inexpensive and available practically everywhere. Most commonly, they are compressed black bundles of sawdust and coal, along with binders and fillers like clay and sodium nitrate. Some are presoaked in lighter fluid so they start easier, but they can impart a chemical taste to food if you don't completely burn off the lighter fluid before you begin cooking.

Standard briquettes don't burn as hot as lump charcoal and the amount of smoke produced is minimal at best. But they do produce predictable, even heat over a long period of time. A batch of 80 to 100 briquettes will last for about an hour, which is plenty of time to barbecue most foods without having to replenish the fire, whereas a pure lump-charcoal fire may provide only half as much barbecuing time before it requires more coals.

Q: ARE THERE ANY OTHER CHOICES?

A: Pure hardwood (or 'all-natural') briquettes are a great option, if you can find them. They have the same pillow shape of standard briquettes, but they burn at higher temperatures, and with none of the questionable fillers and binders. Usually, they are made of crushed hardwoods bound together with nothing but natural starches. You'll probably pay more for these coals, but many serious barbecuers and barbecue competitors consider them the gold standard of charcoal.

Q: IF SOMEONE IS ENTIRELY NEW TO CHARCOAL BARBECUING (AND MAYBE A LITTLE INTIMIDATED), WHAT'S THE BEST WAY TO GET STARTED?

A: My advice is to start by learning to light the charcoal safely and reliably using a chimney starter. This simple device consists of a metal cylinder with holes cut out along the bottom, a wire rack inside and two handles attached to the outside. Here's how to use the chimney. First, remove the top grate – or cooking grate – from your barbecue and place the chimney starter on the charcoal grate below. Next, place a couple sheets of wadded-up newspaper under the wire rack, fill the upper chamber of the cylinder with charcoal, and light the newspaper through the holes on the side. (As an alternative, use paraffin cubes in place of the newspaper.) The beauty of this method is that the chimney sucks the hot air up from the bottom and makes it circulate through the coals, lighting them much faster and more evenly than if you spread the coals out.

Lump charcoal will burn strong and be ready for barbecuing in about 15 minutes. Charcoal briquettes will take a little longer to light fully, generally 20 to 30 minutes.

When the charcoal is lightly coated all over with white ash (or lump charcoal is lit round the edges of all the pieces), it is ready to go. To empty it on to the charcoal grate, put on two insulated barbecue mitts or oven gloves. Grab hold of the heatproof handle in one hand and the swinging handle in the other. The swinging handle is there to help you lift the chimney and safely aim the contents just where you want them. For safety's sake, always wear insulated barbecue mitts or oven gloves when doing this. And never place a hot, empty chimney starter on the grass or a deck. Be sure to put it on a heatproof surface away from children and pets.

If you don't have a chimney starter, build a pyramid of coals on top of a few paraffin cubes, then light the cubes. When the coals in the middle are lit, use tongs to pile the unlit coals on top. When all the coals are glowing bright orange and covered with ash, arrange them the way you want them on the charcoal grate.

Q: ARE YOU SAYING I SHOULDN'T USE LIGHTER FLUID?

A: That's right. Lighter fluid is a petroleum-based product that can really ruin the flavour of your food. I know there are some people who grew up with the stuff and still think a hamburger is supposed to taste like petrol, but for the rest of us, we would never think of using it.

Q: HOW DO I KNOW HOW MUCH CHARCOAL TO USE?

A: That depends on the size of your barbecue and how much food you want to cook. Let's assume you have a classic 56-cm (22½-inch) diameter kettle barbecue and you are cooking for four to six people. The simplest way to measure the right amount of coals is to use your chimney starter. (See, aren't you glad you got one?) Use it like a measuring cup for charcoal. Filled to the rim (with 80 to 100 standard briquettes), a chimney starter will provide enough charcoal to spread in a single, tightly packed layer across about two-thirds of the charcoal grate. That's usually enough charcoal to cook a couple of courses for four to six people. If you plan on barbecuing for longer than 45 minutes, you will probably need to add more charcoal.

Because lump charcoal comes in irregular shapes and sizes, it is harder to pack tightly in a chimney starter. So do yourself a favour; after you have spread the burning lump charcoal across the charcoal grate, fill in any gaps by adding a few more fist-sized lumps to the fire. The bed of coals should extend at least 10 cm (4 inches) beyond every piece of food on the cooking grate above, to ensure that every piece of food cooks evenly.

Q: WHY WOULDN'T I FILL THE WHOLE CHARCOAL GRATE WITH BURNING COALS?

A: If you covered the entire grate with coals, then you would have only direct heat available to you. Everything on the cooking grate would be right on top of burning coals. That's fine for some foods like burgers and hot dogs, but a lot of other foods do best barbecued over both direct and indirect heat. Bone-in chicken pieces are a prime example. Have you ever seen what happens to them when they cook only over direct heat? They burn. The outside turns black before the meat along the bone has a chance to cook properly. The correct way to barbecue foods like this is to brown them for a while over direct heat and then move them over indirect heat to finish cooking.

Also, if the food being cooked over direct heat causes flare-ups, you have a convenient place to put the food while you figure out what to do next. At the very least, you can just close the lid and let the food finish cooking over indirect heat.

ARRANGING THE COALS

Q: WHAT EXACTLY IS THE DIFFERENCE BETWEEN DIRECT AND INDIRECT HEAT?

A: With direct heat, the fire is right below the food. With indirect heat, the fire is off to one side of the barbecue, or on both sides of the barbecue, and the food sits over an unlit part.

Direct heat works great for small, tender pieces of food that cook quickly, such as hamburgers, steaks, chops, boneless chicken pieces, fish fillets, shellfish and sliced vegetables. It sears the surfaces of these foods, developing flavours, texture and delicious caramelization while it also cooks the food all the way to the centre.

Indirect heat works better for larger, tougher foods that require longer cooking times, such as whole joints, whole chickens and ribs. As I mentioned, it is also just the right method for finishing thicker foods or bone-in cuts that have been seared or browned first over direct heat.

Q: DOES THE DIRECT METHOD COOK MY FOOD DIFFERENTLY FROM THE INDIRECT METHOD?

A: Yes. A direct fire creates both radiant heat and conductive heat. Radiant heat from the coals quickly cooks the surface of the food closest to it. At the same time, the fire heats the cooking grate rods, which conducts heat directly to the surface of the food and creates those unmistakable and lovely grill marks.

If the food is off to the side of the fire, or over indirect heat, the radiant heat and the conductive heat are still factors, but they are not as intense. If the lid of the barbecue is closed however, as it should be, there is another kind of heat generated: convective heat. It radiates off the coals, bounces off the lid and goes round and round the food. Convection heat doesn't sear the surface of the food the way radiant and conductive heat do. It cooks it more gently all the way to the centre, like the heat in an oven, which lets you cook joints, whole birds and other large foods to the centre without burning them.

 Q: ARE THERE ANY OTHER GOOD WAYS TO ARRANGE THE COALS?

A: The basic configuration I've described, with the coals to one side of the barbecue, is called a two-zone fire because you have one zone of direct heat and one zone of indirect heat. The temperature of a two-zone fire can be high, medium or low, depending on how much charcoal is burning and how long it has been burning. Remember, charcoal loses heat over time.

You also can create a three-zone fire, which provides even more flexibility. On one side of the barbecue, pile coals two or three briquettes deep. Then, slope the coals down to a single layer across the centre of the barbecue, and place no coals on the opposite side. When the coals are completely ashen and have burnt down for 10 to 20 minutes longer, after being emptied from the chimney – voila! – you have direct high heat on one side, direct medium heat in the centre and indirect heat on the opposite side.

There are also times when you might prefer a three-zone 'split' fire, where the coals are separated into two equal piles on opposite sides of the charcoal grate. This gives you two zones for direct heat (high, medium or low) and one zone between them for indirect heat. This works nicely for cooking a joint over indirect heat, such as pork loin or beef fillet, because you have the same level of heat on either side of the meat.

Q: WHAT'S THE RING OF FIRE?

A: It's another way of arranging charcoal for both direct and indirect heat. The ring of coals around the perimeter provides direct heat while the empty centre of the ring provides an area of indirect heat.

Q: WHAT'S THE BULL'S-EYE?

A: The bull's-eye is the flip side of the ring of fire. With the coals piled in the centre of the charcoal grate, you have a small area of direct heat, but a lot of area around the perimeter for indirect heat. This is a convenient arrangement for slow cooking or warming several small pieces of food, such as bone-in chicken pieces.

Q: WHAT'S THE PURPOSE OF A DRIP PAN ON A CHARCOAL GRATE?

A: The pan catches drippings, so it extends the life of your barbecue by keeping it clean. If you fill the pan with water, the water will absorb and release heat slowly, adding a bit of moisture to the cooking process.

JUDGING THE HEAT LEVEL

 HOW DO I KNOW I HAVE THE RIGHT LEVEL OF HEAT?

A : As soon as briquettes are lightly covered with grey ash (or lump charcoal is lit round the edges of all the pieces), and you've poured the coals on to the charcoal grate, you have very high heat, actually too high for almost any food to handle without burning quickly.

Spread the coals out the way you like, set the cooking grate in place and close the lid. It's important now to preheat the barbecue. You should do this for 10 to 15 minutes, to make the cooking grate hot enough for searing and to make it easier to clean. The heat will loosen all the little bits and pieces clinging to the cooking grate, left over from the last time you barbecued, and a barbecue brush will easily remove them.

There are two reliable ways to judge how hot a charcoal fire is. One is to use the thermometer in the lid of your barbecue, if there is one. With the lid closed, the temperature should climb past 260°C (500°F) initially. Then, once it has reached its peak, the temperature will begin to fall. You can begin grilling whenever the temperature has fallen into the desired range.

HEAT	TEMPERATURE RANGE	WHEN YOU WILL NEED TO PULL YOUR HAND AWAY
High	230° to 290°C (450° to 550°F)	2 to 4 seconds
Medium	180° to 230°C (350° to 450°F)	5 to 7 seconds
Low	130° to 180°C (250° to 350°F)	8 to 10 seconds

The second way is less technical but surprisingly reliable. It involves extending the palm of your hand over the barbecue at a safe distance above the charcoal grate. Imagine a soda can standing on the cooking grate, right over the coals. If your palm were resting on top of the can, it would be about 12 cm (5 inches) from the cooking grate. That's where you should measure the heat of charcoal.

If you need to pull your hand away after 2 to 4 seconds, the heat is high. If you need to pull your hand away after 5 to 7 seconds, the heat is medium. If you need to pull it away after 8 to 10 seconds, the heat is low. Use common sense and always pull your hand away from the heat before it hurts – you don't want to get burned.

Q: WHAT SHOULD I DO TO MAINTAIN THE HEAT FOR A LONG PERIOD OF TIME?

A: Under normal circumstances, a typical charcoal briquette fire will lose about 38°C (100°F) of heat over 40 to 60 minutes. A typical lump charcoal fire will lose heat even faster. To maintain the barbecue's temperature, you'll need to add new coals during cooking. If you are using standard briquettes, remember that they take 20 minutes or more to reach their highest heat, so plan accordingly. You'll have to add them 20 to 30 minutes before you need them. Alternatively, you can light the briquettes ahead of time in a chimney starter, keep them burning in a safe place and add them when you need instant results. For me, adding lit coals is a much better way to barbecue because I find the taste of food suffers when it absorbs the aromas of partially lit (standard) briquettes.

Lump charcoal and all-natural briquettes light faster than most standard briquettes so they require less lead time. Add them just 5 to 10 minutes before you need to raise the heat. Smaller pieces of lump charcoal will burn out quickly, so you will need to add them more often. Larger lumps will take a little more time to get hot, but they will last longer. Fortunately, lump charcoal and all-natural briquettes don't produce any unwanted aromas in the early stages of their burning.

For a fairly even fire, add about 10 to 15 briquettes, or an equivalent amount of lump charcoal, every 45 minutes to an hour.

Q: HOW SHOULD I WORK THE AIR VENTS ON MY BARBECUE?

A: The vents on the top and bottom of the barbecue control the airflow inside the barbecue. The more air flowing into the barbecue, the hotter the fire will grow and the more frequently you will have to replenish it. To slow the rate of your fire's burn, close the top vent as much as halfway and keep the lid on as much as possible. The bottom vent should be left open whenever you are barbecuing so you don't kill your fire.

All kinds of charcoal, especially briquettes made with fillers, will leave behind some ash after all the combustible carbon has burned. If you allow the ashes to accumulate on the bottom of the barbecue, they will cover the vent and starve the coals of air, eventually extinguishing them. So, every hour or so, give the vent a gentle sweep, to clear them of ashes, by opening and closing the bottom vent several times in a row.

sidebar
BARBECUE BASICS

STARTING A GAS BARBECUE

Q: WHAT'S THE PROCESS FOR LIGHTING A GAS BARBECUE?

A: There's nothing complicated about lighting a gas barbecue. However, gas barbecue operation does vary, so be sure to consult the owner's manual that came with your grill. To light a Weber® gas barbecue, first open the lid so unlit gas fumes don't collect in the cooking box. Next, slowly open the valve on your propane tank (or natural gas line) all the way and wait a minute for the gas to travel through the gas line. Then turn on the burners, setting them all to high. Close the lid and preheat the barbecue for 10 to 15 minutes.

Q: WHAT IF I SMELL GAS?

A: That might indicate a leak around the connection or in the hose. Turn off all the burners. Close the valve on your propane tank (or natural gas line) and disconnect the hose. Wait a few minutes and then reconnect the hose. Try lighting the barbecue again. If you still smell gas, shut the barbecue down and call the manufacturer.

DIRECT AND INDIRECT HEAT ON A GAS BARBECUE

Q: HOW DO I SET UP MY GAS BARBECUE TO COOK WITH DIRECT HEAT?

A: On a gas barbecue, simply leave all the burners on and adjust them for the heat level you want. For example, if you want direct medium heat, turn all the burners down to medium, close the lid and wait until the thermometer indicates that the temperature is in the range of 180° to 230°C (350° to 450°F). Then set your food on the cooking grate right over the burners. If your gas barbecue does not have a thermometer, use the 'hand test' (see page 15).

Q: WHAT'S THE SETUP FOR INDIRECT HEAT?

A: On a gas barbecue, you can switch from direct to indirect heat almost immediately. Just turn off one or more of the burners and place the food over an unlit burner. If your barbecue has two burners, turn off the one towards the back of the barbecue. If your barbecue has more than two burners, turn off the one(s) in the middle. The burners that are left on can be set to high, medium or low heat, as desired. Whenever the food is over an unlit burner and the lid is closed, you're cooking over indirect heat.

BARBECUE KNOW-HOW

Q: DO I NEED TO CLEAN THE COOKING GRATES EVERY TIME I USE THE BARBECUE?

A: You really should clean the grates every time, not only to be tidy, but also because any residue left on the cooking grates may cause your food to stick. You will find that food releases from the grates much more easily, and with more impressive grill marks, if the cooking grates are clean.

The easiest way to clean your cooking grates is to preheat the barbecue, with the lid down, to about 260°C (500°F). Then, while wearing an insulated barbecue mitt or oven glove, use a long-handled barbecue brush to scrape off any bits and pieces that may be stuck to the cooking grates.

Q: WHAT ABOUT CLEANING THE REST OF THE BARBECUE?

A: Once a month or so, you should do a more thorough cleaning of your barbecue. Be sure to read the instructions in your owner's manual beforehand. Wipe down the barbecue with a sponge and warm, soapy water. Scrape off any debris that has accumulated under the lid. Remove the cooking grates, brush the burners and clean out the bottom of the cooking box and the drip pan. For full care and upkeep instructions, consult your owner's manual. With charcoal barbecues, remember that ash naturally has a small amount of water in it. Don't leave it sitting in your barbecue for a long period of time; it can rust some parts of your barbecue.

Q: DO I NEED TO OIL THE COOKING GRATES BEFORE I BARBECUE?

A: I do not recommend it. Many barbecuers do, and that's fine, but keep in mind that oil will drip though the cooking grates and may cause flare-ups on both charcoal and gas barbecues. You can avoid wasting oil and improve your chances of a food releasing more easily by oiling the food, not the grates.

Q: WHAT SHOULD I DO IF FLARE-UPS HAPPEN?

A: A certain number of flare-ups are to be expected. When oil and fat drip into a hot barbecue, especially a charcoal barbecue, they tend to produce flames. If the flames are barely reaching the surface of the food and then they subside, don't worry about it. If, however, the flames are rising through the cooking grates and surrounding your food, you need to act quickly. Otherwise, the foods will pick up a sooty taste and colour, and could burn.

On a charcoal barbecue, most flare-ups begin within a few seconds of putting food on the barbecue, or right after you turn food over. Your first reaction should be to put the lid on the barbecue and close the top vent about halfway. By decreasing the amount of air getting to the fire, you may extinguish a flare-up. You can check the status of the flare-up by carefully looking through the partially open vent. If the flames are still threatening, open the lid and move the food over indirect heat. That's one very important reason why you should always have an indirect heat zone available. After a few seconds, the oil and fat will usually burn off and the flare-up will subside. When the flare-up dies down, resume cooking your food over direct heat.

You are less likely to have flare-ups with a gas barbecue because many of them have a system that prevents fat and oil from falling directly onto the burners. For example, most Weber® gas barbecues have angled steel bars on top of the burners. Not only do they prevent almost all flare-ups, they also transform dripping juices and fat into wonderfully aromatic smoke. The solutions to flare-ups on a gas barbecue are the same as they are on a charcoal barbecue. First, make sure the lid is closed. Then, if necessary, move the food over indirect heat.

Q: WHEN SHOULD I BARBECUE WITH THE LID ON?

A: As often as possible. Whether using a charcoal barbecue or a gas barbecue, the lid is really important. It limits the amount of air getting to the fire, thus preventing flare-ups, and it helps to cook food on the top and bottom simultaneously. While the bottom of the food is almost always exposed to more intense heat, the lid reflects some heat down and speeds up the overall cooking time. Without the lid, the fire would lose heat more quickly and many foods would take much longer to cook, possibly drying out. Plus, using the lid keeps the cooking grate at a higher

temperature, giving you more conductive heat, which creates better searing and caramelization. Finally, the lid traps all those good smoky aromas inside the barbecue and surrounds your food with them. Otherwise, the smoke will drift away and serve no real purpose. One exception to this rule occurs when you are barbecuing very thin pieces of food, like bread slices and tortillas. They cook (and potentially burn) so quickly that it's wise to leave the lid off and watch them carefully.

A: If you want to cook large hunks of meat – like pork loins, whole chickens, turkey, duck and beef joints – a rotisserie attachment is a good investment. Any of those meats can be barbecued right on the cooking grate over indirect heat, but the advantage of a rotisserie is that the food slowly self-bastes as it rotates and absorbs the flavours of the fire.

To ensure that the meat stays in place as it turns and cooks uniformly, use butcher's string to truss your food into a compact shape. Then secure the food on the spit, making sure it is centred as evenly as possible. This will put less strain on the motor. Always preheat the barbecue first. When ready to cook, set the spit in place, put a disposable foil tin underneath the roast to catch the grease, turn on the motor and close the lid.

Q: SO WHAT SHOULD I BUY: A CHARCOAL OR GAS BARBECUE?

A: That decision depends a lot on what kind of barbecuer you are. There are some barbecuers who put a high priority on enjoying the food as quickly, cleanly and conveniently as possible. For them, a gas barbecue makes the most sense. The fire is ready in 10 to 15 minutes. The temperature stays right where you need it for as long as you need it, and clean-up is minimal. Then there are some barbecuers who relish the opportunity to build their own fires and tend the coals. Glowing embers and wood smoke thrill them so much that charcoal barbecuing is well worth the extra time and cleanup required. They believe with every last taste bud that the flavour of food cooked over a live fire is better. So, you tell me: which type of barbecuer are you?

SMOKING AND BARBECUING

Q: SUPPOSE I WANT TO TRY SMOKING FOODS. HOW DO I DO THAT?

A: Congratulations, you get a gold star. Every barbecuer ought to try smoking with hardwoods. Done right, it lends food an irresistible flavour.

Smoking on a kettle barbecue is really easy to do, especially if you are already comfortable barbecuing with indirect heat. Begin by filling a chimney starter about one-third full with briquettes. When they are fully lit, pour all of the charcoal on one side of the cooking grate (if desired, use a charcoal basket, which holds the coals close together so they burn more slowly) and place an aluminium foil tin on the other side. Then, carefully add about 600 ml (1 pint) of water to the tin. The water in the tin is important because it helps to maintain a low cooking temperature. It also adds some moisture to the food, which in many cases will cook for hours and hours, so it could dry out otherwise. Allow 30 minutes to 1 hour for the coals to burn down to the correct

temperature and the water to heat up. Next, drop damp wood chips or dry wood chunks directly onto the coals. Then place your food on top of the cooking grate over the water pan and cover your barbecue. Expect to add more coals every hour or so to maintain the heat.

Wood chips, even when they have been soaked in liquid, will smoke sooner than wood chunks, but they often burn out in a matter of minutes. Wood chunks tend to burn for an hour or more. I suggest using chunks and positioning them on the outer edge of a charcoal fire to prolong and extend smoking times even further.

You've got a lot of options in the hardwoods category, including the most popular ones: oak, hickory and mesquite. Of those, mesquite has the strongest aroma, so be careful about using too much of it for too long. In fact, be careful about using too much of any kind of wood. A common rookie mistake is to keep adding wood throughout hours and hours of cooking. The aromas of the smoke can eventually overpower the food, so start with just a few handfuls, then stop. Next time, if you want a little more smokiness, add an additional handful or two.

In my opinion, oak and hickory complement beef, lamb and pork really well. Milder woods pair nicely with milder foods, for example, apple wood, pecan and alder with chicken and fish. Don't worry about using the 'wrong' wood for any kind of food. It's almost impossible to make a mistake here. Some people latch on to a favourite kind of wood and use it to smoke almost anything. That's fine. The differences between the hardwoods are pretty subtle.

But please don't add soft, resinous woods like pine, cedar and aspen to your fire. They create an acrid (and sometimes toxic) smoke. And never use any wood that has been treated with chemicals.

Q: IF SMOKING IS USUALLY DONE WITH LOW TEMPERATURES, HOW DO I GET MY KETTLE BARBECUE TO DO THAT?

A: Many foods are smoked and simultaneously cooked in the temperature range of 130° to 180°C (250° to 350°F). You can maintain the correct level of heat by controlling the amount of charcoal and the airflow. This is why you begin the fire with a chimney filled only about one-third full with charcoal (about 30 briquettes). Adding 10 to 15 briquettes (or an equivalent amount of lump charcoal) every hour or so will help to maintain the temperature. So will opening and closing the vents on the lid. Opening the vents will help the fire burn faster and hotter. Closing them partially (not all the way, or you might put out the fire) will restrict the airflow and drop the temperature. Having a thermometer on the lid is very helpful here.

Q: CAN I SMOKE FOOD WITH A GAS BARBECUE?

A: Yes, some of today's gas barbecues come equipped with a metal smoker box that sits on top of a dedicated burner. Just turn on the burner and add as many wood chips as you like. You can control how quickly they smoke by turning the knob of the burner higher or lower. Some of the boxes have a separate compartment for water, which will provide a steaming effect on the food, too.

A: A water smoker allows you to smoke meat at temperatures well below 150°C (300°F) for many hours. The Weber version is basically an upright bullet-shaped unit with three sections. The charcoal burns in the bottom section. For smoky barbecue aromas, add a few fist-sized chunks of hardwood to the coals right from the beginning. The meat will absorb the smoke best when it is uncooked.

The water sits in a pan in the middle section, preventing any fat from dripping on to the coals and, more importantly, keeping the temperature nice and low. The meat sits on one or two racks in the top section.

A water smoker has vents on both the bottom and top sections. Generally, it's a good idea to leave the top vent wide open so that smoke can escape. Use the bottom vents as your primary way of regulating the temperature. The less air you allow into the smoker, the lower the temperature will go.

Generally speaking, if the ring in the bottom section of the smoker is filled with lit charcoal, and the water pan is nearly filled, the temperature will stay in the range of 110° to 130°C (225° to 250°F) for 4 to 6 hours. This is an ideal range for barbecuing food like pork ribs, turkeys and large beef joints.

When you see that very little smoke is coming out of the top vent, add another chunk or two through the door on the side. Wood chunks burn slowly and evenly, so they are a better choice than wood chips in this situation. For cooking sessions longer than 6 hours, you will probably need to add more charcoal occasionally. The timing will depend on your type of charcoal and how fast it burns. If you are using charcoal made with unnatural fillers, you may want to light the briquettes in a chimney starter first; some people can taste 'off' flavours in food cooked over unlit briquettes.

During long cooking times, also be sure to replenish the water pan every few hours with warm water. But keep the lid on the smoker as much as possible. That's critical for maintaining even heat.

MUST-HAVE TOOLS

Once you have a good barbecue that allows you to control the fire easily and cook your food over both direct and indirect heat, it's time to equip yourself with the right tools. I've broken down my recommendations into two groups. The first ten tools are essential for most tasks. The other ten will make many jobs a lot easier.

TONGS

Oh, the tongs. Definitely the hardest working tool of all. You will need one pair to load raw food on the barbecue and move it around. You will need another pair (clean tongs that haven't touched any raw meat, fish or poultry) to remove the barbecued food. Dedicate a third pair for rearranging charcoal.

BARBECUE BRUSH

Spring for a solid, long-handled model with stainless-steel bristles. Use the brush to clean off the grates before and after barbecuing, and you will eliminate many problems with food sticking to the grates. And your food won't taste like last night's dinner. Replace the brush when the bristles wear down to about one-half their original length.

GRILL PAN

At first I didn't see the wisdom of a grill pan, but I came around on the issue when I saw (and tasted) how well a perforated grill pan can handle delicate fish fillets and small foods like chopped vegetables that might otherwise fall through the cooking grate. If you preheat a stainless-steel grill pan properly, it will brown the food nicely and allow the smokiness from the barbecue to flavour the food.

CHIMNEY STARTER

Brilliantly simple, a chimney starter lets you start the coals faster and more evenly than you could with lighter fluid. And who needs all those chemicals in lighter fluid? Look for a chimney starter with a capacity of at least 5 litres (8 pints) of briquettes, roughly 80 to 100 pieces. Also, it should have two handles: a heatproof side handle for lifting the chimney and a hinged top handle to provide support when dumping hot coals onto the charcoal grate.

4

5

INSTANT-READ THERMOMETER

You only have to overcook a fine cut of meat once to learn the importance of a good digital thermometer. Small and relatively inexpensive, an instant-read thermometer is essential for quickly gauging the internal temperature of the meat. To get the most accurate read, insert it into the thickest part of the cut and avoid touching any bone, because the bone conducts heat.

ROASTING TRAY

I learned the value of a sturdy roasting tray when I was in culinary school, where there were dozens within reach in every kitchen. A shallow tray, like the one pictured here, is a great portable work surface for oiling and seasoning food, and there's nothing better to use as a landing pad for food coming off the barbecue.

6

7

BASTING BRUSH

In the past, basting brushes were made of wooden/plastic handles and synthetic/natural-boar bristles. Today you can find them made of stainless steel with silicone bristles that have beads at the tips to help load the brush with a sauce or marinade. While most old-style brushes had to be hand washed, this new high-tech style can go right into the dishwasher. Nice.

BARBECUE MITTS

You'll need these to shield your hand and forearm when managing a charcoal fire or reaching towards the back of any hot barbecue. You will probably put them through the wash a lot, so invest in mitts or oven gloves of good-quality materials and workmanship. Silicone barbecue mitts are easy to care for because you can just wipe them off when they get dirty, but insulated cloth mitts will give better dexterity.

SPATULA

Look for a long-handled spatula or fish slice designed with a bent (offset) neck so that the blade is set lower than the handle. This will make it easier to lift food off the barbecue without hitting your knuckles. The blade should be at least 10 cm (4 inches) wide; you'll need a longer blade for turning whole fish.

SKEWERS

Bamboo skewers are simple and inexpensive, though they need to be soaked in water for at least 30 minutes prior to loading, in order to keep the wood from burning. If you don't want the hassle, use metal skewers, or freeze bamboo skewers in a bag after soaking them (see page 155). The flat metal skewers and double-pronged ones are nice because they prevent the food from spinning when you turn the skewers.

NICE TO HAVE TOOLS

TIMER

As the old saying goes, timing is everything. It's never truer than when you are trying to pull off a perfect meal at the barbecue. A rotary kitchen timer is adequate, but you can also ante up for a more elaborate digital timer, preferably one that lets you track a couple of barbecuing times simultaneously.

WIRELESS MEAT THERMOMETER

While an instant-read thermometer is a must-have, a wireless thermometer is a cool little luxury. It's a high-tech gadget that monitors the temperature of meat using a wireless probe. You can walk away from the barbecue and a remote beeper will tell you when your food is ready.

SMALL SHOVEL

Seeing this tool on the list might surprise you, but a small shovel is really helpful for pushing charcoal around. You can buy a shovel specifically for the task at a barbecue retailer, or buy a small shovel (one with no plastic parts) from a hardware, DIY or garden shop.

ROTISSERIE

It's true that you can roast a chicken, turkey or pork loin on the barbecue without a rotisserie, but there is something wonderfully medieval about food spinning over a fire. Many people also argue that the rotisserie causes the meat to self-baste while cooking. I agree that food comes out juicier, so I am pro-rotisserie.

DISPOSABLE TINS

Available in large and small sizes, disposable foil tins offer many conveniences. Use them to move food to and from the barbecue, keep food warm on the cooking grate, soak wood chunks in them or set them under the cooking grate to catch drippings and keep a charcoal barbecue clean.

CAST-IRON FRYING PAN

A big cast-iron frying pan allows you to make favourites in this book, like paella, gingerbread and a stunning pineapple upside-down cake. Once it gets hot on the barbecue, you can sauté, stew or pan-roast just about anything in it without ever worrying that the pan will discolour or deteriorate. It will last you forever.

RESEALABLE PLASTIC BAGS

Marinating foods in plastic bags allows you to force some of the marinade up and over the food, particularly when you set a bag snugly in a bowl, giving you better coverage and faster marinating times. Resealable bags also avoid dreaded spills in your refrigerator.

RIB RACK

This wire rack holds multiple slabs of ribs upright so that heat circulates around the ribs, cooking them evenly, and it encourages the pork fat to drip down and away from the ribs. Plus, it frees up space on the cooking grates for barbecuing other food at the same time.

FISH BASKET

Many people resist barbecuing fish, especially whole fish, for fear that it will stick and fall apart on the cooking grate. For them, there are hinged baskets that provide one degree of separation from the cooking grate, which makes turning a cinch. Using one of these sure beats the alternative of cooking the fish inside the house and smelling it for days.

MICROPLANE GRATER

This is terrific at grating garlic, whole nutmeg and hard cheeses. It's even better used to zest citrus fruits. You'll see Microplane graters in several shapes and sizes. I prefer the long, thin one shaped like a paint brush.

RED MEAT

TECHNIQUES

RECIPES

HOW TO BARBECUE BURGERS
THINGS YOU NEED TO KNOW

1 WHAT MAKES THEM JUICY

Fat makes burgers juicy. That's a big reason why minced chuck (from the shoulder) is better for burgers than minced round (from the rump). Chuck is typically about 18 per cent fat, whereas round is often down around 12 per cent fat. The reality is that most minced beef in supermarkets comes from all kinds of parts of the animal, but that shouldn't stop you from asking the person behind the counter to mince some chuck just for you, maybe mixing in some sirloin for extra flavour.

2 SEASONING WORKS

Minced beef alone makes a pretty dull-tasting hamburger, so make sure that the meat is mixed throughout with at least salt and pepper. Other ingredients, like Worcestershire sauce, hot sauce or grated onions, will improve not only the taste but also the juiciness of your hamburgers.

3 SHAPING UP

The ideal thickness for a raw patty is 1.5 cm (¾ inch). If it's any thinner, it's likely to overcook and dry out before a nice crust develops on the outside. If it's much thicker, the crust might turn black and unappetizing before the centre reaches the safe internal doneness level of medium.

4 LEVELING OFF

Burgers tend to puff up in the centre as they cook, making the tops rounded and awkward for piling on the toppings. A good trick for avoiding this problem is pressing a little indentation into the top of each raw burger with your thumb or the back of a spoon. Then, when the centre pushes up, the top of each burger will be relatively level.

5 FLIPPING ONLY ONCE

You should flip each burger only once, and only when it's ready to flip. You'll know when by slipping the edge of a spatula or fish slice underneath the edge of the burger and lifting up very gently. If the meat is sticking to the cooking grate, back off and try again a minute later. When you can lift the edge of the burger without sticking, it's ready to flip.

CLASSIC PATTY MELTS ON RYE

SERVES: 6
PREP TIME: 25 MINUTES

HEAT: DIRECT HIGH HEAT 230° TO 290°C (450° TO 550°F)
AND DIRECT MEDIUM HEAT 180° TO 230°C
(350° TO 450°F)
GRILLING TIME: 11 TO 13 MINUTES

3 tablespoons rapeseed or other vegetable oil
2 large yellow onions, halved and thinly sliced
½ teaspoon sugar
Sea salt
50 g (2 oz) unsalted butter, softened
12 slices crusty rye bread, each about 8 mm (⅓ inch) thick
1 kg (2 lb) minced chuck
2 tablespoons Worcestershire sauce
½ teaspoon freshly ground black pepper
125 g (4 oz) Havarti or Emmental cheese, grated
Dijon or spicy brown mustard, optional

1. Warm the oil in a large frying pan over a medium heat.
Add the onions, sprinkle with the sugar, cover and cook for
15 to 20 minutes, stirring occasionally, until the onions are
tender and golden brown. Season to taste with salt, then
remove from the heat.

2. Butter the bread on each side and set aside.

3. Prepare the barbecue for direct cooking over a high heat. Mix
the minced chuck with the Worcestershire sauce, 1 teaspoon
of salt and the pepper in a large bowl, incorporating the spices
evenly. Gently shape into 6 equal-sized burgers, each about
1.5 cm (¾ inch) thick. With your thumb or the back of a spoon,

make a shallow indentation about 2.5 cm (1 inch) wide in the
centre of each burger.

4. Brush the cooking grates clean. Cook the burgers over **direct
high heat** for 8 to 10 minutes, with the lid closed as much as
possible but turning once. Transfer the burgers to a work surface.

5. Lower the temperature of the barbecue to medium heat. Grill
the bread slices over **direct medium heat** for about 1 minute
until toasted on one side only. Transfer the bread, toasted sides
up, to a work surface.

6. Evenly divide the caramelized onions on 6 of the toasted
bread slices and top each with a burger. Scatter the cheese over
the tops and place the remaining bread slices, toasted sides
down, on top of the burgers. Using a fish slice, carefully place
the patty melts back on to the cooking grate and grill over **direct
medium heat** for about 1 minute until the bread on the bottom
is toasted, and then carefully turn the sandwiches and toast the
other side. Serve the patty melts warm with mustard, if desired.

*The sturdy texture of
crusty rye bread
holds up well under
the weight of all the
wonderfully messy
ingredients in a
patty melt.*

CALIFORNIA BURGERS WITH GUACAMOLE MAYONNAISE

SERVES: 4
PREP TIME: 25 MINUTES

HEAT: DIRECT HIGH HEAT 230° TO 290°C (450° TO 550°F)
GRILLING TIME: 18 TO 20 MINUTES

MAYONNAISE
2 tablespoons grated white onion
1 ripe Haas avocado, stoned and peeled
2 tablespoons mayonnaise
2 plum tomatoes, cored, deseeded and chopped
1 tablespoon finely chopped fresh coriander
2 teaspoons fresh lime juice
1 small garlic clove, grated
Sea salt

2 poblano chillies
750 g (1½ lb) minced chuck
1½ teaspoons sea salt
1 teaspoon freshly ground black pepper

4 hamburger buns

1. Rinse the grated onion in a sieve under cold water and allow the excess water to drain off. Mash the avocado and mayonnaise together in a bowl with a fork. Stir in the onion, tomatoes, coriander, lime juice and garlic, then season generously with salt. Cover with clingfilm, pressing the film directly on to the surface, and set aside. (The mayonnaise can be prepared up to 8 hours ahead.)

2. Prepare the barbecue for direct cooking over a high heat. Brush the cooking grates clean. Cook the chillies over **direct high heat** for about 10 minutes, with the lid closed as much as possible but turning occasionally, until the skin has blackened on all sides. Remove them from the barbecue and allow them to cool completely. Peel off and discard the blackened skin, and then remove and discard the stem, seeds and ribs. Chop the chillies into 1-cm (½-inch) dice.

3. Mix the minced chuck, chillies, salt and pepper together in a large bowl, then shape into 4 equal-sized burgers, each about 1.5 cm (¾ inch) thick. With your thumb or the back of a spoon, make a shallow indentation about 2.5 cm (1 inch) wide in the centre of each burger so the centres are about 1 cm (½ inch) thick. This will help the burgers cook evenly and prevent them from puffing on the barbecue.

4. Grill the burgers over **direct high heat** for 8 to 10 minutes, with the lid closed as much as possible, turning once when the burgers release easily from the grate without sticking, until cooked to medium. During the last minute of cooking time, toast the buns, cut sides down, over a direct heat. Top the burgers with the mayonnaise and serve warm.

HOW TO SPICE UP MAYONNAISE

1. Tame the sharp flavour and crunch of raw onion in your mayonnaise by grating the onion on the medium-sized holes of a grater, then rinse the grated onion in a sieve for a mild taste.

2. A Microplane grater with tiny holes will quickly make a paste out of fresh garlic.

3. Swipe the paste right off the back side of the grater and into your mayonnaise.

CABERNET BURGERS WITH ROSEMARY FOCACCIA

SERVES: 4
PREP TIME: 25 MINUTES

HEAT: DIRECT HIGH HEAT 230° TO 290°C (450° TO 550°F)
AND DIRECT MEDIUM HEAT 180° TO 230°C
(350° TO 450°F)
GRILLING TIME: 10 TO 14 MINUTES

GLAZE
500 ml (17 fl oz) Cabernet Sauvignon wine
1 tablespoon light brown sugar

BUTTER
50 g (2 oz) unsalted butter, softened
1 tablespoon very finely chopped fresh rosemary leaves

BURGERS
750 g (1½ lb) minced chuck
4 tablespoons Cabernet glaze (above)
2 teaspoons sea salt
½ teaspoon freshly ground black pepper

4 slices Cheddar cheese
8 slices ripe tomato, each about 1 cm (½ inch) thick
Extra-virgin olive oil
Sea salt
4 focaccia squares, each about 11 cm (4½ inches),
sliced in half horizontally, or 4 focaccia buns, split
100 g (3½ oz) rocket leaves

4 thick rashers cooked, crisp bacon

Thanks to a red wine reduction, the burger on the left has improved dramatically in flavour, moisture and appearance.

1. Combine the wine and brown sugar in a heavy-based saucepan over a medium heat and cook for 20 to 25 minutes until reduced to 125 ml (4 fl oz). Set aside to cool.

2. Mix the butter and rosemary together in a small bowl.

3. Prepare the barbecue for direct cooking over a high heat. Combine the burger ingredients in a large bowl and shape into 4 equal-sized burgers, each about 1.5 cm (¾ inch) thick. With your thumb or the back of a spoon, make a shallow indentation about 2.5 cm (1 inch) wide in the centre of each burger.

4. Brush the cooking grates clean. Barbecue the burgers over **direct high heat** for 8 to 10 minutes with the lid closed as much as possible. Brush with the glaze every 2 minutes and turn them once when the burgers release easily from the grate without sticking, until cooked to medium. During the last minute of cooking, place a slice of cheese on each burger to melt.

5. Lower the temperature of the barbecue to a medium heat. Brush the tomato slices with oil, season to taste with salt and cook over **direct medium heat** for 2 to 4 minutes, turning once, until soft. Spread the cut sides of the focaccia with the rosemary butter and heat over **direct medium heat** for about 1 minute, cut sides down, until lightly toasted. Assemble each burger with rocket, a burger, a rasher of bacon and 2 slices of tomato. Serve warm.

BRIE AND SHALLOT PARISIAN BURGERS

SERVES: 4
PREP TIME: 30 MINUTES

HEAT: DIRECT HIGH HEAT 230° TO 290°C (450° TO 550°F)
GRILLING TIME: 8 TO 10 MINUTES

150 g (5 oz) shallots, thinly sliced
2 tablespoons extra-virgin olive oil

BURGERS
1½ pounds minced chuck
3 tablespoons fine dried breadcrumbs
3 tablespoons beef or chicken stock
1 teaspoon sea salt
½ teaspoon freshly ground black pepper

50 g (2 oz) Brie cheese (not the triple cream variety)
4 round crusty rolls, each about 10 cm (4 inches)
    in diameter
75 g (3 oz) wholegrain mustard
100 g (3½ oz) rocket leaves, to serve

1. Combine the shallots with the oil in a frying pan over a low heat, and cook for about 20 minutes, stirring often until they are browned but not scorched. Allow to cool to room temperature.

2. Prepare the barbecue for direct cooking over a high heat. Mix the burger ingredients together in a large bowl, then shape into 4 equal-sized burgers, each about 1.5 cm (¾ inch) thick. Make a hole in the centre of each burger for the cheese.

3. Trim away the rind of the Brie and bury the cheese, about 15 g (½ oz) for each burger, into the hole of each. Close the opening to seal the cheese inside. It's important that there is 8 mm (⅓ inch) of meat on the top and bottom of the cheese so it doesn't seep out during barbecuing.

4. Brush the cooking grates clean. Barbecue the burgers over **direct high heat** for 8 to 10 minutes, with the lid closed as much as possible, until cooked to medium, but turning once when the burgers release easily from the grate without sticking. During the last minute of cooking time, toast the buns, cut sides down, over a direct heat.

5. Assemble the burgers with shallots, mustard and rocket. Serve warm.

HOW TO MAKE 'OUTSIDE-IN' CHEESEBURGERS

A fun way to turn a cheeseburger outside-in is by nestling a little knob of cheese in the centre and letting it soften slowly while the burger barbecues.

1. Trim off any unwanted rind.

2. Cut the pieces small enough so that the cheese won't seep out of the burger.

3. Nestle each piece right in the centre of each burger.

4. Seal each burger tightly to enclose the cheese completely.

KOFTA IN PITTA POCKETS WITH CUCUMBER AND TOMATO SALAD

SERVES: 6
PREP TIME: 25 MINUTES

HEAT: DIRECT AND INDIRECT HIGH HEAT
    230° TO 290°C (450° TO 550°F)
GRILLING TIME: 8 TO 10 MINUTES

DRESSING
125 g (4 oz) natural Greek yogurt
125 g (4 oz) sesame tahini
15 g (½ oz) fresh coriander or mint leaves,
    or a combination, finely chopped
3 tablespoons fresh lemon juice
2 tablespoons extra-virgin olive oil
½ teaspoon sea salt

SALAD
175 g (6 oz) cherry tomatoes, quartered
100 g (3½ oz) cucumber, chopped
40 g (1½ oz) red onion, finely chopped
Sea salt

KOFTA
750 g (1½ lb) minced chuck
25 g (1 oz) flat leaf parsley, very finely chopped
1 tablespoon very finely chopped garlic
2 teaspoons ground coriander
1½ teaspoons ground cumin
1½ teaspoons sea salt
½ teaspoon freshly ground black pepper
½ teaspoon ground allspice
¼ teaspoon ground cardamom
¼ teaspoon ground turmeric

Extra-virgin olive oil
3 wholewheat pittas

1. Combine the dressing ingredients in a small bowl. If the dressing is too thick, whisk in up to 3 tablespoons of water until your desired consistency is reached.

2. Combine the salad ingredients in another bowl, including salt to taste.

3. Prepare the barbecue for direct and indirect cooking over a high heat. Combine the kofta ingredients in a large bowl and shape into 6 equal-sized koftas, each about 1.5 cm (¾ inch) thick. With your thumb or the back of a spoon, make a shallow indentation about 2.5 cm (1 inch) wide in the centre of each kofta, then brush them with oil.

4. Sprinkle the pittas with water and wrap them in foil.

5. Brush the cooking grates clean. Barbecue the koftas over **direct high heat** for 8 to 10 minutes, with the lid closed as much as possible but turning once when they release easily from the grate without sticking, until medium. While they cook, warm the pitta pockets over **indirect high heat** for 4 to 5 minutes, turning once.

6. Cut each pitta in half. Scoop about 3 tablespoons of the salad into each pitta. Spoon some of the dressing over the salad. Place a kofta into each pitta pocket and spoon in more dressing, if desired. Serve warm.

HOW TO SEASON KOFTA

1. The bold flavours of this dish rely on a panoply of international ingredients.

2. Kofta refers to any kind of ground meat mixed with grains, vegetables or spices.

3. Pressing a shallow indentation in each kofta prevents the meat from puffing up like a meatball during cooking.

As with any type of burger, the key to keeping this one flat instead of puffed up is to make a shallow indentation in the meat while it is raw. During the last minute of barbecuing, scatter crumbled goats' cheese on top so that it oozes a little into the burger.

LAMB BURGERS WITH TAPENADE AND GOATS' CHEESE

SERVES: 6
PREP TIME: 25 MINUTES

HEAT: DIRECT HIGH HEAT 230° TO 290°C (450° TO 550°F)
GRILLING TIME: 8 TO 10 MINUTES

TAPENADE
1 garlic clove
75 g (3 oz) stoned kalamata olives
75 g (3 oz) stoned green olives
2 tablespoons small capers, rinsed
2 tablespoons extra-virgin olive oil
½ teaspoon Dijon mustard
½ teaspoon dried herbes de Provence

1.1 kg (2¼ lb) minced lamb
½ teaspoon dried herbes de Provence
½ teaspoon sea salt
½ teaspoon freshly ground black pepper
150 g (5 oz) goats' cheese, crumbled
6 hamburger buns
3 plum tomatoes, thinly sliced

1. Fit a food processor with the metal chopping blade. With the machine running, drop the garlic through the feed tube and very finely chop. Add the rest of the tapenade ingredients and pulse until coarsely chopped. (The tapenade can be made, and then covered and refrigerated, for up to 1 week ahead. Bring to room temperature before serving.)

2. Prepare the barbecue for direct cooking over a high heat. Mix the lamb, herbs, salt and pepper together in a large bowl, then shape in to 6 equal-sized burgers, each about 10 cm (4 inches) across and 1.5 cm (¾ inch) thick. With your thumb or the back of a spoon, make a shallow indentation about 2.5 cm (1 inch) wide in the centre of each burger.

3. Brush the cooking grates clean. Barbecue the burgers over **direct high heat** for 8 to 10 minutes, with the lid closed as much as possible but turning once until medium. During the last minute of cooking, top each burger with the cheese to allow the cheese to soften, and toast the buns.

4. Assemble the burgers with tomato slices and tapenade. Serve warm.

LAMB MEATBALLS WITH CHOPPED SALAD AND MINTED YOGURT

SERVES: 6
PREP TIME: 30 MINUTES

HEAT: DIRECT MEDIUM-HIGH HEAT
    ABOUT 200°C (400°F)
GRILLING TIME: 4 TO 6 MINUTES
SPECIAL EQUIPMENT: METAL OR BAMBOO SKEWERS (IF
    BAMBOO, SOAK IN WATER FOR AT LEAST 30 MINUTES)

SALAD
4 tablespoons extra-virgin olive oil
2 tablespoons red wine vinegar
1 teaspoon finely grated lemon rind
2 teaspoons very finely chopped garlic
3 large plum tomatoes, deseeded and diced
½ cucumber, deseeded and diced
½ small red onion, finely diced
40 g (1½ oz) feta cheese, crumbled
15 g (½ oz) flat leaf parsley, chopped
½ teaspoon sea salt
¼ teaspoon freshly ground black pepper

MEATBALLS
750 g (1½ lb) ground lamb
1 tablespoon very finely chopped garlic
2 teaspoons ground cumin
1 teaspoon sea salt
½ teaspoon freshly ground black pepper

Extra-virgin olive oil

SAUCE
375 g (12 oz) natural Greek yogurt
2 tablespoons fresh lemon juice
15 g (½ oz) mint leaves, coarsely chopped
½ teaspoon sea salt

4–6 naans

1. Whisk the oil, vinegar, lemon rind and garlic together in a large non-metallic bowl. Add in the rest of the salad ingredients and gently toss with the dressing.

2. Mix all the meatball ingredients in a bowl. Do not overwork the mixture or the meatballs will be tough. Shape about 24 meatballs. Thread 4 meatballs on to each skewer and lightly brush with oil.

3. Prepare the barbecue for direct cooking over a medium-high heat.

4. Combine the yogurt and lemon juice in a small bowl. Fold in the mint and season with the salt.

5. Brush the cooking grates clean. Grill the meatballs over **direct medium-high heat** for 4 to 6 minutes, with the lid closed as much as possible but turning occasionally, until they have browned but are still slightly pink in the centre. During the last 30 seconds of barbecuing time, heat the naan over a direct heat.

6. Cut the naan in half, or into pieces large enough to hold 4 meatballs. Top with a generous spoonful of sauce and some salad.

Skewering these meatballs allows you to turn 4 of them at a time, rather than having to turn them individually. Skewers are ready to turn only when the meat releases from the cooking grate without any sticking.

HOW TO BARBECUE MEAT LOAF

1. Light panko breadcrumbs hold these meat loaves together without making them dense.

2. Check the internal temperature near the top because that part takes the longest to cook.

3. To remove each meat loaf in one whole piece, support both ends with fish slices.

BARBECUED MEAT LOAF

SERVES: 8 TO 10
PREP TIME: 20 MINUTES

HEAT: INDIRECT MEDIUM-LOW HEAT
  ABOUT 150°C (300°F)
GRILLING TIME: 50 TO 60 MINUTES
SPECIAL EQUIPMENT: INSTANT-READ THERMOMETER

MEAT LOAF
625 g (1¼ lb) minced beef
625 g (1¼ lb) minced pork
125 g (4 oz) panko breadcrumbs
150 g (5 oz) yellow onion, finely chopped
1 egg
1 teaspoon Worcestershire sauce
1 teaspoon garlic granules
1 teaspoon dried tarragon
1 teaspoon sea salt
1 teaspoon freshly ground black pepper

SAUCE
125 ml (4 fl oz) bottled barbecue sauce
65 g (2½ oz) ketchup

1. Gently combine the meat loaf ingredients using your hands in a large bowl.

2. Divide the meat loaf mixture in half and form into 2 loaves, each about 10 cm (4 inches) wide and 15 to 18 cm (6 to 7 inches) long. Place the loaves on a roasting tray. Prepare the barbecue for indirect cooking over a medium-low heat.

3. Mix the sauce ingredients in a small bowl. Set aside half of the sauce to serve with the meat loaf. Top each meat loaf with 3 tablespoons of the remaining sauce and coat thoroughly.

4. Brush the cooking grates clean. Pick up each loaf from the roasting tray with a metal fish slice, and place directly on the cooking grate. Grill the meat loaves over ***indirect medium-low heat*** for 50 to 60 minutes, with the lid closed, until a thermometer inserted horizontally through the top of each loaf registers 68°C (155°F). Remove the loaves from the barbecue and allow to rest for 10 to 15 minutes. Once removed from the barbecue, the loaves will continue to cook, allowing them to reach the 70°C (160°F) recommended for minced beef and pork. Cut the loaves into 1-cm (½-inch) slices and serve with the reserved sauce.

TO MAKE MEAT LOAF SANDWICHES
Cut the meat loaf into 1-cm (½-inch) slices and slather both sides with some of the reserved sauce. Barbecue over ***direct low heat***, 130° to 180°C (250° to 350°F), with the lid closed as much as possible but turning once, for 4 to 6 minutes. Serve on sourdough bread. This is also great with melted provolone cheese.

'TUBE STEAKS' WITH PICKLED ONIONS

SERVES: 8
PREP TIME: 15 MINUTES
MARINATING TIME: 2 TO 3 HOURS

HEAT: DIRECT MEDIUM HEAT 180° TO 230°C
   (350° TO 450°F)
GRILLING TIME: 5 TO 7 MINUTES

PICKLED ONIONS
1 small white or yellow onion
1 small red onion
125 ml (4 fl oz) cider vinegar
125 ml (4 fl oz) distilled white vinegar
100 g (3½ oz) sugar
1 tablespoon sea salt
2 teaspoons celery seeds
1 teaspoon crushed red chilli flakes

8 all-beef hot dogs, about 125 g (4 oz) each
8 hot dog buns
Mustard
Ketchup

1. Trim off the ends of the onions. Cut each onion in half lengthways, then with a very sharp knife cut the onions into paper-thin slices and place in a shallow, non-metallic dish. Combine the remaining onion ingredients in a bowl and whisk thoroughly until the sugar and salt have dissolved. Pour the vinegar mixture over the onions and stir to coat them evenly. Set aside at room temperature for about 3 hours, stirring occasionally. Drain the pickled onions and set aside.

2. Using a sharp knife, cut a few shallow slashes in each hot dog.

3. Prepare the barbecue for direct cooking over a medium heat. Brush the cooking grates clean. Barbecue the hot dogs over **direct medium heat**, with the lid closed as much as possible, until lightly marked on the outside and hot all the way to the centre, for 5 to 7 minutes, turning occasionally.

4. Place the hot dogs in buns. Squeeze your condiment of choice alongside each hot dog and top with pickled onions. Serve warm.

HOW TO PICKLE ONIONS

1. Peel and halve the onions, and make sure the root and stem ends are completely removed.

2. Cut the onions into paper-thin slices, place them in a shallow glass dish and pour the pickling liquid over them.

3. Stir to coat them evenly and set aside to marinate for about 3 hours.

HOW TO BARBECUE STEAK

THINGS YOU NEED TO KNOW

1 SALTING EARLY PAYS OFF

You might have heard the warning that you shouldn't salt meat too far ahead of cooking because it can draw out moisture. It's true that salt draws moisture towards itself, but over the course of 20 to 30 minutes that's a good thing, because the salt begins to dissolve into that little bit of moisture. When the steak hits the hot cooking grate, the sugars and proteins in the moisture combine with the salt and other seasonings to create a delicious crust. Any moisture you might lose is well worth the flavour of that crust.

2 TAKING OFF THE CHILL SPEEDS UP COOKING

The goal of barbecuing a steak is to brown and lightly char the surface while also cooking the interior to a perfectly juicy doneness, right? If the steak is too cold, the interior might require so much cooking time to reach that perfect doneness that the steak overcooks deep below the surface, turning grey and dry. Allow your steaks to stand at room temperature for 20 to 30 minutes before barbecuing. They will cook faster all the way to the centre and stay juicier.

3 SEARING EQUALS FLAVOUR

One good habit that separates professional chefs from many home cooks is that chefs spend more time searing their steaks. They understand that searing develops literally hundreds of flavours and aromas on the surface of steak, so they allow their steaks to sizzle over a direct heat until the surfaces are dark, dark brown. Don't allow anyone to tell you that searing 'locks in the juices'. That's a myth. But searing does make steak tasty.

4 THICKER STEAKS SHOULD SLIDE OVER

Most steaks barbecue beautifully over direct high heat alone. The only time you might need to move them is if/when they cause flare-ups. Some steaks, however, are so thick that if you left them over a direct heat alone, they would burn on the outside before they reached the internal doneness you like. If your steaks are much thicker than 2.5 cm (1 inch), consider the sear-and-slide approach. After you have seared both sides nicely over direct high heat, slide the steaks to a part of the barbecue that is not so hot, perhaps over indirect heat, and finish cooking them safely there.

5 YOU CAN'T PUT MOISTURE BACK INSIDE A STEAK

As steaks grill over a high heat, they lose moisture. Fat and juices are literally pushed out of the meat. That's the price we pay for making the steaks easier to digest. Perhaps the most important part of barbecuing a steak is taking it off the heat before it has lost too much moisture. There is a short window of time, usually just a minute or two, when steaks go from medium rare to medium, or from medium to medium well. Catching that window requires vigilance. Don't walk away from a steak on the barbecue. And remember, it's always better to take it off when it's underdone and then return it to the barbecue than it is to let a steak overcook.

1. Buying a whole sirloin is a great way to save money on steaks.

2. You'll need to trim away most of the thick 'fat cap' on the top side.

3. Next, remove the long section of scraggy meat and fat on the thinnest edge.

4. Cutting the sirloin yourself allows you to make the steaks just the right thickness.

5. After cutting the steaks, go back and trim the fat around the outer edges to about 5 mm (¼ inch).

6. Grill some of the steaks now and freeze the remaining ones for another day. (For how to freeze steaks, see page 296.)

RED MEAT

HOW TO PREP AND BARBECUE SIRLOIN STEAKS

1. Lean sirloins benefit from the rich flavour and slickness of extra-virgin olive oil.

2. Rub the oil evenly all over the steaks to prevent them from sticking to the cooking grate.

3. The oil also helps the seasonings adhere to the meat.

4. Sometimes coarse salt and freshly ground pepper are all you need for a great-tasting steak.

5. Bring the barbecue temperature to 260°C (500°F). A hot cooking grate will sear the steaks quickly.

6. Once the cooking grates are smoking hot, they are easy to clean with a stainless-steel bristle brush.

7. Lay each steak on the cooking grate over a high heat as if it were the small hand of a clock pointing to 10 o'clock, then close the lid.

8. After a couple of minutes, lift each steak with tongs – not a fork! Piercing the steaks would mean losing delicious juices.

9. Rotate the steaks so that they point to 2 o'clock, close the lid and allow them to sear for another minute or two.

10. Flip each steak and check out those handsome cross-hatch grill marks.

11. Putting cross-hatches on the second side is optional. The key now is to finish the steaks, with the lid down, without overcooking them. An internal doneness of 52°C (125°F) will give you a medium-rare steak.

12. As the steaks rest for a few minutes after grilling, the internal temperature will climb several degrees and the juices w redistribute evenly.

Occasionally the fat and juices dripping from a steak will cause flare-ups on the barbecue. Don't panic. Simply slide the steak to a cooler area of the grate. If your steak already has good charring on both sides, finish cooking it over indirect heat, with the lid closed. If you want more charring, slide the steak back over a high heat once the flare-ups have died out.

SIRLOIN STEAKS WITH RED-EYE BARBECUE SAUCE

SERVES: 4
PREP TIME: 20 MINUTES

HEAT: DIRECT HIGH HEAT 230° TO 290°C (450° TO 550°F)
GRILLING TIME: 6 TO 8 MINUTES

SAUCE
15 g (½ g) unsalted butter
2 teaspoons very finely chopped shallot
1 teaspoon very finely chopped garlic
137 g (4½ oz) ketchup
4 tablespoons brewed dark-roast coffee or espresso
1 tablespoon balsamic vinegar
1 tablespoon light brown sugar
2 teaspoons ground ancho chilli powder

4 sirloin steaks, each 300 to 375 g (10 to 12 oz) and about
    2.5 cm (1 inch) thick, trimmed of excess fat
2 tablespoons extra-virgin olive oil
¾ teaspoon sea salt
¾ teaspoon freshly ground black pepper

1. Melt the butter in a saucepan over a medium heat. Add the shallot and cook for about 3 minutes, stirring often, until it begins to brown. Add the garlic and cook for about 1 minute until fragrant. Stir in the rest of the sauce ingredients and bring to a simmer. Reduce the heat to low and simmer for about 10 minutes, stirring often, until slightly reduced. Transfer to a bowl to cool.

2. Lightly brush the steaks on both sides with the oil and season evenly with the salt and pepper. Allow the steaks to stand at room temperature for 20 to 30 minutes before grilling. Prepare the barbecue for direct cooking over a high heat.

3. Brush the cooking grates clean. Grill the steaks over **direct high heat**, with the lid closed as much as possible but turning once, until cooked to your desired doneness, 6 to 8 minutes for medium rare. Remove from the barbecue and allow the steaks to rest for 3 to 5 minutes. Serve the steaks warm with the sauce on the side.

Grilled red onions make a great addition to a steak sandwich, and here they benefit from soaking twice in a bold sweet-and-sour marinade: once before grilling and once afterwards.

STEAK SANDWICHES WITH GRILLED ONIONS AND CREAMY HORSERADISH SAUCE

SERVES: 4
PREP TIME: 15 MINUTES
MARINATING TIME: 30 MINUTES

HEAT: DIRECT HIGH HEAT 230° TO 290°C (450° TO 550°F) AND
    DIRECT MEDIUM HEAT 180° TO 230°C (350° TO 450°F)
GRILLING TIME: 7 TO 9 MINUTES

MARINADE
500 ml (17 fl oz) red wine
200 ml (8 fl oz) soy sauce
4 tablespoons balsamic vinegar
3 tablespoons dark brown sugar
1 tablespoon finely chopped garlic
1 teaspoon freshly ground black pepper
125 ml (4 fl oz) extra-virgin olive oil

½ teaspoon bicarbonate of soda

4 sirloin steaks, each about 375 g (12 oz) and about
    2.5 cm (1 inch) thick
2 red onions, sliced into 5-mm (¼-inch) rings

125 ml (4 fl oz) soured cream
4 tablespoons prepared horseradish
1 teaspoon finely chopped thyme
Sea salt
Freshly ground black pepper

4 French rolls
2 bunches watercress, trimmed and rinsed

1. Combine the marinade ingredients in a large bowl, whisking in the oil until blended. Divide the marinade, pouring 750 ml (1¼ pints) into a non-metallic ovenproof dish and leaving the rest in the bowl. Add the bicarbonate of soda to the marinade in the dish for a tenderizing effect (the mixture may fizz a little).

2. Put the steaks into the dish with the marinade and turn to completely coat them. Allow them to marinate at room temperature for 30 minutes, turning once.

3. Place the sliced onions in the bowl with the marinade and gently stir to coat them evenly. Set aside and allow them to marinate alongside the steaks.

4. Mix the soured cream and horseradish in a bowl, then stir in the thyme and season to taste with salt and pepper. Cover and refrigerate until ready to use.

5. Prepare the barbecue for direct cooking over a high heat on one side of the barbecue and a medium heat on the other. Brush the cooking grates clean. Remove the steaks from the dish, allowing most of the marinade to drip back into the dish. Discard the marinade. Grill the steaks over **direct high heat**, with the lid closed as much as possible but turning once, until cooked to your desired doneness, 6 to 8 minutes for medium rare. While the steaks are grilling, carefully remove the onions from the marinade, keeping the bowl of marinade close by, and grill the onions over **direct medium heat** for 6 to 8 minutes, turning once. Remove the onions from the barbecue and plunge back into the bowl of marinade. Toss to coat and allow the onions to soak up the marinade while the steaks rest for 3 to 5 minutes. Slice and toast the cut sides of the rolls over **direct medium heat**, for about 1 minute.

6. To assemble the sandwiches, slice the steaks on the bias into thin strips. Pile the bottom of a French roll with onions and layer with strips of steak. Top with horseradish sauce and watercress.

HOW TO CHECK STEAKS FOR DONENESS

1. Because steaks get firmer as they grill, one way to judge their doneness is by lightly squeezing the sides with tongs. It takes time to learn just how firm each type of steak will feel at each level of doneness, but this is how many restaurant chefs work, and it's a technique worth practising.

2. Another popular method is to press the surface of a steak with your fingertip. When the meat is no longer soft, but is not yet firm either, you know a steak has reached medium-rare doneness. See below for more hints on judging doneness by touch.

3. A more scientific approach is to use an instant-read thermometer. If you are sure to position the thermometer sensor right in the middle of the steak, you'll have a perfectly accurate reading of doneness.

4. Perhaps the most straightforward approach is to have a look at the colour of the meat inside the steak. On the underside of the steak (the side that will face the plate), cut a little slit down to the centre of the meat and peek inside. When it's cooked just the way you want it, turn the steak over and press the surface with your fingertip. Note how it feels so that next time you won't need to cut into your steak.

HOW TO CHECK DONENESS BY TOUCH

1. Most raw steaks are as soft as the base of your thumb when your hand is relaxed.

2. If you touch your index finger and thumb together, and then press the base of your thumb, that's how most steaks feel when they are rare.

3. If you touch your middle finger and thumb together, and then press the base of your thumb, that's how most steaks feel when they are medium rare.

PANZANELLA STEAK SALAD

SERVES: 4 TO 6
PREP TIME: 20 MINUTES

HEAT: DIRECT AND INDIRECT HIGH HEAT 230° TO 290°C
(450° TO 550°F)
GRILLING TIME: 12 TO 16 MINUTES
SPECIAL EQUIPMENT: BAMBOO SKEWERS,
SOAKED IN WATER FOR AT LEAST 30 MINUTES

DRESSING
3 tablespoons red wine vinegar
1 teaspoon sea salt
1 teaspoon freshly ground black pepper
2 teaspoons very finely chopped garlic
125 ml (4 fl oz) extra-virgin olive oil

2 sirloin steaks, each about 375 g (12 oz) and 2.5 cm
(1 inch) thick, trimmed of excess fat
275 g (8 oz) crusty bread, cut into 3.5-cm (1½-inch) cubes
6 plum tomatoes, about 750 g (1½ lb), cut in half
lengthways and deseeded
1 medium yellow onion, cut into 1-cm (½-inch) slices
150 g (5 oz) cup oil-cured black olives, drained and stoned
50 g (2 oz) basil leaves, torn into pieces

1. Combine the dressing ingredients in a small bowl, gradually
whisking in the oil until it has emulsified.

2. Put the steaks in a shallow dish, pour 3 tablespoons of the
dressing on top, and turn to coat them evenly. Allow them to
stand at room temperature for 20 to 30 minutes before grilling.
Set aside the remaining dressing.

3. Put the bread cubes into a large bowl, add 2 tablespoons of
the dressing and toss to coat them evenly. Thread the bread
cubes on to skewers. Brush the cut sides of the tomatoes and
the onion slices with 2 tablespoons of the dressing.

4. Prepare the barbecue for direct and indirect cooking over a
high heat.

5. Brush the cooking grates clean. Grill the tomatoes and onions
over **direct high heat** and the bread skewers over **indirect high
heat**, with the lid closed as much as possible, but turning as
needed, until the tomatoes are lightly charred, the onions are
browned and the bread is toasted. The tomatoes will take 2 to
4 minutes and the onions and bread skewers will take 6 to
8 minutes. Remove the food from the barbecue as it is done.

6. Brush the cooking grates clean. Grill the steaks over **direct high
heat**, with the lid closed as much as possible but turning once,
until cooked to your desired doneness, 6 to 8 minutes for medium
rare. Remove from the barbecue and let rest for 3 to 5 minutes.

7. Pull off and discard the tomato skins. Cut the onion, tomatoes
and steak into bite-sized chunks, then place in a large serving
bowl. Add the remaining dressing, olives, bread cubes and basil
and gently mix. Serve immediately.

HOW TO PREP PANZANELLA STEAK SALAD

1. Toss big cubes of dense bread
in salad dressing for flavour and
even browning.

2. Skewer the bread cubes to
make them easier to handle on the
barbecue.

3. Firm but ripe plum tomatoes
maintain their shape even when
you lightly char them.

4. Grilling the bread cubes
over an indirect heat allows you to
brown them slowly, with little
risk of burning.

SIRLOIN STEAK PAILLARDS

SERVES: 4
PREP TIME: 20 MINUTES

HEAT: DIRECT HIGH HEAT 230° TO 290°C (450° TO 550°F)
GRILLING TIME: ABOUT 3 MINUTES

4 sirloin steaks, each 200 to 250 g (7 to 8 oz) and
    1 to 1.5 cm (½ to ¾ inch) thick, trimmed of all fat
    and silver skin
Extra-virgin olive oil
Sea salt
Freshly ground black pepper

DRESSING
4 tablespoons soured cream
4 tablespoons mayonnaise
2 tablespoons Dijon mustard
½ teaspoon Worcestershire sauce

1 beefsteak tomato, about 375 g (12 oz), cut into
    4 even slices
4 thin slices red onion
50 g (2 oz) triple cream cheese, cut into thin wedges,
    at room temperature

1. One at a time, place each steak between 2 sheets of
clingfilm and pound to an even 5-mm (¼-inch) thickness.
Lightly brush the paillards with oil and season them evenly
with salt and pepper.

2. Combine the dressing ingredients in a small bowl, including
salt to taste.

3. Prepare the barbecue for direct cooking over a high heat.

4. Lightly brush each tomato slice with oil and season to taste
with salt and pepper. Brush the cooking grates clean. Grill the
tomatoes over **direct high heat** for 2 to 3 minutes until slightly
charred on one side. Transfer to a roasting tray, grilled sides up.

5. Grill the paillards over **direct high heat** for 1½ to 2 minutes,
with the lid open and turning when the first side is nicely
marked. The second side will only take 10 to 15 seconds for
medium-rare doneness (the paillards will continue to cook as
they rest).

6. Transfer the paillards, with the first grilled sides facing up, to
a serving platter or individual plates. Place a slice of tomato in
the centre of each paillard.

7. Evenly divide the dressing over the tomatoes. Separate the
slices of onion into rings and place a small mound on the
tomatoes. Finish with a piece of cheese and a grinding of
pepper on top of each.

Three stages of a steak paillard. On the left, a sirloin just as
you find it at the butcher's. In the centre, a steak trimmed
of all the fat around the edges, to make it easier to pound.
On the right, an evenly pounded paillard ready for greasing,
seasoning and grilling.

HOW TO BUTCHER A BONE-IN RIB JOINT

Many chefs and carnivores will tell you that their favourite steak for barbecuing is a rib-eye. The meat is magnificently tender and flavourful, due in large part to the generous interior marbling of milky white fat. Sadly, though, many supermarket butchers cut rib-eyes too thin, so the steaks tend to overcook rather quickly, squandering some of their magnificence. One solution is to cut your own rib-eyes from a bone-in rib roast, also known as a prime rib.

1. Use a long, sharp knife to cut right along the ribs, separating them from the meat.

2. Now cut along the bone at the base of the joint to separate the meat from the bones completely.

3. Don't throw away those ribs. Barbecue them! See page 85.

4. Trim off most of the surface fat from your boneless rib roast.

5. At this point, you could grill the whole boneless joint in one piece for a big event (see page 91), or you can slice it into thick steaks and freeze the ones you don't use right away. (For how to freeze steaks, see page 296.)

6. Use the blade of a carving knife to measure a consistent thickness for each steak.

7. Make a shallow slit at each point where you plan to slice.

8. Slice the steaks as evenly as possible. Avoid sawing back and forth, which tears the surface of the meat and gives the steaks a ragged appearance.

HOW TO PREP RIB-EYE STEAKS

1. As with any steak, trim off any sections along the edges that include more fat than meat.

2. A flavourful cut like rib-eye requires no marinade or elaborate sauce, but consider using a bold blend of dry seasonings as a complement to the meat's richness.

3. With so much marbling in the steak, just a light coating of oil is all you'll need to prevent sticking on the barbecue.

4. Allow your seasoned steaks to stand at room temperature for 20 to 30 minutes before cooking to take the chill off. They will cook a little faster and stay juicier.

RIB-EYE STEAKS
WITH ESPRESSO-CHILLI RUB

SERVES: 4
PREP TIME: 10 MINUTES

HEAT: DIRECT HIGH HEAT 230° TO 290°C (450° TO 550°F)
GRILLING TIME: 6 TO 8 MINUTES
SPECIAL EQUIPMENT: SPICE MILL

RUB
2 teaspoons cumin seeds, toasted
2 tablespoons dark-roast coffee or espresso beans
1 tablespoon ground ancho chilli
1 teaspoon sweet paprika
1 teaspoon sea salt
1 teaspoon freshly ground black pepper

4 rib-eye steaks, each about 250 g (8 oz) and 2.5 cm (1 inch) thick
Extra-virgin olive oil

1. Grind the cumin seeds and coffee beans together in a spice mill. Transfer to a small bowl, add the remaining rub ingredients and stir to combine.

2. Lightly brush the steaks with oil and season evenly with the rub, pressing the rub into the meat. Cover and allow to stand at room temperature for 20 to 30 minutes before grilling. Prepare the barbecue for direct cooking over a high heat.

3. Brush the cooking grates clean. Grill the steaks over **direct high heat**, with the lid closed as much as possible but turning once, until cooked to your desired doneness, 6 to 8 minutes for medium rare. (If flare-ups occur, move the steaks temporarily over indirect high heat.) Remove from the barbecue and allow to rest for 3 to 5 minutes. Serve warm.

HOW TO PREP ESPRESSO-CHILLI RUB

1. A coffee grinder works well for grinding spices, too. Clean it out later by whirling raw white rice in it to absorb the spice residue.

2. Grind your cumin and coffee to a coarse texture, similar to that of sea salt.

HOW TO MAKE PAN-ROASTED CHILLI SALSA

1. The distinctive flavour of the salsa on the opposite page comes mostly from an ancho chilli, which is a dried poblano chilli. It is not terribly spicy, but it has a brilliant sweet heat, especially when it is toasted first.

2. Cut off and discard the stem of the chilli, then slice open the chilli so that you can lay it flat like a book.

3. A lot of the heat is in the seeds, so tap the chilli on a board or use a knife to remove them, if you like.

4. Use a fish slice to flatten the chilli in a hot, dry frying pan. This step brings out big flavour. Next, soak the chilli in hot water for 20 to 30 minutes.

5. You can blacken and blister tomatoes, onions, a jalapeño chilli and garlic in the same pan. Don't be afraid to get them dark and caramelized.

6. Puréeing all the ingredients with some fresh lime juice, salt and oregano gives you an exciting salsa to serve with steaks. If it seems a little thick, thin it out with a touch of the water used to soak the ancho chilli.

RIB-EYE STEAKS WITH PAN-ROASTED CHILLI SALSA

SERVES: 4
PREP TIME: 20 MINUTES

HEAT: DIRECT HIGH HEAT 230° TO 290°C (450° TO 550°F)
GRILLING TIME: 6 TO 8 MINUTES
SPECIAL EQUIPMENT: 30-CM (12-INCH) CAST-IRON PAN

SALSA
1 dried ancho chilli
1 tablespoon extra-virgin olive oil
4 ripe tomatoes, quartered, with stalks and seeds removed
1 slice white onion, about 1.5 cm (¾ inch) thick
1 jalapeño chilli, stem removed
1 large garlic clove (do not peel)
1 teaspoon fresh lime juice
½ teaspoon sea salt
¼ teaspoon dried oregano

RUB
1 tablespoon sea salt
2 teaspoons paprika
1 teaspoon onion granules
1 teaspoon freshly ground black pepper

4 rib-eye steaks, each about 250 g (8 oz) and 2.5 cm
(1 inch) thick
Extra-virgin olive oil

1. Bring 500 ml (17 fl oz) water to a simmer in a small saucepan. Preheat a 30-cm (12-inch) cast-iron or ovenproof frying pan over a medium heat on your side burner or hob.

2. Remove and discard the stem from the ancho chilli, then open like a book and discard the seeds. Flatten the chilli and place it in the hot, dry pan. Press down on the chilli with a fish slice to flatten it and dry fry until the aroma is obvious and you begin to see wisps of smoke. Transfer the chilli to the pan of hot water and soak for 20 to 30 minutes until it is very soft. Reserve the water; you may need a little to thin out the salsa.

3. Meanwhile, add the oil, tomatoes, onion, jalapeño and garlic to the pan and fry over a medium heat for 10 to 15 minutes, turning occasionally, until the vegetables have blackened and blistered in spots. Remove the vegetables as they are finished cooking (they may not finish cooking at the same time). Allow them to cool until you can handle the garlic, then squeeze the garlic out of its skin into a blender or food processor. Add the ancho chilli, tomatoes, onion, jalapeño, lime juice, salt and oregano and process to make a salsa. For a thinner consistency, add a little of the water used to soak the ancho chilli.

4. Mix the rub ingredients together in a small bowl. Lightly brush the steaks on both sides with oil. Season evenly with the rub. Allow the steaks to stand at room temperature for 20 to 30 minutes before grilling. Prepare the barbecue for direct cooking over a high heat.

5. Brush the cooking grates clean. Grill the steaks over **direct high heat**, with the lid closed as much as possible but turning once until cooked to your desired doneness, 6 to 8 minutes for medium rare. (If flare-ups occur, move the steaks temporarily over indirect high heat.) Remove from the barbecue and allow to rest for 3 to 5 minutes. Serve warm with the salsa.

RED MEAT

55

HOW TO BARBECUE PIADINI

1. Your dough should be at room temperature and you should have flour on both your board and your rolling pin.

2. Roll each piece of dough to a diameter of 20 to 25 cm (8 to 10 inches) and a thickness of about 8 mm (⅓ inch). Stack the dough rounds between sheets of parchment paper.

3. Grill the dough rounds over direct medium heat, with the lid closed, until they bubble on top and turn gold brown on the bottom. Then turn them over with a fish slice to toast the other side.

4. While the second side grills, distribute the cheese on top so that it begins to melt. Rotate each dough round and move it around the barbecue as needed for even cooking.

STEAK AND GORGONZOLA PIADINI

SERVES: 4
PREP TIME: 30 MINUTES
RISING TIME: 1½ TO 2 HOURS

HEAT: DIRECT HIGH HEAT 230° TO 290°C (450° TO 550°F)
   AND DIRECT MEDIUM HEAT 180° TO 230°C
   (350° TO 450°F)
GRILLING TIME: 14 TO 18 MINUTES
SPECIAL EQUIPMENT: ELECTRIC STAND MIXER

DOUGH
350 ml (12 fl oz) warm water (40° to 93°C/100° to 110°F)
1 sachet fast-action dried yeast
½ teaspoon sugar
625 g (1¼ lb) strong plain white flour, plus more for rolling
   the dough
3 tablespoons extra-virgin olive oil
2 teaspoons sea salt

DRESSING
2 tablespoons extra-virgin olive oil
2 teaspoons balsamic vinegar
½ teaspoon very finely chopped garlic
½ teaspoon Dijon mustard
¼ teaspoon sea salt
⅛ teaspoon freshly ground black pepper

2 rib-eye steaks, each 175 g to 250 g (6 to 8 oz) and about
   2.5 cm (1 inch) thick
Extra-virgin olive oil
Sea salt
Freshly ground black pepper
250 g (8 oz) gorgonzola dolce or other soft, mild blue cheese,
   broken into small pieces
75 g (3 oz) baby rocket or spinach

1. Combine the water, yeast and sugar in the bowl of an electric stand mixer. Stir briefly and allow to stand for 5 minutes, or until the top surface has a thin, frothy layer. (This indicates that the yeast is active.) Add the flour, the oil and salt. Fit the mixer with the dough hook and mix on low speed for about 1 minute or until the dough begins to come together. Increase the speed to medium and continue to mix for about 10 minutes until the dough is slightly sticky, smooth and elastic. Form the dough into a ball and place in a lightly greased bowl. Turn it over to coat all sides and tightly cover the bowl with clingfilm. Allow the dough to rise in a warm place for 1½ to 2 hours until it has doubled in size.

2. Whisk the dressing ingredients together in a small bowl.

3. Trim most of the exterior fat from the steaks and then allow to stand at room temperature for 20 to 30 minutes before grilling. Prepare the barbecue for direct cooking over a high heat.

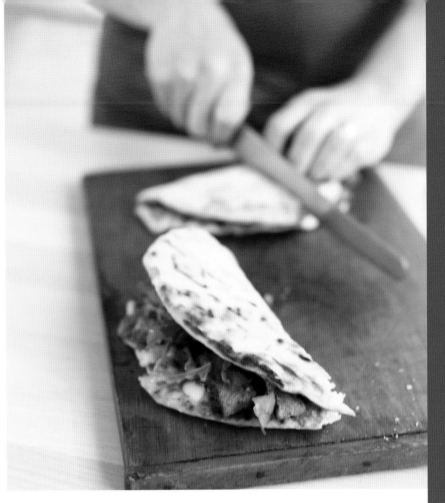

Piadini are thin folded flat breads with a long history in Romagna, Italy. Filled with meat, cheeses and vegetables, they make a fun snack or not-so-ordinary sandwiches.

4. Knock back the dough in the bowl. Transfer to a lightly floured surface and cut into 4 equal-sized pieces. Cut parchment paper into 25-cm (10-inch) squares and lightly grease each sheet on one side. Roll each piece of dough flat into rounds 20 to 25 cm (8 to 10 inches) in diameter. Lay each dough round on a greased sheet of paper and lightly grease the top of each round.

Stack the dough rounds between the sheets of paper and set aside on a roasting tray.

5. Lightly brush both sides of the steaks with oil and season them evenly with salt and pepper. Brush the cooking grates clean. Grill the steaks over *direct high heat*, with the lid closed as much as possible but turning once, until cooked to your desired doneness, 6 to 8 minutes for medium rare. (If flare-ups occur, move the steaks temporarily over indirect high heat.) Remove from the barbecue, cover and keep warm.

6. Reduce the temperature of the barbecue to a medium heat. Lay 2 dough rounds over *direct medium heat*, with the paper sides facing up. Grab one corner of the paper with tongs and peel it off. Grill the rounds for 2 to 3 minutes, rotating them occasionally for even cooking, until they are golden and marked on the underside.

7. Turn the crusts over and distribute one quarter of the cheese over each crust, leaving a 1-cm (½-inch) border round the edges. Continue grilling over *direct medium heat* for about 2 minutes, rotating the crusts occasionally for even cooking, until the crusts are crisp and the cheese has melted. Transfer the grilled crusts to a work surface. Repeat with the remaining crusts.

8. Place the greens in a salad bowl, pour the dressing over the greens and toss to combine.

9. Cut the steaks into thin slices, removing any pockets of fat, and distribute evenly over the crusts, then top with equal portions of the salad. Fold each piadini in half and eat it like a sandwich or, for easier eating or sharing, cut each piadini in half with a serrated knife after folding.

HOW TO CUT BONE-IN STEAKS FROM A RIB JOINT

You can tell a lot about the taste and tenderness of a cut of meat by where it comes from on the animal. The parts of the animal that get a lot of exercise, like the shoulder and the back end (the topside), develop more tough connective tissue than the parts of the animal that don't work so hard, like the sirloin and rib sections. From the sirloin, we get tender steaks like the porterhouse, the T-bone, and, of course, the sirloin. The rib section, pictured below, is where you'll find incredibly tender and succulent rib steaks.

1. Stand the rib joint on end so that you can clearly see the tips of the bones.

2. The advantage of barbecuing rib-eye steaks with the bones attached is that the bones will add mouthwatering flavour to the steaks and help keep the meat moist during cooking.

3. Using a very sharp knife, slice between the bones, trying not to saw back and forth too much. A hollow-ground knife will give the cleanest cut and best appearance.

4. What you have now is a big, brawny masterpiece called a bone-in rib-eye steak.

HOW TO MAKE GARLIC PASTE

Fresh garlic on a steak lights up all the endorphins in my brain. When time is short and I'm craving a full-throttled steak experience, I always turn to chopped garlic. The only problem is, I often grill my steak over very high heat, and so the bits and pieces of garlic sometimes burn, turning them bitter. I avoid this problem by making a garlic paste instead. The paste melts into the surface of the meat, and all the fat and juices collected there prevent it from burning.

1. Begin by thinly slicing the garlic with a chef's knife.

2. Finely chop the garlic, keeping the knife tip on the board and moving the blade from side to side.

3. Add some sea salt for flavour, crumbling it between your fingers if it is very coarse.

4. The salt will also hold the garlic together while you chop it very finely.

5. Now, drag the side of the knife over the garlic, putting extra pressure near the tip, to smash the garlic into a paste.

6. Keep swishing the knife back and forth until the garlic is so thin it's almost transparent. Now it's ready to smear on your steaks.

GARLIC-CRUSTED RIB-EYE STEAKS WITH GRILLED BROCCOLINI

SERVES: 4
PREP TIME: 15 MINUTES

HEAT: DIRECT AND INDIRECT HIGH HEAT
   230° to 290°C (450° to 550°F)
GRILLING TIME: 11 TO 15 MINUTES

PASTE
4 large garlic cloves
1 tablespoon sea salt
15 g (½ oz) flat leaf parsley, finely chopped
4 tablespoons extra-virgin olive oil
2 teaspoons balsamic vinegar
1 teaspoon freshly ground black pepper

4 bone-in rib-eye steaks, 200 to 375 g (10 to 12 oz) each and
   about 2.5 cm (1 inch) thick, trimmed of excess fat
175 g (6 oz) broccolini, with stalks no wider than 1 cm (½ inch)
Extra-virgin olive oil
Sea salt

1. Finely chop the garlic on a chopping board, then sprinkle with the salt. Use the side of a knife to smash the garlic into a paste. Put the garlic paste into a small bowl and add the remaining paste ingredients.

2. Smear the paste evenly over both sides of each steak. Allow the steaks to stand at room temperature for 20 to 30 minutes before grilling.

3. Meanwhile, soak the broccolini in a large bowl of water for 20 to 30 minutes so that they absorb the water. This will help them to steam a little on the barbecue.

4. Prepare your grill for direct and indirect cooking over a high heat.

5. Pour off the water from the bowl of broccolini. Lightly drizzle some oil over the broccolini and season with ½ teaspoon salt. Toss to coat them evenly with oil and salt.

6. Brush the cooking grates clean. Grill the steaks over **direct high heat**, with the lid closed as much as possible but turning once, until cooked to your desired doneness, 6 to 8 minutes for medium rare. (If flare-ups occur, move the steaks temporarily over indirect high heat.) Remove from the barbecue and allow to rest while you grill the broccolini.

7. Use tongs to lift the broccolini and allow any excess oil to drip back into the bowl. Grill the broccolini over **direct high heat** for 3 to 4 minutes, with the lid closed as much as possible but turning occasionally, until lightly charred. Finish cooking the broccolini over **indirect high heat** for 2 to 3 minutes. Serve warm with the steaks.

HOW TO MAKE TEA PASTE

1. A bit of Earl Grey tea leaves adds a deep, unexpected fragrance to this spice rub.

2. To get the best peppery zing, grind whole black peppercorns in a spice mill with the other seasonings. As with other spices, whole peppercorns retain more aromatic flavour than pre-ground pepper.

3. Pulse all the seasonings into a coarse blend to release their flavours, then mix them in a bowl with oil to make a paste.

SERVES: 4

PREP TIME: 25 MINUTES

HEAT: DIRECT MEDIUM HEAT 180° TO 230°C
   (350° TO 450°F)

GRILLING TIME: ABOUT 8 MINUTES

SPECIAL EQUIPMENT: SPICE MILL, 30-CM (12-INCH)
   CAST-IRON FRYING PAN

PASTE

2 teaspoons (about 2 tea bags) Earl Grey tea leaves

1 teaspoon whole black peppercorns

1 teaspoon dried tarragon

1 teaspoon sea salt

½ teaspoon dried thyme

3 tablespoons extra-virgin olive oil

4 fillet steaks, each about 250 g (8 oz) and
   3.5 cm (1½ inches) thick

MUSHROOMS

250 g (8 oz) button mushrooms

25 g (1 oz) unsalted butter

2 tablespoons extra-virgin olive oil

4 large garlic cloves, thinly sliced

¼ teaspoon sea salt

⅛ teaspoon freshly ground black pepper

15 g (½ oz) flat leaf parsley, roughly chopped

1 teaspoon sherry or red wine vinegar

1. Whirl the tea leaves, peppercorns, tarragon, salt and thyme in a spice mill until finely ground. Pour the spice mix into a bowl, add the oil and stir to make a paste.

2. Brush all sides of each fillet with the paste, then allow to stand at room temperature for 20 to 30 minutes before grilling.

3. Before you grill the steaks, prepare the mushrooms and have all the other ingredients in place. Lay the mushrooms on their sides and cut off a 5-mm (¼-inch) slice lengthways, then roll the mushrooms over so the flat sides are on your chopping board and the mushrooms no longer roll around. Cut the mushrooms lengthways into 5-mm (¼-inch) slices.

4. Prepare the barbecue for direct cooking over a medium heat.

5. Brush the cooking grates clean. Grill the steaks over **direct medium heat**, with the lid closed as much as possible but turning once, until cooked to your desired doneness, about 8 minutes for medium rare. Remove from the barbecue and allow the steaks to rest while you sauté the mushrooms.

6. Melt the butter with the oil in a 30-cm (12-inch) cast-iron frying pan over a high heat on your barbecue's side burner or your hob. Add the mushrooms and spread them out so that most are touching the bottom of the pan. Cook the mushrooms

without moving them for 2 minutes, then stir and add the garlic, salt and pepper and cook for a further 2 to 3 minutes, stirring 2 or 3 times, until the mushrooms are barely tender. Add the parsley and vinegar and mix well. Season to taste with salt and pepper, if needed. Spoon the hot mushrooms over the steaks.

HOW TO BROWN MUSHROOMS

1. Cut off one round edge to make a flat, stable surface.

2. Then cut into 5-mm (¼-inch) slices.

3. Melt the butter with a little oil, which helps to prevent the butter from burning.

4. Spread the mushrooms in a single layer and don't touch them for 2 minutes.

5. Add the salt towards the end of cooking because it draws moisture out of the mushrooms and hinders browning.

6. A little sherry vinegar near the end of cooking cuts the richness of the butter.

7. By resisting the urge to stir the mushrooms often, you will brown them better and create deeper flavours.

HOW TO MAKE FLAVOURED BUTTER

If you like to barbecue steaks – or any kind of meat, fish or poultry for that matter – I think you should have at least one flavoured butter waiting for you at all times in the refrigerator or freezer. One of the surest ways to please your palate and delight your guests is to crown each barbecued steak with a savoury slice of butter blended with the flavours of your choice. The heat of the steak will melt the butter and send the flavours running to mingle with the meat juices for a luxurious sauce.

1. Start by mixing softened butter with fresh herbs and other seasonings, along with shallots that have been simmered in red wine.

2. Shape the butter into a little log on parchment paper.

3. Wrap the log tightly in the paper and squeeze both ends to compact it.

4. Twist the ends of the parchment wrapper in opposite directions and store the flavoured butter in the refrigerator or freezer.

5. When it's time to serve, trim off one end. Remember to remove the frozen butter from the freezer in enough time to thaw.

6. Cut as many slices as you need and pull off the paper. Re-wrap any that is left over and return to the refrigerator or freezer.

HOW TO MAKE CROSS-HATCH MARKS

1. For a nice diamond pattern on your steaks, position them at a 45-degree angle to the bars of the cooking grate.

2. After searing for a couple of minutes, rotate your steaks 90 degrees.

3. Turn the steaks over and, if you like, mark the other side in the same way.

PORTERHOUSE STEAKS WITH RED WINE-SHALLOT BUTTER

SERVES: 4 TO 6
PREP TIME: 15 MINUTES

HEAT: DIRECT HIGH HEAT 230° TO 290°C (450° TO 550°F)
GRILLING TIME: 8 TO 10 MINUTES

BUTTER
3 tablespoons hearty red wine
2 tablespoons very finely chopped shallot
125 g (4 oz) unsalted butter, softened
1 tablespoon very finely chopped flat leaf parsley,
1 tablespoon very finely chopped tarragon
½ teaspoon sea salt
¼ teaspoon freshly ground black pepper

4 porterhouse steaks, each about 500 g (1 lb)
    and 2.5 cm (1 inch) thick
2 tablespoons extra-virgin olive oil
2 teaspoons sea salt
½ teaspoon freshly ground black pepper

1. Bring the wine and shallot to the boil in a small, heavy-based saucepan over a high heat. Boil for 3 to 5 minutes until the wine

is reduced to a glaze and is absorbed mostly by the shallots. Transfer to a bowl and allow to cool completely.

2. Add the butter, parsley, tarragon, salt and pepper to the shallot-wine reduction and mix to combine. Scoop the mixture out of the bowl on to a sheet of parchment or greaseproof paper. Loosely shape the mixture into a log about 2.5 cm (1 inch) in diameter. Roll the log in the paper and twist the ends in opposite directions to form an even cylinder. Refrigerate until about 1 hour before serving. (The butter can be made up to 1 week ahead.)

3. Allow the steaks to stand at room temperature for 20 to 30 minutes before grilling. Prepare the barbecue for direct cooking over a high heat.

4. Lightly brush the steaks with the oil and season evenly with the salt and pepper. Brush the cooking grates clean. Grill the steaks over *direct high heat*, with the lid closed as much as possible but turning once, until cooked to your desired doneness, 8 to 10 minutes for medium rare. (If flare-ups occur, move the steaks temporarily over indirect high heat.) Remove the steaks from the barbecue and allow to rest for 3 to 5 minutes. Serve the steaks hot with the butter smeared over the top.

HOW TO BARBECUE REALLY THICK STEAKS

One of the noblest dishes in the pantheon of international barbecued steaks is Bistecca alla Fiorentina, an enormous porterhouse steak jockeyed over and beside the hot coals until the outside is crisply charred and the interior is just rosy red and deliciously tender. The seasonings are pure and simple – nothing more than coarse salt, preferably sea salt, and freshly ground black pepper. The finishing touches are a squeeze of lemon juice and a drizzle of the best olive oil in the house.

1. Whereas most steaks do best when you don't fiddle with them on the barbecue, this one is so thick and monstrous that you will need to move it every few minutes.

2. Charcoal fires are inherently uneven, so don't be surprised if one part of the steak browns faster than another. Move the steak around to compensate for the unevenness.

3. This is a case where the charcoal is as much an ingredient in the recipe as the seasonings. The smokiness permeates the meat and delivers great primordial flavours.

BISTECCA ALLA FIORENTINA

SERVES: 4
PREP TIME: 5 MINUTES

HEAT: DIRECT AND INDIRECT MEDIUM HEAT
180° TO 230°C (350° TO 450°F)
GRILLING TIME: 25 TO 27 MINUTES

1 porterhouse steak, about 1.25 kg (2½ lb) and
5.5 cm (2¼ inches) thick
Grey or coarse sea salt
Freshly ground black pepper
2 lemons
Extra-virgin olive oil

1. Allow the steak to rest at room temperature for 1 hour before cooking. During this hour, you can prepare and cook the grill-baked beans, and then keep them warm.

2. Prepare the barbecue for direct and indirect cooking over a medium heat.

3. Liberally season the steak on both sides with salt and pepper. Rub the seasoning into the meat.

4. Grill the steak over **direct medium heat** for 10 to 12 minutes, rotating the steak 45 degrees about every 3 minutes to create a nice crust and turning once. Move the steak over **indirect medium heat** and continue to cook until the internal temperature reaches 52°C (125°F) for rare, about 15 minutes, rotating the steak as needed for even cooking. Allow the steak to rest for about 10 minutes before carving.

5. To carve the steak, cut the fillet side first as close to the bone as possible. Repeat the procedure for the strip steak. Slice each piece crossways into 1-cm (½-inch) slices, keeping the slices intact. Transfer to a serving platter and reassemble the steak with the bone. Drizzle some extra-virgin olive oil over the slices and serve with fresh lemon and grill-baked beans.

GRILL-BAKED BEANS ALLA CONTADINA

PREP TIME: 10 MINUTES

HEAT: INDIRECT MEDIUM HEAT 180° TO 230°C
(350° TO 450°F)
GRILLING TIME: ABOUT 15 MINUTES

2 cans (425 g/14 oz each) cannellini beans, rinsed
175 g (6 oz) vegetable stock
4 tablespoons bottled tomato sauce
1 tablespoon extra-virgin olive oil
1 teaspoon very finely chopped fresh thyme
½ teaspoon sea salt
1 teaspoon very finely chopped garlic
1 tablespoon plus 1 teaspoon very finely chopped
flat leaf parsley

1. Prepare the barbecue for indirect cooking over a medium heat.

2. Place the beans in a 23-cm (9-inch) square ovenproof dish.

3. Combine the stock, tomato sauce, oil, thyme and salt in a small bowl, then pour over the beans. Lightly press the beans so they are all immersed in the liquid. Bake the beans over **indirect medium heat** for about 15 minutes, with the lid closed, until they are bubbling and most of the liquid has reduced.

4. Blend the garlic with the parsley and scatter over the beans. Serve with the steak.

HOW TO CARVE BISTECCA

1. The porterhouse is a large cut that includes a T-shaped bone, with meat from the sirloin on one side and the fillet on the other.

2. The traditional way to serve it is to cut all the meat from the bone in 2 big sections and then slice it.

3. Cut the sirloin crossways in nice thick slices.

4. Also cut the fillet section in thick slices, and then arrange all the slices back along the bone.

SKIRT STEAKS WITH RED POTATOES AND FETA

SERVES: 4
PREP TIME: 15 MINUTES

HEAT: INDIRECT AND DIRECT HIGH HEAT
    230° TO 290°C (450° TO 550°F)
GRILLING TIME: 34 TO 46 MINUTES
SPECIAL EQUIPMENT: PERFORATED GRILL PAN, LARGE
    DISPOSABLE FOIL TIN

RUB
1 teaspoon sea salt
1 teaspoon ground cumin
½ teaspoon granulated garlic
¼ teaspoon freshly ground black pepper

750 g (1½ lb) small red-skinned potatoes, 3.5 cm to 5 cm
    (1½ to 2 inches) in diameter, cut into quarters
2 tablespoons extra-virgin olive oil
½ teaspoon sea salt
2 skirt steaks, about 375 g (12 oz) each, trimmed of
    excess surface fat
65 g (2½ oz) feta cheese, crumbled
2 tablespoons chopped flat leaf parsley
Sea salt
Freshly ground black pepper

1. Prepare the barbecue for indirect and direct cooking over a high heat.

2. Combine the rub ingredients in a small bowl.

3. Combine the potatoes, oil and salt in a large bowl and stir to coat them evenly.

4. Preheat a grill pan over **_indirect high heat_** for about 10 minutes. Add the potatoes to the pan and grill them for 30 to 40 minutes, with the lid closed as much as possible

but turning them 2 or 3 times, until the potatoes are golden brown and tender.

5. After the potatoes have cooked for about 10 minutes, season the steaks evenly with the rub, pressing the spices into the meat. Allow the meat to stand at room temperature for 20 to 30 minutes before grilling.

6. When the potatoes are fully cooked, transfer them to a large disposable foil tin. Add the cheese and parsley and mix well, then season to taste with salt and pepper. To keep the potatoes warm, place the pan over indirect heat while the steaks cook.

7. Grill the steaks over **_direct high heat_**, with the lid closed as much as possible but turning once, until cooked to your desired doneness, 4 to 6 minutes for medium rare. Transfer the steaks to a chopping board and allow to rest for 3 to 5 minutes. Keep the potatoes warm on the barbecue. Cut the meat across the grain into thin slices. Serve warm with the potatoes.

HOW TO PREP SKIRT STEAK

1. Trim away most of the fat that clings to both sides of the skirt steaks with a sharp knife.

2. Thoroughly trimming the fat will help prevent flare-ups.

3. Working with lengths of about 30 cm (12 inches) makes steaks easier to handle on the barbecue.

4. Season the meat generously with the rub, patting and massaging it in with your fingertips so it won't fall off during grilling.

CARNE ASADA WITH BLACK BEAN AND AVOCADO SALSA

SERVES: 4 TO 6
PREP TIME: 20 MINUTES

HEAT: DIRECT HIGH HEAT 230° TO 290°C (450° TO 550°F)
GRILLING TIME: 4 TO 6 MINUTES

SALSA
1 can (425 g/14 oz) black beans, rinsed
1 ripe Haas avocado, finely chopped
150 g (5 oz) white onion, finely chopped and rinsed in a sieve
175 g (6 oz) ripe tomato, finely chopped
2 tablespoons roughly chopped fresh coriander
1 tablespoon fresh lime juice
½ teaspoon sea salt
¼ teaspoon chipotle chilli powder
¼ teaspoon ground cumin
⅛ teaspoon freshly ground black pepper

RUB
1 teaspoon chipotle chilli powder
1 teaspoon sea salt
½ teaspoon ground cumin
¼ teaspoon freshly ground black pepper

750 g (1½ lb) skirt steak, trimmed of excess fat
Extra-virgin olive oil

Raw onions can taste a little harsh in a salsa, but a good rinse will take the edge off.

1. Combine the salsa ingredients in a non-metallic bowl. Cover with clingfilm, pressing the film directly on to the surface and set aside at room temperature for as long as 2 hours before serving.

2. Mix the rub ingredients together in a small bowl. Cut the steak into 30-cm (12-inch) lengths to make them easier to handle on the barbecue. Lightly coat both sides of the steaks with oil. Season evenly with the rub and allow to stand at room temperature for 20 to 30 minutes before grilling. Prepare the barbecue for direct cooking over a high heat.

3. Brush the cooking grates clean. Grill the steaks over **direct high heat**, with the lid closed as much as possible but turning once, until cooked to your desired doneness, 4 to 6 minutes for medium rare. Remove the steaks from the barbecue and allow them to rest for 3 to 5 minutes.

4. Cut the steaks across the grain into 1-cm (½-inch) slices. Serve warm with the salsa.

HOW TO PREP SHALLOTS

1. Trim off most of each root end.

2. Peel off the papery skin.

3. Spread the shallots on foil and drizzle with oil.

4. Wrap the foil over the shallots to make a neat packet.

HOW TO PREP FEATHER STEAKS

1. Some feather steaks, like the one on the right, have a tough streak running down the centre.

2. It's more difficult to see it after the steak is cooked.

3. To ensure that every slice is tender, cut away that tough area before serving.

BISTRO STEAKS
WITH MUSTARD CREAM SAUCE

SERVES: 4
PREP TIME: 15 MINUTES

HEAT: INDIRECT AND DIRECT MEDIUM HEAT
  180° TO 230°C (350° TO 450°F)
GRILLING TIME: ABOUT 1 HOUR

8 large shallots, about 375 g (12 oz) total
Extra-virgin olive oil
1¾ teaspoons sea salt
1 teaspoon dried thyme
1 teaspoon paprika
¾ teaspoon freshly ground black pepper
4 feather steaks, each 175 to 250 g (6 to 8 oz) and about
  2.5 cm (1 inch) thick
125 ml (4 fl oz) soured cream
1 tablespoon Dijon mustard

1. Prepare the barbecue for indirect and direct cooking over a medium heat.

2. Peel and trim the shallots, removing most of each root end. Cut the larger shallots in half lengthways or pull apart the distinct halves. Pile the shallots in the middle of a large square of aluminium foil. Drizzle with 1 tablespoon of oil and season with ¼ teaspoon of the salt. Fold up the sides and seal to make a packet. Grill over **indirect medium heat** for 20 to 30 minutes, with the lid closed as much as possible but turning once or twice, until a knife slides easily in and out of the shallots. Open the packet and continue to cook the shallots in the foil for 20 to 30 minutes more, turning the shallots very gently once or twice, until nicely browned. Remove the packet from the barbecue.

3. Mix the remaining 1½ teaspoons of salt with the thyme, paprika and pepper in a small bowl. Lightly coat the steaks on both sides with oil, then season evenly with the spices. Allow the steaks to stand at room temperature for 20 to 30 minutes before grilling.

4. Combine the soured cream and mustard in a small bowl.

5. Brush the cooking grates clean. Grill the steaks over **direct medium heat**, with the lid closed as much as possible but turning once, until cooked to your desired doneness, 8 to 10 minutes for medium rare. At the same time reheat the packet of shallots over **indirect medium heat**. Remove the steaks from the barbecue and allow them to rest for 3 to 5 minutes before slicing. While the steaks rest, remove any charred outer layers from the shallots.

6. Cut each steak lengthways on either side of the gristle that runs down the middle. Thinly slice the steak against the grain and overlap the slices on serving dishes. Serve the steaks warm with the shallots and sauce.

SESAME-GINGER FLANK STEAK WITH ASPARAGUS AND GOMASHIO

SERVES: 4 TO 6
PREP TIME: 25 MINUTES
MARINATING TIME: 3 TO 4 HOURS

HEAT: DIRECT MEDIUM HEAT 180° TO 230°C
(350° TO 450°F)
GRILLING TIME: 12 TO 16 MINUTES
SPECIAL EQUIPMENT: PESTLE AND MORTAR

MARINADE
5 tablespoons soy sauce
2 tablespoons sugar
3 tablespoons rice wine vinegar
2 tablespoons toasted sesame oil
1 tablespoon very finely chopped garlic
1½ tablespoons grated fresh root ginger
1½ teaspoons sambal oelek or other ground fresh chilli paste
150 g (5 oz) spring onions, white and light green parts, finely chopped
15 g (½ oz) fresh coriander, coarsely chopped

1 flank steak, 750 g to 1kg (1½ to 2 lb) and about 1.5 cm (¾ inch) thick

GOMASHIO
40 g (1½ oz) sesame seed
1 teaspoon sea salt

ASPARAGUS
1 large bunch asparagus, about 500 g (1 lb)
1 tablespoon extra-virgin olive oil
½ teaspoon sea salt

2 tablespoons finely chopped fresh coriander or flat leaf parsley

1. Whisk the soy sauce, sugar, vinegar, oil, garlic, ginger and chilli paste together in a small bowl. Add the spring onions and coriander. Place the steak in a glass or stainless-steel dish and pour in the marinade, turning the steak to coat both sides. Cover and refrigerate for 3 to 4 hours, turning the steak once or twice.

2. Toast the sesame seeds in a clean, dry non-stick frying pan over a low heat for 2 to 3 minutes, shaking and stirring until the seeds are golden brown, but before they begin to pop. Turn them out on to a plate and allow to cool for 10 minutes. Add the sea salt and combine in a pestle and mortar. Lightly crush the seeds so that some texture remains; do not make a fine powder. (The unused portion can be stored in a glass jar in the refrigerator for up to 2 months.)

3. Snap or cut off the dry, woody ends from the asparagus spears. Lightly coat them with the oil and season with the salt.

4. Prepare the barbecue for direct cooking over a medium heat.

HOW TO MAKE GOMASHIO

1. Toast the sesame seeds just until they start to colour.

2. Grind coarsely with sea salt to make a delicious seasoning.

HOW TO SLICE FLANK STEAK

1. For the sake of tenderness, cut flank steak crossways, or against the grain.

2. Keep the slices no thicker than about 8 mm (⅓ inch).

5. Remove the steak from the refrigerator and allow to stand at room temperature for 20 to 30 minutes before grilling. Brush the cooking grates clean. Grill the steak over **direct medium heat**, with the lid closed as much as possible but turning once, until cooked to your desired doneness, 8 to 10 minutes for medium rare. Transfer to a chopping board and allow to rest while you grill the asparagus.

6. Arrange the asparagus perpendicular to the bars on the cooking grate. Grill over **direct medium heat** for 4 to 6 minutes, with the lid closed as much as possible but rolling the spears a couple of times, until lightly charred and crisp-tender. Remove them from the barbecue and arrange on one side of a large platter.

7. Thinly slice the steak on the bias, then arrange it next to the asparagus. Sprinkle over the gomashio and coriander. Serve warm.

HOW TO STUFF AND ROLL FLANK STEAK

1. Trim the silver skin and most of the fat from the surface of the meat.

2. Holding your knife parallel to the board, make a shallow cut along the length of the steak.

3. Slice again, making the cut a little deeper.

4. Keep making strokes with the tip of your knife as you open up the meat with your other hand.

5. Continue cutting until you come within about 1 cm (½ inch) from the opposite edge.

6. Now open the steak like a book, laying it flat.

7. Turn the steak over and carefully trim off the seam that sticks up.

8. Turn the steak back over so the cut side is facing up.

9. With the grain of the meat running horizontally, spread the stuffing mixture to within 2.5 cm (1 inch) of the outer edges and a few centimetres (inches) from the top.

10. Roll up the meat from the bottom edge to the top.

11. With no stuffing at the top of the meat, all the ingredients will stay nicely inside the roll.

12. Tie the roll every couple of centimetres (inches) with lengths of butcher's string.

RED MEAT

70

FLANK STEAK WITH ROASTED PEPPER AND FETA STUFFING

SERVES: 6
PREP TIME: 40 MINUTES

HEAT: INDIRECT MEDIUM HEAT 180° TO 230°C
    (350° TO 450°F)
GRILLING TIME: 20 TO 30 MINUTES
SPECIAL EQUIPMENT: BUTCHER'S STRING

75 g (3 oz) feta cheese, drained and crumbled
50 g (2 oz) dried breadcrumbs
1 small red pepper, roasted, peeled, deseeded and diced
1 large garlic clove
25 g (1 oz) flat leaf parsley
1 tablespoon fresh thyme
½ teaspoon sea salt
¼ teaspoon freshly ground black pepper

2 flank steaks, about 750 g (1½ lb) each
1 tablespoon extra-virgin olive oil
Sea salt
Freshly ground black pepper

1. Combine the cheese, breadcrumbs and diced pepper in a bowl. Finely chop the garlic and herbs together and add to the bowl, then blend thoroughly with a fork. Season with the salt and pepper.

2. Lay out the flank steak on a chopping board. Starting near one end of the steak, carefully insert a boning knife horizontally into one long edge (the edge parallel to the grain), splitting the steak evenly top to bottom. Continue this cut until the entire steak can be opened up like a book (see directions at left). Repeat with the other flank steak.

3. Prepare your barbecue for indirect cooking over a medium heat.

4. Evenly spread the stuffing mixture over the inside of the butterflied steaks to within 2.5 cm (1 inch) of the edges and a few centimetres (inches) from the top (you may not need all of it). Be careful not to overstuff or it will just fall out and make it more difficult to roll. Roll up the steaks around the filling, with the grain running the length of the roll. Tie the rolls every few centimetres (inches) with butcher's string. Brush the outside of the rolls with oil and lightly season with salt and pepper.

5. Brush the cooking grates clean. Grill over **_indirect medium heat_**, with the lid closed as much as possible but turning once, until cooked to your desired doneness, 20 to 30 minutes for medium rare. Transfer to a carving board, lightly cover with foil, and allow to rest for 10 minutes before slicing.

6. To serve, cut the rolls into 1- to 1.5-cm (½- to ¾-inch) slices. Serve warm

ARGENTINE BEEF SKEWERS WITH CHIMICHURRI SAUCE

SERVES: 4 TO 6
PREP TIME: 20 MINUTES

HEAT: DIRECT HIGH HEAT 230° TO 290°C (450° TO 550°F)
GRILLING TIME: 6 TO 8 MINUTES
SPECIAL EQUIPMENT: BAMBOO SKEWERS,
    SOAKED IN WATER FOR AT LEAST 30 MINUTES

SAUCE
50 g (2 oz) flat leaf parsley leaves and tender stems
25 g (1 oz) fresh basil leaves
40 g (1½ oz) white onion, finely chopped and rinsed
25 g (1 oz) carrot, finely chopped
1 garlic clove
½ teaspoon sea salt
6 tablespoons extra-virgin olive oil
2 tablespoons rice vinegar

RUB
1½ teaspoons sea salt
½ teaspoon paprika
½ teaspoon ground coriander
½ teaspoon ground cumin
¼ teaspoon freshly ground black pepper

1 kg (2 lb) rump steak, 2.5 to 3 cm (1 to 1¼ inches) thick,
    cut into 2.5-cm (1-inch) cubes
Extra-virgin olive oil
18 large cherry tomatoes

1. Finely chop the parsley, basil, onion, carrot, garlic and salt in a food processor or blender. With the machine running, add the oil and vinegar in a steady stream, using just enough oil to create a fairly thick sauce.

2. Mix the rub ingredients together in a small bowl.

3. Place the meat cubes in a large bowl. Lightly coat the meat with oil and then season with the rub, stirring to coat the meat evenly. Allow the meat to stand at room temperature for 20 to 30 minutes before grilling. Prepare the barbecue for direct cooking over a high heat.

4. Thread the meat and tomatoes alternately on to skewers. Brush the cooking grates clean. Grill the skewers over **direct high heat,** with the lid closed as much as possible but turning occasionally, until cooked to your desired doneness, 6 to 8 minutes for medium rare. Serve warm with the sauce on the side or drizzled over the top.

HOW TO CUBE RUMP STEAK

When making kebabs, the goal is to create cubes of the same size and thickness so they all cook at the same rate.

1. Start with a nice even piece of steak at least 2.5 cm (1 inch) thick.

2. Cut it down the centre and side to side in whichever way leaves you with 2.5-cm (1-inch) cubes.

3. With so many flat sides, you now have plenty of opportunities to lightly char and flavour the surface of the meat.

4. If some cubes end up a little smaller than most, combine all the small ones on a skewer or two of their own and grill them for a shorter time.

The centre-cut section of a beef fillet is almost always the most expensive part. Save that to slice into steaks. To make skewers or kebabs, use the tail ends of the fillet and enjoy all the buttery texture for far less cost. Some folded lemon slices complement the flavours in the finadene, which is a very popular marinade and sauce on the tropical island of Guam.

BEEF KEBABS WITH FINADENE

SERVES: 4 TO 6
PREP TIME: 20 MINUTES
MARINATING TIME: 1 TO 2 HOURS

HEAT: DIRECT HIGH HEAT 230° TO 290°C (450° TO 550°F)
GRILLING TIME: 4 TO 6 MINUTES
SPECIAL EQUIPMENT: BAMBOO SKEWERS,
    SOAKED IN WATER FOR AT LEAST 30 MINUTES

SAUCE
125 ml (4 fl oz) soy sauce
40 g (1½ oz) white onion, very finely chopped
3 tablespoons fresh lemon juice
3 tablespoons water
1 teaspoon very finely chopped jalapeño chilli

1 beef fillet roast, about 1.25 kg (2½ lb)
4 tablespoons extra-virgin olive oil
2 lemons, thinly sliced

1. Mix the sauce ingredients together in a bowl. In a separate small bowl reserve 5 tablespoons of the sauce to spoon over the barbecued meat.

2. Trim any excess fat and sinew from the surface of the meat. Cut it crossways into steaks about 3 cm (1¼ inches) thick, then cut each steak into pieces 2.5 to 3 cm (1 to 1½ inches) thick, cutting away and discarding any clumps of fat and sinew. Place the meat into a large, resealable plastic bag, pour in the remaining sauce and add the oil. Press the air out of the bag, seal tightly and turn the bag several times to incorporate the oil and evenly coat the meat, then refrigerate for 1 to 2 hours.

3. Thread the meat on to skewers, placing a folded slice of lemon between each piece so that the meat cooks evenly. Allow the kebabs to stand at room temperature for 20 to 30 minutes before grilling. Prepare the barbecue for direct cooking over a high heat.

4. Brush the cooking grates clean. Grill the skewers over **_direct high heat_**, with the lid closed as much as possible but turning 2 or 3 times, until the meat is cooked to your desired doneness, 4 to 6 minutes for medium rare. Serve warm with the reserved sauce spooned over the top.

HOW TO PREP CUCUMBER

1. Grate the cucumber coarsely on the side of a box grater.

2. Arrange the pieces in the middle of a sturdy piece of kitchen paper.

3. Squeeze gently to remove the water, then mix the cucumbers into the sauce.

LAMB SOUVLAKI WITH CUCUMBER-YOGURT SAUCE

SERVES: 4
PREP TIME: 20 MINUTES
MARINATING TIME: 3 TO 4 HOURS

HEAT: DIRECT HIGH HEAT 230° TO 290°C (450° TO 550°F)
GRILLING TIME: 6 TO 7 MINUTES
SPECIAL EQUIPMENT: BAMBOO SKEWERS, SOAKED IN WATER FOR AT LEAST 30 MINUTES

MARINADE
125 ml (4 fl oz) extra-virgin olive oil
1 tablespoon finely chopped garlic
1 tablespoon very finely chopped fresh oregano leaves, or 1 teaspoon crumbled dried oregano
1 teaspoon sea salt
¼ teaspoon freshly ground black pepper

1 boneless leg of lamb, about 750 g (1½ lb), trimmed of excess fat and cut into 3.5-cm (1½-inch) chunks
2 red or green peppers, cored, deseeded and cut into 2.5-cm (1-inch) squares
24 large cherry tomatoes

SAUCE
½ cucumber, coarsely grated
250 g (8 oz) natural Greek yogurt
2 tablespoons very finely chopped red onion
1 teaspoon finely grated lemon rind
1 tablespoon fresh lemon juice
½ teaspoon very finely chopped garlic
Sea salt
Freshly ground black pepper

1. Whisk the marinade ingredients together in a small bowl. Thread the lamb chunks, pepper squares and tomatoes alternately on to skewers. Place in a shallow dish, pour the marinade over the skewers and turn to coat them evenly. Cover and refrigerate for 3 to 4 hours, turning occasionally. Allow to stand at room temperature for 20 to 30 minutes before grilling.

2. Squeeze the grated cucumber to remove as much liquid as possible. Transfer the cucumber to a small bowl and stir in the yogurt, onion, lemon rind, lemon juice and garlic. Season to taste with salt and pepper, cover and refrigerate until serving.

3. Prepare the barbecue for direct cooking over a high heat. Brush the cooking grates clean. Remove the skewers from the dish and discard the marinade. Grill the skewers over **direct high heat**, with the lid closed as much as possible but turning occasionally, until the meat is cooked to your desired doneness, 6 to 7 minutes for medium rare. Serve the skewers warm with the sauce.

PORCINI-RUBBED VEAL CHOPS WITH HERBED MASCARPONE

SERVES: 4
PREP TIME: 15 MINUTES

HEAT: DIRECT MEDIUM HEAT 180° TO 230°C
   (350° TO 450°F)
GRILLING TIME: ABOUT 6 MINUTES
SPECIAL EQUIPMENT: SPICE MILL

MASCARPONE
5 tablespoons mascarpone cheese
1 teaspoon very finely chopped sage
¼ teaspoon sea salt
¼ teaspoon freshly ground black pepper

25 g (1 oz) dried porcini mushrooms
2 teaspoons sea salt
1 teaspoon freshly ground black pepper

4 veal rib chops, each about 250 g (8 oz) and
   2.5 cm (1 inch) thick
Extra-virgin olive oil

1. Mix the mascarpone ingredients together in a small bowl. Cover and allow to stand at room temperature for 1 hour.

2. Grind the mushrooms into a powder in a spice mill (this should yield 2 tablespoons). Put the powder into a small bowl and mix with the salt and pepper. Pour some oil on to a roasting tray and then sprinkle the seasoning over the oil. Dredge the chops through the oil mixture to coat them evenly. Cover and allow them to stand at room temperature for 20 to 30 minutes before grilling. Prepare the barbecue for direct cooking over a medium heat.

3. Brush the cooking grates clean. Grill the chops over **direct medium heat**, with the lid closed as much as possible but turning once, until cooked to your desired doneness, about 6 minutes for medium rare. Remove from the barbecue and allow the chops to rest for 3 to 5 minutes. Serve the chops hot with the herbed mascarpone.

If your impression of veal comes mostly from over-breaded and overcooked escallops, you owe it to yourself to try this chop. Quickly grilling a lean, bone-in veal chop over a fragrant fire, Tuscan style, results in a succulent, tender taste experience.

HOW TO PREP VEAL CHOPS

1. Dried porcini mushrooms star in this veal chop recipe. Pulverize them first in a spice mill or coffee grinder.

2. Brush some good olive oil on to a roasting tray and sprinkle the pulverized mushrooms, salt and pepper over the oil.

3. Press the veal chops into the oil and seasonings.

4. Drag each chop back and forth on both sides to get an even coating.

HOW TO FRENCH A RACK OF LAMB

1. 'Frenching' means removing the fat on the bones extending from a rack (or chop) and cleaning them thoroughly for a nice presentation.

2. Each rack of lamb has a 'fat cap' that runs on top of the rib bones and meat. Make a cut through the fat at the base of the bones.

3. Use the knife to help lift off the fat cap.

4. Use your knife to cut out the rib meat between the bones and to scrape the bones clean.

5. Then trim off the fat clinging to the loin meat, to prevent flare-ups.

6. Ideally the meat will be pinkish red, not purple. A dark colour indicates an older animal.

HOW TO BARBECUE RACK OF LAMB

Lamb chops are a buttery-soft luxury. You can certainly barbecue them individually, but they are likely to be juicier and more succulent if you cook whole racks first and then cut them into chops.

1. Prepare your barbecue by spreading the coals over one-half to three-quarters of the charcoal grate.

2. Grill the lamb as much as possible over a direct heat.

3. If flare-ups occur, move the racks to the other side of the barbecue, over indirect heat.

4. Once the internal temperature reaches 52°C (125°F), remove the racks from the barbecue, loosely cover them with foil and allow them to rest for about 5 minutes before cutting into chops.

RACK OF LAMB WITH ORANGE-POMEGRANATE SYRUP

SERVES: 4 TO 6

PREP TIME: 40 MINUTES

HEAT: DIRECT MEDIUM HEAT 180° TO 230°C
    (350° TO 450°F)

GRILLING TIME: 15 TO 20 MINUTES

2 lamb racks, 500 to 750 g (1 to 1½ lb) each

PASTE
2 tablespoons extra-virgin olive oil
1 tablespoon very finely chopped garlic
1 tablespoon chilli con carne seasoning
2 teaspoons sea salt
1 teaspoon freshly ground black pepper

SYRUP
125 ml (4 fl oz) fresh orange juice
4 tablespoons pomegranate juice
2 tablespoons runny honey
1 tablespoon balsamic vinegar
½ teaspoon sea salt

1. French the lamb racks as shown on the previous page.

2. Mix the paste ingredients in a small bowl. Spread the paste over the lamb racks and allow them to stand at room temperature for 20 to 30 minutes before grilling.

3. Combine the orange juice, pomegranate juice, honey and balsamic vinegar in a small saucepan over a high heat and bring to the boil. Once boiling, reduce the heat to medium and simmer for 15 to 20 minutes until the liquid has reduced to about 5 tablespoons. Season the light syrup with the salt and allow to cool. (You can refrigerate the syrup for up to 3 days.)

4. Prepare the barbecue for direct cooking over a medium heat. Brush the cooking grates clean. Grill the lamb, bone sides down first, over **direct medium heat**, with the lid closed as much as possible but turning once or twice and moving the racks over indirect heat if flare-ups occur, until cooked to your desired doneness, 15 to 20 minutes for medium rare. Remove from the barbecue when the internal temperature reaches 52°C (125°F). Allow the lamb to rest for 5 minutes before carving into chops (the internal temperature will rise during resting).

5. If necessary, warm the syrup over a low heat until it reaches your desired consistency. Serve the lamb warm with the syrup drizzled on top.

Of course you can buy pre-cut lamb rib chops, but cutting them yourself from a frenched rack of lamb will probably save you some money and assure you that each chop is the same thickness. For a clear look at where the bones are, face the meaty side of each rack down on a chopping board. Cut right between each pair of ribs.

LAMB CHOPS WITH INDIAN SPICES

SERVES: 4
PREP TIME: 10 MINUTES
MARINATING TIME: 1 TO 2 HOURS

HEAT: DIRECT HIGH HEAT 230° TO 290°C (450° TO 550°F)
GRILLING TIME: 4 TO 6 MINUTES

MARINADE
4 tablespoons extra-virgin olive oil
2 tablespoons fresh lime juice
1 tablespoon very finely chopped garlic
1½ teaspoons sea salt
1 teaspoon ground coriander
1 teaspoon ground cumin
½ teaspoon ground ginger
½ teaspoon freshly ground black pepper

16 rib lamb chops, each about 1.5 cm (¾ inch) thick, trimmed of excess fat

Lime wedges, to serve, optional

1. Whisk the marinade ingredients together in a small bowl.

2. Arrange the chops on a large, rimmed plate. Spoon or brush the marinade over the chops, turning to coat them evenly. Cover with clingfilm and refrigerate for 1 to 2 hours.

3. Remove the chops from the refrigerator 20 to 30 minutes before grilling. Prepare the barbecue for direct cooking over a high heat.

4. Brush the cooking grates clean. Grill the chops over **direct high heat**, with the lid closed as much as possible but turning once, until nicely marked on both sides and grilled to your desired doneness, 4 to 6 minutes for medium rare.

5. Remove the chops from the barbecue and allow them to rest for 3 to 5 minutes. Serve warm with lime wedges, if desired, for squeezing over.

LAMB CHOPS IN UZBEK MARINADE

SERVES: 4
PREP TIME: 10 MINUTES
MARINATING TIME: 3 TO 5 HOURS

HEAT: DIRECT HIGH HEAT 230° TO 290°C (450° TO 550°F)
GRILLING TIME: ABOUT 8 MINUTES

MARINADE/SAUCE
1 small yellow onion, cut into chunks
4 canned plum tomatoes
125 ml (4 fl oz) extra-virgin olive oil
4 large garlic cloves
2 tablespoons red wine vinegar
1 tablespoon sweet paprika
1 tablespoon dried thyme
1 tablespoon ground coriander
2 teaspoons ground cumin
2 teaspoons sea salt
½ teaspoon ground cayenne pepper
½ teaspoon freshly ground black pepper

8 lamb loin chops, each about 3.5 cm (1½ inches) thick
Extra-virgin olive oil

1. Process the marinade ingredients in a food processor for 1 to 2 minutes until very smooth.

2. Arrange the chops side by side in a shallow dish. Pour the marinade over the chops and turn to coat them on all sides. Cover with clingfilm and marinate in the refrigerator for 3 to 5 hours.

3. Remove the chops from the dish and wipe off most of the marinade. Discard the marinade. Lightly brush the chops with oil and allow to stand at room temperature for 20 to 30 minutes before grilling. Prepare the barbecue for direct cooking over a high heat.

4. Brush the cooking grates clean. Grill the chops over **direct high heat**, with the lid closed as much as possible but rotating and turning the chops once or twice for even cooking, until they are cooked to your desired doneness, about 8 minutes for medium rare. Each time you lift the chops off the grate to rotate them or turn them over, place them down on a clean area of the grate, and brush away the bits of marinade that will cling to the grate as you go.

5. Remove the chops from the barbecue and allow them to rest for 3 to 5 minutes. Serve warm.

After marinating lamb chops in a thick, coarse purée, wipe off most of the marinade before putting the chops on the barbecue. Otherwise, the coating would prevent the chops from searing nicely and developing a good char on the outside. Don't worry; the flavours of the marinade will have imbued the meat itself.

RED MEAT

HOW TO MAKE BASIL-GARLIC OIL

1. Bring a saucepan of salted water to the boil. Add the basil leaves and blanch them for 10 seconds.

2. Immediately remove the basil with a slotted spoon and plunge the leaves into a bowl of iced water to stop them cooking and to retain the green colour.

3. Lay the basil leaves on kitchen paper and pat them dry.

4. Combine the basil leaves, oil and garlic in a food processor or blender.

5. Process until the basil is puréed, then season the mixture with salt and crushed red chilli flakes.

6. Drizzle the basil-garlic oil over barbecued meats. Save any remaining oil by straining out the solids and storing it in the refrigerator for up to a week.

HOW TO PREP SHOULDER CHOPS

1. Lamb shoulder chops typically cost about one-third the price of loin and rib chops, and their flavour is excellent.

2. First brush them with good-quality olive oil and some bold seasonings like dried herbes de Provence.

3. Their texture, though, can be a little tough, so it's best to slow-cook them over indirect heat, which renders them tender.

HERBES DE PROVENCE

Dried herbes de Provence is an aromatic blend of dried herbs frequently used in the south of France. It typically includes thyme, marjoram, parsley, tarragon, lavender, celery seeds and bay leaf.

LAMB SHOULDER CHOPS WITH RATATOUILLE SALAD AND BASIL-GARLIC OIL

SERVES: 4
PREP TIME: 25 MINUTES

HEAT: DIRECT AND INDIRECT MEDIUM HEAT
   180° TO 230°C (350° TO 450°F)
GRILLING TIME: 51 TO 58 MINUTES

OIL
1 tablespoon plus ½ teaspoon sea salt
50 g (2 oz) basil leaves
175 g (6 fl oz) extra-virgin olive oil
1 medium garlic clove, peeled
¼ teaspoon crushed red chilli flakes

RATATOUILLE
1 large red pepper
1 aubergine, cut into 1-cm (½-inch) slices
2 small courgettes, cut in half lengthways
1 yellow onion, cut crossways into 4 thick slices
Extra-virgin olive oil
4 plum tomatoes
Sea salt
Freshly ground black pepper

2 teaspoons dried herbes de Provence
4 lamb shoulder chops, 300 to 375 g (10 to 12 oz) each

1. Bring a small saucepan of water, with 1 tablespoon of the salt, to the boil over a high heat. Add the basil leaves and blanch them for 10 seconds, then immediately remove the basil and plunge them into a bowl of iced water. Transfer to kitchen paper and pat away the excess water. Process the basil, oil and garlic in a blender or food processor until the basil is puréed. Season with the remaining ½ teaspoon salt and the red chilli flakes, then pour into a small jug and set aside.

2. Prepare the barbecue for direct and indirect cooking over a medium heat.

3. Remove the stalk, ribs and seeds from the pepper and cut into 4 pieces. Lightly brush the aubergine, courgette and onion with oil. Brush the cooking grates clean. Grill all the vegetables over ***direct medium heat*** for 6 to 8 minutes, turning occasionally, until the pepper is charred and blistered, the aubergine, courgette and onion are tender, and the tomato skins are seared and blistered. Transfer the vegetables to a platter as they are done, and season to taste with salt and pepper. Cut the vegetables into bite-sized pieces and drizzle with 2 tablespoons of basil-garlic oil. Set aside.

4. Mix 2 teaspoons sea salt, ½ teaspoon pepper and the dried herbs together in a bowl. Lightly brush the lamb with oil and season with the spices.

5. Brush the cooking grates clean. Grill the lamb over ***indirect medium heat*** for 45 to 50 minutes, with the lid closed as much as possible but turning once or twice, until the chops are fork tender.

6. Place equal portions of ratatouille on each of 4 dinner plates. Add a chop to each plate and garnish with another drizzle of basil-garlic oil on the plate around the lamb and vegetables.

HOW TO CUT SHORT RIBS

1. Short ribs are cut two different ways for Korean barbecue. You can buy 'flanken-style' short ribs, like what you see towards the bottom of this picture, or you can buy the more-conventional short ribs, like the thicker pieces towards the top of this picture.

2. To prepare the more-conventional short ribs, begin by making a horizontal cut just over the bone of each rib.

3. Stop just before you cut all the way through the meat.

4. Continue to make horizontal cuts and butterfly the meat until it is about 1 cm (½ inch) thick.

5. Next, cut very shallow slits in the meat to tenderize it.

HOW TO BARBECUE FLANKEN-STYLE RIBS

1. Flanken-style ribs are thin enough that they require no cutting. Simply marinate them for a few hours in the refrigerator. When you lift them, allow the excess liquid to drip back into the bowl before laying them on the barbecue.

2. Grill the ribs over direct hight heat, leaving the lid off so that you can keep an eye on them and turn them as they char.

KOREAN BEEF BARBECUE

SERVES: 4 TO 6
PREP TIME: 10 MINUTES
MARINATING TIME: 2 TO 4 HOURS

HEAT: DIRECT HIGH HEAT 230° TO 290°C (450° TO 550°F)
GRILLING TIME: 3 TO 5 MINUTES

MARINADE
1 Asian pear (baseball size), peeled, cored and
    roughly chopped
3 spring onions, trimmed and roughly chopped
6 large garlic cloves
500 ml (17 fl oz) water
175 ml (6 fl oz) soy sauce
75 g (3 oz) sugar
4 tablespoons rice vinegar

12 flanken-style beef ribs, about 2 kg (4 lb) total
    and 1 cm (½ inch) thick
2 tablespoons toasted sesame seed

1. Finely chop the pear, spring onions and garlic in a food
processor. Add the remaining marinade ingredients and process
until well combined.

2. Put the ribs in a large bowl and pour in the marinade.
Mix well to coat the ribs evenly, then cover and refrigerate for
2 to 4 hours.

3. Prepare the barbecue for direct cooking over a high heat.

4. Brush the cooking grates clean. One at time, lift the ribs and
allow the liquid and solid bits to fall back into the bowl. Discard
the marinade. Grill the ribs over **direct high heat** for 3 to 5
minutes, with the lid open and turning occasionally, until they
are nicely charred on both sides and cooked to a medium or
medium-rare doneness. Remove from the barbecue and
sprinkle with the sesame seeds.

The crisp, translucent flesh of Asian pears makes a sweet juice
that is excellent for marinating beef.

HOW TO BARBECUE BEEF RIBS

1. Look for the meatiest beef ribs you can find and season them generously.

2. Line them up on their sides in a disposable foil tin.

3. Add beef stock to create a moist cooking environment.

4. Cover the tin with foil, which will trap steam and help to tenderize the meat.

5. Seal the edges tightly so that the liquid does not evaporate.

6. The ribs should cook over indirect heat, with the lid closed, for the first hour.

7. It's important to maintain the barbecue's temperature at about 180°C (350°F).

8. At the start of the second hour, add more charcoal to maintain the heat.

9. Uncover the tin and turn the ribs over so they cook evenly.

10. Wearing barbecue mitts or oven gloves, seal the tin again for the second hour of cooking.

11. Remove the ribs from the tin and brush them with the sauce.

12. Finish them over a direct heat for a beautifully caramelized surface.

BEEF RIBS WITH BARBACOA SAUCE

SERVES: 2 TO 4
PREP TIME: 45 MINUTES

HEAT: INDIRECT AND DIRECT MEDIUM HEAT
180° TO 230°C (350° TO 450°F)
GRILLING TIME: ABOUT 2¼ HOURS
SPECIAL EQUIPMENT: LARGE DISPOSABLE FOIL TIN,
CAST-IRON FRYING PAN

RUB
2 teaspoons garlic granules
1 teaspoon ground cinnamon
1 teaspoon sea salt
1 teaspoon freshly ground black pepper

½ rack beef ribs (7 ribs), about 2.5 kg (5 lb)
500 ml (17 fl oz) beef stock

SAUCE
3 dried ancho chillies
150 g (5 oz) onion, finely chopped
1 teaspoon dried oregano
1 teaspoon ground cumin
1 garlic clove, very finely chopped
2 tablespoons cider vinegar
1 tablespoon light brown sugar
¾ teaspoon sea salt
137 g (4½ oz) ketchup

1. Combine the rub ingredients in a small bowl.

2. Prepare the barbecue for indirect and direct cooking over a medium heat.

3. Cut the rack into individual ribs and arrange them on a roasting tray. Evenly coat each rib with the rub and then place them side by side in a large disposable foil tin, layering a few ribs if necessary. Add the beef stock to the tin and tightly cover with aluminium foil.

4. Place the tin over **_indirect medium heat_**, close the lid, and cook for 1 hour. After the first hour, using tongs and wearing insulated barbecue mitts, carefully remove the aluminium foil cover and turn the ribs over. Put the foil cover back on the tin and continue to cook over **_indirect medium heat_** for another hour. If using a charcoal barbecue, to maintain the heat, add 6 to 8 unlit briquettes to each pile of lit charcoal about every hour.

5. While the ribs are cooking, make the sauce. Heat a cast-iron frying pan over a medium-high heat. Add the chillies and cook for 3 to 5 minutes, occasionally pressing the chillies against the bottom of the pan, until they are lightly toasted, pliable and dark brick red in spots. The chillies may start to puff while in the pan. Allow the toasted chillies to cool until easy to handle, then split them open and remove and discard the stems, seeds and ribs. Transfer to a bowl, cover with 600 ml (1 pint) hot tap water and allow them to stand for about 20 minutes until they become soft. Strain into a small bowl, reserving the chilli soaking liquid.

6. Combine the soaked chillies, onion, oregano, cumin and garlic in a blender or food processor. Add 125 ml (4 fl oz) of the reserved soaking liquid and blend to make a thick paste, adding more reserved liquid, if necessary. Combine the chilli paste, vinegar, brown sugar and salt in a saucepan over a medium heat, and bring to the boil, stirring often. Reduce the heat to medium-low and cook for about 5 minutes until slightly thickened. Remove the pan from the heat and stir in the ketchup. Transfer to a bowl and allow the sauce to cool.

7. When the ribs are tender and the meat has visibly shrunk back from the bones, wearing insulated barbecue mitts, carefully remove the tin from the barbecue. Remove the ribs from the tin drippings and place them on a roasting tray. Discard the tin and the drippings. Liberally brush the ribs with the sauce and then grill the ribs over **_direct medium heat_** for 3 to 5 minutes. Brush the ribs again with more sauce, turn them over and grill for a further 3 to 5 minutes. Transfer the ribs to a platter and allow to rest for 5 minutes. Serve with the remaining sauce.

LEG OF LAMB
WITH MOROCCAN SPICES

SERVES: 6 TO 8
PREP TIME: 20 MINUTES
MARINATING TIME: 1 HOUR

HEAT: DIRECT AND INDIRECT HIGH HEAT
  230° TO 290°C (450° TO 550°F)
GRILLING TIME: 21 TO 27 MINUTES

MARINADE
75 g (3 oz) yellow onion, chopped
1 tablespoon grated lemon rind
4 tablespoons fresh lemon juice
3 tablespoons extra-virgin olive oil
2 garlic cloves
1½ teaspoons crushed red chilli flakes
1 teaspoon ground coriander
1 teaspoon ground cumin
1 teaspoon paprika
1 teaspoon ground ginger
1 teaspoon sea salt

1 boneless leg of lamb, about 1.5 kg (3 lb), butterflied
  and trimmed of any excess fat and sinew

1. Combine the marinade ingredients in a food processor and
pulse to make a smooth paste, scraping down the side of the
bowl as necessary. Place the lamb in a large, resealable plastic
bag and pour in the marinade. Press the air out of the bag and
seal tightly. Turn the bag to distribute the marinade and
refrigerate for 1 hour. Allow the lamb to stand at room
temperature for 20 to 30 minutes before grilling. Prepare the
barbecue for direct and indirect cooking over a high heat.

2. Remove the lamb from the bag, letting the marinade cling to
the lamb. Discard the marinade in the bag. Brush the cooking
grates clean. Grill the lamb over **direct high heat** for about
6 minutes, with the lid closed as much as possible but turning
once, until nicely browned on both sides. Slide the lamb
over **indirect high heat** and cook, with the lid closed, to your
desired doneness, 15 to 20 minutes for medium rare. Remove
the lamb from the barbecue and allow to rest for about
5 minutes before carving. Cut the lamb across the grain
into thin diagonal slices and serve warm.

HOW TO BUTTERFLY A LEG OF LAMB

1. A boneless leg of lamb is actually several
muscles held together. The different muscles
have various shapes and thicknesses.

2. In order to grill the whole leg evenly, you need
to make the thickest parts thinner.

3. You do that by making angled cuts at the
thickness you want and then spreading the meat
open like a book.

PANIOLO TRI-TIP ROAST WITH ORANGE BARBECUE SAUCE

SERVES: 6
PREP TIME: 20 MINUTES

HEAT: DIRECT AND INDIRECT MEDIUM HEAT
    180° TO 230°C (350° TO 450°F)
GRILLING TIME: 23 TO 30 MINUTES

PASTE
2 tablespoons extra-virgin olive oil
2 tablespoons very finely chopped fresh root ginger
2 tablespoons light brown sugar
2 teaspoons coarse sea salt or alaea (Hawaiian sea salt)
2 teaspoons very finely chopped garlic
1 teaspoon chilli-garlic sauce, such as Sriracha

1 tri-tip roast, about 1 kg (2 lb) and 3.5 cm (1½ inches) thick,
    fat and silver skin removed

SAUCE
250 ml (8 fl oz) thawed frozen orange juice concentrate
2 tablespoons light brown sugar
2 tablespoons cider vinegar
2 tablespoons soy sauce

1. Combine the paste ingredients in a bowl. Coat the joint evenly with the paste and allow the roast to stand at room temperature for 20 to 30 minutes before grilling. Prepare the barbecue for direct and indirect cooking over a medium heat.

2. Combine the sauce ingredients in a saucepan over a medium heat and bubble for 10 to 15 minutes, whisking frequently, until thickened and reduced to about 175 ml (6 fl oz). Set aside and reheat just before serving.

3. Brush the cooking grates clean. Grill the roast over **direct medium heat** for 8 to 10 minutes, turning once, until well marked on both sides. Move the tri-tip over **indirect medium heat** and cook to your desired doneness, 15 to 20 minutes for medium rare. Keep the lid closed as much as possible during grilling but turn the joint over every 5 minutes or so. Remove the joint from the barbecue, cover with foil, and allow it to rest for 5 to 10 minutes. Cut the joint across the grain into thin slices. Serve warm with the sauce.

Much of what gives this Hawaiian-style tri-tip roast such great flavour is the paste, which features fresh root ginger. Before very finely chopping the ginger, scrape off the skin with the back of a spoon. Also, be careful not to overcook the joint. It's a very lean cut of meat and it's best served medium rare.

HOW TO PREP BEEF FILLET

1. Slide a sharp knife just under any large clumps of fat, being careful not to cut into the meat. Also remove the strips of silver skin, which are tough and chewy.

2. Tie the 'cleaned' joint every couple of inches to make it even and compact. Because the tail is thinner than the rest of the joint, fold it underneath and tie it snugly for a more even thickness end to end.

3. Cut off the loose ends of the string.

4. Rub oil all over the joint and season it with herbs and spices.

5. Grill the joint first over a direct heat to brown it on all sides.

6. Finish cooking it over indirect heat so that the exterior does not burn before the interior is cooked.

HERB-CRUSTED BEEF FILLET WITH WHITE WINE CREAM SAUCE

SERVES: 10 TO 12
PREP TIME: 40 MINUTES

HEAT: DIRECT AND INDIRECT MEDIUM HEAT
   180° TO 230°C (350° TO 450°F)
GRILLING TIME: 35 TO 45 MINUTES
SPECIAL EQUIPMENT: BUTCHER'S STRING

RUB
1½ tablespoons dried tarragon
2½ teaspoons sea salt
2 teaspoons freshly ground black pepper
1½ teaspoons dried thyme
1 teaspoon dried sage, packed

1 whole beef fillet, 3 to 3.5 kg (6 to 7 lb), untrimmed
Extra-virgin olive oil

SAUCE
75 g (3 oz) shallot, very finely chopped
125 ml (4 fl oz) rice vinegar
1½ teaspoons dried tarragon
¼ teaspoon dried thyme
125 ml (4 fl oz) dry white wine
125 ml (4 fl oz) chicken stock
350 ml (12 fl oz) whipping cream
25 g (1 oz) flat leaf parsley, very finely chopped

Sea salt

1. Mix the rub ingredients together in a small bowl.

2. Trim and discard the excess fat and silver skin from the fillet. Part of the thin 'tail' end of the fillet may separate as it is trimmed, but leave it connected to the main muscle as much as possible. Lay the fillet out flat and straight, with the smoothest side up, aligning the narrow pieces at the tail end. Neatly fold the tail end of the fillet under itself to form an even thickness (one end may be larger). Tie the joint snugly with butcher's string at 5-cm (2-inch) intervals. Secure the folded end with 2 strings. Lightly coat the joint with oil, then season the joint all over with the rub.

3. Allow the joint to stand at room temperature for 30 minutes to 1 hour before grilling. Prepare the barbecue for direct and indirect cooking over a medium heat.

4. Combine the shallot, vinegar, tarragon and thyme in a large frying pan over a high heat, and cook for 3 to 4 minutes, stirring often, until the vinegar has evaporated. Add the wine and stock and boil for 3 to 4 minutes until reduced to about 125 ml (4 fl oz). Add the cream and continue boiling for a further 5 to 7 minutes until the surface is covered with large, shiny bubbles and the sauce is reduced to about 375 ml (12 fl oz). Remove the pan from the heat, adjust the seasonings and set aside. Reheat and add parsley just before serving.

5. Brush the cooking grates clean. Sear the joint over ***direct medium heat*** for about 15 minutes, turning a quarter turn once every 3 to 4 minutes. Slide the joint over ***indirect medium heat*** and cook, turning once, until it reaches your desired doneness, 20 to 30 minutes for medium rare. Keep the lid closed as much as possible during grilling. Remove the joint from the barbecue, loosely cover with foil and allow to rest for 10 to 15 minutes. The internal temperature will rise during this time.

6. Snip and remove all the string from the joint. Cut the meat crossways into 1- to 2.5-cm (½- to 1-inch) slices. Season to taste with salt. Serve warm with the sauce.

HOW TO PREP BONELESS RIB ROAST

1. For a special occasion, consider buying a rib roast a few days before you plan to serve it and dry-ageing it in your refrigerator. (For safety reasons, never do this for more than 4 days.) Patted dry and set on a rack over a roasting tray in the refrigerator, the meat will develop more concentrated flavours and a softer texture.

2. After you have seasoned the meat, allow it to stand at room temperature for 30 to 40 minutes so that the outer ring of the joint won't overcook before the centre reaches your ideal temperature on the barbecue.

HOW TO SMOKE A BONELESS RIB ROAST

1. Spread a layer or two of lit coals on one-half of the charcoal grate. Position some wood chunks alongside the coals. On the opposite side, set up a water pan, which will absorb some heat and release it slowly.

2. Initially position the joint with the thicker end towards the coals.

3. An instant-read thermometer takes all the guesswork out of doneness. For medium rare, remove the joint when it hits the 49° to 52°C (120° to 125°F) range. The internal temperature will climb as the meat rests.

The sweet, haunting aromas of smoldering oak are a distinctive part of this recipe. Bags of wood chunks are pretty easy to find in shops specializing in selling barbecues, but if you happen to have dried oak logs lying around, you can make your own chunks. Saw the logs into smaller sections and use a chisel and hammer to break off most of the bark; it tends to add a bit of bitterness to the smoke. Next split the wood into fist-sized pieces. Unlike wood chips, chunks don't need to be soaked. Alongside the coals, they will burn slowly and permeate the meat with a taste of the great outdoors.

OAK-SMOKED BONELESS RIB ROAST WITH SHIRAZ SAUCE

SERVES: 10
PREP TIME: 30 MINUTES

HEAT: INDIRECT MEDIUM HEAT 180° TO 190°C
   (350° TO 375°F)
GRILLING TIME: ABOUT 1½ HOURS
SPECIAL EQUIPMENT: LARGE DISPOSABLE FOIL TIN,
   INSTANT-READ THERMOMETER

1 boneless rib roast, about 2.2 kg (5½ lb), trimmed
   of excess surface fat
Sea salt
Freshly ground black pepper
4 tablespoons Dijon mustard
50 g (2 oz) yellow onion, coarsely grated
3 garlic cloves, very finely chopped
2 oak wood chunks (not soaked)

SAUCE
40 g (1½ oz) unsalted butter, cold
3 tablespoons very finely chopped shallot
1 garlic clove, very finely chopped
1 litre (1¾ pints) beef stock, preferably home-made
375 ml (12 fl oz) Shiraz wine
1 tablespoon soy sauce
1½ teaspoons tomato purée
¼ teaspoon dried thyme
½ bay leaf

1. Season the joint with 2 teaspoons salt and 1 teaspoon pepper. Mix the mustard, onion and garlic together in a small bowl. Spread this mixture over the top of the joint and allow it to stand at room temperature for 30 to 40 minutes before grilling.

2. Prepare the barbecue for indirect cooking over a medium heat (see instructions at left). Add 2 wood chunks alongside the coals. Brush the cooking grates clean. Position the joint with the thicker end facing the coals. Grill over *indirect medium heat* for about 1½ hours, with the lid closed as much as possible but rotating the joint 180 degrees halfway through the grilling time, until the internal temperature reaches 49° to 52°C (120° to 125°F) for medium rare. Keep the barbecue's temperature between 180° and 190°C (350° and 375°F).

3. Melt 15 g (½ oz) of the butter in a medium, heavy-based saucepan over a medium heat (keep the remaining butter refrigerated). Add the shallot and cook for about 2 minutes until softened. Add the garlic and cook for about 1 minute until fragrant. Add the stock, wine, soy sauce, tomato purée, thyme and bay leaf, and bring to the boil over a high heat. Cook for about 30 minutes, uncovered, until reduced to about 500 ml (17 fl oz). Season to taste with salt and pepper. Remove the bay leaf and keep the sauce warm.

4. Remove the joint from the barbecue, loosely cover with foil, and rest for 20 to 30 minutes. The internal temperature will rise during this time. Carve the joint into 1-cm (½-inch) slices, reserving the juices. Just before serving, whisk the remaining cold butter into the sauce, and stir in the carving juices. Serve warm with the sauce.

HOW TO BARBECUE BRISKET

1. The first layer of flavour to apply is the sweet heat of a good spice rub and mustard. Next, cook the seasoned brisket on a smoker for 4 to 5 hours so that it absorbs a good amount of flavourful wood smoke. The brisket should be in a large disposable foil tin to catch some of the juices, and the thick layer of fat should be on top so that it bastes the meat below it.

2. When the internal temperature of the meat reaches 70°C (160°F), take it out of the foil tin and double-wrap the brisket in aluminium foil. This will trap some moisture and help to break down the tough fibres in the meat.

3. When the internal temperature reaches 88° to 90.5°C (190° to 195°F) in the thickest section, remove the brisket from the smoker and allow the precious meat juices to collect in the foil. The brisket will stay warm and continue to cook for an hour or two.

4. Carefully unwrap the foil, set the brisket aside and bend the foil to funnel the juices into a serving bowl.

5. Slice a section of fat from the top side of the brisket so you can see which way the grain of the meat runs. For the sake of tenderness, you want to slice against the grain.

6. Slice the brisket nice and thin with a sharp knife. That beautiful pink ring is a result of the wood smoke. Now spoon those meat juices over the top and enjoy eating it.

TRULY BARBECUED BRISKET

SERVES: 6
PREP TIME: 15 MINUTES
MARINATING TIME: 6 TO 8 HOURS

HEAT: INDIRECT LOW HEAT 110° TO 130°C (225° TO 250°F)
GRILLING TIME: 6 TO 8 HOURS, PLUS 1 TO 2 HOURS
    RESTING TIME
SPECIAL EQUIPMENT: LARGE DISPOSABLE FOIL TIN,
    INSTANT-READ THERMOMETER

RUB
4 teaspoons sea salt
2 teaspoons ancho chilli powder
2 teaspoons light brown sugar
2 teaspoons garlic granules
2 teaspoons paprika
1 teaspoon celery seeds
1 teaspoon coarsely ground black pepper

1 brisket (flat cut), 2.5 to 3 kg (5 to 6 lb), untrimmed
4 tablespoons yellow mustard
6 hickory or oak wood chunks (not soaked)
500 ml (17 fl oz) favourite barbecue sauce

1. Mix the rub ingredients together in a small bowl.

2. Lay the brisket, fat side up, on a large chopping board. Trim the layer of fat to a 1-cm (½-inch) thickness. Turn the brisket over and trim any hard fat or thin membrane covering the meat.

3. Season the brisket evenly with the mustard and then the rub. Cover and refrigerate for 6 to 8 hours.

4. Place the brisket, fat side up, in a large disposable foil tin.

5. Prepare your smoker, following manufacturer's instructions, for indirect cooking over a low heat.

6. Place the tin with the brisket on the cooking grate. Smoke the brisket for 4 to 5 hours, starting with 2 chunks of wood, at 110° to 130°C (225° to 250°F), until the internal temperature of the meat reaches 70° to 77°C (160° to 170°F). Every hour or so, add another chunk of wood to the coals and, if necessary, add more coals to maintain the temperature of the smoker at 110° to 130°C (225° to 250°F).

7. When the internal temperature of the meat has reached 70° to 77°C (160° to 170°F), the collagen in the meat will have dissolved. At that point, remove the brisket and tin from the smoker (close the lid to maintain the heat). Baste the brisket with some of the juices and fat collected in the tin, then wrap the joint in 2 large sheets of heavy-duty foil. Discard the tin.

8. Return the brisket to the smoker and cook for 2 to 3 hours, without adding more wood chunks, until the internal temperature of the brisket has reached 88° to 90.5°C

(190° to 195°F) in the thickest section. The probe of the thermometer should slide in and out of the brisket with just a little resistance.

9. Remove the brisket from the smoker and allow it to rest inside the foil at room temperature for 1 to 2 hours. It will stay hot and continue to tenderize.

10. Carefully unwrap the brisket, being careful not to lose any of the juices inside the foil. Move the brisket to a large chopping board and pour the juices into a small bowl.

11. If necessary, cut off a small chunk of brisket to identify the direction of the grain. Cut the brisket across the grain into 3-mm (⅛-inch) slices. Spoon or brush some of the juices over the slices. Serve warm with barbecue sauce on the side.

■■■

Brisket is the Mt Everest of barbecue. Not only is it huge, but it also poses challenges all along the way. If your first couple of attempts don't work out exactly as you had hoped, persevere. The rewards of mastering your own barbecued brisket are unspeakably good. Among a cadre of outdoor cooks you will have earned long-standing respect and admiration.

■■■

PORK

TECHNIQUES

RECIPES

HOW TO BARBECUE BRATWURST

1. Before cooking, prick several small holes in each bratwurst to prevent them from bursting open.

2. For the first stage of cooking, you will need a very hot fire on one side of the cooking grate.

3. Arrange the bratwurst in a single layer in a disposable tin with the cider and sliced onions.

4. Simmer the bratwurst for about 20 minutes, turning them occasionally. If the liquid boils, slide the tin over indirect heat.

5. Strain the onions and return them to the tin to caramelize with brown sugar.

6. Finish barbecuing the bratwurst over direct heat to lightly char the surfaces.

CIDER-SIMMERED BRATS WITH APPLES AND ONIONS

SERVES: 5
PREP TIME: 15 MINUTES

HEAT: DIRECT HIGH HEAT 230° TO 290°C
(450° TO 550°F) AND DIRECT MEDIUM HEAT
180° TO 230°C (350° TO 450°F)
GRILLING TIME: 6 TO 8 MINUTES
SPECIAL EQUIPMENT: 2 LARGE DISPOSABLE FOIL TINS

MUSTARD
2 tablespoons apple sauce
2 tablespoons Dijon mustard
2 tablespoons wholegrain mustard

750 ml (1¼ pints) cider
2 yellow onions, halved and cut into 5-mm (¼-inch) slices
5 fresh bratwurst, pierced several times
1 tablespoon brown sugar
5 submarine sandwich or hot dog buns, halved lengthways
2 Granny Smith apples, cored and thinly sliced

1. Mix the mustard ingredients together in a small bowl. Cover and let stand at room temperature until ready to serve.

2. Prepare the barbecue for direct and indirect cooking over a high heat. Brush the cooking grates clean. Put the cider, onions and bratwurst into a large disposable foil tin. Place the tin over **direct high heat** and bring the liquid to a simmer. Keep the barbecue lid closed as much as possible but turn the bratwursts occasionally, until they are evenly coloured and have lost their raw look. If the liquid starts to boil, move the tin over indirect heat to prevent the bratwurst from splitting open.

3. Lower the temperature of the barbecue to a medium heat. Transfer the brats to another large disposable aluminium tin. Strain the onions in a colander over the tin with the brats (the liquid will keep the brats warm while you cook the onions). Return the onions to the original tin and stir in the brown sugar. Cook the onions over **direct medium heat** for about 15 minutes, with the lid closed as much as possible but stirring occasionally, until they are golden brown. Move the onions over indirect heat to keep them warm.

4. Remove the brats from the liquid and grill them over **direct medium heat** for 6 to 8 minutes, turning once or twice, until browned. During the last minute, place the buns on the barbecue to toast.

5. Place the brats in the buns. Spread each with the mustard, and top with the glazed onions and a few apple slices. Serve hot.

One key to the juiciness of these burgers is mixing apple sauce into the minced pork. Another key is including green apples in the slaw. A box grater conveniently separates the moist flesh of a cored apple from its tough skin.

PORK BURGERS WITH APPLE-TARRAGON SLAW

SERVES: 4
PREP TIME: 20 MINUTES

HEAT: DIRECT MEDIUM HEAT 180° TO 230°C
   (350° TO 450°F)
GRILLING TIME: 12 TO 15 MINUTES

SLAW
175 g (6 oz) green cabbage, thinly sliced
65 g (2½ oz) tart green apple, coarsely grated
50 g (2 oz) carrot, coarsely grated
2 tablespoons finely chopped tarragon
2 tablespoons cider vinegar
1 tablespoon sugar
½ teaspoon celery seeds
¼ teaspoon sea salt

BURGERS
750 g (1½ lb) minced pork
75 g (3 oz) apple sauce
1½ teaspoons sea salt
1 teaspoon hot sauce, or to taste
½ teaspoon freshly ground black pepper

4 hamburger buns

1. Mix the slaw ingredients together in a large bowl. Cover and refrigerate until ready to assemble the burgers.

2. Gently mix the burger ingredients together in a large bowl. Gently shape into 4 equal-sized burgers, each about 1.5 cm (¾ inch) thick. With your thumb or the back of a spoon, make a shallow indentation about 2.5 cm (1 inch) wide in the centre of each burger. Prepare the barbecue for direct cooking over a medium heat.

3. Brush the cooking grates clean. Grill the burgers over **_direct medium heat_** for 12 to 15 minutes with the lid closed as much as possible but turning once when the burgers release easily from the grate without sticking, until cooked through. During the last minute of grilling time, toast the buns, cut sides down, over **_direct medium heat_**. Place the burgers on the buns and top with the slaw. Serve warm.

BUTTERMILK BISCUITS
WITH PEPPER JELLY–GLAZED HAM

SERVES: 6

PREP TIME: 20 MINUTES

HEAT: INDIRECT HIGH HEAT ABOUT 200°C (400°F) AND
DIRECT MEDIUM HEAT 180° TO 230°C (350° TO 450°F)

GRILLING TIME: 16 TO 21 MINUTES

BISCUITS

550 g (1 lb 2 oz) plain flour
4 teaspoons baking powder
1 teaspoon bicarbonate of soda
1 teaspoon sea salt
250 g (8 oz) solid white vegetable fat, cold
350 ml (12 fl oz) buttermilk, cold
1 tablespoon unsalted butter, melted

250 g (8 oz) medium or hot jalapeño jelly
1 kg (2 lb) gammon steak, about 1 cm (½ inch) thick

1. Prepare the barbecue for indirect cooking over a high heat.

2. Combine the flour, baking powder, bicarbonate of soda and
salt in a large bowl. Cut in the shortening with your fingertips or
a pastry blender until the mixture resembles coarse breadcrumbs. Add the buttermilk and stir just until the mixture sticks
together. Turn the dough out on to a lightly floured surface and
knead lightly for 20 to 30 seconds. Lightly dust your hands
with flour and gently pat out the dough to a thickness of about
1.5 cm (¾ inch). Dip a 6-cm (2½-inch) round biscuit cutter in
flour and cut out rounds of dough. Gather scraps of dough and
pat out, using a light touch so you don't overwork the dough.
Cut to make a total of 12 biscuits. Place the biscuits close
together on a greased baking sheet. Brush the tops with
melted butter.

3. Grill the sheet of biscuits over **indirect high heat** (keeping
the barbecue 's temperature as close to 200°C/400°F as
possible) with the barbecue lid closed as much as possible
but checking occasionally and moving or rotating the sheet as
needed so the bottoms of the biscuits do not burn, until they
are lightly browned. Remove the biscuits from the barbecue
and set aside to keep warm.

4. Prepare the barbecue for direct cooking over medium heat.

5. Warm one-third of the jalapeño jelly in a small saucepan over
low heat until it melts. Brush the cooking grates clean. Grill the
gammon steaks over **direct medium heat** for 4 to 6 minutes,
with the lid closed as much as possible but turning once and
basting with jalapeño jelly before and after turning, until the
steaks are nicely marked and crispy on the edges.

6. Cut the ham into pieces about the same size as the biscuits.
Split each biscuit horizontally. Serve the ham warm in biscuits
with the remaining jalapeño jelly on top.

HOW TO MAKE
BUTTERMILK BISCUITS

1. Mix the dry ingredients in a medium bowl . Add cold
vegetable fat. Use a pastry blender or fork to 'cut in' the
fat until the mixture resembles coarse crumbs with a few
larger clumps.

2. Add buttermilk and stir just until the mixture
comes together.

3. Pat the dough on a floured surface into a round about
1.5 cm (¾ inch) thick. Use a floured biscuit cutter to cut out
rounds of dough.

HOW TO BARBECUE PORK CHOPS

5 THINGS YOU NEED TO KNOW

1 NOT YOUR GRANDFATHER'S PORK

Today's pigs come to market younger and smaller than the pigs of yesteryear. They have had less time to develop much collagen and connective tissue – that is, the stuff that can make pork chewy. Pork chops, therefore, are definitely tender enough for barbecuing. That's the good news.

2 IT'S BRINE TIME

The bad news is that today's pigs are also much leaner than the pigs of yester-year. In fact, pork chops are about as lean as chicken today, which means it doesn't take long for them to dry out on the barbecue. So it is always a good idea to brine pork chops first. Brining means soaking them in a flavourful salty liquid that the meat can absorb, giving them more moisture (and flavour) from the start.

3 CHOOSE YOUR CHOP WELL

Pork chops are cut from a pig's loin, which runs from the shoulder to the hip. The chops from the shoulder (blade chops and country-style ribs) are the most marbled and flavourful, but also the chewiest. The chops from the hip (sirloin chops) are quite dry and tough, so I don't recommend those for barbecuing. The chops from the mid-section of the loin (rib chops and loin chops) can be quite tender and juicy, if you cook them right.

4 EASY DOES IT

We don't serve pork chops charred on the outside and rare or medium rare in the middle, like steaks. We serve them with a relatively even doneness from top to bottom. This means a gentler heat on the barbecue so that the centres of the chops can reach the right degree of doneness well before the outsides are overdone.

5 THAT TOUCH OF PINK

There is really only one correct doneness level for pork chops. You'll know it when you see it and when you taste it. As the chop cooks, the colour of the meat inside will turn from reddish-pink to a very light pink. That's it. Stop there. If you cook pork chops any further than that, the meat will be grey and bland.

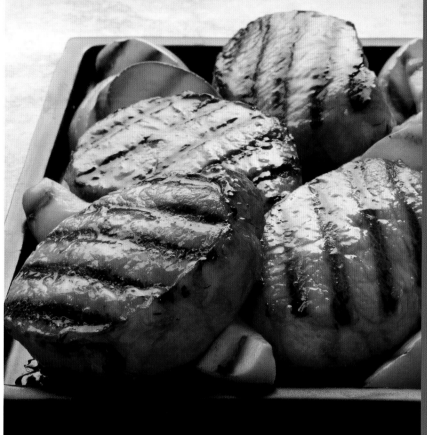

Good barbecuing is all about layering flavours from the inside out. In this recipe, pork chops benefit dramatically from a cider brine that penetrates right to the centre of the meat, plus an apple-brandy glaze that coats the outside.

CIDER-BRINED PORK CHOPS WITH GRILLED APPLES

SERVES: 4
PREP TIME: 15 MINUTES
BRINING TIME: 1 TO 1½ HOURS

HEAT: DIRECT MEDIUM HEAT 180° TO 230°C
(350° TO 450°F)
GRILLING TIME: ABOUT 12 MINUTES

BRINE
350 ml (12 fl oz) cider
100 g (3½ oz) sea salt
1 tablespoon dried rosemary
1 tablespoon dried sage
1½ teaspoons dried thyme
½ teaspoon whole black peppercorns

4 centre-cut pork loin chops, each about 350 g (12 oz) and
    3.5 cm (1½ inches) thick, trimmed of excess fat
Extra-virgin olive oil

GLAZE
6 tablespoons apple jelly
2 tablespoons unsalted butter
2 tablespoons Calvados or other apple brandy

4 Granny Smith apples, each cut into 6 wedges with the
    cores removed

1. Mix the brine ingredients together in a large bowl. Put the chops in a large, resealable plastic bag and pour in the brine. Press the air out of the bag and seal tightly. Place the bag in a bowl or a rimmed dish and refrigerate for 1 to 1½ hours, turning the bag every 30 minutes.

2. Remove the chops from the bag and discard the brine. Rinse the chops under cold water and pat dry with kitchen paper. Lightly brush the chops with oil and let stand at room temperature for 20 to 30 minutes before cooking. Prepare the barbecue for direct cooking over a medium heat.

3. Warm the jelly and butter in a small saucepan over a medium-low heat, stirring until the jelly melts. Remove the pan from the heat and stir in the Calvados. If the glaze cools, reheat gently until fluid. Set aside half of the glaze to serve as a sauce with the barbecued pork. Brush the remaining glaze all over the apple slices and then the chops.

4. Brush the cooking grates clean. Grill the chops over ***direct medium heat*** for about 10 minutes, with the lid closed as much as possible, but turning then once, until they are slightly pink in the centre. Remove the chops from the barbecue and allow to rest for 3 to 5 minutes. While they rest, cook the apples over ***direct medium heat***, about 2 minutes, turning once, until crisp-tender. Serve the chops and apples warm with the reserved glaze.

HOW TO PREP LEEKS

1. Remove the tough green tops from small, slender leeks and trim off just enough of the root end to get rid of the stringy parts.

2. Cut each leek in half lengthways to expose the many layers inside, making sure to leave some root end intact so the layers remain attached.

3. Because leeks grow underground, you will often find dirt and sand trapped between the layers. Spread the layers open under running water to clean them before barbecuing.

HOW TO MAKE PORK PAILLARDS

1. Begin with boneless centre-cut pork chops at least 2.5 cm (1 inch) thick. Cut into the centre of the fat side to within about 1 cm (½ inch) of the other side, so that each chop opens up like a butterfly.

2. Flatten the meat with the palm of your hand and trim off any excess fat around the perimeter.

3. Lay each chop between 2 large sheets of clingfilm. Use the flat side of a meat tenderizer (or the bottom of a small, heavy frying pan) to flatten the meat to an even thickness of about 5 mm (¼ inch).

HOW TO BARBECUE PORK PAILLARDS

1. While thick pork chops do best over a medium heat, thinly-pounded paillards should be grilled quickly over a very high heat.

2. Grill the first side of each paillard with the lid closed until it has nice grill marks, usually about 3 minutes.

3. The second side should need no more than 1 minute to finish cooking.

PORK PAILLARDS
WITH ROMESCO SAUCE

SERVES: 4
PREP TIME: 25 MINUTES

HEAT: DIRECT LOW HEAT 130° TO 180°C (250° TO 350°F)
AND DIRECT HIGH HEAT 230° TO 290°C (450° TO 550°F)
GRILLING TIME: 19 TO 24 MINUTES

4 boneless centre-cut pork chops, 175 to 200 g (6 to 7 oz) each
    and about 2.5 cm (1 inch) thick
Extra-virgin olive oil
Sea salt
Freshly ground black pepper
8 small leeks, no wider than 2.5 cm (1 inch) in diameter,
    optional

SAUCE
100 g (3½ oz) roasted red pepper, roughly chopped
25 g (1 oz) flaked almonds, toasted
1 tablespoon ketchup
1 tablespoon extra-virgin olive oil
1 tablespoon fresh lemon juice
1 teaspoon roughly chopped garlic
½ teaspoon paprika
⅛ teaspoon ground cayenne pepper

1 tablespoon flat leaf parsley, finely chopped

1. Butterfly each chop from the fat side and trim them of
excess fat. One at a time, place each chop between 2 sheets
of clingfilm and pound to an even 5-mm (¼-inch) thickness.
Lightly brush the paillards with oil and season all sides with salt
and pepper.

2. Remove the dark green tops off of each leek, cutting about
5 cm (2 inches) above the point where the leaves begin to
darken. Trim just enough of each root end to remove the stringy
parts, but leave enough of each root end so the layers remain
attached. Cut each leek in half lengthways. Remove the tough
outer leaves on each leek. Rinse the leeks under water, opening
up the layers to remove any dirt, then pat dry. Lightly coat the
leeks with oil and season to taste with salt and pepper.

3. Prepare the barbecue for direct cooking over a low heat.

4. Brush the cooking grates clean. Grill the leeks over **direct
low heat** for 15 to 20 minutes, with the lid closed as much as
possible but turning every couple of minutes for even cooking,
and moving over indirect heat if the leeks become too dark
before they are tender, until softened and slightly charred on
all sides.

5. Combine the sauce ingredients in a food processor. Pulse
until you get a semi-smooth consistency, then season to taste
with salt.

6. Increase the temperature of the barbecue to a high heat.
Brush the cooking grates clean. Grill the paillards over **direct
high heat** for about 3 minutes on the first side, turning when the
meat is nicely marked. The second side will need only a minute
to finish cooking.

7. Transfer the paillards, with the first grilled side facing up, to a
serving platter or individual plates. Divide the sauce evenly and
spoon over the meat. Arrange 2 leeks on top of each paillard.
Garnish with some parsley over the top.

Once the sandwiches are assembled, you can reheat the meat and melt the cheese by wrapping each sandwich in parchment paper or aluminium foil and barbecuing them over direct medium heat, turning them occasionally.

PORK, ROASTED PEPPER AND CHEESE SANDWICHES

SERVES: 4
PREP TIME: 30 MINUTES
MARINATING TIME: 30 MINUTES

HEAT: DIRECT HIGH HEAT 230° TO 290°C (450° TO 550°F)
AND DIRECT MEDIUM HEAT 180° TO 230°C
(350° TO 450°F)
GRILLING TIME: 18 TO 22 MINUTES

MARINADE
2 tablespoons fresh lemon juice
1 teaspoon dried oregano
1 teaspoon finely chopped rosemary
1 teaspoon very finely chopped garlic
1 teaspoon sea salt
¼ teaspoon crushed red chilli flakes
5 tablespoons extra-virgin olive oil

6 boneless centre-cut loin pork chops, each 50 to 125 g
  (2 to 4 oz) and about 1 cm (½ inch) thick, trimmed of
  excess fat
2 red peppers
4 crusty French rolls, split in half crossways
4 slices pepper jack or Cheddar cheese
65 g (2½ oz) baby spinach leaves, rinsed and dried

1. Combine the lemon juice, oregano, rosemary, garlic, salt and chilli flakes in a small bowl, then whisk in the oil. Reserve 2 tablespoons of the marinade to use as a dressing.

2. Working with 1 chop at a time, place each chop between 2 sheets of clingfilm. Using a flat meat tenderizer, pound the chop until it is an even 5 mm (¼ inch) thick. When all the chops are pounded, place them in a large, resealable plastic bag, arrange them flat and pour in the marinade. Press the air out of the bag and seal tightly. Turn the bag to distribute the marinade, place the bag on a plate and allow to marinate at room temperature for 30 minutes. Prepare the barbecue for direct cooking over a high heat.

3. Brush the cooking grates clean. Grill the peppers over **direct high heat** for 10 to 12 minutes, with the lid closed as much as possible but turning every 3 to 5 minutes, until blackened and blistered all over. Place the peppers in a bowl, cover with clingfilm and allow to stand for 10 to 15 minutes. Remove the peppers from the bowl and peel away and discard the charred skins. Cut off the tops and remove the seeds. Cut lengthways into 1-cm (½-inch) wide strips.

4. Remove the chops from the bag and discard the marinade. Sear the chops over **direct high heat** for about 4 minutes, with the lid closed as much as possible but turning once. During the last minute of cooking, toast the cut sides of the rolls over direct heat.

5. Toss the spinach with the 2 tablespoons of reserved marinade in a bowl. Build the sandwiches with a slice of cheese, 1 to 1½ pork chops, cut to fit the roll, strips of roasted pepper and spinach.

6. Lower the temperature of the barbecue to a medium heat. Completely wrap each sandwich in a 30 by 30-cm (12 by 12-inch) sheet of parchment paper, twisting the ends in opposite directions to enclose the sandwiches. Grill over **direct medium heat** for 4 to 6 minutes, until the cheese melts and the sandwiches are hot.

PORK LOIN CHOPS
WITH SOFRITO BARBECUE SAUCE

SERVES: 4
PREP TIME: 30 MINUTES

HEAT: DIRECT MEDIUM HEAT 180° TO 230°C
    (350° TO 450°F)
GRILLING TIME: 7 TO 9 MINUTES

SAUCE
250 g (8 oz) yellow onion, cut into 5 mm (¼ inch) dice
3 tablespoons extra-virgin olive oil
1 small bay leaf
1 tablespoon finely chopped garlic
1 tablespoon sherry vinegar
125 ml (4 fl oz) apple juice
1 can (425 g/14 oz) fire-roasted tomatoes
1 teaspoon paprika
½ teaspoon dried oregano
¼ teaspoon crushed red chilli flakes
¼ teaspoon sea salt
¼ teaspoon freshly ground black pepper

RUB
1 teaspoon sea salt
½ teaspoon paprika
½ teaspoon dried oregano
½ teaspoon freshly ground black pepper

4 bone-in pork loin rib chops, each 2.5 cm (1 inch) thick
Extra-virgin olive oil

1. Combine the onion, oil and bay leaf in a frying pan over a medium heat. When the onion starts to sizzle, adjust the heat to medium-low and cook for about 30 minutes, stirring frequently and adding the garlic to the pan after 15 minutes, until the onions are evenly browned. Add the vinegar and cook until it has almost evaporated. Add the apple juice and simmer until the liquid in the pan has reduced by half. Add the rest of the sauce ingredients and continue to simmer for about 5 minutes.

2. Remove the bay leaf. Transfer the sauce to a food processor or blender and purée until smooth. Reserve 125 ml (4 fl oz) of the sauce for basting and the rest to serve with the chops.

3. Combine the rub ingredients in a small bowl. Lightly coat the chops with oil and season with the rub. Allow the chops to stand at room temperature for 20 to 30 minutes before grilling. Prepare the barbecue for direct cooking over a high heat.

4. Brush the cooking grates clean. Grill the chops over **direct medium heat** for 4 to 5 minutes, with the lid closed as much as possible but turning once, until they are nicely marked on each side. Then brush both sides with the reserved sauce and continue cooking for 3 to 4 minutes, turning once or twice, until the sauce cooks into the meat a bit and the centres are barely pink. Remove the chops from the barbecue and allow to rest for 2 to 3 minutes. Serve warm with the reserved sauce.

HOW TO BARBECUE PORK CHOPS WITH SOFRITO BARBECUE SAUCE

1. In Spain and throughout much of Latin America, it is common to begin sauces with a sofrito, which is slowly browned onions and garlic followed by tomatoes.

2. Combined with apple juice and spices, this sofrito becomes a barbecue sauce. Use it for brushing onto the chops and as a dipping sauce.

3. Mark the pork chops well on both sides before brushing on the sauce, then let the sauce flavours cook into the meat.

To remove the tough silver skin from the surface, slip the tip of a narrow, sharp knife under a piece of silver skin, then grab the loosened end and stretch it taut. Slide the knife just over the pinkish meat below, angling it upwards to avoid cutting into the meat. The goal is to 'clean' the fillets without losing any more meat than necessary.

PORK FILLETS WITH CREAMY CORN

SERVES: 4 TO 6
PREP TIME: 25 MINUTES
MARINATING TIME: 1 TO 3 HOURS

HEAT: DIRECT MEDIUM HEAT 180° TO 230°C
(350° TO 450°F)
GRILLING TIME: 25 TO 30 MINUTES

PASTE
3 large garlic cloves
15 g (½ oz) oregano leaves and tender stems
1 teaspoon sea salt
4 tablespoons extra-virgin olive oil
2 tablespoons cider vinegar
½ teaspoon freshly ground black pepper

2 pork fillets, about 500 g (1 lb) each
5 ears fresh corn, husked
Extra-virgin olive oil
50 g (2 oz) red onion, finely chopped
3 spring onions, thinly sliced crossways
250 ml (8 fl oz) double cream
¼ teaspoon sea salt
⅛ teaspoon freshly ground black pepper
1 tablespoon finely chopped oregano
Hot pepper sauce, optional

1. Roughly chop the garlic, then sprinkle the oregano and salt over the garlic. Continue to chop until the garlic and oregano are very finely chopped. Periodically use the side of your knife blade to press the garlic on the cutting board and create a paste. Transfer the garlic paste to a bowl and mix in the oil, vinegar and pepper.

2. Trim the pork fillets of surface fat and silver skin. Brush the paste all over the surface of the meat. Cover and refrigerate for 1 to 3 hours. Allow the meat to stand at room temperature for 20 to 30 minutes before grilling. Prepare the barbecue for direct cooking over a medium heat.

3. Lightly brush the ears of corn with oil. Brush the cooking grates clean. Grill the corn over **direct medium heat** for about 10 minutes, with the lid closed as much as possible but turning occasionally, until browned in spots and barely tender. Using a sharp knife, cut the corn kernels off the cobs.

4. Warm 2 tablespoons of olive oil in a frying pan over a medium heat. Add the onion and spring onions; cook for 3 to 4 minutes, stirring occasionally. Add the corn kernels, cream, salt and pepper and mix well. Reduce the heat to low and simmer for 5 to 7 minutes until about half of the cream has evaporated. Add the oregano and a couple dashes of hot sauce, if desired. Set aside.

5. Grill the pork over **direct medium heat** for 15 to 20 minutes, with the lid closed as much as possible but turning about every 5 minutes, until the outsides are evenly seared and the centres are barely pink. The internal temperature of the tenderloins should be 65°C (150°F) when fully cooked.

6. Remove the pork from the barbecue and allow it to rest for 3 to 5 minutes before slicing. Meanwhile, warm the corn mixture over a medium heat. Cut each fillet crossways into slices about 1 cm (½ inch) thick. Arrange the slices on a platter or individual plates. Serve warm with the creamy corn.

PORK FILLETS WITH SMOKED PAPRIKA ROUILLE

SERVES: 6
PREP TIME: 15 MINUTES

HEAT: DIRECT MEDIUM HEAT 180° TO 230°C
    (350° TO 450°F)
GRILLING TIME: 27 TO 35 MINUTES

ROUILLE
2 red peppers
2–3 small garlic cloves
¾ teaspoon sea salt
100 g (3½ oz) dried breadcrumbs
3 tablespoons fresh lemon juice
¾ teaspoon smoked paprika
150 ml (5 fl oz) extra-virgin olive oil

2 pork fillets, about 500 g (1 lb) each
Extra-virgin olive oil
½ teaspoon sea salt
¼ teaspoon freshly ground black pepper

A rouille is a rust-coloured garlicky paste that it is traditionally added to bouillabaisse (fish stew), but if you thin out a rouille with a bit more extra-virgin olive oil, it also makes a very nice sauce. The key to a smooth texture is adding the oil very slowly while the paste whirls in a food processor or blender. Some food processors have a handy little hole in the feed tube that prevents too much oil from pouring into the emulsion all at once.

1. Prepare the barbecue for direct cooking over medium heat. Brush the cooking grates clean. Grill the peppers over **direct medium heat** for 12 to 15 minutes, with the lid closed as much as possible but turning every 3 to 5 minutes, until blackened and blistered all over. Place the peppers in a bowl, cover with clingfilm and allow to stand for 10 to 15 minutes. Remove the peppers from the bowl and peel away and discard the charred skins, tops and seeds.

2. Very finely chop the garlic in a blender or food processor, then add the roasted peppers, salt and breadcrumbs. Add the lemon juice and paprika and, with the motor running, slowly add the oil. Blend until very smooth and orangey-red in colour. If the rouille is too thick, add about 1 tablespoon of water. Season to taste with more salt, if needed.

3. Trim the fillets of any surface fat and silver skin. Lightly brush with oil and season evenly with the salt and pepper. Allow the meat to stand at room temperature for 20 to 30 minutes before grilling.

4. Grill the fillets over **direct medium heat** for 15 to 20 minutes, with the lid closed as much as possible but turning about every 5 minutes, until the outsides are evenly seared and the centres are barely pink. The internal temperature of the fillets should be 65°C (150°F) when fully cooked.

5. Remove the pork from the barbecue and allow it to rest for 3 to 5 minutes. Cut each fillet crossways into thin slices. Serve warm or at room temperature with the rouille.

Cut each pork fillet crossways into pieces about 3.5 cm (1½ inches) thick. Use the heel of your hand to flatten each piece into a medallion about 2.5 cm (1 inch) thick. For juicy results, marinate the medallions for at least 1 hour and then grill them gently over a medium heat until barely pink in the centre.

PORK MEDALLIONS WITH ASIAN BLACK BEAN SAUCE

SERVES: 4
PREP TIME: 25 MINUTES
MARINATING TIME: 1 HOUR

HEAT: DIRECT MEDIUM HEAT 180° TO 230°C
    (350° TO 450°F)
GRILLING TIME: 4 TO 5 MINUTES

MARINADE
½ teaspoon grated orange rind
4 tablespoons fresh orange juice
4 tablespoons Chinese rice wine or dry sherry
2 tablespoons soy sauce
1 tablespoon hoisin sauce
1 tablespoon very finely chopped fresh root ginger
1 tablespoon toasted sesame oil
¼ teaspoon crushed red chilli flakes

2 pork fillets, about 500 g (1 lb) each, trimmed of silver skin

SAUCE
2 tablespoons Chinese fermented black beans
125 ml (4 fl oz) chicken stock
2 tablespoons Chinese rice wine or dry sherry
1 tablespoon soy sauce
1 teaspoon sugar
1½ teaspoons cornflour
1 tablespoon rapeseed or other vegetable oil
2 teaspoons peeled and very finely chopped fresh root ginger
1 garlic clove, very finely chopped
2 tablespoons fresh orange juice

1. Whisk the marinade ingredients together in a bowl.

2. Cut off the thin, tapered end from each fillet and reserve for another use, or marinate and grill along with the medallions. Cut each fillet crossways into 6 equal-sized pieces, each about 3.5 cm (1½ inches) thick. One at a time, stand the pork rounds on a work surface and, using the heel of your hand, slightly flatten into a round medallion about 2.5 cm (1 inch) thick. Place the medallions in a large, resealable plastic bag and pour in the marinade. Press the air out of the bag and seal tightly. Turn the bag several times to distribute the marinade and refrigerate for at least 1 hour, turning the bag occasionally.

3. Soak the fermented black beans in a small bowl filled with warm water for 10 to 20 minutes, then drain well. Coarsely chop the beans and set aside. Whisk the stock, rice wine, soy sauce and sugar together in a bowl until the sugar has dissolved. Sprinkle in the cornflour and stir to dissolve. Set aside.

4. Warm the oil in a small saucepan over a medium-high heat. Add the ginger and garlic and stir for about 20 seconds, until softened. Stir in the beans, then add the stock mixture and bring to the boil, stirring constantly, until the sauce has slightly thickened. Remove from the heat and stir in the orange juice.

5. Prepare the barbecue for direct cooking over a medium heat. Brush the cooking grates clean. Remove the pork from the bag and discard the marinade. Grill the medallions over **direct medium heat** for 4 to 5 minutes, with the lid closed as much as possible but turning once, until the outsides are evenly seared and the centres are barely pink. Remove from the barbecue and allow to rest for 2 to 3 minutes. Serve hot with the black bean sauce.

SODA-BRINED PORK LOIN WITH CHERRY-CHIPOTLE GLAZE

SERVES: 4 TO 6
PREP TIME: 25 MINUTES
BRINING TIME: 1 TO 2 HOURS

HEAT: DIRECT AND INDIRECT HIGH HEAT 230° TO 290°C
(450° TO 550°F)
GRILLING TIME: 33 TO 42 MINUTES
SPECIAL EQUIPMENT: LARGE DISPOSABLE FOIL TIN

1 litre (1¾ pints) Dr. Pepper® (do not use diet soda)
100 g (3½ oz) sea salt
1 boneless centre-cut pork loin, 750 g to 2 kg (3 to 4 lb)

GLAZE
275 g (9 oz) tart cherry preserve
125 ml (4 fl oz) Dr. Pepper®
125 ml (4 fl oz) water
1–2 tablespoons very finely chopped canned chipotle in adobo
4 teaspoons Dijon mustard

Rapeseed or other vegetable oil

1. Pour the soda into a large bowl and slowly add the salt (the mixture will foam up quite a bit so be sure to use a bowl large enough to prevent overflowing). Stir for 1 to 2 minutes until the salt has dissolved completely. Place a large, disposable plastic bag inside a large bowl, and carefully pour the brine into the bag.

2. Trim excess fat and silver skin from the pork. Submerge the pork in the brine, seal the bag and refrigerate for 1 to 2 hours.

3. Combine the glaze ingredients in a small bowl.

4. Remove the pork from the bag and discard the brine. Pat dry with kitchen paper. Lightly coat the pork with oil and allow to stand at room temperature for 20 to 30 minutes before grilling. Prepare the barbecue for direct and indirect cooking over a high heat.

5. Brush the cooking grates clean. Sear the pork over **direct high heat** for 8 to 12 minutes, with the lid closed as much as possible but turning once, until the surface is well marked but not burned.

6. Place a large disposable tin over **indirect high heat** and pour the glaze into the tin. Transfer the pork to the tin and turn to coat with the glaze. Grill the pork over **indirect high heat** for 25 to 30 minutes, with the lid closed as much as possible but turning in the glaze every 8 to 10 minutes, until barely pink in the centre and the internal temperature reaches 63° to 65°C (145° to 150°F). If the glaze gets too thick or starts to scorch, add a little water or more soda to the tin. Transfer the pork to a chopping board and allow it to rest for about 5 minutes. Cut the pork crossways into 1-cm (½-inch) slices and serve with the remaining tin sauce on the side.

If it's not treated correctly, pork loin can dry out all too quickly on the grill. The surest way to prevent this is to brine it first in a sweet-and-savoury solution, swelling the meat with moisture and flavour. Next, brown the joint over direct heat and finish cooking it over indirect heat, glazing it periodically.

PORK

HOW TO MAKE ROTISSERIE PORK LOIN

1. Large, thick pieces of meat will almost always be juicier after cooking than small narrow ones will, so improve your chances of wonderfully moist results by tying 2 sections of pork loin together.

2. Place one joint on top of the other, with the fat sides on the outside, and tie them together crossways with individual lengths of butcher's string separated by 2.5 cm (1 inch) or so.

3. Cut 2 very long pieces of string, each about 1.2 m (4 feet). Tie one end of each piece to a crossways piece at one end of the roast. Weave the long pieces of string lengthways in and out of the crossways pieces and all the way around the length of the joint.

4. Tie off each lengthways piece of string at the knot where it began, on the first crossways piece. The twine will hold the meat in place as it shrinks a little on the rotisserie.

5. Slide the centre rod (spit) of the rotisserie between the sections of pork loin, making sure to imbed the fork prongs well inside the meat.

6. Allow the meat to rest at room temperature for 1 hour before cooking. Brush it with oil and season it evenly with salt and pepper before putting the rotisserie in position.

7. Natural juices baste the meat inside and out as the joint turns slowly on the rotisserie. Place a foil tin underneath to prevent grease from falling into the barbecue.

8. Check the internal temperature of the meat at the centre of the joint. When it reaches 63° to 65°C (145° to 150°F), turn off the rotisserie and, wearing insulated barbecue mitts or oven gloves, remove it from the barbecue. While the meat rests at room temperature, it will continue to cook.

ROTISSERIE PORK LOIN AGRO DOLCE

SERVES: 12 TO 14
PREP TIME: 45 MINUTES

HEAT: INDIRECT HEAT ABOUT 200°C (400°F)
GRILLING TIME: 1 TO 1¼ HOURS
SPECIAL EQUIPMENT: BUTCHER'S STRING, ROTISSERIE, LARGE DISPOSABLE FOIL TIN

SAUCE
2 tablespoons extra-virgin olive oil
375 g (13 oz) yellow onions, finely diced
½ teaspoon sea salt
750 ml (1¼ pints) red wine
150 g (5 oz) raisins
125 g (4 oz) pitted prunes, stoned and finely diced
1 tablespoon finely grated orange rind
175 ml (6 fl oz) fresh orange juice
⅛ teaspoon ground cloves
Sea salt
Freshly ground black pepper

2 boneless pork loin joints, 1.5 to 1.75 kg (3 to 3½ lb) each
2 tablespoons extra-virgin olive oil
1½ teaspoons sea salt
1 teaspoon freshly ground black pepper

1. Warm the oil in a saucepan over a medium heat. Add the onions and salt and cook for about 15 minutes, stirring often, until the onions are quite soft. Increase the heat to high, add the wine and boil for about 8 minutes until it has reduced by half. Stir in the raisins, prunes and orange rind, reduce the heat to medium and cook for 5 to 10 minutes, stirring occasionally, until the fruit is tender. Add the orange juice and cloves and season to taste with salt and pepper. Keep warm.

2. Trim the pork loins to match in size and then place one joint on top of the other, making sure the sides of the joint with the layers of fat are facing outwards. This fatty layer will help protect the meat while it cooks. Tie the 2 joints together to make one large cylindrical joint. Allow the roast to stand at room temperature for 1 hour before grilling. Brush the roast with the oil and season with the salt and pepper.

3. Prepare the barbecue for rotisserie cooking over indirect heat. If your gas barbecue has one, turn on the infrared burner to *low* and set the outer burner control knobs to *low heat*. The temperature of the barbecue should be around 200°C (400°F). You may need to adjust the outer burners to medium heat.

4. Carefully slide one pronged fork on to the spit, with the tines facing inwards, about 25 cm (10 inches) from the end of the spit. Secure the fork but do not tighten at this time. Slide the spit through the centre of the joint and gently push the joint on to the fork tines so that they are deep inside the joint. Add the other pronged fork to the spit with the tines facing inwards and slide down until they are firmly imbedded into the joint. Secure the fork, but do not completely tighten at this time. Wearing barbecue mitts or oven gloves, place the pointed end of the spit into the rotisserie motor. If necessary, adjust the joint so that it is centred on the spit and tighten the forks into place. Place the foil tin under the joint to catch any grease. Turn on the motor to begin the rotisserie.

5. Grill the joint for 1 to 1¼ hours, until the internal temperature reaches 63° to 65°C (145° to 150°F). To check the temperature, turn off the rotisserie motor and insert a thermometer down the centre of one of the joints. Wearing barbecue mitts or oven gloves, carefully remove the spit from the barbecue. Gently loosen the forks and slide the joint off of the spit. Transfer the pork to a carving board, tent with foil and allow to rest for 15 to 30 minutes (the roast will continue to cook during this time).

6. Slice the joint and serve with the sauce.

HOW TO BARBECUE BONE-IN PORK LOIN

1. A moderately hot fire of about 180°C (350°F) is just right for roasting a bone-in pork loin. Begin with a chimney starter filled about two-thirds full with charcoal briquettes. Let the coals burn down until they are completely covered with ash, and then dump them on to the charcoal grate.

2. Spread the briquettes in a single layer over one side of the charcoal grate and lay an oak log beside them. It will smolder and smoke, filling the pork with haunting outdoorsy aromas.

3. Cook the joint on the cooler side of the barbecue opposite the bed of charcoal, with the bone side facing down and the thick meaty side facing the coals. If the log catches fire, use a spray bottle filled with water to douse the flames.

4. After cooking with the lid on for 45 minutes, rotate the joint 180 degrees so the tips of the bones are facing the coals. As the meat finishes cooking, the barbecue temperature should fall to about 150°C (300°F).

5. Remove the joint from the barbecue when the internal temperature reaches the range of 63° to 65°C (145° to 150°F). Loosely cover the joint with foil and allow it to rest for 15 minutes, which allows the juices to stay in the meat when you slice it.

6. The easiest way to carve the joint is to turn it over so the bone side is facing up. That way you can see exactly where the bones are and slice right between them.

PORK

112

When you buy a bone-in pork loin, make sure the butcher has removed the chine bone (backbone), which runs along the top of all the rib bones. Otherwise it will be nearly impossible to slice between the ribs and serve individual chops. Also, don't be afraid to season the meat generously before cooking. It is a thick joint that can handle plenty of salt and pepper.

SMOKE-ROASTED PORK LOIN WITH REDCURRANT SAUCE

SERVES: 8

PREP TIME: 20 MINUTES

HEAT: INDIRECT MEDIUM HEAT 150° TO 180°C
(300° TO 350°F)

GRILLING TIME: 1½ TO 2 HOURS

1 bone-in pork loin joint, 3.5 to 4 kg (7 to 8 lb)
3 tablespoons extra-virgin olive oil
2 teaspoons sea salt
1 teaspoon freshly ground black pepper

1 oak log, about 45 cm (18 inches) long and 10 cm (4 inches) in diameter

SAUCE
175 g (6 oz) redcurrant preserve
137 g (4½ oz) ketchup
125 ml (4 fl oz) apple juice
2 tablespoons cider vinegar
1 tablespoon soy sauce
1 tablespoon whisky
½ teaspoon crushed red chilli flakes

1. Lightly coat the pork with the oil and season with the salt and pepper. Allow the pork to stand at room temperature for 30 minutes while you prepare the barbecue.

2. Starting with about two-thirds of a chimney of lit coals, arrange them on one-third of the charcoal grate. Place the log alongside the outer edge of the coals; do not place it directly on top of the coals. The log should slowly start to smolder but should not catch on fire. If it does catch on fire, use a spray bottle filled with water to douse the flames. Put the cooking grate in place and set the pork joint, bone side down and with the meaty section facing the fire, over **indirect medium heat** (about 180°C/350°F), and cook for 45 minutes with the lid closed.

3. After 45 minutes, to maintain the heat, add 8 to 10 lit briquettes to the coals and rotate the meat 180 degrees so the bone section is facing the heat. Continue to cook over **indirect medium heat** for 45 minutes to 1¼ hours with the lid closed, until the internal temperature reaches 63° to 65°C (145° to 150°F). The fire should slowly lose heat and finish cooking the joint at about 150°C (300°F).

4. Combine the sauce ingredients in a saucepan over a medium heat. Let the sauce come to a simmer and cook, stirring occasionally until the preserves have melted and the sauce is well combined. Remove the pan from the heat.

5. Transfer the joint to a chopping board, loosely cover with foil and allow to rest 15 to 30 minutes. Slice between each bone. Serve warm with the sauce.

HOW TO BARBECUE PORK SHOULDER

1. A water smoker can maintain temperatures between 110°C (225°F) and 130°C (250°F) for several hours, which is just what you need to break down the connective tissue in pork shoulder joints.

2. Fill the water pan in the middle section of the smoker. It will absorb some of the charcoal's heat and release it slowly with some humidity.

3. After 8 to 10 hours of barbecuing, the meat will be so tender that you can slide the bone out cleanly.

4. Ideally you will need both a fish slice and a pair of tongs to remove the shoulders without the meat falling apart.

5. Shred the meat with your fingers or 2 forks. Discard any clumps of fat, but hold onto the crispy bits of 'bark' that have developed on the outside of the meat.

6. The pinkish colour of the meat is a good sign that smoke has penetrated the surface and filled the pork with authentic barbecue flavour.

PULLED PORK SANDWICHES

SERVES: 10 TO 12
PREP TIME: 25 MINUTES

HEAT: INDIRECT LOW HEAT 110° TO 130°C (225° TO 250°F)
GRILLING TIME: 8 TO 10 HOURS

RUB
2 tablespoons pure chilli powder
2 tablespoons sea salt
4 teaspoons garlic granules
2 teaspoons freshly ground black pepper
1 teaspoon dry mustard

2 bone-in pork shoulder joints, 2.5 to 3 kg (5 to 6 lb) each
3 large handfuls hickory wood chips, soaked in water for at least
    30 minutes

SAUCE
275 g (9 oz) ketchup
175 ml (6 fl oz) cider vinegar
50 g (2 oz) light brown sugar
1½ teaspoons Worcestershire sauce
1 teaspoon hot pepper sauce, or to taste
1 teaspoon sea salt
½ teaspoon dry mustard
¼ teaspoon freshly ground black pepper

12 hamburger buns

1. Prepare your smoker, following manufacturer's instructions, for indirect cooking over a low heat.

2. Mix the rub ingredients together in a small bowl. Season the pork shoulders all over with the rub and press the spices into the meat.

3. Smoke the pork over ***indirect low heat***, with the lid closed but adding a handful of drained wood chips to the coals every hour for the first 3 hours, until the internal temperature of the meat reaches 88°C (190°F). At this point the bone should easily slip out of the meat, and the meat should be falling apart in some areas. The total cooking time will be 8 to 10 hours. Maintain the heat of the smoker at 110° to 130°C (225° to 250°F).

4. Whisk the sauce ingredients together in a large, heavy-based saucepan. Bring to a simmer over a medium heat and cook for about 5 minutes, stirring occasionally. Taste and adjust the seasonings, if necessary. It should be spicy and tangy.

5. Transfer the pork joints to a roasting tray and tightly cover them with aluminium foil. Allow the pork to rest for 30 minutes.

6. Pull the warm meat apart with your fingers, or use 2 forks to shred the meat. Discard any large pieces of fat or sinew. Put the pork into a large bowl and moisten with as much sauce as you like (you may not need all of the sauce). Pile the pork on hamburger buns.

HOW TO MAKE PORCHETTA

1. Trim off the relatively thin pieces of meat on the ends of the pork shoulder joint. Also trim the thick sections of the joint to create a fairly even thickness from end to end.

2. Ideally you will have 250 to 300 g (8 to 10 oz) of trimmed meat and fat to mix with delicious herbs, spices, garlic and olive oil. This will be the porchetta filling.

3. Pulse the ingredients in a food processor 20 to 25 times until they have the look and texture of minced sausagemeat. Then spread the filling over the interior of the joint.

4. Leave a border along the edges of the pork joint so the filling does not spill out when you roll the meat. Press the filling into any grooves in the meat.

5. Now roll up the meat from one short end to the other, creating an evenly shaped and compact cylinder.

6. Use several long pieces of butcher's string to tie the joint both crossways and lengthways. Allow the joint to stand at room temperature for 20 to 30 minutes before cooking.

PORK

PORCHETTA-STYLE PORK SHOULDER

SERVES: 6 TO 8
PREP TIME: 30 MINUTES

HEAT: INDIRECT MEDIUM HEAT 180° TO 200°C
　　(350° TO 400°F)
GRILLING TIME: 2 TO 2½ HOURS
SPECIAL EQUIPMENT: BUTCHER'S STRING

FILLING
125 ml (4 fl oz) extra-virgin olive oil
3 sprigs rosemary leaves
16 large sage leaves
1 tablespoon finely grated lemon rind
1 tablespoon chopped garlic
1 teaspoon sea salt
½ teaspoon whole fennel seeds
½ teaspoon crushed red chilli flakes

1 boneless pork shoulder joint, about 2.5 kg (5 lb), butterflied,
　　ends trimmed to produce 250 to 300 g (8 to 10 oz) meat
　　and fat
1 tablespoon extra-virgin olive oil
½ teaspoon sea salt
½ teaspoon freshly ground black pepper

1. Combine the filling ingredients in a food processor and
process until they form a smooth purée. Add the trimmed
meat and fat and pulse for 20 to 25 pulses, until it resembles
sausagemeat.

2. Place the joint, skin side down, on a work surface. Evenly
distribute the filling over the pork, leaving a border round the
edges of the joint. Roll up the meat and tie with butcher's string
in 5 or 6 places. Rub the outside of the joint with the oil, salt
and pepper, then allow the joint to stand at room temperature
for 20 to 30 minutes before grilling. Prepare the barbecue for
indirect cooking over a medium heat.

3. Brush the cooking grates clean. Grill the joint over **indirect
medium heat** for 2 to 2½ hours, with the lid closed, until the
internal temperature reaches 82° to 85°C (180° to 185°F).

4. Transfer the joint to a chopping board, loosely cover with foil
and allow to rest for 20 to 30 minutes. Remove the string and
carve the meat into thin slices. Serve warm.

■ ■ ■

In and around Rome, Italy, porchetta *is a
bacchanalian dish that involves stuffing a whole pig
with wild fennel, garlic and spices, and then cooking
it on a rotisserie spit. Assuming that you may not
be inclined to tackle such a huge project, here's a
simpler version that calls for a pork shoulder filled
with the authentic flavours.*

■ ■ ■

PORK

HOW TO SEASON PORK ROAST

1. Grate the garlic finely.

2. Make shallow cross-hatch slashes about 5 cm (2 inches) apart through the fat but not into the flesh.

3. Smear the garlic-and-herb paste all over the joint, pressing it into the slashes and crevices.

4. Cover the joint and refrigerate for 12 to 24 hours.

HOW TO BARBECUE PORK ROAST

1. Cook a bone-in pork shoulder over indirect low heat (about 130°C/300°F) so that its collagen and fat will melt and make the meat succulent before the outside burns. This requires starting the fire with a charcoal chimney starter filled about halfway and adding 8 to 10 briquettes every hour or so.

2. When the meat's internal temperature reaches 85° to 88°C (185° to 190°F), remove the joint from the barbecue, wrap it in foil and let the meat rest and juices redistribute for a full hour.

3. Cut the joint into 1-cm (½-inch) slices or tear the meat into bite-sized chucks. Serve with a bold garlic-citrus sauce called mojo (pronounced 'mo-ho').

LATINO PORK ROAST

SERVES: 6 TO 8
PREP TIME: 30 MINUTES
MARINATING TIME: 12 TO 24 HOURS

HEAT: INDIRECT LOW HEAT ABOUT 130°C (250°F)
GRILLING TIME: 5 TO 7 HOURS, PLUS 1 HOUR
    RESTING TIME

PASTE
5 large garlic cloves, very finely grated
3 tablespoons extra-virgin olive oil
3 tablespoons cider vinegar
2 tablespoons dried oregano
1 tablespoon plus 2 teaspoons sea salt
1 tablespoon freshly ground black pepper

1 bone-in pork shoulder joint, with an outer layer of fat,
    3 to 3.5 kg (6 to 7 lb)
4 handfuls oak or hickory wood chips, soaked in water for at
    least 30 minutes

MOJO
Finely grated rind of 1 orange
250 ml (8 fl oz) fresh orange juice
125 ml (4 fl oz) fresh grapefruit juice
50 g (2 oz) white onion, finely chopped
2 tablespoons distilled white vinegar
1 small serrano chilli, very finely chopped
1 garlic clove, finely chopped
1 teaspoon sugar
Sea salt

3 tablespoons fresh coriander, finely chopped

1. Combine the paste ingredients in a small bowl.

2. Score the fat on the joint in a cross-hatch pattern, about 5 cm
(2 inches) apart, cutting through the fat just to the flesh. Rub
the paste all over the joint, then place it in a bowl, cover and
refrigerate for 12 to 24 hours. Allow the joint to stand at room
temperature for 1 hour before grilling.

3. Prepare the barbecue for indirect cooking over a low heat.
Brush the cooking grates clean. Drain 1 handful of the wood
chips and scatter them over the coals or in the smoker box of a
gas barbecue, following the manufacturer's instructions. Grill
the pork, fat side down, over **_indirect low heat_** for 5 to 7 hours,
with the lid closed as much as possible but turning once after
about 3 hours and adding 1 handful of drained wood chips
each hour until they are gone, until the meat is so tender that
it gives no resistance when pierced with a meat fork and the
internal temperature registers 85° to 88°C (185° to 190°F).
Transfer the joint to a platter and loosely cover with aluminium
foil, then allow to rest for about 1 hour.

4. Combine the mojo ingredients, including salt to taste, in a
small serving bowl, stirring to dissolve the sugar and salt. Cover
and set aside. Just before serving, stir in the coriander.

5. Cut the joint into 1-cm (½-inch) slices (it may fall apart into
chunks and not carve neatly, but that's okay). Serve warm with
the mojo.

HOW TO BARBECUE PORK RIBS
THINGS YOU NEED TO KNOW

1 STRIKE THE BALANCE

A perfectly barbecued rack of ribs achieves a seamless harmony of effects. The slightly crisp texture of a handsome, glossy surface gives way to morsels of luscious meat with a fragrant wood-smoke flavour. At each step of cooking your goal is to balance the spices, sauce and smoke with the inherently beautiful flavour of slow-roasted pork, never allowing one effect to outdo the others.

2 USE WHAT YOU HAVE

You can make satisfying barbecued ribs on a gas barbecue, charcoal barbecue or smoker. Each one is capable of slowly tenderizing the rib meat and scenting it with wood smoke, although with a gas barbecue you will need a smoker box attachment.

3 WATCH THAT HEAT

The key to tender ribs is maintaining a low temperature for several hours. Spikes and valleys of heat will tighten and dry out the meat, but consistently low temperatures will produce soft and succulent meat.

4 ALL IN GOOD TIME

It's one thing to wait the required 3 to 4 hours for baby back ribs or 5 to 6 hours for spareribs, but that's not the only timing issue. You must not sauce any ribs too early, especially if you are using a sweet sauce, as the sugars will burn and threaten your precious ribs. Sauce them during the final 30 minutes of cooking, or just before you wrap them in foil.

5 WRAP 'EM UP

Wrapping ribs in foil during the final stages of cooking holds in some moisture and helps to tenderize the meat. This is a little trick that some barbecue professionals dismiss as 'the Texas crutch', but you know what? It works.

HOW TO PREP BABY BACK RIBS

1. At one end of the rack, slide a dinner knife under the membrane and over a bone.

2. Lift and loosen the membrane until it tears.

3. Grab the edge of the membrane with kitchen paper and pull it off.

4. The membrane may come off in one whole piece, or you may need to remove it in smaller pieces.

5. Season the ribs mostly on the meaty side and press the spices into the meat so they don't fall off.

6. Stand the ribs in a rib rack to double the number of ribs you can cook in a limited cooking space.

HOW TO SET UP A CHARCOAL BARBECUE FOR SMOKING

1. If you are using wood chips, soak them first in water for at least 30 minutes so that they smolder and smoke slowly rather than flame up.

2. Dump the charcoal on one side of the charcoal grate. A charcoal basket holds the coals together in a compact bunch and slows down the burning. Tap the edge of the basket with tongs every hour or so to knock the ashes through the basket holes.

3. Place a foil tin on the other side of the charcoal grate and fill it at least halfway with water to create a little steam inside the barbecue. The ribs will cook on the cooking grate directly above the water pan.

4. Drain some wood chips and lay them right on the coals. Replenish them after the first hour of cooking, ideally when you replenish the coals, too.

HOW TO BARBECUE BABY BACK RIBS

1. To protect the meat, begin with the bone side of the ribs facing the coals.

2. After the first hour of cooking, baste the ribs with a vinegar 'mop'.

3. Periodically swap the positions of the ribs in the rib rack for even cooking.

4. Towards the end of cooking, face the meaty sides of the ribs towards the coals to brown and crisp the surface.

5. The meat should be tender enough that it tears when you bend a rack backwards.

6. Lightly brush each rack of ribs with sauce as it comes off the barbecue.

7. Wrap each rack individually in aluminium foil.

8. The ribs will stay warm and continue to cook a bit for at least 30 minutes.

SLOW GOOD BABY BACK RIBS WITH SOO-WEE SAUCE

SERVES: 4 TO 6
PREP TIME: 20 MINUTES

HEAT: INDIRECT LOW HEAT 130° TO 150°C (250° TO 300°F)
GRILLING TIME: 3 TO 4 HOURS
SPECIAL EQUIPMENT: RIB RACK

RUB
2 tablespoons sea salt
2 tablespoons paprika
4 teaspoons garlic granules
4 teaspoons pure chilli powder
2 teaspoons dry mustard
2 teaspoons freshly ground black pepper

4 racks baby back ribs, 1 to 1½ kg (2 to 2½ lb) each

SAUCE
250 ml (8 fl oz) apple juice
137 ml (4½ fl oz) ketchup
3 tablespoons cider vinegar
1 tablespoon soy sauce
2 teaspoons molasses
½ teaspoon pure chilli powder
½ teaspoon garlic granules
½ teaspoon dry mustard
¼ teaspoon sea salt
¼ teaspoon freshly ground black pepper

MOP
175 ml (6 fl oz) red wine vinegar
175 ml (6 fl oz) water
2 tablespoons soy sauce

4 handfuls hickory wood chips, soaked in water for at least 30 minutes

1. Prepare a charcoal barbecue for indirect cooking over a low heat (see page 121).

2. Mix the rub ingredients together in a small bowl.

3. Slide a dull dinner knife tip under the membrane covering the back of each rack of ribs. Lift and loosen the membrane until it breaks, and then grab a corner of it with kitchen paper and pull it off. Season the ribs all over with the rub, putting more of it on the meaty sides than the bone sides. Arrange the ribs in a rib rack, all facing the same direction. The ribs should stand at room temperature for 30 minutes to 1 hour before cooking.

4. When the fire has burned down to about 180°C (350°F), drain 2 handfuls of hickory wood chips and place them on top of the coals. The damp wood will lower the temperature a bit. Put the cooking grate in place. Place the ribs in the rack over **indirect low heat** (positioned over the foil tin) as far from the coals as possible, with the bone sides facing toward the coals. Close the lid. Close the top vent about halfway. Allow the ribs to cook and smoke for 1 hour. During this time, maintain the temperature at 130° to 150°C (250° to 300°F) by opening and closing the top vent. Meanwhile, make the sauce and the mop.

5. Mix the sauce ingredients together in a small saucepan over a medium heat. Simmer for about 5 minutes, then remove the pan from the heat. Taste and add more salt and pepper, if desired.

6. Mix the mop ingredients together in a small bowl.

7. After the first hour of cooking the ribs, add 8 to 10 unlit briquettes and the remaining 2 handfuls of wood chips (drained) to the lit coals. Move the ribs from the rack and spread them out on 2 roasting trays. Brush them generously on both sides with some of the mop. Leaving the lid off for a few minutes while you brush the ribs will help the new briquettes to light. Return the ribs to the rack, all facing the same direction, now with the bone sides facing away from the coals.

8. Close the lid and cook for another hour. During this time, maintain the temperature at 130° to 150°C (250° to 300°F) by opening and closing the top vent.

9. After 2 hours of cooking, add 8 to 10 unlit briquettes to the fire. Move the ribs from the rack and spread them out on 2 baking trays. Brush them generously on both sides with some of the mop, leaving the lid off for a few minutes while you brush the ribs to help the new briquettes to light. Return the ribs to the rack, all facing the same direction, but this time turned over so that the ends facing down before now face up. Also position any ribs that appear to be cooking faster then others toward the back of the rib rack, further away from the coals. This time the bone sides should face the coals.

10. Close the lid and let the ribs cook for a third hour. During this time, maintain the temperature at 130° to 150°C (250° to 300°F) by opening and closing the top vent.

11. After 3 hours of cooking, check to see if any rack is ready to come off the barbecue. They are done when the meat has shrunk back from most of the bones by 5 mm (¼ inch) or more. When you lift a rack by picking up one end with tongs, the rack should bend in the middle and the meat should tear easily. If the meat does not tear easily, continue to cook the ribs. The total cooking time could be anywhere between 3 to 4 hours. Not all racks will cook in the same amount of time. Lightly brush the ribs with some sauce. Transfer the racks to a clean roasting tray and brush the ribs on both sides with some sauce. Wrap each rack individually in aluminium foil and allow to rest for about 30 minutes. Serve warm with the remaining sauce on the side.

HOW TO COOK STACKED RIBS

1. One space-saving solution, whether you are cooking with charcoal or gas, is to stack the racks of ribs on top of each other in the centre of the barbecue.

2. Cook the ribs for about 45 minutes, with the lid closed and low heat radiating from both sides of the barbecue.

3. Then undo the stack of ribs on the cooking grate.

4. Baste the ribs on both sides with some reserved marinade.

5. Stack them again, swapping the positions of the ribs by moving the top rack to the bottom, the bottom rack to the centre, and the middle rack to the top.

6. Continue to cook the ribs, basting and swapping positions of the racks occasionally, until the meat has shrunk back at least 5 mm (¼ inch) from the ends of the bones.

STACKED BABY BACK RIBS

SERVES: 6 TO 8
PREP TIME: 20 MINUTES
MARINATING TIME: 30 MINUTES

HEAT: INDIRECT AND DIRECT LOW HEAT 150° TO 170°C
(300° TO 325°F)
GRILLING TIME: 2¾ TO 3¼ HOURS

MARINADE
250 g (8 oz) sweet chilli sauce
250 ml (8 fl oz) water
Grated rind of 3 limes
5 tablespoons fresh lime juice
4 large garlic cloves
4 tablespoons soy sauce
3 tablespoons roughly chopped fresh root ginger

3 racks baby back ribs, 1 to 1.5 kg (2 to 2½ lb) each
1 tablespoon sea salt

1. Combine the marinade ingredients in a blender or food processor and process for about 1 minute to purée. Set aside 250 ml (8 fl oz) of the marinade to use as a basting sauce.

2. Remove the thin membrane from the back of each rack of ribs (see page 121). Season the ribs on the meaty sides with salt. Brush the remaining marinade over all the ribs. Allow the ribs to stand at room temperature for 30 minutes before cooking. Prepare the barbecue for indirect cooking over a low heat.

3. Brush the cooking grates clean. Stack the ribs on top of each other, with the bone sides facing down, and grill over **indirect low heat** for 45 minutes, with the lid closed.

4. Undo the stack of ribs on the barbecue. Brush the meaty sides with some of the reserved marinade. Stack the ribs, with the bone sides facing down, moving the top rack to the bottom, the bottom rack to the centre, and the middle rack to the top. Cook over **indirect low heat** for another 45 minutes, with the lid closed.

5. Undo the stack of ribs on the barbecue again. Brush the meaty sides with some of the reserved marinade. Stack the ribs, with the bone sides facing down, moving the top rack to the bottom, the bottom rack to the centre, and the middle rack to the top. Cook over **indirect low heat** for 1 to 1½ hours, with the lid closed. During this third round of cooking, move the relative positions of the ribs occasionally so that the racks that are browning a little faster cook in the centre of the stack and the racks that are not as brown cook at the top of the stack. As you move the ribs, brush the meaty sides with the reserved marinade.

6. Undo the stack of ribs and place them side by side, with the bone sides facing down, over **direct low heat** for 10 to 15 minutes, turning occasionally to prevent burning. Brush with a little more of the reserved marinade and continue cooking until the meat is very tender and has shrunk back from the ends of the bones.

7. Transfer the racks to a roasting tray, cover with foil and allow to rest for 15 minutes before cutting into individual ribs. Serve warm.

HOW TO PREP ST LOUIS–STYLE RIBS

1. There is a tough flap of meat, called the skirt, hanging from the bone side of a full rack of spareribs. The first step for converting 'regular' spareribs to the St Louis-style cut is to remove that flap.

2. The next step is to cut off the long strip of cartilaginous meat, called the brisket, which runs along the bottom of the rack.

3. Then trim off any meat dangling from either end of each rack. The goal is to make a handsome rectangular rack of ribs.

4. Use a dinner knife or some other dull instrument to get under the membrane and lift it so that you can grab an edge with kitchen paper. Then peel off and discard the membrane.

5. The rack on top is a St Louis-style cut. It is about the same length as the rack of baby back ribs, shown on the bottom, but the St Louis-style cut is obviously wide and meatier. It's also tougher, so it requires longer cooking.

6. You can bump up the flavour and give the ribs a crispy surface by marinating them in a sweet-and-savoury marinade for a few hours before cooking.

HOW TO USE 'THE TEXAS CRUTCH'

1. In the world of competition barbecue, 'the Texas crutch' refers to the technique of wrapping ribs in foil during the final stages of cooking, often with some liquid trapped inside.

2. The theory is that the humidity inside the foil moistens and tenderizes the meat. Some purists shun this approach – hence the mocking sobriquet. It's unclear why the technique is associated with Texas.

3. Many barbecue teams and home cooks use the technique with great success, either finishing their ribs in foil on their smoker or just allowing their ribs to 'rest' in foil after they have been removed from the smoker.

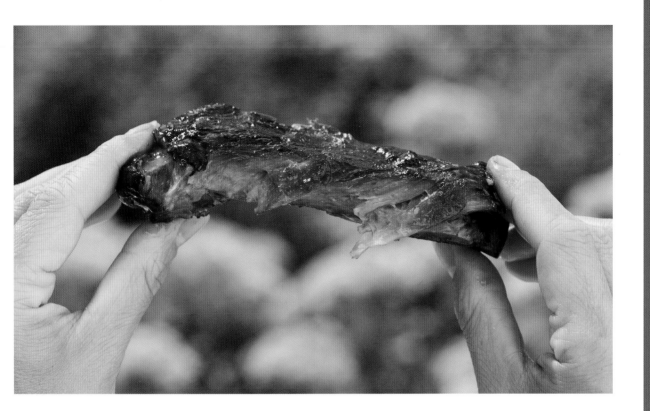

SWEET GINGER-AND-SOY-GLAZED SPARERIBS

SERVES: 6
PREP TIME: 30 MINUTES
MARINATING TIME: 3 HOURS

HEAT: INDIRECT LOW HEAT ABOUT 150°C (300°F)
GRILLING TIME: 4 TO 5 HOURS

MARINADE
100 g (3½ oz) brown sugar
125 ml (4 fl oz) soy sauce
137 ml (4½ fl oz) ketchup
125 ml (4 fl oz) dry sherry
2 tablespoons very finely chopped fresh root ginger
1½ teaspoons very finely chopped garlic

2 racks pork spareribs, about 2 kg (4 lb) each

1. Combine the marinade ingredients in a large bowl.

2. Prepare the racks of spareribs as detailed at left. Put the spareribs, meaty side up, on a chopping board. Follow the line of fat that separates the meaty ribs from the much tougher tips at the base of each rack, and cut off the tips. Turn each rack over. Cut off the flap of meat attached in the centre of each rack. Also cut off the flap of meat that hangs below the shorter end of the ribs. (The flaps and tips may be grilled separately, but they will not be as tender as the ribs.) Remove the thin membrane from the back of each rack of ribs.

3. Place the ribs in one layer on a large roasting tray. Pour the marinade over the ribs and turn to coat them evenly. Cover and refrigerate for 3 hours, turning occasionally. Remove the ribs from the tray and reserve the marinade. Allow the ribs to stand at room temperature for 30 minutes before grilling. Prepare the barbecue for indirect cooking over a low heat.

4. Brush the cooking grates clean. Grill the ribs over **_indirect low heat_** for 2 hours, with the lid closed. Remove the ribs from the barbecue, brush them on both sides with the reserved marinade, wrap them in aluminium foil and continue cooking the ribs for 2 to 3 hours, until the meat has shrunk back about 1 cm (½ inch) from the ends of the rib bones and the meat is tender enough to tear with your fingers.

5. Transfer the ribs (keep them wrapped in foil) to a large tray and allow them to rest for 30 minutes. Serve warm.

HOW TO COOK SPARERIBS ON A SMOKER

1. Fill the ring in the bottom section of the smoker with fully lit charcoal. Briquettes will burn much longer than lump charcoal, so they are a good choice for meats like pork spareribs, which require long, slow smoking.

2. Toss a few chunks of hardwood on the coals right at the start. Don't bother soaking the chunks first. They won't absorb much water, and they are large enough that they will smoke for quite a while. Put the middle section in place and immediately fill the water pan three-fourths of the way with water. The water pan gets hot fast, so don't wait to fill the pan or water will splatter all over!

3. The vent on the lid should be open right from the start. It allows much of the smoke to escape. Otherwise, the meat would be over-powered. Also, the vent keeps the air flowing so the coals stay lit.

4. Regulate the temperature in the smoker by adjusting the bottom vents. If the temperature begins to fall, open the bottom vents a bit more to allow more airflow. If the temperature begins to rise, close the bottom vents to restrict airflow.

5. After the first few chunks of hardwood have burned out, open the side door and drop one or two more on the burning coals. Work quickly when the door is open so you don't allow too much air into the smoker and create havoc with the cooking temperatures.

6. If necessary, for really long cooking times, add a few more handfuls of briquettes to the coals.

SLOW-SMOKED SPARERIBS WITH SWEET-AND-SOUR BARBECUE SAUCE

SERVES: 8
PREP TIME: 30 MINUTES

HEAT: INDIRECT LOW HEAT 110° TO 130°C (225° TO 250°F)
GRILLING TIME: 5 TO 6 HOURS

RUB
3 tablespoons sea salt
2 tablespoons pure chilli powder
2 tablespoons light brown sugar
2 tablespoons garlic granules
2 tablespoons paprika
4 teaspoons dried thyme
4 teaspoons ground cumin
4 teaspoons celery seeds
2 teaspoons freshly ground black pepper

4 racks St Louis-style spareribs (see page 126)

MOP
250 ml (8 fl oz) apple juice
125 ml (4 fl oz) cider vinegar
2 tablespoons Worcestershire sauce

5 fist-sized chunks hickory or apple wood (not soaked)

SAUCE
550 g (1 lb 2 oz) ketchup
250 ml (8 fl oz) apple juice
150 ml (5 fl oz) cider vinegar
2 tablespoons Worcestershire sauce
2 tablespoons runny honey
2 tablespoons reserved rub

1. Prepare your smoker, following manufacturer's instructions, for indirect cooking over a low heat.

2. Mix the rub ingredients together in a medium bowl. Set aside 2 tablespoons for the sauce.

3. See the top of page 126, steps 1 to 4, for how to prep St Louis-style ribs. Season the ribs all over with the rub, putting more of it on the meaty sides than the bone sides.

4. Mix the mop ingredients together in a small bowl.

5. Smoke the spareribs, adding 2 wood chunks at the start of cooking and 1 chunk each hour after that, until the chunks are gone. Cook until the meat has shrunk back from the bones at least 1 cm (½ inch) in several places and the meat tears easily when you lift each rack, basting the ribs on both sides with the mop every 2 hours. The total cooking time could be anywhere between 5 to 6 hours. Not all racks will cook in the same amount of time. Maintain the temperature of the smoker between 110° to 130°C (225° to 250°F) by opening and closing the vents.

6. Mix the sauce ingredients together in a saucepan over a medium heat and cook for about 5 minutes. Remove the pan from the heat.

7. When the meat has shrunk back at least 1 cm (½ inch) in several places, lightly brush the ribs on both sides with sauce.

8. Cook the ribs for a further 30 to 60 minutes. Remove them from the smoker and, if desired, lightly brush the ribs on both sides with sauce again, then cut the racks into individual ribs. Serve warm with the remaining sauce on the side.

Tamarind pods (top) provide a pulp that is responsible for an addictive sour flavour in many South-east Asian dishes. Finding the pods can be a challenge, but Asian food shops and many supermarkets stock tamarind paste (bottom). It needs to be diluted in a liquid to use in a marinade or glaze.

TAMARIND-GLAZED COUNTRY-STYLE RIBS

SERVES: 6
PREP TIME: 10 MINUTES
MARINATING TIME: 20 TO 30 MINUTES

HEAT: INDIRECT MEDIUM HEAT 180° TO 230°C
   (350° TO 400°F)
GRILLING TIME: 45 TO 50 MINUTES

MARINADE
150 g (5 oz) tamarind paste
5 tablespoons soy sauce
75 g (3 oz) light brown sugar
4 tablespoons water
½ teaspoon freshly ground black pepper
½ teaspoon garlic granules
¼ teaspoon ground cayenne pepper

12 country-style pork ribs, 1.5 to 1.75 kg (3 to 3½ lb) total

1. Whisk the marinade ingredients together in a bowl. Set aside 4 tablespoons for brushing on the ribs during grilling.

2. Liberally brush the ribs with the marinade. Allow the ribs to marinate at room temperature for 20 to 30 minutes before cooking. Prepare the barbecue for indirect cooking over a medium heat.

3. Brush the cooking grates clean. Grill the ribs over *indirect medium heat* for 20 minutes with the lid closed. Turn the ribs over, brush with the reserved marinade and continue to cook for a further 25 to 30 minutes.

4. Remove the ribs from the barbecue, tightly wrap with foil and allow them to rest for 30 minutes. Serve warm.

CHILLI VERDE COUNTRY-STYLE RIBS

SERVES: 6 TO 8
PREP TIME: 30 MINUTES

HEAT: DIRECT MEDIUM HEAT 180° TO 230°C
    (350° TO 450°F)
GRILLING TIME: 30 MINUTES
SPECIAL EQUIPMENT: LARGE DISPOSABLE FOIL TIN

1.5 kg (3 lb) boneless country-style pork ribs, 1.5 to 2.5 cm
    (¾ to 1 inch) thick and trimmed of fat
1 medium white onion, cut into 1-cm (½-inch) slices
2 jalapeño chillies
Rapeseed or other vegetable oil

RUB
1 tablespoon ground cumin
1 tablespoon brown sugar
2 teaspoons sea salt
1 teaspoon pasilla or pure chilli powder
1 teaspoon ground coriander
1 teaspoon dried oregano

SAUCE
425 g (14 oz) canned green chillies with juice, diced
1 can (425 g/14 oz) fire-roasted diced tomatoes with juice
400 ml (14 fl oz) chicken stock
1 tablespoon finely chopped garlic
1 teaspoon ground cumin
1 teaspoon dried oregano

12 corn or flour tortillas (18 to 20 cm/7 to 8 inches)
250 ml (8 fl oz) soured cream
1 ripe Haas avocado, peeled, stoned and diced
100 g (3½ oz) Cheddar cheese, grated
25 g (1 oz) fresh coriander, finely chopped
2 limes, cut into wedges

1. Lightly brush the ribs, onion slices and chillies with oil.

2. Mix the rub ingredients together in a small bowl. Generously coat the ribs on both sides with the rub. Allow the ribs to stand at room temperature for 20 to 30 minutes before grilling. Prepare the barbecue for direct cooking over a medium heat.

3. Brush the cooking grates clean. Grill the ribs, onion slices and chillies over **direct medium heat** for 10 to 12 minutes, with the lid closed as much as possible but turning once, until the meat is well browned but still a little pink and the onions and chillies are lightly charred and softened.

4. Remove the meat and vegetables from the barbecue and allow them to cool for a few minutes. Cut the pork into 1.5-cm (¾-inch) cubes. Coarsely chop the onions. Remove and discard the skins, seeds and stems from the chillies and then finely chop them.

5. Combine the sauce ingredients in a large disposable foil tin. Place the pan over **direct medium heat** and bring the sauce to a simmer. Add the meat and vegetables to the sauce. Keep the sauce at a simmer and cook for 15 to 20 minutes, with the lid closed, until the pork is tender when tested with a fork (if the liquid is cooking too fast, move the tin to indirect medium heat). Carefully slide the foil tin on to a roasting tray and remove from the barbecue.

6. Grill the tortillas in a single layer over **direct medium heat** for about 1 minute, turning once, just long enough to warm and soften them. Stack the tortillas and wrap them in a dishtowel.

7. Spoon the pork and a generous amount of sauce into warm bowls. Top with soured cream, avocado, cheese and coriander. Serve with warm tortillas and lime wedges.

Looking more like pork chops than ribs, country-style ribs are cut from the upper shoulder. You can buy them with or without bones. Either way, the meat is a little tough, but simmering it in a spicy chilli verde sauce makes it tender.

PORK

131

POULTRY

TECHNIQUES

RECIPES

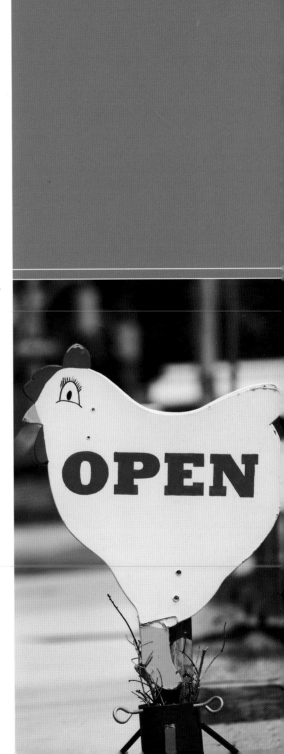

HOW TO BARBECUE CHICKEN INVOLTINI

1. The brilliance of involtini, an Italian dish of stuffed and rolled meat, is that it allows you to fill fairly bland pieces of meat like chicken breasts with gorgeous flavours like fresh basil, Parma ham and provolone cheese.

2. First flatten the chicken breasts, smooth side down, between layers of clingfilm. Next, season each one with sea salt, garlic granules and freshly ground black pepper.

3. Lay a slice of Parma ham on each piece of chicken, then top with a couple pieces of cheese and a couple basil leaves.

4. Roll up the chicken lengthways, keeping it as compact as you can.

5. Tie each piece of chicken with 2 pieces of butcher's string, then lightly brush the surface with olive oil.

6. Grill for about 12 minutes, turning the rolls every few minutes, over direct medium heat until the chicken is fully cooked through and the cheese has begun to melt.

CHICKEN INVOLTINI WITH PARMA HAM AND BASIL

SERVES: 4
PREP TIME: 20 MINUTES

HEAT: DIRECT MEDIUM HEAT 180° TO 230°C (350° TO 450°F)
GRILLING TIME: ABOUT 12 MINUTES
SPECIAL EQUIPMENT: BUTCHER'S STRING

4 boneless, skinless chicken breasts, about
    250 g (8 oz) each, with the fillets removed
1 teaspoon sea salt
1 teaspoon garlic granules
½ teaspoon freshly ground black pepper
4 very thin slices Parma ham
4 thin slices provolone cheese, halved
8 large basil leaves, plus more for garnish
Extra-virgin olive oil
450 ml (½ pint) good-quality tomato sauce

1. Prepare the barbecue for direct cooking over a medium heat.

2. For each piece of chicken, use about 30 cm (12 inches) of clingfilm. Place the chicken, smooth side down, to one side of the plastic, about 5 cm (2 inches) from the edge. Fold the remaining clingfilm over the chicken leaving an inch or so from the folded edge. This will allow the chicken to spread out as it gets thinner. Starting from the thick side, gently pound the chicken with the flat side of a tenderizer or the bottom of a small, heavy frying pan, moving to different areas with every stroke until it is about 5 mm (¼ inch) thick and doubles in size. Do not pound too hard or the chicken might break apart.

3. Season each piece of chicken on both sides with the salt, garlic granules and pepper. Arrange the chicken with the smooth side down on a work surface.

4. Lay a slice of prosciutto on each piece of chicken, then top with 2 halves of the provolone and then 2 basil leaves. Carefully roll up the chicken, keeping it snug as you work. Tie 2 pieces of butcher's string around each piece to keep it together, then trim the loose ends of string. Lightly brush each rolled piece of chicken with oil.

5. Brush the cooking grates clean. Grill the chicken over **direct medium heat** for 12 minutes, with the lid closed as much as possible but giving a quarter turn every 3 minutes, until golden on all sides. Remove from the barbecue and allow to rest for 3 to 5 minutes. Meanwhile, warm the tomato sauce in a small saucepan over a medium-high heat.

6. Remove the string from the chicken pieces, cut into slices, and serve warm on a pool of sauce. Garnish with torn pieces of basil.

HOW TO BARBECUE CHICKEN PAILLARDS

1. On the underside of some shop-bought chicken breast halves is a thin strip of meat called the fillet (or tender). To pound the chicken breasts thinly for this recipe, remove each fillet first and save it for another use.

2. Holding each breast steady with one hand, use your other hand to grab the fillet near the thick end of each breast and pull it off.

3. Place each chicken breast, smooth side down, between 2 sheets of clingfilm and pound it to a thickness of about 5 mm (¼ inch).

4. For an even thickness, aim the back of a small, heavy frying pan at the centre of each breast and push the pan towards the thinner edges as you make contact.

5. Grill each chicken breast over a direct high heat mostly on the first side. When the perimeter of the second side is turning opaque, it's time to turn the breast.

6. Check the doneness by firmness. The chicken should yield just a little to pressure. It should not be soft or firm.

CHICKEN PAILLARDS WITH TOMATO AND OLIVE RELISH

SERVES: 4
PREP TIME: 30 MINUTES

HEAT: DIRECT HIGH HEAT 230° TO 290°C (450° TO 550°F)
GRILLING TIME: 4 TO 5 MINUTES

RUB
1 tablespoon ground fennel seeds
1½ teaspoons sea salt
½ teaspoon garlic granules
½ teaspoon freshly ground black pepper

4 boneless, skinless chicken breasts, about
   175 g (6 oz) each
Extra-virgin olive oil

RELISH
125 g (4 oz) cored and deseeded tomato, cut into 5-mm
   (¼-inch) dice
75 g (3 oz) trimmed celery heart, cut into 5-mm (¼-inch) dice
75 g (3 oz) kalamata olives, rinsed, stoned and cut into
   5-mm (¼-inch) dice
75 g (3 oz) green olives, rinsed, stoned and cut into 5-mm
   (¼-inch) dice
2 tablespoons extra-virgin olive oil
2 teaspoons very finely chopped fresh thyme or ½ teaspoon
   dried thyme leaves
Sea salt
1 lemon

1. Combine the rub ingredients in a small bowl.

2. Remove the fillets from the underside of each breast (save for another use). One at a time, place each breast, smooth side down, between 2 sheets of clingfilm and pound to an even 5-mm (¼-inch) thickness. Lightly brush the chicken with oil and season both sides with the rub.

3. Prepare the barbecue for direct cooking over a high heat.

4. Combine the relish ingredients, including salt to taste, in a large bowl.

5. Brush the cooking grates clean. Grill the chicken, smooth side down, over **direct high heat** for 3 to 4 minutes, with the lid closed as much as possible, until no longer pink. Turn over and grill just to sear the surface for about 1 minute. Transfer the chicken, with the first grilled sides facing up, to a serving platter or individual plates. Spoon the relish over each piece and squeeze fresh lemon juice on top just before serving.

LEMON-OREGANO CHICKEN BREASTS

SERVES: 6
PREP TIME: 15 MINUTES
MARINATING TIME: 1 TO 2 HOURS

HEAT: DIRECT MEDIUM HEAT 180° TO 230°C (350° TO 450°F)
GRILLING TIME: 8 TO 12 MINUTES

MARINADE
6 tablespoons extra-virgin olive oil
Finely grated rind and juice of 2 lemons
1 tablespoon dried oregano
1 tablespoon very finely chopped garlic
2 teaspoons paprika
1½ teaspoons sea salt
½ teaspoon freshly ground black pepper

6 boneless, skinless chicken breasts, about
175 g (6 oz) each

1. Whisk the marinade ingredients together in a bowl.

2. Place the breasts on a large, rimmed plate. Spoon or brush the marinade over the breasts, turning to coat them evenly. Cover with clingfilm and refrigerate for 1 to 2 hours.

3. Prepare the barbecue for direct cooking over a medium heat.

4. Brush the cooking grates clean. Grill the chicken, smooth side down, over **direct medium heat** for 8 to 12 minutes, with the lid closed as much as possible but turning once or twice, until the meat is firm to the touch and opaque all the way to the centre. Serve warm.

HOW TO GRATE LEMON RIND

1. A Microplane grater can quickly remove the outermost skin of a lemon.

2. The oil-rich rind holds a wealth of flavour, but avoid the bitter, white pith.

HOW TO JUICE LEMON

1. Cut off each end of the lemon to expose a small amount of fruit, then cut the lemon in half.

2. This makes the lemon much easier to juice.

TANDOORI CHICKEN BREASTS WITH MANGO-MINT CHUTNEY

SERVES: 4
PREP TIME: 20 MINUTES
MARINATING TIME: 2 HOURS

HEAT: DIRECT MEDIUM HEAT 180° TO 230°C (350° TO 450°F)
GRILLING TIME: 10 TO 14 MINUTES

MARINADE
250 g (8 oz) natural yogurt
3 tablespoons fresh lemon juice
1 tablespoon chopped garlic
1 tablespoon chopped fresh root ginger
2 teaspoons garam masala
2 teaspoons sea salt
1 teaspoon sweet paprika

4 boneless, skinless chicken breasts, about 175 g (6 oz) each

CHUTNEY
2 firm ripe mangoes, sides cut from stone
½ tablespoon rapeseed or other vegetable oil
2 tablespoons finely chopped mint
2 tablespoons cider vinegar
½ teaspoon sugar
¼ teaspoon sea salt
¼ teaspoon freshly ground black pepper

Rapeseed or other vegetable oil

1. Blend the marinade ingredients together in a food processor until uniform in consistency, adding 1 or 2 tablespoons of water, if needed. Place the chicken in a large, resealable plastic bag and pour in the marinade. Press the air out of the bag and seal it tightly. Turn the bag several times to distribute the marinade, then refrigerate for 2 hours, turning occasionally.

2. Prepare the barbecue for direct cooking over a medium heat.

3. Lightly brush the mango sides with the oil. Brush the cooking grates clean. Grill over ***direct medium heat*** for about 2 minutes, flat sides down, with the lid closed, until they brown. Remove the mango from the barbecue and cut cross-hatch marks in the flesh down to the skin, then scoop out the little pieces. Combine the mango with the remaining chutney ingredients in a small bowl.

4. Remove the chicken from the bag and discard the marinade. Wipe off most of the marinade clinging to the chicken and then brush the chicken with oil. Grill over ***direct medium heat*** for 8 to 12 minutes, with the lid closed as much as possible but turning once, until the meat is firm to the touch and no longer pink in the centre. Serve warm with the chutney.

HOW TO CUT A MANGO

1. Inside each mango is a flat stone that runs from side to side.

2. To cut around the stone, rotate the mango so that the stone runs parallel to the blade of your knife.

3. Cut each mango lengthways along each side of the stone.

HOW TO MAKE PLUM SAUCE

1. For the sauce, grill halved red plums until they are soft and sweet.

2. Simmer the grilled plums with port, sugar and shallots. Strain the sauce through a coarse sieve, pressing the solids to extract as much flavour as possible.

HOW TO PREP DUCK BREASTS

1. The skin of a duck breast is very fatty. To avoid flare-ups on the barbecue, one good option is to remove the skin before grilling.

2. Lift the edge of the skin and use the sharp tip of a paring knife to separate the skin from the flesh as you pull back the skin.

3. The secret ingredient used in both the rub and the sauce is smoked sea salt. Look for it in speciality food shops.

4. The salt in the rub not only adds flavour, it also breaks down some muscle fibres, making the duck meat more tender.

DUCK BREASTS WITH PORT-PLUM SAUCE

SERVES: 4
PREP TIME: 30 MINUTES

HEAT: DIRECT MEDIUM HEAT 180° TO 230°C (350° TO 450°F)
GRILLING TIME: ABOUT 12 MINUTES

SAUCE
500 g (1 lb) red plums, halved and stoned
1 tablespoon extra-virgin olive oil
125 ml (4 fl oz) port wine
3 tablespoons sugar
1 shallot, thinly sliced
Smoked sea salt
Freshly ground black pepper

RUB
1 tablespoon smoked sea salt
1 tablespoon sea salt
1 tablespoon light brown sugar

4 duck breasts, 125 to 175 g (4 to 6 oz) each, skinned
1 tablespoon extra-virgin olive oil

1. Prepare the barbecue for direct cooking over a medium heat. Brush the cooking grates clean.

2. Lightly brush the plums with the oil. Grill the plums over **direct medium heat** for about 4 minutes, with the lid closed as much as possible but turning once, until they have light grill marks and are starting to soften. Remove them from the barbecue and place in a saucepan with the port, sugar and shallot. Bring the mixture to the boil, then reduce the heat to medium, cover and simmer for about 10 minutes, stirring occasionally. After the sauce has cooked, use a wooden spoon to gently crush the plums into the sauce. Strain the sauce through a coarse sieve into a bowl, pushing as much plum pulp as possible through the sieve. Discard the remaining plum skin and pulp. Season to taste with smoked salt and pepper. Warm the sauce just before serving.

3. Combine the rub ingredients in a small bowl. Place the duck in a large, resealable plastic bag and add the rub. Seal the bag and toss to coat the duck thoroughly with the rub. Allow to stand at room temperature for 10 minutes, then remove the duck from the bag, pat dry with kitchen paper and brush with the oil.

4. Brush the cooking grates clean. Grill the duck over **direct medium heat** for about 8 minutes for medium rare, with the lid closed as much as possible but turning once. Let the duck rest for 5 minutes before serving. Slice the duck crossways into 5-mm (¼-inch) slices and serve warm with the sauce.

For unforeseen tacos, try salt-cured duck breasts with thinly sliced Chinese cabbage and cooked red onions.

DUCK BREAST TACOS WITH SOUR ORANGE-ONION SALSA

SERVES: 4 TO 6
PREP TIME: 30 MINUTES

HEAT: DIRECT MEDIUM HEAT 180° TO 230°C (350° TO 450°F)
GRILLING TIME: ABOUT 9 MINUTES

4 boneless duck breasts, 125 to 175 g (4 to 6 oz) each
2 tablespoons sea salt
2 tablespoons sugar

SALSA
300 g (10 oz) red onion, thinly sliced
125 ml (4 fl oz) fresh orange juice
4 tablespoons fresh lime juice
4 tablespoons poblano chillies, finely chopped
1 tablespoon sugar
¼ teaspoon sea salt
15 g (½ oz) chopped fresh coriander

Extra-virgin olive oil

16 corn tortillas (18 cm/7 inches in diameter)
1 ripe Haas avocado, peeled, stoned and sliced
125 g (4 oz) red radishes, thinly sliced
100 g (3½ oz) Chinese cabbage, finely sliced

1. Remove and discard the thick layer of fat and skin from the duck breasts (see page 140).

2. Mix the salt and sugar together in a large bowl, then add the duck breasts and turn to coat them. Allow the breasts to stand at room temperature for 20 to 30 minutes before grilling, turning them over once or twice.

3. Combine the onion, orange and lime juices, chilli, sugar and salt in a large frying pan and boil over a medium-high heat for 15 to 18 minutes, stirring occasionally to avoid burning, until most of the liquid has evaporated. Remove the pan from the heat and stir in the coriander.

4. Prepare the barbecue for direct cooking over a medium heat.

5. Pat the breasts dry and generously coat them on both sides with oil.

6. Brush the cooking grates clean. Grill the breasts over **direct medium heat** for about 8 minutes, with the lid closed as much as possible but turning once, until lightly browned on each side and still rosy pink in the centre. Transfer to a chopping board and, while the duck rests, grill the tortillas.

7. Brush the cooking grates clean. Grill the tortillas over **direct medium heat** for about 10 seconds on each side. Stack the hot tortillas and wrap them in a thick dishtowel (or put them in an insulated tortilla server).

8. Thinly slice the duck and serve with the warm tortillas, salsa, avocado, radish and cabbage.

JERK CHICKEN SKEWERS
WITH HONEY-LIME CREAM

SERVES: 4 TO 6
PREP TIME: 30 MINUTES
MARINATING TIME: 2 TO 3 HOURS

HEAT: DIRECT HIGH HEAT 230° TO 290°C (450° TO 550°F)
GRILLING TIME: 6 TO 8 MINUTES
SPECIAL EQUIPMENT: RUBBER OR PLASTIC GLOVES;
    8 TO 12 BAMBOO SKEWERS, SOAKED IN WATER FOR
    AT LEAST 30 MINUTES

PASTE
1 habanero or Scotch bonnet chilli
50 g (2 oz) fresh coriander leaves and tender stems
125 ml (4 fl oz) extra-virgin olive oil
4 spring onions, white and light green parts, roughly chopped
6 garlic cloves
2 tablespoons finely chopped fresh root ginger
2 tablespoons sugar
1 tablespoon fresh lime juice
1 tablespoon ground allspice
2 teaspoons sea salt
1 teaspoon freshly ground black pepper

6 boneless, skinless chicken breasts, 175 to 250 g (6 to 8 oz)
    each

SAUCE
125 ml (4 fl oz) soured cream
½ teaspoon finely grated lime rind
1 tablespoon fresh lime juice
1 tablespoon extra-virgin olive oil
2 teaspoons runny honey
¼ teaspoon sea salt
⅛ teaspoon freshly ground black pepper

1. To avoid burning your skin, wear rubber or plastic gloves when you handle the chilli. After handling the chilli, do not touch your face or any other part of your body, as that may cause a burning sensation. Remove and discard the stem of the chilli, then cut away and discard the hot whitish veins and seeds. Put the rest of the chilli in a food processor. Add the remaining paste ingredients and process until smooth.

2. Trim the chicken of any fat and remove the fillets. Cut it lengthways into even strips, 1 to 1.5 cm (½ to ¾ inch) thick.

3. Place the chicken strips and fillets into a large, resealable plastic bag and spoon in the paste. Work the paste into the chicken, press out the air in the bag and seal tightly. Place in the refrigerator and allow to marinate for 2 to 3 hours.

4. Whisk the sauce ingredients together in a small bowl, then cover with clingfilm and refrigerate. Allow the sauce to stand at room temperature for about 30 minutes before serving. Prepare the barbecue for direct cooking over a high heat.

5. Wearing rubber or plastic gloves, thread the chicken strips on to the skewers, being sure to keep each skewer well within the flesh of the chicken. If you don't have rubber gloves, be sure to wash your hands thoroughly after this step.

6. Brush the cooking grates clean. Grill the skewers over **direct high heat** for 6 to 8 minutes, with the lid closed as much as possible but turning once or twice, until the meat is firm and the juices run clear. Serve warm with the sauce.

HOW TO MAKE CHICKEN SKEWERS

1. Wearing rubber or plastic gloves, remove and discard the incredibly spicy seeds and whitish veins in habanero chilli.

2. Marinate the chicken pieces in the puréed chilli paste, then thread them on to skewers. Make sure that the skewers run through the centre of the chicken pieces.

3. When you are done, you should see wood only at the tip and base of each skewer.

POULTRY

HOW TO PREP CHICKEN BREASTS

1. For the puréed parsley sauce with olive oil, nuts and garlic, you can use all but the tough stalks of parsley. Hold the tough stalks in one hand and use the other to shave off the leaves and tender stalks.

2. This Tunisian-inspired spice paste will be particularly aromatic if you cook the spices first in a dry frying pan over a medium heat.

3. Crush the toasted spices with a pestle and mortar, or use a clean coffee mill or spice mill to grind them to a powder.

4. To get the spices right on to the meat, very gently work your fingertips under the skin at the thin end and lift the skin, but leave it attached at the other end.

5. Spread the spice paste all over the exposed meat.

6. Lay the skin back in place and spread a bit more of the spice paste on top.

POULTRY

TUNISIAN CHICKEN WITH PARSLEY SAUCE

SERVES: 4
PREP TIME: 20 MINUTES

HEAT: DIRECT AND INDIRECT MEDIUM HEAT
   180° TO 230°C (350° TO 450°F)
GRILLING TIME: 23 TO 35 MINUTES
SPECIAL EQUIPMENT: PESTLE AND MORTAR OR
   SPICE MILL

SAUCE
75 g (3 oz) flat leaf Italian parsley leaves and
   tender stalks
40 g (1½ oz) whole unsalted almonds
1 garlic clove
125 ml (4 fl oz) extra-virgin olive oil
2 teaspoons Dijon mustard
1 teaspoon runny honey
¼ teaspoon sea salt

PASTE
4 teaspoons coriander seeds
2 teaspoons caraway seeds
2 teaspoons cumin seeds
2 teaspoons crushed red chilli flakes
2 tablespoons extra-virgin olive oil
1 teaspoon sea salt

4 chicken breasts (with bone and skin), 300 to 375 g
   (10 to 12 oz) each

1. Pulse the parsley, almonds and garlic together in a food processor until finely chopped. With the motor running, slowing add the oil to create an emulsion. Stir in the mustard, honey and salt and emulsify the sauce again just before serving.

2. Toast the seeds and chilli flakes in a frying pan over a medium heat for 2 to 3 minutes, until fragrant, then put into a pestle and mortar or spice mill and grind to a powder. Transfer to a bowl, add the oil and salt and stir to make a paste.

3. Using your fingertips, carefully lift the skin from the chicken breasts, leaving the skin closest to the breastbone attached. Rub 1 teaspoon of the paste under the skin of each chicken breast, then lay the skin back in place and rub the remaining paste evenly over all the pieces of chicken. Place the chicken on a plate and cover with clingfilm. Allow the chicken to stand at room temperature for 20 to 30 minutes before grilling. Prepare the barbecue for direct and indirect cooking over a medium heat.

4. Brush the cooking grates clean. Grill the chicken, skin side down, over ***direct medium heat*** for 3 to 5 minutes, until the skin is browned. Turn over the chicken and continue to cook over ***indirect medium heat*** for 20 to 30 minutes, with the lid closed, until the meat is opaque all the way to the bone. Transfer to a platter and allow to rest for 5 to 10 minutes. Serve the chicken warm with the sauce.

HOW TO BARBECUE CHICKEN WINGS

1. You don't have to use skewers to barbecue chicken wings. You'll get great results without them, but skewers are helpful for spreading the wings flat, as if they were 'in flight'.

2. The flatter the wings, the more contact they have with the cooking grate. That means crispier skins and more flavour.

3. Brushing the wings with a honey-garlic glaze just before serving helps add flavour, too.

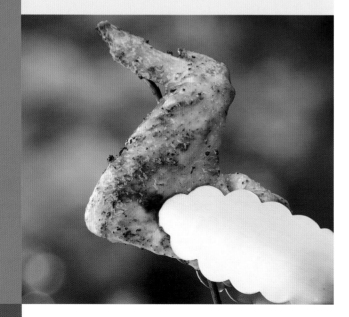

HONEY-GARLIC CHICKEN WINGS

SERVES: 4 TO 6 AS A STARTER
PREP TIME: 20 MINUTES
MARINATING TIME: UP TO 4 HOURS

HEAT: DIRECT AND INDIRECT MEDIUM HEAT
180° TO 230°C (350° TO 450°F)
GRILLING TIME: 19 TO 25 MINUTES
SPECIAL EQUIPMENT: 12 BAMBOO SKEWERS,
SOAKED IN WATER FOR AT LEAST 30 MINUTES

MARINADE
6 tablespoons fresh lemon juice
1 tablespoon finely chopped garlic
1 teaspoon sea salt
½ teaspoon freshly ground black pepper

1 kg (2 lb) chicken wings
175 g (6 oz) runny honey
1 tablespoon hot pepper sauce, or to taste

1. Combine 3 tablespoons of the lemon juice, the garlic, salt and pepper in a large non-metallic bowl. Add the wings and toss to coat them evenly, then cover and refrigerate for up to 4 hours.

2. Combine the remaining 3 tablespoons of lemon juice with the honey and hot pepper sauce in a small bowl.

3. Prepare the barbecue for direct and indirect cooking over a medium heat.

4. Thread each wing on to a bamboo skewer, being sure to skewer each portion of the wing all the way up into the cartilage in the wingtip and then spreading it out as if it were 'in flight'.

5. Brush the cooking grates clean. Brown the wings over **direct medium heat** for 4 to 5 minutes, with the lid closed as much as possible, turning once. Move the wings over **indirect medium heat** and grill for 15 to 20 minutes, basting with the honey mixture once or twice during the last 10 minutes of grilling time, until the meat is no longer pink at the bone. Keep the lid closed as much as possible during grilling. Remove the wings from the barbecue, brush once more with the glaze and serve warm.

HICKORY 'DRUMETTES' WITH BOURBON-MOLASSES GLAZE

SERVES: 6 TO 8 AS A STARTER
PREP TIME: 20 MINUTES

HEAT: INDIRECT MEDIUM HEAT 180° TO 230°C
   (350° TO 450°F)
GRILLING TIME: 20 TO 30 MINUTES

RUB
1 tablespoon smoked paprika
2 teaspoons dry mustard
1 teaspoon sea salt
½ teaspoon garlic granules
½ teaspoon onion granules
¼ teaspoon ground chipotle chilli

20 chicken wing drumettes, about 1.5 kg (3 lb)

GLAZE
2 tablespoons soy sauce
2 tablespoons bourbon
1 tablespoon unsulphured (light) molasses
15 g (½ oz) unsalted butter

2 handfuls hickory wood chips, soaked in water for at
   least 30 minutes

1. Mix the rub ingredients together in a large bowl. Add the drumettes and toss to coat them evenly.

2. Prepare the barbecue for indirect cooking over a medium heat.

3. Bring the glaze ingredients to the boil in a small, heavy-based saucepan over a high heat and cook just until the butter melts. Transfer to a small bowl and allow the glaze to cool.

4. Drain and scatter the wood chips over lit charcoal or put them in the smoker box of a gas barbecue, following manufacturer's instructions. Brush the cooking grates clean. Grill the wings over *indirect medium heat* for 20 to 30 minutes with the lid closed as much as possible but turning and basting with the glaze once or twice during the last 20 minutes of cooking, until the meat is no longer pink at the bone.

HOW TO BARBECUE CHICKEN DRUMETTES

1. Each chicken wing has three parts: a wingtip (left); a 2-bone middle section (middle); and an upper wing (right).

2. The upper wing is called the 'drumette' because it looks like a little drumstick.

3. Grill drumettes over indirect heat to break down some of the chewy characterisic of the meat, and give them some good hickory smoke and a sweet boozy glaze.

HOW TO PREP WHOLE CHICKEN LEGS

1. Turn each chicken leg skin-side down and trim off the excess skin. The fat under that skin tends to melt into the barbecue and pose a threat of flare-ups.

2. The meat near the joint of a chicken leg will take the longest to cook. So cut an opening between the drumstick and thigh to expose that innermost meat and speed up its cooking time.

3. Making some slashes on the outside of the leg will allow the marinade to penetrate faster and deeper.

4. The Provençal flavours in this recipe come primarily from a blend of dried herbs that usually includes thyme, marjoram, parsley, tarragon and bay leaf, as well as lavender and celery seeds. It is sold as dried herbes de Provence.

5. Pour the marinade over the chicken in a large, resealable plastic bag. Press the air out of the bag, seal it tightly and turn it several times, making sure to coat all of the pieces evenly.

6. When you are dealing with raw chicken and a messy marinade, it's always a good idea to avoid spills by putting the bag in a bowl before refrigerating it.

PROVENÇAL MARINATED CHICKEN LEGS

SERVES: 6
PREP TIME: 15 MINUTES
MARINATING TIME: 4 TO 8 HOURS

HEAT: INDIRECT MEDIUM HEAT 180° TO 230°C
    (350° TO 450°F)
GRILLING TIME: 50 MINUTES TO 1 HOUR

MARINADE
250 ml (8 fl oz) dry white wine
5 tablespoons extra-virgin olive oil
3 tablespoons wholegrain mustard
3 tablespoons white wine vinegar
2 tablespoons dried herbes de Provence
3 garlic cloves, very finely chopped
2 teaspoons sea salt
½ teaspoon crushed red chilli flakes

6 whole chicken legs, 300 to 375 g (10 to 12 oz) each

1. Whisk the marinade ingredients together in a bowl.

2. Cut a few deep slashes into the meaty parts of each chicken leg. Place them in a large, resealable plastic bag and pour in the marinade. Press the air out of the bag and seal tightly. Turn the bag to distribute the marinade and refrigerate for 4 to 8 hours, turning occasionally.

3. Prepare the barbecue for indirect cooking over a medium heat.

4. Remove the chicken from the bag, letting the herbs cling to the chicken. Discard the marinade. Brush the cooking grates clean. Grill the chicken over ***indirect medium heat*** for 50 minutes to 1 hour with the lid closed as much as possible but turning once, until the juices run clear and the internal temperature reaches 77°C (170°F) in the thickest part of the thigh (not touching the bone). If desired, to crisp the skin, grill the chicken over ***direct medium heat*** during the last 5 minutes of grilling time, turning once. Remove from the barbecue and cut into thighs and drumsticks.

■ ■ ■

Boneless chicken pieces do well barbecued quickly over direct heat, but bone-in pieces take longer and direct heat alone would burn them, so use indirect heat (or both direct and indirect) for bone-in pieces.

■ ■ ■

POULTRY

149

HOW TO ROAST DUCK LEGS

1. Duck legs have so much fat under their skins that they are prone to flare-ups if you try grilling them over direct heat, but the 'ring of fire' gives you ample room in the centre of the cooking grate to smoke-roast them safely over indirect heat.

2. While the charcoal burns down to the right temperature and the wood chunks begin smoking, trim any fat hanging from the edges of the duck legs.

3. Cook the duck legs, skin side up, until dark brown and crisp. Brush on the orange-hoisin glaze near the end of the cooking time so that it does not burn.

SLOW-ROASTED DUCK LEGS WITH HOISIN-ORANGE GLAZE

SERVES: 4
PREP TIME: 10 MINUTES

HEAT: INDIRECT MEDIUM HEAT ABOUT 160°C (325°F)
GRILLING TIME: ABOUT 1 HOUR

GLAZE
4 tablespoons orange marmalade
4 tablespoons fresh orange juice
4 tablespoons mirin (rice wine)
2 tablespoons hoisin sauce
½ teaspoon crushed red chilli flakes

RUB
2 teaspoons sea salt
¾ teaspoon freshly ground black pepper
¾ teaspoon Chinese five-spice powder

8 whole duck legs, 175 to 250 g (6 to 8 oz) each, trimmed of excess fat
5 apple wood chunks (not soaked)

1. Prepare the barbecue for indirect cooking over a medium heat using the 'ring-of-fire' configuration (see photo above).

2. Combine the glaze ingredients in a small saucepan over a medium-high heat. Bring to a simmer to melt the marmalade, then remove the pan from the heat.

3. Combine the rub ingredients in a small bowl, then season the duck evenly with the rub.

4. Add the wood chunks directly on to burning coals. As soon as the wood starts to smoke, grill the duck, skin side up, over **indirect medium heat** for about 1 hour, with the lid closed as much as possible but turning and basting with the glaze during the last 15 to 20 minutes of grilling time, until the duck is evenly browned and crisp and is fully cooked through. Serve warm.

HOW TO BARBECUE CHICKEN

1. Season the chicken thighs and drumsticks with the spices.

2. After browning the chicken first over direct heat, move it to indirect heat to smoke and finish cooking.

3. A couple handfuls of damp wood chips should provide smoke for 20 to 30 minutes.

4. Spices, smoke and finally a light coating of sauce. That's a triple-play of flavour.

TRIPLE-PLAY BARBECUED CHICKEN

SERVES: 4
PREP TIME: 30 MINUTES

HEAT: DIRECT AND INDIRECT MEDIUM HEAT 180° TO 230°C
(350° TO 450°F)
GRILLING TIME: 43 TO 45 MINUTES

SAUCE
75 g (3 oz) yellow onion, finely chopped
2 teaspoons very finely chopped garlic
2 tablespoons extra-virgin olive oil
275 g (9 oz) ketchup
125 ml (4 fl oz) lemon-lime carbonated beverage (not diet)
4 tablespoons fresh lemon juice
50 g (2 oz) light brown sugar
2 tablespoons wholegrain mustard

RUB
2 teaspoons smoked paprika
2 teaspoons sea salt
Finely grated rind of 1 lemon
½ teaspoon garlic granules
½ teaspoon freshly ground black pepper

4 whole chicken legs, 300 to 375 g (10 to 12 oz) each, cut into
thighs and drumsticks
2 handfuls hickory wood chips, soaked in water for at least
30 minutes

1. Cook the onion and garlic in the oil in a saucepan over a medium heat for about 10 minutes, stirring often, until golden. Add the rest of the sauce ingredients and stir to combine. Bring the sauce to a simmer, reduce the heat to low and cook for 10 to 15 minutes, stirring often, until slightly thickened.

2. Mix the rub ingredients together in a bowl. Sprinkle the rub evenly over the chicken pieces and allow the chicken to stand at room temperature for 20 to 30 minutes before grilling. Prepare the barbecue for direct and indirect cooking over a medium heat.

3. Brush the cooking grates clean. Grill the chicken, skin side down, over **direct medium heat** for 8 to 10 minutes, with the lid closed as much as possible but turning occasionally, until golden brown. Move the chicken pieces over **indirect medium heat**. Drain and scatter the wood chips over the lit charcoal or put them in the smoker box of a gas barbecue, following manufacturer's instructions. Continue to grill the chicken, with the lid closed, for about 20 minutes. Then brush both sides with a thin layer of the sauce and cook for a further 15 minutes, turning occasionally and brushing with the sauce, until the juices run clear and the meat is no longer pink at the bone. Serve warm or at room temperature with the remaining sauce on the side.

HOW TO CEDAR-PLANK BONE-IN CHICKEN THIGHS

1. Soak the cedar plank in beer or water for at least 1 hour.

2. Weight the plank down with something heavy so it doesn't float.

3. Place the soaked plank over direct medium heat and close the lid to start the plank smoking.

4. When the plank starts smoking, turn it over and arrange the marinated chicken thighs on top.

5. Finish cooking the chicken thighs with the plank over indirect heat, basting them occasionally with the reserved marinade. If you left the plank over direct heat for too long, it would ignite.

6. To check for doneness, pull one of the thickest thighs from the barbecue and cut into the underside. If the colour of the meat near the bone is still pink, put it back on the plank until it is fully cooked.

7. Using 2 pairs of tongs, carefully remove the plank and chicken thighs to a heatproof surface.

8. Before serving, glaze the chicken thighs one more time.

CEDAR-PLANKED CHICKEN THIGHS WITH SOY-GINGER GLAZE

SERVES: 4 TO 6

PREP TIME: 30 MINUTES

HEAT: DIRECT AND INDIRECT MEDIUM HEAT 180° TO 230°C
(350° TO 450°F)

GRILLING TIME: 40 TO 50 MINUTES

SPECIAL EQUIPMENT: 1 UNTREATED CEDAR PLANK, 30
TO 45 CM (12 TO 15 INCHES) LONG AND 1 TO 1.5 CM
(½ TO ¾ INCH) THICK, SOAKED IN BEER OR WATER
FOR AT LEAST 1 HOUR

GLAZE

175 g (6 oz) soy sauce

125 ml (4 fl oz) balsamic vinegar

100 g (1½ oz) light brown sugar

1 tablespoon very finely chopped garlic

1 tablespoon very finely chopped fresh root ginger

1 teaspoon crushed red chilli flakes

4 tablespoons toasted sesame oil

10 skinless chicken thighs (with bone), 150 to 175 g
(5 to 6 oz) each

1. Combine the soy sauce, vinegar and sugar in a small,
saucepan over a medium-low heat and simmer for about
20 minutes until reduced by half. Remove the pan from the
heat and add the garlic, ginger and red chilli flakes. Cool slightly
and then whisk in the oil. Reserve 125 ml (4 fl oz) of the glaze
for basting the chicken.

2. Put the thighs in a large bowl, pour in the remaining glaze
and toss to coat. Cover and refrigerate until you are ready
to barbecue.

3. Prepare the barbecue for direct and indirect cooking over a
medium heat. Place the soaked plank over **direct medium heat**
and close the lid. After 5 to 10 minutes, when the plank begins
to smoke and char, turn the plank over.

4. Remove the thighs from the bowl and discard the glaze.
Arrange the thighs on the smoking plank and cook over **direct
medium heat**, with the lid closed, for 5 to 10 minutes. Move
the plank over **indirect medium heat** and continue cooking for
35 to 40 minutes, with the lid closed as much as possible but
basting occasionally with the reserved glaze during the last 10
to 15 minutes of grilling time, until the juices run clear. Remove
the chicken plank and thighs from the barbecue and baste with
the reserved glaze once more before serving.

POULTRY

DRESSING

1 large poblano chilli
125 ml (4 fl oz) soured cream
25 g (1 oz) fresh coriander leaves and tender stems
1 tablespoon fresh lime juice
1 tablespoon extra-virgin olive oil
1 large garlic clove
½ teaspoon ground cumin
½ teaspoon sea salt
¼ teaspoon freshly ground black pepper

SALAD

250 g (8 oz) Cos lettuce, thinly sliced or shredded
175 g (6 oz) yellow or blue corn tortilla chips, crushed
175 g (6 oz) ripe tomato, diced
2 Haas avocados, diced
1 can (425 g/14 oz) pinto or black beans, rinsed

1. Whisk the marinade ingredients together in a medium bowl. Add the chicken thighs, turning several times to coat them evenly, then cover and refrigerate for 30 minutes to 1 hour.

2. Prepare the barbecue for direct cooking over a medium heat. Brush the cooking grates clean. Grill the chilli over **direct medium heat** for 8 to 10 minutes, with the lid closed as much as possible but turning occasionally, until the skin is blackened and blistered. Transfer the chilli to a small bowl, cover with clingfilm and let steam for about 10 minutes. Gently peel the skin from the chilli and remove the seeds. Put the chilli in a blender with the remaining dressing ingredients and process until smooth. Refrigerate until ready to serve.

3. Arrange a bed of lettuce on a large platter and then add the chips, tomato, avocado and beans in separate sections on top.

4. Grill the chicken over **direct medium heat** for 8 to 10 minutes, with the lid closed as much as possible but turning once or twice, until the meat is firm and the juices run clear. Transfer the chicken to a chopping board and cut into 1-cm (½-inch) strips. Place the chicken on a separate section of the platter. Serve the dressing alongside.

LAYERED MEXICAN CHICKEN SALAD

SERVES: 4 TO 6
PREP TIME: 35 MINUTES
MARINATING TIME: 30 MINUTES TO 1 HOUR

HEAT: DIRECT MEDIUM HEAT 180° TO 230°C
(350° TO 450°F)
GRILLING TIME: 16 TO 20 MINUTES

MARINADE

4 tablespoons extra-virgin olive oil
2 tablespoons fresh lime juice
1 teaspoon dried thyme
1 teaspoon dried marjoram
½ teaspoon sea salt
¼ teaspoon freshly ground black pepper

6 boneless, skinless chicken thighs, about 125 g (4 oz) each

HOW TO BARBECUE CHICKEN THIGHS

1. Lay chicken thighs, smooth side down first, over direct heat and resist the urge to turn them for at least 4 minutes. Otherwise, you might rip the meat.

2. However, if the meat is bunched on top of itself, unfold it so that it lies at flat as possible on the grate for better charred flavour.

3. You can check the doneness by bending back a thigh and opening up the meat. If there is no trace of pink, it's done.

KEEPING FROZEN SKEWERS ON HAND

To avoid soaking bamboo skewers each time you need them, soak a big batch once for an hour or so, then drain them and freeze them in a plastic bag. When it's time to barbecue, pull out as many skewers as you need.

Ingredients like chicken pieces will stay juicier longer if they are touching (but not crammed) on the skewers.

PERSIAN CHICKEN KEBABS

SERVES: 4 TO 6
PREP TIME: 15 MINUTES
MARINATING TIME: 30 MINUTES

HEAT: DIRECT MEDIUM HEAT 180° TO 230°C
   (350° TO 450°F)
GRILLING TIME: 8 TO 10 MINUTES
SPECIAL EQUIPMENT: BAMBOO SKEWERS,
   SOAKED IN WATER FOR AT LEAST 30 MINUTES

MARINADE
1 large onion, coarsely chopped
125 ml (4 fl oz) fresh lemon juice
2 tablespoons dried oregano
2 teaspoons sweet paprika
2 teaspoons very finely chopped garlic
250 ml (8 fl oz) extra-virgin olive oil

10 boneless, skinless chicken thighs, about 125 g (4 oz) each,
   cut into 3.5-cm (1½-inch) pieces

1. Purée the onion, lemon juice, oregano, paprika and garlic together in a food processor or blender. With the motor running, slowly add the oil.

2. Place the chicken pieces in a large, resealable plastic bag and pour in the marinade. Press the air out of the bag and seal tightly. Turn the bag to distribute the marinade and allow the chicken to marinate at room temperature for 30 minutes.

3. Prepare the barbecue for direct cooking over a medium heat.

4. Remove the chicken from the marinade and thread on to skewers, so that the pieces are touching (but not crammed together). Discard the marinade.

5. Brush the cooking grates clean. Grill the kebabs over **direct medium heat** for 8 to 10 minutes, with the lid closed as much as possible but turning once, until the meat is fully cooked but not dry. Serve warm.

HOW TO BARBECUE QUESADILLAS

1. Of course most great quesadillas involve guacamole, and that means avocado. To stone one, cut lengthways around the stone and then twist the halves in opposite directions.

2. Tap the exposed stone with the heel of your knife. It will pull out easily from the avocado.

3. You can chop the avocado right in the skin by cross-hatching it and then scooping the little pieces into a bowl with a spoon. Next, mash the avocado pieces with lime juice, garlic and salt.

4. Load up one side of each tortilla with barbecued chicken, vegetables and some grated cheese, but don't add so much that the filling may spill out the sides.

5. Fold the other half of the tortilla on top and firmly press down on it. At this point, you can set the quesadillas aside for a couple hours before grilling them.

6. Grill the quesadillas over direct medium heat until toasted on each side. This is one of the few times when it's best to leave the barbecue lid open, so you can keep an eye on the quesadillas and prevent them from burning.

CHICKEN AND VEGETABLE QUESADILLAS WITH GUACAMOLE

SERVES: 4 TO 6
PREP TIME: 30 MINUTES

HEAT: DIRECT MEDIUM HEAT 180° TO 230°C
 (350° TO 450°F)
GRILLING TIME: 10 TO 13 MINUTES

RUB
1 teaspoon pure chilli powder
1 teaspoon sea salt
½ teaspoon dried oregano
¼ teaspoon garlic granules
¼ teaspoon onion granules
¼ teaspoon freshly ground black pepper

4 boneless, skinless chicken thighs, about 125 g (4 oz) each
2 courgettes, trimmed and halved lengthways
2 ears corn, husked
Extra-virgin olive oil
2 teaspoons chopped oregano
1 teaspoon very finely chopped garlic
1 tablespoon fresh lime juice
Sea salt
Freshly ground black pepper

GUACAMOLE
2 Haas avocados, diced
2 teaspoons fresh lime juice
1 teaspoon very finely chopped garlic
¼ teaspoon sea salt

10 flour tortillas (25 cm/10 inches in diameter)
400 g (13 oz) pepper jack or Cheddar cheese, grated

1. Prepare the barbecue for direct cooking over a medium heat.

2. Combine the rub ingredients in a small bowl. Lightly brush the chicken, courgettes and corn with oil. Season the chicken with the rub.

3. Brush the cooking grates clean. Grill the chicken and vegetables over **direct medium heat**, with the lid closed as much as possible but turning the chicken once and the vegetables occasionally, until the meat is firm and the juices run clear, the courgettes are just tender and the corn kernels are golden brown in spots. The chicken will take 8 to 10 minutes and the vegetables will take 6 to 8 minutes. Remove the chicken and vegetables from the barbecue as they are cooked and allow them to cool.

4. Cut the chicken and courgettes into 5-mm (¼-inch) chunks. Cut the kernels from the cobs. Combine the courgettes and corn with the oregano, garlic and lime juice in a large bowl, then season to taste with salt and pepper. Add the chicken to the vegetable mixture and stir to combine.

5. Mash together the guacamole ingredients In a small bowl.

6. Lay the tortillas in a single layer on a work surface. Evenly divide the chicken and vegetable mixture, and then the cheese, over half of each tortilla. Fold the empty half of each tortilla over the filling, creating a half circle, and press down firmly.

7. Grill the quesadillas over **direct medium heat** for 2 to 3 minutes with the lid open, turning once. Transfer the quesadillas from the barbecue to a chopping board and cut into wedges. Serve warm with the guacamole.

HOW TO SPLIT POUSSINS

1. Use poultry shears to cut along both sides of the backbone, then discard it.

2. Cut through the centre of the breast.

3. The breastbone will stay attached to one of the halves.

4. Poussins cut into halves will absorb marinades more easily and cook faster than whole ones.

POUSSINS MARINATED IN BOURBON, HONEY AND SOY

SERVES: 4
PREP TIME: 30 MINUTES
MARINATING TIME: 4 TO 8 HOURS

HEAT: INDIRECT MEDIUM HEAT 180° TO 230°C
  (350° TO 450°F)
GRILLING TIME: ABOUT 30 MINUTES

MARINADE
350 ml (12 fl oz) soy sauce
175 ml (6 fl oz) bourbon or other whisky
6 garlic cloves, very finely chopped
2 tablespoons runny honey
1½ tablespoons grated fresh root ginger

4 Poussins, 500 to 625 g (1 to 1¼ lb) each
Extra-virgin olive oil
½ teaspoon freshly ground black pepper

1. Combine the marinade ingredients in a medium bowl.

2. Remove and discard the giblets from each poussin. Using poultry shears, cut along both sides of each backbone and discard it, then cut through the centre of each breast.

3. Place the birds side by side in a shallow, non-metallic dish and cover with the marinade. Turn to coat the birds evenly, then cover and refrigerate for 4 to 8 hours. (Do not marinate overnight or the ginger will cause the meat to break down and become mushy.)

4. Remove the poussins from the dish and reserve the marinade. Lightly brush the hens with oil and season with the pepper. Allow them to stand at room temperature for 20 to 30 minutes before grilling. Prepare the barbecue for indirect cooking over medium heat.

5. Pour the reserved marinade into a small saucepan and bring to the boil over a high heat for about 30 seconds. Set aside to use as a basting sauce.

6. Brush the cooking grates clean. Grill the poussins, skin side up, over *indirect medium heat* for about 30 minutes, with the lid closed but basting the birds with the sauce a couple of times during the last 10 minutes of cooking, until the skin is golden brown and the internal temperature in the thickest part of the thigh reaches 77°C (170°F). Remove the birds from the barbecue and serve warm.

HULI-HULI CHICKEN

SERVES: 4 TO 6
PREP TIME: 15 MINUTES
MARINATING TIME: ABOUT 4 HOURS

HEAT: INDIRECT MEDIUM HEAT 180° TO 230°C
    (350° TO 450°F)
GRILLING TIME: 45 MINUTES TO 1 HOUR

MARINADE
250 ml (8 fl oz) thawed pineapple juice concentrate
125 ml (4 fl oz) soy sauce
65 g (2½ oz) ketchup
2 tablespoons very finely chopped fresh root ginger
2 teaspoons very finely chopped garlic

2 whole chickens, 1.5 to 2 kg (3 to 4 lb) each
4 handfuls mesquite wood chips, soaked in water for at
    least 30 minutes

1. Whisk the marinade ingredients together in a bowl.

2. Place one of the chickens, breast side down, on a chopping board. Using poultry shears, cut along each side of the backbone and discard it. Open the chicken like a book, and then cut the chicken in half lengthways along one side of the breastbone. Pull off and discard any lumps of fat. Remove and discard the wingtips. Repeat the process with the other chicken. Place the chicken halves in a large, resealable plastic bag and pour in the marinade. Press the air out of the bag and seal it tightly. Turn the bag several times to coat the chicken evenly with the marinade. Place the bag in a bowl and refrigerate for about 4 hours, turning the bag occasionally.

3. Remove the chicken from the bag and discard the marinade.

4. Prepare the barbecue for indirect cooking over a medium heat.

5. Drain half of the wood chips and toss them on to burning coals or into the smoker box of a gas barbecue, following manufacturer's instructions. Begin cooking the chicken when the wood starts to smoke.

6. Brush the cooking grates clean. Grill the chicken, skin side up first, over ***indirect medium heat*** for 45 minues to 1 hour, with the lid closed as much as possible but turning the chicken every 15 minutes, until the juices run clear and the internal temperature reaches 77°C (170°F) in the thickest part of the thigh (not touching the bone). Drain and add the rest of the wood chips after the first 15 minutes of grilling.

7. Remove from the barbecue and allow the chicken to rest for about 10 minutes before serving.

Huli-Huli is a Hawaiian term meaning 'turn-turn', which is exactly what you need to do here to prevent the sweet marinade from burning. That said, turn the chicken halves carefully with a fish slice so they hold together. And don't forget the wood smoke. It is as important as any ingredient in the recipe.

HOW TO SMOKE BEER CAN CHICKEN

1. Blanketing a chicken with salt and refrigerating it for a couple hours will draw out some moisture and strengthen the chicken flavours. Don't worry; the chicken will not be salty. The next step is to rinse off the salt.

2. After you have rinsed and seasoned the chicken, open a beer can and pour out half of it (into a cold mug). With a can opener, make 2 more holes in the top to allow steam to escape.

3. Fold the wingtips behind the back of the chicken to shield the tips from the heat.

4. Working with a solid surface underneath, slide the chicken over the beer can as far as it will go.

5. Set up the barbecue with a water pan in the middle and coals on either side. Add a couple handfuls of damp chips to each pile of coals.

6. When the wood starts to smoke, place the chicken in the centre of the cooking grate. Position the chicken legs towards the front so they balance the chicken with the can like a tripod.

7. When the chicken is fully cooked (77°C/170°F in the thickest part of the thigh), grab the back with tongs and slide a fish slice under the can to lift it. Be careful; the beer will be very hot. Allow the chicken to cool for about 10 minutes before sliding it off the can.

SMOKED BEER CAN CHICKEN

SERVES: 4
PREP TIME: 10 MINUTES
SALT-CURING TIME: 1½ TO 2 HOURS

HEAT: INDIRECT MEDIUM HEAT 180° TO 230°C
    (350° TO 450°F)
GRILLING TIME: 1¼ TO 1½ HOURS

1 whole chicken, about 2.5 kg (5 lb)
65 g (2½ oz) sea salt

RUB
2 teaspoons onion granules
2 teaspoons garlic granules
1 teaspoon chili con carne seasoning
½ teaspoon freshly ground black pepper

1 can (425 ml/14 fl oz) beer, at room temperature
4 handfuls hickory wood chips, soaked in water for at
    least 30 minutes

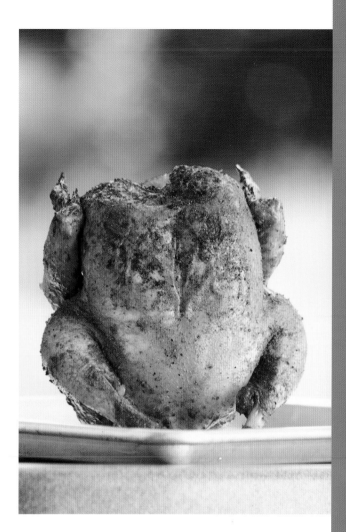

1. Remove and discard the neck, giblets and any excess fat
from the chicken. Sprinkle the salt over the entire surface and
inside the cavity of the chicken, covering it all like a light blanket
of snow. Cover the chicken with clingfilm and refrigerate for
1½ to 2 hours.

2. Mix the rub ingredients together in a small bowl.

3. Rinse the chicken inside and out with cold water. Gently
pat the chicken dry with kitchen paper. Season it all over with
the rub. Fold the wingtips behind the chicken's back. Allow
the chicken to stand at room temperature for 20 to 30 minutes
before grilling. Prepare the barbecue for indirect cooking over a
medium heat.

4. Open the beer can and pour out about half the beer. Using a
can opener, make 2 more holes in the top of the can. Place the
beer can on a solid surface. Ease the chicken cavity over the
beer can.

5. Drain and add the wood chips directly on to burning
coals or to the smoker box of a gas barbecue, following
manufacturer's instructions. When the wood chips begin to
smoke, transfer the bird-on-a-can to the barbecue, balancing
the bird on its two legs and the can, like a tripod. Grill over
indirect medium heat for 1¼ to 1½ hours, with the lid closed,
until the juices run clear and the internal temperature registers
77°C (170°F) in the thickest part of the thigh (not touching the
bone). Carefully remove the chicken and can from the barbecue
(do not spill contents of the beer can, as it will be very hot).
Allow the chicken to rest for about 10 minutes before lifting it
from the beer can and cutting into serving pieces. Serve warm.

HOW TO COOK ROTISSERIE CHICKEN

1. To truss the chicken, remove the wingtips and slide a 1.2-metre (4-feet) length of string under the legs and back.

2. Lift both ends of the string and cross it between the legs, then run one end under one drumstick.

3. Run the other end under the other drumstick and pull both ends to draw the drumsticks together.

4. Bring the string along both sides of the chicken so that it holds the legs and wings against the body.

5. Tie a knot in the ends between the neck and the top of the breast. If necessary, push the breast down a little to expose more of the neck.

6. Marinate the chicken in a bag with the buttermilk mixture for 2 to 4 hours in the refrigerator.

7. Position one set of fork prongs on the far end of the centre rod (spit) and slide the spit into the opening between the neck and the knotted string, though the chicken, and out the other side, just underneath the drumsticks. Slide the other set of fork prongs on the spit and drive the prongs into the back of the chicken. Make sure the chicken is centred on the spit before tightening the fork prongs into place.

8. Position the chicken over a drip pan of water. Turn on the motor and let the chicken cook over indirect heat. Adjust the burners as necessary to maintain a cooking temperature of about 200°C (400°F). Brush the chicken a few times with the glaze during the last 30 minutes of cooking, but keep the lid closed as much as possible. For a crispier skin, turn on the infrared burner at the back of the barbecue during the final minutes of cooking.

ROTISSERIE BUTTERMILK CHICKEN WITH APRICOT GLAZE

SERVES: 4
PREP TIME: 25 MINUTES
MARINATING TIME: 2 TO 4 HOURS

HEAT: INDIRECT MEDIUM HEAT ABOUT 200°C (400°F)
GRILLING TIME: 1 TO 1¼ HOURS
SPECIAL EQUIPMENT: BUTCHER'S STRING,
    ROTISSERIE, LARGE DISPOSABLE FOIL TIN,
    INSTANT-READ THERMOMETER

MARINADE
500 ml (17 fl oz) buttermilk
15 g (½ oz) roughly chopped fresh rosemary leaves
4 large garlic cloves, finely chopped
2 tablespoons sea salt
1 teaspoon freshly ground black pepper

1 whole chicken, 4.4 to 5 kg (4½ to 5 lb)

GLAZE
250 ml (8 fl oz) apricot nectar
3 tablespoons maple syrup
1 tablespoon Dijon mustard
1 tablespoon white wine vinegar

1. Combine the marinade ingredients in a large bowl.

2. Truss the chicken with butcher's string (see preceding page). Place the chicken in a large, resealable plastic bag and pour in the marinade. Press the air out of the bag and seal it tightly. Turn the bag several times to coat the chicken evenly, place in a large bowl, starting with the breast side facing down, and marinate in the refrigerator for 2 to 4 hours, turning the bag once or twice. Allow the chicken to stand at room temperature for about 30 minutes before grilling. Prepare the barbecue for indirect cooking at 200°C (400°F), with the outside burners on medium to high and the middle burners turned off.

3. Whisk the glaze ingredients together in a small saucepan over a medium-high heat, then bring to the boil, reduce the heat and simmer for about 5 minutes until you have about 250 ml (8 fl oz) remaining. Reserve half of the glaze to use as a sauce.

4. Remove the chicken from the bag. Wipe off most of the marinade and discard the marinade. Following the barbecue's instructions, secure the chicken in the middle of a rotisserie spit, put the spit in place and turn on the motor. Place a large disposable foil tin under the chicken to catch drippings and pour about 250 ml (8 fl oz) of warm water into the tin. Grill the chicken over ***indirect medium heat*** for 1 to 1¼ hours, with the lid closed but brushing the chicken with the glaze a few times during the last 30 minutes of grilling, until the internal temperature reaches 77°C (170°F) in the thickest part of the thigh (not touching the bone).

5. When the chicken is fully cooked, turn off the rotisserie motor and, wearing insulated mitts, carefully remove the spit from the barbecue. Tilt the chicken upright over the disposable foil tin so that the liquid that has accumulated in the chicken's cavity pours into the tin. Slide the chicken from the spit on to a chopping board. Allow it to rest for about 10 minutes before carving into serving pieces. Serve warm with the reserved sauce.

HOW TO ROAST CHICKEN

Most chickens in supermarkets today have been bred primarily for their appearance. Large-scale farmers select their breeds for plump breast meat and raise the chickens in cramped cages, feeding them cheap diets that promote quick growth but contribute very little to flavour. One way around the blandness problem is to buy old-fashioned breeds instead. They might be a little more difficult to find, and they will cost you more, but they do taste better. Another way around the blandness problem is to roast mass-market chickens with plenty of butter, fresh herbs and seasonings under the skin.

1. Starting at the bottom of the breast, work your fingertips gently under the skin and over the meat. Try not to tear the skin.

2. Use just one finger to reach down each drumstick and along the thigh meat.

3. Smear the flavoured butter over the breast meat and cover as much of the thigh meat as possible without tearing the skin. Use the remaining flavoured butter to coat the outside of the chicken evenly.

4. Wrap a piece of butcher's string under and around the drumsticks, cross it in the centre and pull the ends to draw the drumsticks together.

5. Cross the string above the drumsticks and tie a knot. This will hold the chicken in a compact shape and help the meat cook more evenly.

6. Roast the chicken inside a disposable foil tin to catch the melted butter and drippings. Baste the chicken occasionally with what's in the tin and rotate the tin as necessary for even browning.

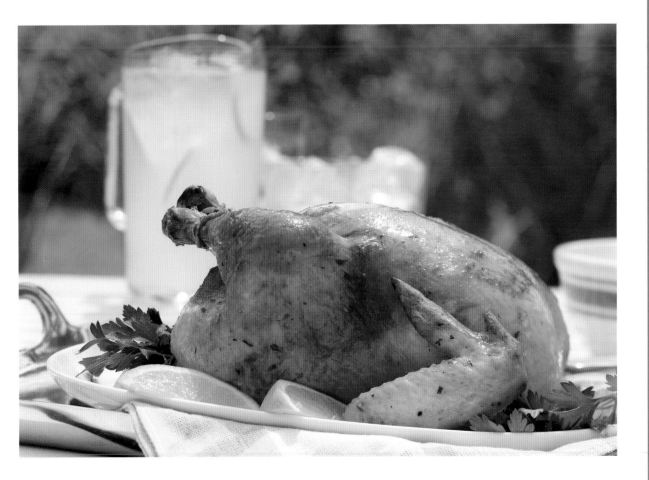

ORANGE-TARRAGON ROASTED CHICKEN

SERVES: 4

PREP TIME: 15 MINUTES

HEAT: INDIRECT MEDIUM HEAT 180° TO 230°C
(350° TO 450°F)

GRILLING TIME: 1¼ TO 1½ HOURS

SPECIAL EQUIPMENT: LARGE DISPOSABLE FOIL TIN,
BUTCHER'S STRING

BUTTER
50 g (2 oz) unsalted butter, softened
1 tablespoon finely chopped tarragon
2 teaspoons finely grated orange rind
½ teaspoon sea salt
¼ teaspoon freshly ground black pepper

1 whole chicken, 2.5 to 2.75 kg (5 to 5½ lb)
1 teaspoon sea salt
½ teaspoon freshly ground black pepper

1. Use the back of a fork to mix and mash the butter ingredients
together in a small bowl.

2. Remove and discard the neck, giblets and any excess
fat from the chicken. Loosen the chicken skin gently with
your fingertips and spread the butter under the skin on to the
breast meat and as much as you can reach on the drumsticks
and thighs.

3. Season the chicken inside and out with the salt and pepper.
Truss the chicken legs with butcher's string. Place the chicken,
breast side up, in a large disposable foil tin. Allow the chicken to
stand at room temperature for 20 to 30 minutes before grilling.
Prepare the barbecue for indirect cooking over a medium heat.

4. Brush the cooking grates clean. Grill the chicken over
indirect medium heat for 1¼ to 1½ hours, with the lid
closed but rotating the tin as needed for even browning and
occasionally basting the chicken with the melted butter
collected in the bottom of the tin, until the juices run clear and
the internal temperature in the thickest part of the thigh reaches
77°C (170°F). When fully cooked, transfer the chicken to a
platter and loosely cover with aluminium foil. Allow to rest for
about 10 minutes. Remove the string and carve the chicken.
Serve warm.

HOW TO BARBECUE BUTTERFLIED CHICKEN

1. Pull out and discard the loose clumps of fat that are typically just inside the chicken. Otherwise they might drip into the barbecue and cause flare-ups.

2. Turn the chicken over so that the back is facing up and the neck end is closest to you. Use poultry shears to cut along both sides of the backbone, then discard it.

3. Open the chicken like a butterfly spreading its wings, and press down to flatten it.

4. Run your fingertips along both sides of the breastbone to expose it.

5. Dig your fingers down along the breastbone until it comes loose from the meat, then pull it out and discard it.

6. Fold the wingtips behind the chicken's back to prevent them from burning.

7. Now you have overcome one of the key cooking challenges of a whole chicken: an uneven shape. By butterflying (or spatchcocking) the bird, you have created a relatively even shape.

8. Grill the chicken, bone side down first, with a heavy weight on top. Use a medium-low heat to gently cook the meat.

9. After about 25 minutes, carefully turn the chicken over with a spatula or fish slice and put the weight back on top. With the skin side down, flare-ups are more likely. If necessary, turn off the middle burners or move the chicken to finish cooking over indirect heat.

NUTMEG CHICKEN UNDER A CAST-IRON FRYING PAN

SERVES: 4
PREP TIME: 30 MINUTES
MARINATING TIME: 2 HOURS

HEAT: DIRECT MEDIUM-LOW HEAT ABOUT 180°C (350°F)
GRILLING TIME: 40 MINUTES TO 1 HOUR
SPECIAL EQUIPMENT: CAST-IRON FRYING PAN OR
    SHALLOW ROASTING TIN AND 2 FOIL-WRAPPED
    BRICKS, INSTANT-READ THERMOMETER

MARINADE
4 tablespoons extra-virgin olive oil
2 tablespoons very finely chopped fresh rosemary
1 tablespoon very finely chopped fresh garlic
1 tablespoon freshly grated nutmeg
1 tablespoon sea salt
1 tablespoon sugar
1 teaspoon freshly ground black pepper

1 whole chicken, about 2.5 kg (5 lb)

1. Combine the marinade ingredients in a large, shallow bowl.

2. Place the chicken, breast side down, on a chopping board. Using sturdy poultry shears or a very sharp knife, cut from the neck to the tail end, along either side of the backbone, to remove it. Take special care if you are using a knife; you'll be cutting through small bones and will have to use some force.

3. Once the backbone is out, you'll be able to see the interior of the chicken. Make a small slit in the cartilage at the bottom end of the breastbone. Then, placing both hands on the rib cage, crack the chicken open like a book. Run your fingers along either side of the cartilage in between the breasts to loosen it from the flesh. Grab the bone and pull up on it to remove it along with the attached cartilage. The chicken should now lay flat.

4. Place the chicken inside the bowl or a roasting tin and turn to coat it evenly with the marinade. Cover with clingfilm and refrigerate for about 2 hours.

5. Prepare the barbecue for direct cooking over a medium-low heat.

6. Brush the cooking grates clean. Place the chicken, bone side down, over **direct medium-low heat** for 20 to 30 minutes, with the lid closed, and put a heavy cast-iron frying pan or a roasting tin weighted down with 2 foil-wrapped bricks, directly on top. Remove the pan, turn the chicken over, replace the weight, close the lid and cook for a further 20 to 30 minutes until the juices run clear and an instant-read thermometer inserted into the thigh (not touching the bone) registers 77°C (170°F). Remove from the barbecue and allow to rest for 3 to 5 minutes. Serve warm.

HOW TO BARBECUE BACON-WRAPPED TURKEY BREAST

1. With the smooth side facing the board, open up the breast and cut down the centre (but not all the way through) to make the breast as flat and even as possible.

2. Lay the butterflied turkey breast between 2 large sheets of clingfilm and pound it to a thickness of 1.5 to 2.5 cm (¾ to 1 inch).

3. Spread the stuffing evenly over the turkey breast, but leave a margin all the way round the perimeter. Don't over-stuff the breast.

4. Roll up the breast lengthways to create a cylinder. If any excess stuffing falls out, discard it.

5. Arrange the bacon slices on a work surface in 6 tightly spaced parallel rows, overlapping the ends of 2 slices to make each row.

6. Place the rolled turkey breast in the centre of the bacon and then criss-cross the bacon around the turkey.

7. Tie the turkey crossways with butcher's string at 2.5-cm (1-inch) intervals.

8. Thread a long piece of string lengthways, in and out of the crossways pieces, and tie the ends together to create a uniform roast and to secure the bacon.

9. Set a disposable foil tin under the cooking grate to catch the bacon grease. Grill the roast over the tin, using indirect heat, until the internal temperature of the meat and stuffing reaches 74°C (165°F), turning to ensure even cooking.

BACON-WRAPPED TURKEY BREAST WITH HERB STUFFING

SERVES: 4 TO 6
PREP TIME: 30 MINUTES

HEAT: INDIRECT HIGH HEAT 230° TO 290°C (450° TO 550°F)
GRILLING TIME: 1 TO 1¼ HOURS
SPECIAL EQUIPMENT: BUTCHER'S STRING, LARGE DISPOSABLE FOIL TIN, INSTANT-READ THERMOMETER

STUFFING
75 g (3 oz) fresh breadcrumbs
4 tablespoons chicken stock
1 tablespoon finely chopped garlic
2 teaspoons finely chopped rosemary
2 teaspoons finely chopped oregano
1 teaspoon finely grated lemon rind
½ teaspoon sea salt
½ teaspoon freshly ground black pepper

500 g (1 lb) bacon rashers
1 boneless, skinless turkey breast, about 1 kg
    (2 lb), butterflied

1. Combine the stuffing ingredients in a bowl. The stuffing should be moist, mounding nicely on a spoon, but should not be sopping wet. Add more stock if needed.

2. Carefully place a large disposable foil tin underneath the cooking grate to catch the bacon grease. Prepare the barbecue for indirect cooking over a high heat.

3. Place the butterflied turkey breast on a work surface between 2 sheets of clingfilm and pound to an even thickness. Spread the stuffing evenly over the turkey breast and then roll up the breast lengthways to create a cylinder. Arrange the bacon slices on a work surface in 6 tightly spaced, parallel rows, overlapping the ends of 2 slices to make each row. Place the rolled turkey breast in the centre of the bacon and then criss-cross the bacon around the turkey. Tie the turkey with butcher's string to create a uniform roast and to secure the bacon.

4. Brush the cooking grates clean. Centre the turkey over the drip tin and grill over ***indirect high heat*** for 1 to 1¼ hours, with the lid closed as much as possible but turning occasionally to ensure the bacon gets crisp on all sides, until the internal temperature reaches 77°C (165°F). Transfer to a carving board and allow to rest for 10 minutes (the internal temperature will rise during this time). Remove the string and carve into 2.5-cm (1-inch) slices.

HOW TO COOK TURKEY

THINGS YOU NEED TO KNOW

Every December millions of British cooks tighten up with stress at the thought of how to cook a golden, succulent turkey for Christmas. Let me tell you; it's not that difficult. Focus on a handful of critical elements.

1 BRINING A DAY AHEAD

Because turkey meat is so lean and bland, some kind of brining is important. In the following recipe I call for a dry brine, which just means coating the turkey with sea salt the day before cooking. Overnight, in the refrigerator, the salt will draw out some moisture, which will mix with the salt, and then the meat will reabsorb much of that flavourful moisture.

2 MAINTAINING AN EVEN TEMPERATURE

An even temperature in the range of 180 to 200°C (350° to 400°F) is also key here. That's easy enough to achieve on a gas barbecue, assuming there is plenty of gas in the tank. It's a bit more challenging with a charcoal barbecue. Before cooking your first turkey with charcoal, make sure you have had some good experiences maintaining a live fire over the course of several hours.

3 SHIELDING THE BREAST MEAT

Because the breast meat cooks faster than the leg meat, you should protect the breast and slow down its rate of cooking. I do that by facing the breast down inside a stock-and-vegetable-filled pan for the first hour of cooking.

4 CATCHING THE PERFECT DONENESS

In a very short period of time, a turkey can turn from moist and fabulous to dry and stringy, so it's imperative that you use an instant-read thermometer and remove the turkey from the barbecue when the internal temperature in the thickest part of the thigh reaches 77°C (170°F).

5 GETTING ENOUGH REST

Finally, don't skip the resting step after your turkey comes off the barbecue. During that period, the turkey will finish cooking and the juices will redistribute nicely.

HOW TO PREP TURKEY THE DAY BEFORE

1. Generously season the turkey, inside and out, with sea salt and freshly ground black pepper.

2. Refrigerate the seasoned turkey on a roasting tray, uncovered, for 12 hours. It's okay if the skin looks dry and tightened at the end of the time.

HOW TO SMOKE TURKEY

1. Remove the turkey from the refrigerator and allow it sit at room temperature for 1 hour. Brush the legs, breast and wings with butter.

2. Place 1 large disposable foil tin inside the other and add the vegetables, herbs and 450 ml (¾ pint) of chicken stock.

3. Arrange the charcoal in a half circle on one side of the charcoal grate. A drip tin filled with warm water will help you maintain the temperature of the fire.

4. Place the turkey, breast side down, over the vegetables, inside the foil tins.

5. Add wood chips to the charcoal and set the pan over the water tin, with the legs facing the hottest side of the barbecue.

6. Keep the grill temperature inside the range of 180 to 200°C (350° to 400°F), adding charcoal as needed.

7. After grilling for 1 hour, flip over the turkey so that the breast side is facing up.

8. Continue grilling and smoking the turkey, occasionally adding damp wood chips.

9. After the turkey has been on the grill for 1½ hours, cover any parts that are getting too dark.

HOW TO CARVE TURKEY

1. Remove each half of the turkey breast by cutting lengthways along each side of the breastbone.

2. Pull the first half of the breast away from the breastbone, using a sharp knife to carefully release the meat from the rib cage.

3. It is much easier to carve a half of a turkey breast into crossways slices than it is to carve the breast while it is still attached to the body.

HICKORY-SMOKED TURKEY WITH BOURBON GRAVY

SERVES: 8 TO 12
PREP TIME: 20 MINUTES
DRY BRINING TIME: 12 HOURS

HEAT: INDIRECT MEDIUM HEAT 180° TO 230°C
   (350° TO 400°F)
GRILLING TIME: ABOUT 2½ HOURS
SPECIAL EQUIPMENT: 3 LARGE DISPOSABLE FOIL TINS,
   INSTANT-READ THERMOMETER, FAT SEPARATOR

1 turkey, about 6 kg (12 lb)
2 tablespoons sea salt
2 teaspoons freshly ground black pepper
40 g (1½ oz) unsalted butter, softened

AROMATICS
150 g (5 oz) yellow onion, chopped
65 g (2½ oz) carrot, chopped
50 g (2 oz) celery, chopped
1 teaspoon dried rosemary
1 teaspoon dried thyme
1 teaspoon dried sage

450 ml (¾ pint) chicken stock, plus more for the gravy
4 handfuls hickory wood chips, soaked in water for at least
   30 minutes

GRAVY
75 g (3 oz) plain flour
3 tablespoons bourbon or whisky
½ teaspoon sea salt
¼ teaspoon freshly ground black pepper

1. The day before cooking, prepare the turkey. Remove the giblets from the turkey and set aside for another use. Rinse the turkey with cold water, then shake off the excess water, but do not pat dry. Combine the salt and pepper and rub it all over the turkey, inside and out. Place the turkey on a roasting tray and refrigerate, uncovered, for 12 hours.

2. Remove the turkey from the refrigerator. The skin may look dry, and that's okay. Do not rinse the turkey. Allow the turkey to stand at room temperature for 1 hour. Brush the legs, breast and wings with the butter.

3. Place one foil tin inside the other and combine the aromatics in the top tin. (Do not use a high-quality metal roasting tin, as the smoke may discolour it.) Add 500 ml (17 fl oz) of the chicken stock. Place the turkey, breast side down, inside the foil tins and over the aromatics.

4. Drain and add 2 handfuls of the wood chips directly on to burning coals or to the smoker box of a gas barbecue, following manufacturer's instructions. Grill the turkey over **_indirect medium heat_** for 1 hour, with the lid closed, keeping the barbecue 's temperature between 180 to 200°C (350° to 400°F).

5. After grilling for 1 hour, wearing barbecue mitts or an oven glove and using a pair of tongs, flip over the turkey so that the breast side is facing up. For charcoal grilling, add 12 to 15 unlit briquettes to the coals to maintain the heat of the barbecue. Add the remaining 2 handfuls of the wood chips. Continue grilling and smoking the turkey for 1½ hours, until it is golden brown and a thermometer inserted in the thickest part of the thigh (not touching the bone) reaches 77°C (170°F). After the turkey has been on the barbecue for 1½ hours, check to see if the wing tips or the ends of the drumsticks are getting too dark. If so, wrap them with foil.

6. Carefully remove the turkey and roasting tins from the barbecue. Transfer the turkey to a carving board and allow to rest for 20 to 30 minutes. Save the juices and vegetables to make the gravy.

7. Strain the tin juices into a fat separator, pressing the vegetables firmly with a wooden spoon to extract as much liquid as possible. Discard the vegetables left in the sieve. Allow the tin juices to stand until the fat rises to the surface, about 2 minutes. Pour the tin juices into a 1-litre (1¾-pints) measuring cup. Add more chicken stock, if needed, to make 750 ml (1¼ pints). Measure the turkey fat; you should have 125 ml (4 fl oz). Add melted butter, if needed.

8. Warm the fat in a heavy-based saucepan over a medium heat, for about 2 minutes. Whisk in the flour and let it bubble until golden brown. Whisk in the stock mixture and the bourbon. Gently heat until lightly thickened, stirring often. Season with the salt and pepper.

9. Carve the turkey and serve with the gravy.

MAPLE-PLANKED TURKEY BURGERS

SERVES: 6
PREP TIME: 20 MINUTES

HEAT: DIRECT MEDIUM HEAT 180° TO 230°C (350° TO 450°F)
GRILLING TIME: 20 TO 30 MINUTES
SPECIAL EQUIPMENT: 2 UNTREATED MAPLE PLANKS,
    EACH 30 TO 45 CM (12 TO 15 INCHES) LONG AND
    1 TO 1.5 CM (½ TO ¾ INCH) THICK, SOAKED IN BEER
    OR WATER FOR AT LEAST 1 HOUR

SAUCE
137 g (4½ oz) ketchup
5 tablespoons Worcestershire sauce
3 tablespoons soy sauce
1 tablespoon cider vinegar
1 tablespoon light brown sugar
1½ teaspoons dry mustard
1½ teaspoons ground cumin
1 teaspoon hot sauce, or to taste

1 kg (2 lb) minced turkey thigh meat
40 g (1½ oz) shallot, finely chopped
65 g (2½ oz) old-fashioned porridge oats
1 teaspoon sea salt
½ teaspoon freshly ground black pepper

6 hamburger buns
18 sweet pickle slices
18 red onion slices

1. Combine the sauce ingredients in a bowl. Set aside about 125 ml (4 fl oz) of the sauce to serve with the burgers.

2. Mix the minced turkey with the shallot, oats, salt and pepper and form into 6 burgers, each about 2 cm (¾ inch) thick. With your thumb or the back of a spoon, make a shallow indentation about 2.5 cm (1 inch) wide in the centre of each burger so the centres are about 1 cm (½ inch) thick.

3. Prepare the barbecue for direct cooking over a medium heat.

4. Brush the cooking grates clean. Drain the planks and heat them over **direct medium heat** for 5 to 10 minutes with the lid closed, until they begin to char and lightly smoke. Turn the planks over and place 3 burgers on each plank. Grill the burgers over **direct medium heat** for 15 to 20 minutes, with the lid closed as much as possible, turning and basting with the sauce once after 10 minutes.

5. During the last minute of grilling time, lightly toast the cut sides of the buns over **direct medium heat**. Serve the burgers on buns with pickles, the reserved sauce and slices of onion.

HOW TO SMOKE TURKEY BURGERS ON PLANKS

1. Cook the burgers for about 10 minutes on the planks, then begin basting them with sauce and turn them over.

2. Cook for 5 to 10 minutes, basting now and again, until there's no red left in the centre and the internal temperature registers 74°C (165°F).

3. You will find that burgers made with dark thigh meat give you much juicer results than those made with light breast meat.

HOW TO REMOVE CORN KERNELS

1. Cut off the stem end of an ear of corn to create a flat surface.

2. Stand the ear of corn, stem side down, in a dish or bowl. Cut from top to bottom so the kernels fall into the dish or bowl.

HOW TO SHRED CABBAGE

1. Split a head of cabbage in half lengthways and cut out the tough, triangular core of each half.

2. Lay each half flat on a chopping board and slice as thinly as you can.

SOUTHWESTERN TURKEY BURGERS WITH SALSA SLAW

SERVES: 4
PREP TIME: 20 MINUTES

HEAT: DIRECT MEDIUM HEAT 180° TO 230°C (350° TO 450°F)
GRILLING TIME: 8 TO 10 MINUTES

SLAW
150 g (5 oz) savoy cabbage, finely shredded
250 g (8 oz) fresh tomato salsa (see page 291), drained
15 g (½ oz) fresh coriander, finely chopped
3 tablespoons soured cream

BURGERS
750 g (1½ lb) minced turkey thigh meat
50 g (2 oz) fresh corn kernels
4 tablespoons finely chopped pickled jalapeño chilli,
    or to taste
1 tablespoon pure chilli powder
2 teaspoons very finely chopped garlic
1½ teaspoons sea salt
1 teaspoon ground cumin

4 wholegrain hamburger buns

1. Mix the slaw ingredients together in a bowl. Cover and refrigerate. Stir and then drain well just before serving.

2. Prepare the barbecue for direct cooking over a medium heat.

3. Gently mix the burger ingredients together, then shape into 4 burgers, each about 2 cm (¾ inch) thick. With your thumb or the back of a spoon, make a shallow indentation about 2.5 cm (1 inch) wide in the centre of each burger so the centres are about 1 cm (½ inch) thick. This will help the burgers cook evenly and prevent them from puffing on the barbecue.

4. Brush the cooking grates clean. Grill the burgers over **direct medium heat** for 8 to 10 minutes, with the lid closed as much as possible but turning once, until fully cooked but still juicy. During the last minute of grilling time, lightly toast the cut sides of the buns over **direct medium heat**. Top the burgers with slaw and serve on the toasted buns.

POULTRY

SEAFOOD

TECHNIQUES

RECIPES

Before grilling, remove any tough little side muscles still attached to the scallops (top photo). After grilling, the interior of the scallops should be barely opaque, like the one in the centre. The scallop on the left is a little underdone and the scallop on the right is overdone (bottom photo).

SCALLOPS WITH GRILL-ROASTED TOMATO SAUCE

SERVES: 4
PREP TIME: 25 MINUTES
MARINATING TIME: 10 TO 15 MINUTES

HEAT: DIRECT MEDIUM HEAT 180° TO 230°C
(350° TO 450°F)
GRILLING TIME: 14 TO 16 MINUTES

SAUCE
500 g (1 lb) plum tomatoes
3 spring onions, tops and root ends trimmed
1 teaspoon finely grated lemon rind
2 tablespoons fresh lemon juice
1 tablespoon sugar
1 teaspoon yellow mustard seeds
1 teaspoon fennel seeds
½ teaspoon sea salt

12 jumbo sea scallops, about 50 g (2 oz) each

MARINADE
15 g (½ oz) unsalted butter, melted
1 tablespoon extra-virgin olive oil
1 teaspoon grated lemon rind
1 tablespoon fresh lemon juice
½ teaspoon sea salt
¼ teaspoon freshly ground black pepper

1 tablespoon finely chopped basil or flat leaf parsley

1. Prepare the barbecue for direct cooking over a medium heat. Brush the cooking grates clean.

2. Grill the tomatoes and spring onions over **direct medium heat**, with the lid closed as much as possible, until the tomato

skins blister and brown and the spring onions are lightly browned, turning as needed. The tomatoes will take about 10 minutes and the spring onions will take 4 to 5 minutes. Transfer the vegetables to a chopping board. Carefully pull off and discard the tomato skins and trim and discard the stem ends. Chop the tomatoes into 5-mm (¼-inch) pieces, and then transfer the tomatoes with their juices to a large frying pan. Thinly slice the spring onions, including the tops, and add to the tomatoes along with the rest of the sauce ingredients. Simmer the sauce over medium heat for 5 to 6 minutes, stirring occasionally, until the flavors blend. Keep warm. (The sauce can be made a day ahead and reheated.)

3. Remove the small, tough side muscle that may be left on each scallop. Combine the marinade ingredients in a small bowl. Toss the scallops in the marinade and allow them to stand at room temperature for 10 to 15 minutes.

4. Brush the cooking grates clean. Lift the scallops from the bowl and lay slightly apart on the cooking grate. Discard the marinade. Grill over **direct medium heat** for 4 to 6 minutes with the lid closed as much as possible but turning once, until lightly browned and just opaque in the centre (check one by cutting it open).

5. Add the basil to the tomato sauce. Divide the sauce evenly on 4 warmed plates and top with hot scallops.

PARMA HAM-BELTED SCALLOPS WITH LENTIL SALAD

SERVES: 4
PREP TIME: 25 MINUTES
MARINATING TIME: 1 HOUR

HEAT: DIRECT MEDIUM HEAT 180° TO 230°C
(350° TO 450°F)
GRILLING TIME: 4 TO 6 MINUTES

12 jumbo sea scallops, about 50 g (2 oz) each
6 thin slices Parma ham, cut in half lengthways

MARINADE
3 tablespoons very finely chopped shallot
3 tablespoons fresh lemon juice
2 tablespoons extra-virgin olive oil
1½ tablespoons Dijon mustard
¾ teaspoon dried tarragon
¼ teaspoon freshly ground black pepper

LENTILS
6 thin slices Parma ham, finely chopped
2 tablespoons extra-virgin olive oil
75 g (3 oz) button mushrooms, finely chopped
50 g (2 oz) very finely chopped shallot
½ teaspoon dried tarragon
200 g (7 oz) green lentils
750 ml (1¼ pints) chicken or vegetable stock
1 teaspoon finely grated lemon rind
15 g (½ oz) fresh flat leaf parsley, finely chopped
Sea salt
Freshly ground black pepper

1. Remove the small, tough side muscle that may be left on each scallop.

2. Wrap one slice of Parma ham around each scallop and secure with a cocktail stick.

3. Mix the marinade ingredients together in a shallow non-metallic dish. Gently turn the scallops in the marinade and then lay them flat in the dish. Cover with clingfilm and refrigerate for 1 hour. Meanwhile, prepare the lentils.

4. Combine the chopped Parma ham, oil, mushrooms, shallot and tarragon in a large saucepan over a medium-high heat. Stir often for 5 to 7 minutes until the vegetables are limp and slightly browned.

5. Sort through the lentils and discard any debris. Rinse and drain the lentils and add them to the pan along with the stock and bring to the boil. Reduce the heat, cover and simmer for 40 to 55 minutes until the lentils are tender. Stir in the lemon rind and parsley, then season to taste with salt and pepper. Keep warm.

6. Prepare the barbecue for direct cooking over a medium heat. Brush the cooking grates clean. Grill the scallops, unwrapped sides down, over **direct medium heat** for 4 to 6 minutes, with the lid closed as much as possible but turning them once, until they are lightly browned and opaque in the centre. Remove from the barbecue and serve warm with the lentils.

HOW TO PREP SCALLOPS

1. Cut each Parma ham slice to fit the scallops.

2. Wrap a strip of Parma ham around each scallop and secure it with a cocktail stick.

3. Grill the scallops for 2 or 3 minutes until they can easily lift off the grate without sticking.

4. Turn the scallops over and finish cooking. Grill so the flat sides of each lie flat on the grate.

CEDAR-PLANKED SCALLOPS WITH GRILLED CORN SALAD

SERVES: 4 TO 6
PREP TIME: 25 MINUTES

HEAT: DIRECT MEDIUM HEAT 180° TO 230°C
(350° TO 450°F)
GRILLING TIME: 23 TO 32 MINUTES
SPECIAL EQUIPMENT: 1 UNTREATED CEDAR PLANK,
30 TO 32 CM (12 TO 15 INCHES) LONG AND
1 TO 1.5 CM (½ TO ¾ INCH) THICK, SOAKED IN
WATER FOR AT LEAST 1 HOUR

MARINADE
5 tablespoons extra-virgin olive oil
5 tablespoons fresh lime juice
1 tablespoon honey
1 teaspoon sea salt

20 large sea scallops, each about 3 cm (1¼ inches) in diameter

SALAD
½ small red onion, cut into 3 wedges
3 ears fresh sweetcorn, shucked
1 red pepper
Extra-virgin olive oil
Sea salt
Freshly ground black pepper
½ teaspoon ground cumin
1 teaspoon hot sauce, or to taste

1. Whisk the marinade ingredients together in a bowl. Transfer 3 tablespoons of the marinade to a large bowl to use for dressing the salad. Set the 2 bowls aside.

2. Remove the small, tough side muscle that may be left on each scallop. Refrigerate until ready to cook.

3. Prepare the barbecue for direct cooking over a medium heat. Lightly brush the onion, corn, and pepper with oil and season evenly with salt and pepper. Brush the cooking grates clean. Grill the vegetables over *direct medium heat*, with the lid closed as much as possible but turning the vegetables as needed, until the onion has softened and started to collapse, the corn kernels are mostly brown, with some beginning to char and the pepper is blackened and blistered all over. The onion will take about 4 minutes, the corn will take 6 to 8 minutes and the pepper, 10 to 12 minutes. Place the pepper in a bowl, cover with cling-film and allow it to cool.

4. When the vegetables are cool enough to handle, cut the onion into a small dice, cut the kernels off the cobs and remove and discard the charred skin, stem, ribs and seeds from the pepper. Cut the pepper into a medium dice, saving the juice. Combine the onion, corn, pepper with juice, cumin and hot sauce into the large bowl with the 3 tablespoons of reserved marinade.

5. Place the soaked plank over *direct medium heat* and close the lid. After 5 to 10 minutes, when the plank begins to smoke and char, turn the plank over. Put the scallops in the bowl with the marinade and toss to coat. Place the scallops in a single layer on the plank. Close the barbecue lid and cook for 8 to 10 minutes, until they are slightly firm on the surface and opaque in the centre. Serve the scallops warm with the salad.

HOW TO CUT ONION WEDGES

1. The layers of the onion wedges will hold together on the barbecue if you leave part of the root end attached.

2. After you have cut your wedges, peel off the papery skin.

CHECKING DONENESS

When smoked scallops are done, they will feel slightly firm on top and look lightly coloured all over by the smoke.

THAI PRAWNS
WITH WATERMELON SALSA

SERVES: 4
PREP TIME: 25 MINUTES
MARINATING TIME: 30 MINUTES

HEAT: DIRECT HIGH HEAT 230° TO 290°C (450° TO 550°F)
GRILLING TIME: 3 TO 5 MINUTES
SPECIAL EQUIPMENT: 8 BAMBOO SKEWERS,
    SOAKED IN WATER FOR AT LEAST 30 MINUTES

SALSA
2 tablespoons very finely chopped shallot
2 teaspoons rice vinegar
1 teaspoon sugar
1–2 tablespoons very finely chopped jalapeño chilli
325 g (11 oz) seedless watermelon, cut into 1-cm (½-inch) cubes
1 7.5-cm (3-inch) piece cucumber, halved lengthways,
    deseeded and thinly sliced into half-moons
1 teaspoon very finely chopped mint
¼ teaspoon sea salt

MARINADE
25 g (1 oz) fresh coriander leaves and tender stems
15 g (½ oz) mint leaves
3 garlic cloves
2 tablespoons coarsely chopped fresh root ginger
2 tablespoons rice vinegar
2 tablespoons sunflower or other vegetable oil
2 teaspoons sugar
1 teaspoon Thai red curry paste
¼ teaspoon sea salt

625 g (1¼ lb) extra-large prawns, peeled and deveined but with
    tails left on

1. Mix the shallot, vinegar, sugar and jalapeño together in a
large bowl. Add the watermelon, cucumber, mint and salt and
toss gently to combine. To fully incorporate the flavours, allow
the salsa to sit at room temperature for 30 to 60 minutes.

2. Combine the marinade ingredients in a food processor.
Process to create a coarse purée, occasionally scraping down
the side of the bowl to incorporate the ingredients evenly.

3. Transfer the marinade to a bowl. Add the prawns, and toss to
coat them evenly. Cover the bowl and refrigerate for 30 minutes,
turning the prawns after 15 minutes. Prepare the barbecue for
direct cooking over a high heat.

4. Remove the prawns from the bowl and discard the marinade.
Thread the prawns on to skewers. Brush the cooking grates
clean. Grill the skewers over **direct high heat** for 3 to 5 minutes,
with the lid closed as much as possible but turning once,
until the prawns are firm to the touch, lightly charred and just
turning opaque in the centre. Serve the prawns warm or at room
temperature with the salsa.

Fresh and frozen prawns can range from very small, less than
2.5 cm (1 inch) to 33 cm (13 inches) for Black Tiger prawns, and
the terms 'standard', 'medium', 'large', 'king' and 'jumbo' are used
inconsistently, with the very smallest prawns called 'shrimp'. To add
to the confusion, large and jumbo warm-water prawns (freshwater
or seawater) can both be sold as 'kings'. Supermarkets and fish-
mongers generally sell all prawns by weight and you have to make
your choice based on sight. Choose the size most suitable for your
recipe raw or cooked. Prawns the size of the two largest examples
above are the best choice for grilling, because they are easy to peel
and they don't dry out as quickly as smaller prawns would.

SEAFOOD

PRAWN PO'BOYS WITH CREOLE RÉMOULADE

SERVES: 6
PREP TIME: 20 MINUTES

HEAT: DIRECT HIGH HEAT 230° TO 290°C (450° TO 550°F)
GRILLING TIME: 3 TO 5 MINUTES
SPECIAL EQUIPMENT: PERFORATED GRILL PAN

RÉMOULADE
125 g (4 oz) mayonnaise
2 tablespoons Creole or Dijon mustard
2 tablespoons sweet pickle relish
1 tablespoon prepared horseradish
2 teaspoons very finely chopped tarragon
1 teaspoon very finely chopped garlic
½ teaspoon hot sauce, or to taste
½ teaspoon sweet paprika
½ teaspoon sea salt
¼ teaspoon freshly ground black pepper

1 kg (2 lb) large prawns, peeled and deveined with
    tails removed
2 tablespoons extra-virgin olive oil
1 tablespoon Creole seasoning
6 soft French sandwich rolls, split horizontally
Lettuce, chopped
18 ripe tomato slices

Rémoulade is a mayonnaise-based spread flavoured with mustard and other condiments. Among mustards, Creole is one of the spiciest, thanks to its horseradish and vinegar-marinated brown mustard seeds.

1. Combine the rémoulade ingredients in a small bowl. Cover and refrigerate until serving.

2. Prepare the barbecue for direct cooking over a high heat. Preheat the grill pan for about 10 minutes.

3. Toss the prawns with the oil and then evenly coat with the Creole seasoning. Spread the prawns on the grill pan and grill over **direct high heat** for 2 to 4 minutes, with the lid closed as much as possible but turning once, until firm to the touch and just turning opaque in the centre. Remove from the barbecue and keep warm.

4. Grill the rolls, cut sides down, over **direct high heat** for 30 seconds to 1 minute, until lightly toasted. Spread the rémoulade on the cut sides of the rolls and add lettuce, tomatoes and prawns. Serve warm.

ORANGE-FENNEL PRAWNS OVER WATERCRESS

SERVES: 4
PREP TIME: 25 MINUTES
MARINATING TIME: 1 HOUR

HEAT: DIRECT HIGH HEAT 230° TO 290°C (450° TO 550°F)
GRILLING TIME: 2 TO 4 MINUTES
SPECIAL EQUIPMENT: PERFORATED GRILL PAN

MARINADE
Grated rind of 2 oranges
125 ml (4 fl oz) fresh orange juice
5 tablespoons extra-virgin olive oil
2 tablespoons fresh lime juice
1 tablespoon very finely chopped garlic
1 teaspoon ground fennel
1 teaspoon sea salt
½ teaspoon ground cayenne pepper

750 g (1½ lb) large prawns, peeled and deveined with tails left on
100 g (3½ oz) watercress leaves and tender stems

1. Mix the marinade ingredients together in a bowl. Set aside 125 ml (4 fl oz) of the marinade to use as a dressing for the salad.

2. Place the prawns in a large, resealable plastic bag and pour in the marinade. Press the air out of the bag and seal tightly. Turn the bag several times to distribute the marinade, lay the bag flat on a plate and refrigerate for 1 hour.

3. Prepare the barbecue for direct cooking over high heat. Preheat the grill pan for about 10 minutes.

4. Drain the prawns in a sieve. Spread the prawns in a single layer on the grill pan and cook over **direct high heat** for 2 to 4 minutes, with the lid closed as much as possible but shaking the pan once or twice and turning the prawns over for even cooking, until they are slightly firm on the surface and completely opaque in the centres. Remove the pan from the barbecue and rest it on a baking tray. Transfer the prawns to a large bowl to stop the cooking.

5. Add the watercress to the prawns in the large bowl. Spoon the reserved dressing over the watercress and prawns (you may not need all of it). Toss to coat the ingredients evenly. Serve right away.

HOW TO PEEL AND DEVEIN PRAWNS

1. Grab the shell just above the tail and break it loose.

2. Peel off the shell along with all the little legs.

3. With a sharp paring knife, make a shallow slit along the back of each prawn.

4. Lift any black vein out of the slit and discard it.

HOW TO BARBECUE PRAWN POPS

1. By using 2 spoons moving in opposite directions, you can make little oval-shaped mixtures called quenelles.

2. Move the top spoon over and behind the prawn mixture while moving the bottom spoon under and in front.

3. Continue to move the spoons over the surface of the mixture a few times to smooth it out and shape it.

4. Slide a short bamboo skewer through the centre of each quenelle, and turn the prawn mixture on a greased roasting tray.

5. Grill the pops over a high heat, with the bare ends of the skewers shielded by a folded sheet of aluminium foil.

6. Cook them long enough on the first side so that you can roll them over without any sticking, rather than picking them up with tongs and squeezing them.

VIETNAMESE PRAWN POPS WITH PEANUT SAUCE

SERVES: 4 TO 6
PREP TIME: 30 MINUTES
CHILLING TIME: 30 MINUTES TO 1 HOUR

HEAT: DIRECT HIGH HEAT 230° TO 290°C (450° TO 550°F)
GRILLING TIME: 4 TO 6 MINUTES
SPECIAL EQUIPMENT: BAMBOO SKEWERS,
    SOAKED IN WATER FOR AT LEAST 30 MINUTES

SAUCE
250 ml (8 fl oz) unsweetened coconut milk, stirred
125 g (4 oz) peanut butter, stirred
1 teaspoon finely grated lime rind
3 tablespoons fresh lime juice
1 tablespoon soy sauce
1 tablespoon brown sugar
1 teaspoon hot chilli sauce, such as Sriracha
½ teaspoon grated fresh root ginger

PRAWN POPS
500 g (1 lb) minced pork
375 g (13 oz) prawns, peeled and deveined
25 g (1 oz) basil, coarsely chopped
15 g (½ oz) panko breadcrumbs
2 large garlic cloves
1 tablespoon soy sauce
½ teaspoon freshly ground black pepper

4 tablespoons sunflower or other vegetable oil

1. Combine the sauce ingredients in a heavy-based saucepan over a medium heat. Cook (but do not simmer) for 2 to 3 minutes, whisking constantly, just until the sauce is smooth and slightly thickened (the sauce will thicken further as it cools). Remove the pan from the heat.

2. Put the prawn pop ingredients in a food processor or blender and process until a chunky paste is formed. Pour the vegetable oil on to a baking tray and brush it evenly all over the surface. Using 2 spoons, shape the mixture into small quenelles or ovals, placing them on the greased tray as you make them. Turn them, making sure they are well coated with oil. Refrigerate the quenelles for 30 minutes to 1 hour to firm up the texture.

3. Prepare the barbecue for direct cooking over a high heat.

4. Place a quenelle on the end of each skewer. Brush the cooking grates clean. Grill the prawn pops over **direct high heat** for 4 to 6 minutes, with the lid closed as much as possible but turning once or twice, until they are opaque throughout, (cut one open with a sharp knife to test for doneness). Arrange the prawn pops on a serving platter. Serve warm with the dipping sauce.

HOW TO MAKE ROASTED CHILLI AND AVOCADO SAUCE

1. Roast mildly spicy Anaheim chillies over direct medium heat until the skins are blackened and blistered.

2. Discard the chilli stems, skins and seeds. Then combine the roasted chillies in a food processor with soured cream, mayonnaise, dill, garlic, salt and pepper.

3. Give the sauce a good whizz, stopping occasionally to scrape down the sides of the bowl.

4. If the sauce seems a little thick, add a touch of water to thin it out. The sauce will keep well in the refrigerator for a couple of days.

HOW TO PREP THE PRAWNS

1. Choose prawns that are the same size so that you can nestle them together with no empty spaces between them.

2. Begin by skewering one prawn through both the head and tail ends. Skewer the next prawn through the head end only, with the tail end pointing in the opposite direction. Skewer the remaining prawn just like the second one, with all their tails facing the same way.

3. The prawns are nestled closely together on the skewers, without spaces in between. This means they will stay juicy on the barbecue a little bit longer.

JUICY PRAWNS WITH ROASTED CHILLI AND AVOCADO SAUCE

SERVES: 4 TO 6
PREP TIME: 20 MINUTES

HEAT: DIRECT MEDIUM HEAT 180° TO 230°C
    (350° TO 450°F) AND DIRECT HIGH HEAT
    230° TO 290°C (450° TO 550°F)
GRILLING TIME: 10 TO 16 MINUTES
SPECIAL EQUIPMENT: 8 TO 10 FLAT-SIDED OR ROUND
    BAMBOO SKEWERS, SOAKED IN WATER FOR AT LEAST
    30 MINUTES

SAUCE
3 Anaheim chillies, each about 15 cm (6 inches) long
1 Haas avocado
4 tablespoons soured cream
4 tablespoons mayonnaise
2 tablespoons roughly chopped dill
1 large garlic clove
½ teaspoon sea salt
¼ teaspoon freshly ground black pepper

RUB
1 teaspoon garlic granules
1 teaspoon paprika
¾ teaspoon sea salt
½ teaspoon ground cumin
¼ teaspoon freshly ground black pepper

500 g (1 lb) large prawns, peeled and deveined, with tails left on
Extra-virgin olive oil

1. Prepare the barbecue for direct cooking over a medium heat. Brush the cooking grates clean. Grill the chillies over **direct medium heat** for 8 to 12 minutes, with the lid closed as much as possible but turning occasionally, until they are blackened and blistered in spots all over. Put the chillies in a bowl, cover with clingfilm, and allow to steam for 10 minutes. When cool enough to handle, remove and discard the stem ends, skins and seeds. Drop the chillies into a food processor or blender and add the remaining sauce ingredients. Process to create a smooth dipping sauce. If the sauce seems too thick, add a little water. Spoon the sauce into a serving bowl.

■ ■ ■

The 'fresh' prawns glistening on a bed of shaved ice at the market were almost certainly frozen previously, on the boat or at the harbour, and then they were thawed at the market. In fact, prawns will be closer to 'fresh' if you buy them frozen and thaw them yourself just before cooking.

■ ■ ■

2. Mix the rub ingredients together in a small bowl.

3. Lay 5 to 7 prawns on a work surface and arrange them so that the prawns on one end lays one way and all the rest lay in the same direction (see photo at left). Choose prawns that are the same size so that you can nestle them together with no empty spaces between them. This will help to keep the prawns from spinning, when you turn them, and prevent them from drying out on the barbecue. Pick up and skewer each prawn through the centre, pushing the prawns together on each skewer. Repeat the process with the remaining prawns and skewers. Lightly brush the skewers with oil and then season them evenly with the rub.

4. Increase the temperature of the barbecue to a high heat. Brush the cooking grates clean. Grill the prawns over **direct high heat** for 2 to 4 minutes, with the lid closed as much as possible but turning once, until slightly firm on the surface and opaque in the centre. Remove from the barbecue and serve warm with the dipping sauce.

HOW TO MAKE PAELLA

Paella is a rice dish that is traditionally cooked outdoors in a wide, shallow pan of the same name. Spreading the rice out in such a wide pan helps it to absorb the aromas of burning logs or charcoal. A big cast-iron frying pan substitutes well for the traditional paella pan, but there is no substitute for paella's quintessential spice: saffron.

1. Heat the stock with prawn shells, white wine, bay leaves, smoked paprika, salt, red chilli flakes and saffron.

2. Grill the prawns over direct high heat, but cook them only about halfway. They will finish cooking in the rice.

3. Cook the Parma ham in the pan until it releases its fat and begins to crisp.

4. Cook the onions, pepper and garlic with the Parma ham to create an aromatic base of flavours.

5. Add a medium- or round-grain rice, such as Arborio or Valencia, not a long-grain rice.

6. Stir to cook the rice lightly and to coat all the grains in the pan juices.

7. Add the hot, strained stock and close the lid of the barbecue so that the liquid gently simmers and the wood smoke does not escape.

8. At some point you may need to rotate the pan or move it to another part of the barbecue to even out the cooking.

9. The rice is done when it has absorbed most of the stock and the texture is tender but not mushy.

PAELLA

SERVES: 6 TO 8

PREP TIME: 40 MINUTES

SOAKING TIME FOR WILD MUSSELS: 30 MINUTES TO
    1 HOUR (SEE AUTHOR'S NOTE ON PAGE 190)

HEAT: DIRECT HIGH HEAT 230° TO 290°C (450° TO 550°F)
    AND DIRECT MEDIUM HEAT 180° TO 230°C
    (350° TO 450°F)

GRILLING TIME: 35 TO 37 MINUTES

SPECIAL EQUIPMENT: 30-CM (12-INCH) CAST-IRON
    FRYING PAN

250 g (8 oz) large prawns, tails left on and shells reserved
    for the stock
2 teaspoons extra-virgin olive oil
Sea salt
Freshly ground black pepper

STOCK
Shells from peeled prawns
1 litre (1¾ pints) chicken stock
175 ml (6 fl oz) dry white wine
2 bay leaves
1½ teaspoons smoked paprika
1 teaspoon sea salt
½ teaspoon dried red chilli flakes
¼ teaspoon crushed saffron threads

12 live mussels, scrubbed and beards removed
3 tablespoons extra-virgin olive oil
125 g (4 oz) thick-sliced Parma ham, cut into 5-mm
    (¼-inch) dice
150 g (5 oz) red onion, finely chopped
75 g (3 oz) red pepper, finely chopped
1 tablespoon very finely chopped garlic
400 g (14 oz) medium-grain rice, such as Arborio
175 g (6 oz) frozen baby peas

1. Peel and devein the prawns, reserving the shells to make
the stock. Toss the prawns with the oil in a large bowl and
season evenly with salt and pepper. Cover and refrigerate
until ready to grill.

2. Bring the prawn shells and the stock ingredients to a simmer
in a saucepan over a high heat. Strain, discarding the shells
and bay leaves, and reserve the stock. (The stock can be made
up to 2 hours ahead.)

3. Check each mussel and discard those with broken shells,
any that don't close up when you lightly tap on their shells
and any others that feel unusually heavy because of sand
trapped inside.

4. Prepare the barbecue for direct cooking over a high heat on
one side and medium heat on the other side. Brush the cooking
grates clean. Grill the prawns over ***direct high heat*** for about
2 minutes until cooked halfway, turning once (the prawns will
finish cooking in the stock). Remove from the barbecue and set
aside to cool.

5. Place a 30-cm (12-inch) cast-iron frying pan on the cooking
grate over ***direct high heat.*** Heat the oil in the skillet. Add the
Parma ham and cook for about 3 minutes, stirring occasionally,
until it begins to crisp. Add the onion, pepper and garlic and
cook for about 5 minutes, stirring occasionally and rotating the
pan for even cooking, until the onion is translucent. Slide the
pan away from the fire.

6. Place the pan over ***direct medium heat***, stir in the rice and
cook for about 2 minutes until well coated with the pan juices.
Stir in the prawn stock and the frozen peas. Close the barbecue
lid and let the rice cook at a brisk simmer for about 15 minutes,
until the rice is al dente. Nestle the prawns into the rice. Add
the mussels, hinged sides down. Cook, with the barbecue lid
closed, for 8 to 10 minutes until the mussels open.

7. Remove the pan from the heat, cover with aluminium foil
and allow to stand for 5 minutes. Remove and discard any
unopened mussels. Serve hot straight from the pan.

WILD VERSUS FARM-RAISED MUSSELS

Check each mussel and discard those with broken shells, any that don't close up when you lightly tap on their shells and any others that feel unusually heavy because of sand trapped inside. Soak the mussels in cold, salted water for 30 minutes to 1 hour, then drain. The soaking is to remove sand, but that's only an issue with wild mussels (pictured at left) that grow in sandy places. If you use farm-raised mussels (pictured at right), you can skip the soaking step.

COCONUT-CURRY MUSSELS

SERVES: 4
PREP TIME: 15 MINUTES
SOAKING TIME FOR WILD MUSSELS: 30 MINUTES
    TO 1 HOUR

HEAT: DIRECT MEDIUM HEAT 180° TO 230°C
    (350° TO 450°F)
GRILLING TIME: 17 TO 22 MINUTES
SPECIAL EQUIPMENT: LARGE DISPOSABLE FOIL TIN

SAUCE
1 can (425 ml/14 fl oz) coconut milk, light or regular
1 tablespoon Thai green curry paste
1 tablespoon fresh lime juice
2 teaspoons light brown sugar
2 teaspoons fish sauce
2 tablespoons groundnut oil
1 tablespoon finely chopped fresh root ginger
1 tablespoon finely chopped garlic

1 kg (2 lb) live mussels, scrubbed and beards removed
15 g (½ oz) fresh coriander leaves, finely chopped

Crusty bread, to serve (optional)

1. Prepare the barbecue for direct and indirect cooking over a medium heat.

2. Whisk the coconut milk, curry paste, lime juice, brown sugar and fish sauce together in a bowl.

3. Combine the groundnut oil, ginger and garlic in a large disposable foil tin. Place the tin over **direct medium heat**, close the barbecue lid and let the aromatics cook for about 1 minute. Add the coconut milk mixture to the foil tin and gently stir to combine. Cook for 5 to 6 minutes to bring the sauce to the boil.

4. Add the mussels to the sauce. Cover the foil tin with a roasting tray (to trap the steam and cook the mussels), close the barbecue lid, and cook for 8 to 10 minutes. Check the mussels to see if they are open. If not, continue to cook for a further 3 to 5 minutes. Wearing barbecue mitts or oven gloves, carefully remove the roasting tray from the foil tin and carefully remove the foil tin from the barbecue. Remove and discard any unopened mussels. Sprinkle the coriander on top. Serve the mussels and sauce in bowls with crusty bread, if desired.

CAJUN-STYLE CLAMBAKE

SERVES: 4
PREP TIME: 45 MINUTES

HEAT: DIRECT MEDIUM HEAT 180° TO 230°C
   (350° TO 450°F)
GRILLING TIME: 20 TO 25 MINUTES

125 g (4 oz) unsalted butter, melted
5 tablespoons fresh lemon juice
1 tablespoon Cajun seasoning
1 tablespoon very finely chopped garlic
2 teaspoons chopped thyme leaves
4 red potatoes, halved and sliced into 2.5 mm (⅛-inch)
   half-moons
375 g (13 oz) jumbo prawns, peeled and deveined with
   tails left on, cold
1 kg (2 lb) littleneck clams, rinsed and scrubbed
375 g (13 oz) andouille sausage, thinly sliced
2 ears fresh sweetcorn, each shucked and cut into
   4 pieces

1. Combine the butter, lemon juice, seasoning, garlic and thyme in a small bowl.

2. Prepare the barbecue for direct cooking over a medium heat.

3. Cut 8 sheets of aluminium foil, each about 30 by 50 cm (12 by 20 inches). Line a 20- by 20-cm (8- by 8-inch) cake tin with 2 sheets of aluminium foil, arranged in a criss-cross pattern. Layer the bottom of the foil-lined tin with the sliced potatoes. (This will help insulate the shellfish and keep them from overcooking.) Top the potatoes evenly with the prawns, clams, sausage and corn pieces. Drizzle each packet evenly with the butter mixture. Close the packet by bringing the ends of the 2 inner sheets together, folding them on top of the filling and then bringing the ends of the 2 outer sheets together, folding them down. Repeat this procedure to make 3 more packets.

4. Grill the packets over **_direct medium heat_** for 20 to 25 minutes, with the lid closed, until the clams have opened, the prawns have turned opaque and the potatoes are cooked. To check for doneness, using tongs, gently unfold one of the packets and carefully remove a potato, being careful not to puncture the bottom of the foil. Gently pierce the potato with a knife to ensure doneness. When everything is cooked, remove the packets from the barbecue. Carefully open each packet to let the steam escape and then pour the contents into warmed bowls and serve immediately.

HOW TO PREP FOR A CLAMBAKE

1. Rinse and scrub the clams under cold water. To remove sand and grit from inside the shells, soak them in iced water mixed with salt (1 teaspoon of salt per 250 ml/8 fl oz of water) for a few hours.

2. You can peel and devein the prawns ahead of time.

3. In a foil-lined tin, arrange the sliced potatoes on the bottom so that they will protect the other ingredients from the heat.

4. Be generous with the butter mixture.

5. Fold up the ends of the foil tightly to prevent any liquid from escaping.

6. You will remove each packet from its tin and cook it directly on the barbecue so that all the ingredients steam and simmer inside.

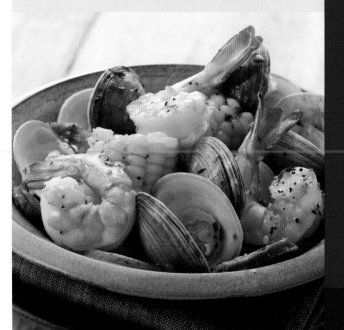

HOW TO CHAR-GRILL OYSTERS

1. For barbecuing, choose oysters like these, with deep rounded shells to hold in their juices.

2. Holding each oyster in a towel with the flat side facing up, push the tip of an oyster knife into the small opening at the hinge of the shell.

3. Twist the knife and wiggle it back and forth to pop open the shell.

4. Drag the knife along the seam between the top and bottom shells.

5. Use the side of the knife to cut the oyster meat loose from the top shell.

6. Slide the knife under the oyster meat to release it from the bottom shell.

7. As you finish shucking each oyster, lay it flat on a roasting tray, keeping as much liquid as possible in the shells.

8. The grilling goes quickly, so have all your sauces and serving platters ready.

9. Spoon the sauces into the raw oysters, but don't overfill the shells.

10. A very hot charcoal fire is crucial for cooking oysters in just a few minutes.

11. As soon as the juices start to bubble, remove the oysters from the barbecue.

12. The meat of the oyster should be warm but not cooked all the way through.

CHAR-GRILLED OYSTERS

SERVES: 4 TO 6
PREP TIME: 30 MINUTES

HEAT: DIRECT HIGH HEAT 230° TO 290°C (450° TO 550°F)
GRILLING TIME: 2 TO 4 MINUTES
SPECIAL EQUIPMENT: OYSTER KNIFE

24 large, fresh oysters
Lemon wedges
Hot sauce
Cocktail sauce

1. Grip each oyster, flat side up, in a folded dishtowel. Find the small opening between the shells near the hinge and pry it open with an oyster knife. Try not to spill the delicious juices, known as the 'oyster liqueur', in the bottom shell. Cut the oyster meat loose from the top shell and then loosen the oyster from the bottom shell by running the oyster knife carefully underneath the body. Discard the top, flatter shell, keeping the oyster and juices in the bottom, deeper shell.

2. Prepare the barbecue for direct cooking over a high heat.

3. Spoon some of your favourite dipping sauce on top of each oyster (recipes follow).

4. Brush the cooking grates clean. Grill the oysters, shell sides down, over **direct high heat** for 2 to 4 minutes, with the lid closed as much as possible, until the oyster juices start to bubble and the edges curl. Using tongs, carefully remove the oysters from the barbecue. Serve with lemon wedges, hot sauce, cocktail sauce and your favourite dipping sauce.

GARLIC-THYME BUTTER
MAKES: ENOUGH FOR 24 OYSTERS

50 g (2 oz) unsalted butter, divided
1 tablespoon very finely chopped garlic
2 teaspoons sherry vinegar
4 tablespoons dry white wine
2 teaspoons very finely chopped thyme
¼ teaspoon sea salt

1. Melt 15 g (½ oz) of the butter in a small frying pan over a medium heat. Add the garlic and sauté for about 2 minutes until it starts to brown. Add the vinegar and wine and simmer for about 2 minutes until the sauce reduces by half. Remove from the heat, whisk in the remaining butter and stir in the thyme and salt.

GRAPEFRUIT-BASIL AÏOLI
MAKES: ENOUGH FOR 24 OYSTERS

4 tablespoons mayonnaise
1 tablespoon chopped basil
1½ teaspoons finely grated grapefruit rind
2 teaspoons fresh grapefruit juice
1 teaspoon very finely chopped garlic
¼ teaspoon sea salt

1. Combine the ingredients in a small bowl and mix thoroughly.

ASIAN BUTTER SAUCE
MAKES: ENOUGH FOR 24 OYSTERS

1 tablespoon sesame oil
2 teaspoons very finely chopped fresh root ginger
2 tablespoons oyster sauce
1 teaspoon soy sauce
¼ teaspoon ground mustard
50 g (2 oz) unsalted butter, cut into small chunks

1. Combine the oil and ginger in a small frying pan over a medium heat and cook until the oil begins to foam. Remove from the heat and stir in the oyster sauce, soy sauce and mustard. Whisk in the butter a few chunks at a time until incorporated.

GORGONZOLA-TOMATO SAUCE
MAKES: ENOUGH FOR 24 OYSTERS

15 g (½ oz) unsalted butter
1 tablespoon very finely chopped shallot
1 teaspoon very finely chopped garlic
125 ml (4 fl oz) vegetable juice
2 teaspoons prepared horseradish
½ teaspoon sea salt
40 g (1½ oz) Gorgonzola cheese, crumbled

1. Melt the butter in a small saucepan over a medium heat. Add the shallot and garlic and sauté for about 2 minutes. Add the vegetable juice, horseradish and salt. Bring the sauce to a simmer. Remove the pan from the heat. After you've added the sauce to the oysters, sprinkle the cheese on top and then grill.

HOW TO PREP AND BARBECUE LOBSTER TAILS

1. Different varieties and sizes of lobster tail are available. Shown here, left to right, are New Zealand, 175 to 250 g (6 to 8 oz); Maine, 150 to 175 g (5 to 6 oz); West Australian, 250 to 300 g (8 to 10 oz); and South African, 135 to 150 g (4½ to 5 oz). Adjust cooking times according to size.

2. Use kitchen shears to cut through the centre of the shell on the underside of each tail.

3. Turn each tail over and cut through the harder back shell all the way to the fins.

4. Use a sharp, heavy knife to cut each tail in half lengthways, passing through the openings you have already made.

5. Grill the tails, meat side down, until the surface of the meat turns opaque.

6. Then turn the tails over on to their shells and brush with garlic butter while the meat turns opaque all the way to the centre.

LOBSTER ROLLS

SERVES: 4

PREP TIME: 25 MINUTES

HEAT: DIRECT MEDIUM HEAT 180° TO 230°C
(350° TO 450°F)

GRILLING TIME: 6 TO 7 MINUTES

3 large garlic cloves, lightly crushed
75 g (3 oz) salted butter
4 lobster tails, about 175 g (6 oz) each
Sea salt
4 tablespoons mayonnaise
75 g (3 oz) plum tomato, cut into 5-mm (¼-inch) dice
2 tablespoons very finely chopped spring onion, white and light
green parts
2 teaspoons fresh lemon juice
Hot sauce
2 teaspoons chopped chervil
4 hot dog buns, sliced vertically from the top
75 g (3 oz) Cos lettuce heart, shredded

1. Warm the garlic and butter in a small saucepan over a
medium-low heat until the butter melts. Set aside about 2 tablespoons for brushing on the buns.

2. Prepare the barbecue for direct cooking over a medium heat.
Carefully cut the lobster tails in half lengthways. Season the meat

with a little salt and brush some of the garlic butter over the
surface of each one. Brush the cooking grates clean. Grill the tails,
meat side down, over **direct medium heat** for 2 to 3 minutes, with
the lid open, until the meat is opaque. Turn the tails over, brush
with more garlic butter and continue to grill for about a further
3 minutes, until the meat is slightly firm. Set aside to cool.

3. Combine the mayonnaise, tomato, spring onion and lemon
juice in a bowl and season to taste with salt and hot sauce.
Remove the lobster meat from the shells and cut into 1-cm
(½-inch) pieces. Add the lobster meat to the mayonnaise
mixture. For best flavour, chill for at least 1 hour. Mix in the
chervil just before serving.

4. Using a serrated knife, trim
some of the crust from the
sides of the buns. Brush the
remaining garlic butter on the
cut sides (outside only) of the
buns and toast over **direct
medium heat** for about
1 minute, turning once, until
golden brown on both sides.

5. Place Cos lettuce on the bottom of each roll and then top with
the lobster mixture.

HOW TO PREP AND BARBECUE DUNGENESS CRABS

1. Lay each live crab flat on its back. Use a cleaver and mallet to cut right down the centre and all the way through.

2. Cut off the dangling tail flap attached to the underside of one half.

3. Also cut off the tail flap dangling on the other half.

4. Find the parts of the mouth that protrude from the front of each half and cut those off.

5. Turn each half over and pull off the top shell.

6. Remove the feathery gills, known as 'dead man's fingers'.

7. Rinse out the brownish viscera in a bowl of cold water.

8. The half on the left is cleaned. The one on the right is not.

9. Cut through the shell between each leg with the cleaver or a sharp knife.

10. You should have five legs from each half crab.

11. Use a clean hammer or a nutcracker to crack the shells prior to grilling.

12. Grill the crab legs over direct high heat for a couple of minutes on each side to absorb the charcoal aromas.

13. Move the crab legs to a frying pan with butter, garlic, wine, lemon and chillies.

14. Turn and coat the crab legs in the buttery mixture as they finish cooking.

DUNGENESS CRABS WITH WHITE WINE-GARLIC BUTTER

SERVES: 2 AS A MAIN COURSE OR 4 STARTERS
PREP TIME: 30 MINUTES

HEAT: DIRECT HIGH HEAT 230° TO 290°C (450° TO 550°F)
GRILLING TIME: 9 TO 11 MINUTES
SPECIAL EQUIPMENT: 30-CM (12-INCH) CAST-IRON
FRYING PAN

2 large live Dungeness crabs
125 g (4 oz) unsalted butter, cut into 8 equal-sized pieces
2 tablespoon very finely chopped garlic
Finely grated rind and juice of 1 lemon
½ teaspoon dried red chilli flakes
½ teaspoon sea salt
¼ teaspoon freshly ground black pepper
150 ml (¼ pint) dry white wine
1 baguette, torn into bite-sized pieces, to serve

1. Prepare the barbecue for direct cooking over a high heat.

2. To kill each crab, place it on its back and hold it down with a large cleaver. Use a hammer to tap the top edge of the cleaver and cut the crab in half lengthways all the way through. Remove and discard the dangling tail flaps and mouth parts. Turn the crab over. Pull off and discard the top shell. Remove and discard the gills. Rinse each half of the crab in a bowl of cold water or under cold running water and use your finger to scoop out and discard the dark viscera. Slice each half into 5 pieces by cutting between each leg and through the body. Using the hammer again (or a nutcracker or crab cracker), crack each section of each leg to make eating easier after the crabs are cooked.

3. Combine the butter, garlic, lemon rind, lemon juice, red chilli flakes, salt and pepper in a 30-cm (12-inch) cast-iron frying pan. Mix well.

4. Place the pan over **direct high heat** and cook for 2 to 3 minutes, with the lid open, until the butter has melted and the garlic turned golden. Add the wine and cook until it comes to the boil. Remove the pan from the barbecue and set it down on a heatproof surface.

5. Grill the crab pieces over **direct high heat** for about 4 minutes, with the lid open and turning once, then move them to the pan. Return the pan over **direct high heat** and gently turn the crab pieces with tongs to coat them with the sauce. Cook for 2 to 3 minutes, until the liquid boils and the crab is fully cooked. Serve warm with pieces of bread to dip into the liquid remaining in the pan.

CRAB AND AVOCADO QUESADILLAS

SERVES: 4 TO 6
PREP TIME: 20 MINUTES

HEAT: DIRECT MEDIUM HEAT 180° TO 230°C
  (350° TO 450°F)
GRILLING TIME: 2 TO 4 MINUTES

500 g (1 lb) fresh crabmeat
20 g (¾ oz) basil, finely chopped
Finely grated rind of 2 lemons
Juice of 2 lemons
1 tablespoon very finely chopped jalapeño chilli
½ teaspoon sea salt
¼ teaspoon freshly ground black pepper
125 ml (4 fl oz) soured cream
6 flour tortillas (20 cm/8 inches)
2 ripe Haas avocados, deseeded, peeled and cubed
175 g (6 oz) tomatoes, finely diced
200 g (7 oz) Monterey Jack or Cheddar cheese, grated
Extra-virgin olive oil

1. Combine the crabmeat, basil, half of the lemon rind, the lemon juice, jalapeño, salt and pepper in a bowl and mix well.

2. Combine the soured cream with the remaining half of the lemon rind in a separate bowl. Set aside.

3. Prepare the barbecue for direct cooking over a medium heat.

4. Lay the tortillas in a single layer on a work surface. Evenly divide the crabmeat mixture, avocados, tomatoes and cheese over half of each tortilla. Fold the empty half of each tortilla over the filling, creating a half circle, and press down firmly. Lightly brush the tortillas with oil. Brush the cooking grates clean. Grill the quesadillas over *direct medium heat* for 2 to 4 minutes, with the lid closed as much as possible but carefully turning over once, until the cheese melts and the tortillas are well marked. Cut each quesadilla into wedges. Serve with the soured cream mixture.

The difference in quality between fresh and canned crabmeat is striking. While crabmeat hand-picked from freshly caught, seasonal crabs is sweet and luscious, what you often find in cans is pasteurized and metallic in flavour. Even the crabmeat from previously frozen crabs can't compete with the truly fresh stuff. For this recipe, the variety of crab (such as Dungeness or rock) is far less important than freshness. However, don't bother spending high prices on 'jumbo' crab, the big unbroken pieces of meat. 'Backfin' or broken pieces of crabmeat will work just great.

SEAFOOD ZUPPA

SERVES: 4

PREP TIME: 30 MINUTES

HEAT: DIRECT MEDIUM HEAT 180° TO 230°C (350° TO 450°F) AND DIRECT HIGH HEAT 230° TO 290°C (450° TO 550°F)

GRILLING TIME: 17 TO 19 MINUTES

SPECIAL EQUIPMENT: PERFORATED GRILL PAN

ZUPPA
2 small fennel bulbs
1 lemon, ends trimmed and cut in half
2 red peppers, cut into flat pieces
4–5 shallots, about 250 g (8 oz), peeled
Extra-virgin olive oil
250 ml (8 fl oz) clam juice
250 ml (8 fl oz) vegetable stock
½ teaspoon paprika
⅛ teaspoon crushed red chilli flakes
⅛ teaspoon saffron threads
Sea salt
Freshly ground black pepper

4 large or jumbo scallops, 40 to 50 g (1½ to 2 oz) each
8 jumbo prawns, peeled and deveined
1 skinless sea bass fillet, about 250 g (8 oz), cut into
    4 pieces
1 skinless swordfish fillet, about 250 g (8 oz), cut into
    4 pieces

4 thick slices bread
15 g (½ oz) flat leaf parsley, finely chopped

1. Prepare the barbecue for direct cooking over a medium heat.

2. Preheat the grill pan over ***direct medium heat*** for about 10 minutes. While the pan preheats, prepare the vegetables. Cut off the thick stalks above the fennel bulbs and save for another use. Cut each fennel bulb into quarters and then remove the thick triangular-shaped core. Slice the fennel vertically into 5-mm (¼-inch) thick slivers. Place the fennel, lemon halves, peppers and shallots in a bowl, add 4 tablespoons oil, and toss to coat the vegetables evenly. Place the vegetables on the grill pan and grill over ***direct medium heat*** for about 10 minutes, with the lid closed as much as possible but turning as needed, until the vegetables are tender.

3. Place the vegetables in a large bowl, cover the bowl with aluminium foil. Steam for 10 minutes. Remove and discard any charred skin from the shallots. Coarsely chop the shallots along with the red peppers. Combine the fennel, peppers, shallots and the juice of one grilled lemon half in a blender and purée until smooth. Add the clam juice and vegetable stock and purée again (the blender will be very full). Pour the zuppa through a strainer into a saucepan and discard any bits left in the strainer. Season with the paprika, chilli flakes and saffron. Keep warm over a low heat. Add additional grilled lemon juice, salt and pepper to taste.

4. Increase the temperature of the barbecue to a high heat. Remove the small, tough side muscle that may be left on each scallop. Lightly coat the shellfish and fish fillets with oil and season with salt and pepper. Brush the cooking grates clean. Grill the seafood over ***direct high heat***, with the lid closed as much as possible but turning the pieces once, until the prawns is lightly charred on the outside and just turning opaque in the centre, the scallops are slightly firm on the surface and opaque in the centre, and the fish fillets are just beginning to separate into layers and the colour is opaque at the centre. The prawns will take 3 to 5 minutes, the scallops will take 4 to 6 minutes and the fillets will take 6 to 8 minutes.

5. Toast the bread over direct heat for about 1 minute, turning once. Evenly divide the shellfish and fish among individual bowls. Ladle the zuppa into each bowl. Garnish with parsley and serve with the bread.

HOW TO BARBECUE FISH
THINGS YOU NEED TO KNOW

1 PRACTICE MAKES PERFECT

Many barbecuers consider fish fillets and steaks their biggest challenge. They remember the times when fish stuck to the grate and fell to pieces when they tried to take it off the barbecue. To greatly improve your chances of success, learn to grill firm fish first, especially the ones that are a bit oily, including salmon, swordfish and tuna.

2 DON'T OVERDO IT

Fish and seafood don't have the muscle structure and firmness that many four-legged creatures have. Therefore marinades work more quickly to break down the structure of fillets and steaks. So, to prevent mushy textures, limit marinating times to just a few hours. And, above all else, don't overcook fillets and steaks.

3 FEED THE FIRE

Don't be afraid of high heat. It creates a bit of a crust on the surface of fish, and the crust helps the fish release from the cooking grate. The thinner the fillets or steaks you have, the higher the heat should be.

4 NO FLIP-FLOPPING

Every time you turn fish on the barbecue, you create a new possibility for sticking, so turn it only once.

5 QUICK FINISH

Grill the first side longer than the second. This assures you a nicely developed crust on the first side. Plus, if you are grilling with the lid closed (as you should), the second side will begin to cook while the first side is on the grate. So the second side will not need as long on the grate.

SALMON WITH NECTARINE SALSA

SERVES: 4
PREP TIME: 20 MINUTES

HEAT: DIRECT HIGH HEAT 230° TO 290°C (450° TO 550°F)
GRILLING TIME: 8 TO 11 MINUTES

SALSA
2 nectarines, about 500 g (1 lb), cut into 1-cm (½-inch) dice
65 g (2½ oz) red pepper, cut into 5-mm (¼-inch) dice
40 g (1½ oz) red onion, cut into 5-mm (¼-inch) dice
15 g (½ oz) chervil, finely chopped
1 jalapeño chilli, deseeded and finely diced
2 tablespoons finely chopped mint
1 tablespoon honey
1 tablespoon fresh lime juice
¼ teaspoon dried red chilli flakes
¼ teaspoon sea salt

4 salmon fillets (with skin), 175 to 250 g (6 to 8 oz) each and
    about 2.5 cm (1 inch) thick
½ teaspoon sea salt
¼ teaspoon crushed red chilli flakes
2 tablespoons fresh lime juice
1 tablespoon extra-virgin olive oil

1. Combine the salsa ingredients in a non-metallic bowl. Cover and refrigerate until ready to serve.

2. Prepare the barbecue for direct cooking over a high heat.

3. Season the salmon on both sides with the salt and chilli flakes and then drizzle with the lime juice and oil. Brush the cooking grates clean. Grill the salmon, flesh side down, over **direct high heat** for 6 to 8 minutes, with the lid closed as much as possible, until you can lift the fillets off the grate with tongs without sticking. Turn the fillets over and cook them for a further 2 to 3 minutes for medium rare, or longer for more well done. Slip a fish slice between the skin and the flesh, and transfer the fillets to serving plates. Serve warm with the salsa.

HOW TO BARBECUE SALMON

1. Start with generously greased fillets, flesh side down, on a clean, hot grate.

2. Grill them over high heat and roll them over when the flesh side releases easily.

3. When the salmon is done, wiggle a fish slice into the seam between the flesh and skin.

4. Scoop the flesh off the skin and pat yourself on the back. Serving the skin is optional.

The sauce for this recipe features some classic Thai ingredients, including coconut milk and red curry paste. The cream that rises to the top of chilled coconut milk contains a good amount of oil, so use it to fry the curry paste, releasing its spicy flavours, before adding the rest of the milk and the other sauce ingredients.

SALMON WITH RED CURRY-COCONUT SAUCE

SERVES: 4 TO 6
PREP TIME: 25 MINUTES

HEAT: DIRECT HIGH HEAT 230° TO 290°C (450° TO 550°F)
GRILLING TIME: 3 TO 6 MINUTES
SPECIAL EQUIPMENT: 12 BAMBOO SKEWERS,
    SOAKED IN WATER FOR AT LEAST 30 MINUTES

300 ml (½ pint) chilled coconut milk
3½ tablespoons Thai red curry paste
1 tablespoon fish sauce
1 tablespoon soy sauce
1½ teaspoons light brown sugar
1 skinless salmon fillet, about 1 kg (2 lb)
2 tablespoons sunflower or other vegetable oil
2 tablespoons finely chopped spring onion

1. Scoop 4 tablespoons of the coconut cream from the top of the chilled coconut milk and transfer it to a small saucepan over a medium heat and bring to the boil. Add 2 tablespoons of the curry paste and cook for 3 to 5 minutes, stirring constantly, until very fragrant. Stir the remaining coconut milk to achieve a smooth consistency, and then slowly incorporate it into the curry paste mixture. Add the fish sauce, soy sauce and sugar and return the mixture to the boil, stirring constantly. Reduce the heat to maintain a steady simmer and cook for 5 to 10 minutes, stirring frequently, until thickened to a thin sauce consistency. Set aside.

2. Prepare the barbecue for direct cooking over a high heat.

3. Remove any remaining pin bones from the salmon fillet. Cut the fillet into 1.5-cm (¾-inch) thick slices. Thread them on to skewers.

4. Combine the remaining 1½ tablespoons curry paste with the oil in a small bowl and generously brush the salmon with the mixture. Brush the cooking grates clean. Grill the skewers over **direct high heat** for 2 to 4 minutes, with the lid closed as much as possible, until you can lift them off the cooking grate with tongs without sticking. Turn the skewers over and cook them for a further 1 to 2 minutes for medium, or longer for more well done. Reheat the sauce and spoon it on to a serving dish, or divide evenly among individual plates. Top with the salmon and scatter the spring onion over the top. Serve warm.

CEDAR-PLANKED SALMON WITH TARATOR SAUCE

SERVES: 4

PREP TIME: 20 MINUTES

HEAT: DIRECT MEDIUM HEAT 180° TO 230°C
(350° TO 450°F)

GRILLING TIME: 20 TO 30 MINUTES

SPECIAL EQUIPMENT: 1 UNTREATED CEDAR PLANK,
30 TO 38 CM (12 TO 15 INCHES) LONG AND
1 TO 1.5 CM (½ TO ¾ INCH) THICK, SOAKED IN
SALTED WATER FOR AT LEAST 1 HOUR

SAUCE
2 pieces firm white bread, crusts removed
2 garlic cloves
50 g (2 oz) hazelnuts, lightly toasted and skinned
3 tablespoons fresh lemon juice
125 ml (4 fl oz) extra-virgin olive oil
15 g (½ oz) flat leaf parsley leaves
Sea salt
Freshly ground black pepper

1 salmon fillet (skin on), about 1 kg (2 lb)
75 g (3 oz) brown sugar

1. Soak the bread briefly in water, then squeeze dry and set aside. Combine the garlic and hazelnuts in a food processor and process until the nuts are finely ground. Add the bread and lemon juice and process until smooth. With the motor running, add the oil in a slow, steady stream. Add the parsley, ½ teaspoon salt and ¼ teaspoon pepper and pulse quickly. Season to taste with additional salt, pepper and lemon juice, if desired. Cover with clingfilm and chill until required.

2. Prepare the barbecue for direct cooking over a medium heat. Remove any remaining pin bones from the fillet. Cut the fillet crossways to make 4 servings, but do not cut through the skin. Generously season with salt and pepper.

3. Place the soaked plank over **direct medium heat** and close the lid. After 5 to 10 minutes, when the plank begins to smoke and char, turn the plank over and then lay the fillet on the plank. Carefully sprinkle the brown sugar over the entire surface of the fillet. Close the lid and let the salmon cook for 15 to 20 minutes until lightly browned on the surface for medium rare, or longer for more well done. Cooking time will vary according to the thickness of the fillet. Serve warm with the sauce on the side.

HOW TO PLANK SALMON

Cooking salmon on a cedar plank prevents the fish from sticking to the cooking grate and imbues it with delicious smoky flavours.

1. Run your fingertips over the salmon to feel for any bones. Use needle-nose pliers or tweezers to grab the ends of any tiny pin bones and pull them out.

2. Cut the raw fish into individual portions, right down to the skin but not through it, to make it easier to serve later.

3. Lay the salmon on a lightly charred, smoldering plank and sprinkle brown sugar over the top.

4. The sugar will melt and caramelize on the surface while the cedar smoke permeates the flesh.

HOW TO PREP FENNEL

1. Cut off the thick stalks above the bulb, leaving the root end attached to hold the bulb together, then cut the bulb in half through the root end.

2. Chop some of the flavourful fronds to season the salad.

3. Simmer the fennel halves in salted water until just tender. Immediately plunge the fennel into iced water to stop the cooking.

4. Trim off the root end and thinly slice the fennel.

HOW TO BONE SALMON STEAKS

1. Find any pin bones and remove them with needle-nose pliers.

2. Trim off any thin, dangling flaps of flesh.

3. Starting at the top of the steak, cut alongside the bone.

4. Continue to cut all along the bone and rib sections.

5. Cut along the other side of the bones, too.

6. The goal is to isolate the bones only, without cutting away much of the flesh.

7. Cut the bones free near the top, leaving just a little bit of bone attached to hold the flesh together.

8. Bring the sides together and secure the ends with a shortened bamboo skewer.

SALMON WITH FENNEL AND OLIVE SALAD

SERVES: 4
PREP TIME: 30 MINUTES

HEAT: DIRECT HIGH HEAT 230° TO 290°C (450° TO 550°F)
GRILLING TIME: 8 TO 11 MINUTES
SPECIAL EQUIPMENT: 8 BAMBOO SKEWERS,
    SOAKED IN WATER FOR AT LEAST 30 MINUTES

SALAD
1 fennel bulb
75 g (3 oz) green olives with pimentos, quartered
3 spring onions, white and light green parts, finely chopped
2 tablespoons chopped fennel fronds
1 tablespoon extra-virgin olive oil
½ teaspoon finely grated lemon rind

4 salmon steaks or fillets, each 175 to 250 g (6 to 8 oz)
    and 2.5 to 3.5 cm (1 to 1½ inches) thick
2 tablespoons extra-virgin olive oil
½ teaspoon sea salt
¼ teaspoon freshly ground black pepper

1. If the fennel stalks have the fronds attached, trim off the fronds and chop enough to make 2 tablespoons; set aside. Cut off the thick stalks above the bulb and save the stalks for another use. Leave the root end attached to hold the bulb together. Cut the fennel bulb in half. Fill a small saucepan with water. Lightly salt the water and bring to the boil over a medium-high heat. Reduce the heat to medium and gently simmer the fennel bulb for 3 minutes. Remove from the water and immediately plunge into iced water to rapidly cool it. Remove the bulb from the water, trim off the root end and thinly slice.

2. Combine the salad ingredients in a bowl. Toss to coat and set aside to let the flavours marinate while you grill the salmon.

3. Prepare the barbecue for direct cooking over a high heat.

4. Prepare the salmon steaks as detailed at left. Brush the salmon with the oil and season with the salt and pepper. Brush the cooking grates clean. Grill the salmon over **direct high heat** for 6 to 8 minutes, with the lid closed as much as possible, until you can lift the steaks off the grate with tongs without sticking. Turn the steaks over and cook for a further 2 to 3 minutes for medium, or longer for more well done. If using fillets, to easily remove the skin, just slip a fish slice between the skin and the flesh, and lift the salmon flesh from the barbecue. Transfer the salmon to plates and top with the salad.

A potent ingredient in any barbecuer's pantry, chipotles are dried and smoked jalapeño chillies. They are often found packed in adobo, which is a tomato-based sauce with vinegar, onions, garlic and spices. How to freeze left-over chillies: spoon one chilli, with a little of the sauce, into each space of an icecube tray. After they have frozen, pop them out of the tray, tightly wrap them with clingfilm, and place them in a resealable freezer bag.

BAJA FISH WRAPS WITH CHIPOTLE-LIME SLAW

SERVES: 6
PREP TIME: 20 MINUTES

HEAT: DIRECT HIGH HEAT 230° TO 290°C (450° TO 550°F)
GRILLING TIME: 7 TO 8 MINUTES

RUB
½ teaspoon pure chilli powder
½ teaspoon ground cumin
½ teaspoon sea salt
¼ teaspoon ground cayenne pepper
¼ teaspoon ground cinnamon

4 halibut or salmon fillets or 2 of each (with skin), about 175 g (6 oz) each and 2.5 to 3.5 cm (1 to 1½ inches) thick
Sunflower or other vegetable oil

SLAW
275 g (9 oz) green cabbage, very thinly sliced
15 g (½ oz) coriander, coarsely chopped
4 tablespoons mayonnaise
2 tablespoons fresh lime juice
2 teaspoons sugar
1 teaspoon very finely chopped canned chipotle chilli in adobo (see above)
½ teaspoon sea salt

6 flour tortillas (10 to 12 inches)

1. Mix the rub ingredients together in a small bowl. Lightly brush the fillets with oil and then apply the rub evenly. Cover and set aside in the refrigerator.

2. Combine the slaw ingredients in a large bowl and toss to coat. Set aside until ready to assemble the wraps. Prepare the barbecue for direct cooking over a high heat.

3. Brush the cooking grates clean. Grill the fillets over **direct high heat** for about 4 minutes, with the lid closed as much as possible, until you can lift them with a fish slice off the cooking grate without sticking. Turn the fillets over and cook them for a further 2 to 3 minutes, until they are opaque in the centre. Transfer them to a plate. Warm the tortillas over **direct high heat** for 30 seconds to 1 minute, turning once.

4. To assemble the wraps, break a fillet into large chunks and arrange on one half of a warm tortilla, then top with some of the slaw. Roll the tortilla to enclose the fillings, fold in the sides, and continue rolling to the end. Cut the wrap in half. Serve warm or at room temperature.

Halibut has a nice, mild, sweet flavour, but the flesh is quite lean, so it dries out quickly if it's overcooked. The key is to remove it from the barbecue before it begins to flake apart. Check each fillet first with a paring knife to make sure the flesh is no longer translucent at the centre.

HALIBUT FILLETS WITH BOMBAY TOMATO SAUCE

SERVES: 4
PREP TIME: 30 MINUTES

HEAT: DIRECT MEDIUM HEAT 180° TO 230°C (350° TO 450°F) AND DIRECT HIGH HEAT 230° TO 290°C (450° TO 550°F)
GRILLING TIME: 19 TO 23 MINUTES
SPECIAL EQUIPMENT: 30-CM (12-INCH) CAST-IRON FRYING PAN

SAUCE
3 tablespoons groundnut oil
1 yellow onion, halved and thinly sliced
1 tablespoon very finely chopped garlic
2 teaspoons finely grated fresh root ginger
1 teaspoon ground coriander
1 teaspoon paprika
½ teaspoon turmeric
½ teaspoon sea salt
¼ teaspoon ground cayenne pepper
2 cans (425 g/14 oz) peeled, chopped tomatoes with juice
175 ml (6 fl oz) unsweetened coconut milk, stirred

4 tablespoons groundnut oil
1 teaspoon finely grated fresh root ginger
1 teaspoon sea salt
½ teaspoon freshly ground black pepper
¼ teaspoon turmeric
4 halibut fillets, each 175 to 250 g (6 to 8 oz) and about 2.5 cm (1 inch) thick
2 tablespoons torn basil leaves, optional

1. Prepare the barbecue for direct cooking over a medium heat on one side and high heat on the other side. Brush the cooking grates clean. Warm the oil in a 30-cm (12-inch) cast-iron frying pan over *direct medium heat*. Add the onion and cook for about 5 minutes, stirring often until it softens and begins to brown. Add the garlic, ginger, coriander, paprika, turmeric, salt and cayenne. Mix well and cook for 2 to 3 minutes, stirring often to avoid burning. Add the tomatoes and coconut milk, then taste and adjust the seasoning, if needed. Allow the sauce to simmer for 5 minutes or so while you prepare the halibut.

2. Mix the oil, ginger, salt, pepper and turmeric together in a small bowl. Brush the halibut on both sides with the oil mixture.

3. Grill the fillets over *direct high heat* for 4 to 5 minutes, with the lid closed, until they release easily from the cooking grate. Lift the fillets, one at a time, with a fish slice and turn them over into the pan with the sauce, so that the grilled side is facing up. Nestle the fillets into the sauce, close the lid, and let the fillets cook over *direct medium heat* for 3 to 5 minutes until they have just begun to flake when you poke them with the tip of a knife.

4. Remove from the barbecue. Scatter the basil and serve warm.

HOW TO PREP HALIBUT

1. The first step is to skin the fish. Along one end of the fillet, cut a slit all the way through the skin large enough to get your finger though it.

2. Holding the skin steady with your finger in the slit, angle the blade of a large, sharp knife inside the seam between the flesh and skin.

3. Cut away from you and over the top of the skin, always with the knife angled slightly downwards.

4. Grill the fillets on one side only until they release easily from the grate.

5. Move the fillets to a frying pan with warm tomato sauce, grilled sides facing up.

6. The sauce helps to keep the fillets moist as they finish cooking.

HOW TO SKIN MAHI-MAHI FILLETS

1. Angle the blade of a large, sharp knife into the seam between the flesh and skin on one end of a fillet.

2. Hold the fillet steady with your other hand and slide the knife right over the skin.

3. For safety's sake, cut away from your body, in case the knife slips, and tilt the blade downwards so you don't cut into the flesh of the fillet.

HOW TO MAKE CORN AND MUSHROOM SALSA

1. The cooking goes quickly, so have all your ingredients chopped and weighed beforehand. Chefs refer to this as their 'mise en place'.

2. Cook the corn in a smoking-hot frying pan, stirring occasionally to prevent the kernels from popping right out of the pan.

3. The goal is to caramelize the natural sugars in the corn, turning the kernels golden brown and super sweet.

4. Cook the mushrooms in the same hot pan. The less you stir them, the browner and more delicious they will be.

5. Cook the tomatillos, black beans and garlic just until the garlic begins to brown, too.

6. Combine all the vegetables in the pan, adjust the seasonings and cook just long enough to marry the flavours.

HOW TO CHECK FOR DONENESS

When you insert the end of a metal skewer into the centre of a fillet and then quickly and carefully touch the end of the skewer on the outside of the base of your thumb, it should feel warm. If it feels less than warm, the fish is under-cooked. If it feels hot, the fish is overcooked.

MAHI-MAHI
WITH CORN AND MUSHROOM SALSA

SERVES: 4
PREP TIME: 25 MINUTES
MARINATING TIME: UP TO 1 HOUR

HEAT: DIRECT HIGH HEAT 230° TO 290°C (450° TO 550°F)
GRILLING TIME: 13 TO 15 MINUTES
SPECIAL EQUIPMENT: 30-CM (12-INCH) CAST-IRON
    FRYING PAN

RUB
1 teaspoon pure chilli powder
1 teaspoon garlic granules
1 teaspoon paprika
1 teaspoon sea salt
½ teaspoon ground coriander
½ teaspoon ground cumin
½ teaspoon freshly ground black pepper

4 skinless mahi-mahi fillets, each about 250 g (8 oz)
    and 1.5 mm (¾ inch) thick
4 tablespoons extra-virgin olive oil

SALSA
Kernels cut from 2 ears fresh sweetcorn
1 large Portabello mushroom, stems removed and the
    caps diced
3–4 medium tomatillos, cored and cut into 5-mm to 1-cm
    (¼- to ½-inch) pieces
3 tablespoons extra-virgin olive oil
75 g (3 oz) canned black beans, drained
2 teaspoons very finely chopped garlic
2 tablespoons fresh coriander, roughly chopped
2 teaspoons fresh lime juice
½ teaspoon sea salt
¼ teaspoon freshly ground black pepper
Hot pepper sauce

1. Mix the rub ingredients together in a small bowl. Generously coat the mahi-mahi fillets on both sides with the oil. Season evenly with the rub. Cover and refrigerate for up to 1 hour.

2. Assemble all salsa ingredients so that everything is ready for quick cooking.

3. Prepare the barbecue for direct cooking over a high heat.

4. Warm 1 tablespoon of the oil in a 30-cm (12-inch) cast-iron frying pan over a ***direct high heat***. When it is smoking hot, add the corn and spread the kernels in an even layer. Cook for about 2 minutes, stirring 2 or 3 times, until most of the kernels have turned golden brown and crisp-tender, then transfer to a bowl. Add another tablespoon of oil to the pan, and when the oil begins to smoke, add the mushrooms and spread them out in a single layer. Cook without touching them for 30 seconds, then give them a stir and cook for about 3 minutes, until the mushrooms are browned and tender. Add the mushrooms to the bowl with the corn. Add another tablespoon of the oil to the pan and immediately add the tomatillos, black beans and garlic. Mix well and cook for about 30 seconds, until the garlic begins to brown. Add the corn kernels and the mushrooms from the bowl, the remaining salsa ingredients and heat for about 1 minute. Taste and adjust the seasonings, if necessary. Pour the salsa into the bowl and let cool while you grill the fish.

5. If cooking over charcoal, you'll probably need to add more briquettes to the fire so it is hot enough to grill the fish properly. Grill the mahi-mahi fillets over ***direct high heat*** for 6 to 8 minutes, with the lid closed as much as possible but turning once, until the fish is fully cooked but still moist.

6. Serve the fish fillets warm with the salsa served on the side.

■■■

Recipe from the chefs at Weber Grill® Restaurant

■■■

GRILLED AHI POKE

SERVES: 4 AS A STARTER
PREP TIME: 15 MINUTES

HEAT: DIRECT HIGH HEAT 230° TO 290°C (450° TO 550°F)
GRILLING TIME: ABOUT 2 MINUTES

2 tablespoons dried Japanese arame or other thin
    edible seaweed
40 g (1½ oz) white onion, finely chopped
4 tablespoons spring onion, white and light green parts, thinly
    sliced
2 tablespoons soy sauce
1 tablespoon dark sesame oil
1 teaspoon grated fresh root ginger
½ teaspoon very finely chopped serrano chilli

2 sushi-grade ahi tuna fillets, each about 175 to 250 g
    (6 to 8 oz) and 1.5 to 2.5 cm (¾ to 1 inch) thick
Sunflower or other vegetable oil
Coarse sea salt or alaea (Hawaiian sea salt)
Freshly ground black pepper
2 tablespoons toasted sesame seed
1 lemon, cut into wedges, optional

1. If using dried seaweed, place the seaweed in a small
bowl, add enough water to cover and set aside to soften for
15 minutes. Drain and coarsely chop before using.

2. Prepare the barbecue for direct cooking over a high heat.

3. Mix the onion, spring onion, soy sauce, sesame oil, ginger
and chilli together in a bowl. Add the seaweed.

4. Brush the tuna with oil and lightly season with salt and
pepper, patting the seasoning into the fish. Brush the cooking
grates clean. Grill the tuna over **direct high heat** for about
2 minutes, with the barbecue lid open and turning once, just
until seared on both sides but still rare inside.

5. Transfer the tuna to a chopping board and cut into 1- to
1.5-cm (½- to ¾-inch) cubes. Add to the bowl containing
the onion mixture and toss to combine. Divide equally into
individual bowls. Sprinkle with the sesame seeds. Serve warm
with lemon wedges, if desired.

Poke is a beloved Hawaiian dish of finely chopped raw fish
tossed with edible seaweed, seeds or nuts and a dressing. In
this recipe, the flavour and texture of the fish benefit from a
quick sear on the barbecue. If you use dried seaweed, be sure
to rehydrate it in water for about 15 minutes.

SMOKED TUNA SALAD
WITH GRILLED MANGO

SERVES: 4 TO 6
PREP TIME: 30 MINUTES

HEAT: DIRECT MEDIUM HEAT 180° TO 230°C
   (350° TO 450°F)
GRILLING TIME: ABOUT 10 MINUTES
SPECIAL EQUIPMENT: 4 TO 6 CEDAR PAPERS, SOAKED IN
   WATER FOR 10 MINUTES; BUTCHER'S STRING

DRESSING
125 g (4 oz) runny honey
3 tablespoons Dijon mustard
2 tablespoons rice wine vinegar
2 tablespoons mayonnaise
½ teaspoon sea salt
¼ teaspoon chilli con carne seasoning

2 firm but ripe mangoes
Sunflower or other vegetable oil
300 g (10 oz) sugar snap peas
¼ teaspoon sea salt
2 tuna steaks, each about 500 g (1 lb) and 2.5 cm (1 inch) thick
150 g (5 oz) mixed baby greens, rinsed and crisped
125 g (4 oz) roasted and salted cashews
Freshly ground black pepper

1. Whisk the dressing ingredients in a small bowl until thoroughly combined. Set aside 5 tablespoons of the dressing for the tuna.

2. Slice the sides from the mangoes, cutting along either side of the stone. Carefully, without cutting through the skin, slice 3 to 4 short lines along the inside of the flesh. Using the point of the knife, cut 3 to 4 lines in the opposite direction of the first set of cuts to create mango cubes. Brush the mango halves with oil.

3. Place the snap peas just off the centre on a 30 by 30-cm (12 by 12-inch) sheet of aluminium foil and season them with the salt. Fold the foil over the snap peas and seal to create a pouch.

4. Slice each tuna steak to create equal strips that will fit on the cedar papers. Liberally brush the tuna with the reserved dressing and roll up in the cedar paper, tying to keep the paper secure.

5. Prepare the barbecue for direct cooking over a medium heat. Brush the cooking grates clean. Grill the cedar bundles over **direct medium heat** for about 6 minutes, with the lid closed as much as possible but turning once, until the tuna is pink but still juicy. Keep an eye on the cedar paper. If it catches on fire, use a spray bottle to mist out the flames. Remove the cedar bundles from the barbecue, cut the string, remove the tuna from the cedar paper and let cool. Gently flake the tuna.

6. Place the mangos and the foil pouch with the snap peas over **direct medium heat** and cook for about 4 minutes, with the lid closed as much as possible but turning once. Remove from the barbecue. Open the foil pouch to let the steam escape so the peas do not overcook. When the mangoes are cool enough to handle, hold each mango slice in both hands and press up on the skin side to expose the cubes. Slice the cubes off the skin.

7. Divide the salad greens evenly on serving plates. Top with grilled mango, peas, flaked tuna and cashews. Drizzle with some dressing and finish with a grinding of pepper.

HOW TO SMOKE TUNA IN CEDAR PAPERS

1. Submerge the cedar papers and string in water for 10 minutes.

2. Cut thick tuna steaks into strips that will fit inside the papers. Lay a strip of tuna on each paper parallel to the grain of the wood. Brush the tuna with some of the dressing.

3. Roll up the sides of the paper over the tuna and secure with string.

4. Grill for a few minutes on each side to produce some smoke while the fish cooks.

A cardinal rule for grilling seafood is that freshness and firmness always matter more than a particular type of fish. Don't go to the store thinking, for example, that only grouper will work for this recipe. If the grouper is not fresh that day, choose whatever else is firm and fresh. Good options here are swordfish, scallops, prawns and sea bass.

GRILLED FISH IN A CARIBBEAN CITRUS MARINADE

SERVES: 6
PREP TIME: 15 MINUTES
MARINATING TIME: 3 HOURS

HEAT: DIRECT HIGH HEAT 230° TO 290°C (450° TO 550°F)
GRILLING TIME: 8 TO 10 MINUTES (FILLETS) OR
    4 TO 6 MINUTES (SHELLFISH)

MARINADE
2 teaspoons grated orange rind
125 ml (4 fl oz) fresh orange juice
1 teaspoon grated lime rind
4 tablespoons fresh lime juice
4 tablespoons extra-virgin olive oil
25 g (1 oz) pure chilli powder
1½ tablespoons very finely chopped garlic
1½ teaspoons ground coriander
1 teaspoon very finely chopped jalapeño chilli
¾ teaspoon ground allspice
¾ teaspoon freshly ground black pepper
¼ teaspoon ground cayenne pepper

6 fish fillets, such as grouper, sea bass, plaice, cod or
    halibut (with skin), each 150 to 175 g (5 to 6 oz) and
    about 2.5 cm (1 inch) thick or 750 g (1½ lb) large prawns
    or scallops
Extra-virgin olive oil
Sea salt

1. Combine the marinade ingredients in a non-metallic bowl. Reserve 5 tablespoons of the marinade to serve with the grilled fish.

2. Place the fillets or shellfish side by side in another non-metallic dish, such as an 20 by 20-cm (8 by 8-inch) ovenproof dish. Pour the remaining marinade over the fish or shellfish and turn to coat them. Cover and refrigerate the fish and reserved marinade for 3 hours.

3. Prepare the barbecue for direct cooking over a high heat.

4. Remove the fillets or shellfish from the dish and discard the marinade. Lightly brush with oil and season with some salt.

5. Brush the cooking grates clean. Grill the fillets, skin side up, over **direct high heat** for 8 to 10 minutes, with the lid closed as much as possible but turning once after 6 to 7 minutes when they release easily from the cooking grate, until just opaque in the centre. If using prawns or scallops, grill over **direct high heat** for 4 to 6 minutes, turning once. Serve with the reserved marinade spooned over the fillets or shellfish.

SWORDFISH ESCABÈCHE

SERVES: 4
PREP TIME: 30 MINUTES
MARINATING TIME: UP TO 2 HOURS

HEAT: DIRECT MEDIUM HEAT 180° TO 230°C
(350° TO 450°F)
GRILLING TIME: 14 TO 18 MINUTES

MARINADE
125 ml (4 fl oz) extra-virgin olive oil
3 tablespoons sherry vinegar
1 tablespoon very finely chopped garlic
1 teaspoon dried oregano
¾ teaspoon sea salt
½ teaspoon crushed red chilli flakes
¼ teaspoon freshly ground black pepper

8 button mushrooms
2 plum tomatoes, cored and halved lengthways
1 large Anaheim chilli
1 small yellow squash, halved lengthways
4 swordfish steaks, 250 to 300 g (8 to 10 oz) each and about
2.5 cm (1 inch) thick

ESCABÈCHE
250 ml (8 fl oz) chicken stock
1 tablespoon sherry vinegar
¼ teaspoon dried oregano
⅛ teaspoon freshly ground black pepper

1. Whisk the marinade ingredients together in a small bowl. Transfer 4 tablespoons of the marinade to another bowl. Add the vegetables to the second bowl and mix to coat them evenly.

2. Place the swordfish steaks flat on a plate large enough to fit them in a single layer. Spoon the remaining marinade over the steaks, turning them over to coat them evenly. Cover with clingfilm and refrigerate for as long as 2 hours.

3. Prepare the barbecue for direct cooking over a medium heat. Brush the cooking grates clean. Grill the vegetables over **direct medium heat** for 6 to 8 minutes, with the lid closed as much as possible but turning occasionally, until they are lightly marked and tender. Remove the vegetables from the barbecue.

4. Place the chilli in a bowl and cover with clingfilm. When cool enough to handle, remove and discard the stem, seeds and skin. Roughly chop all the vegetables.

5. In a frying pan over a medium-high heat, combine the escabèche ingredients and bring the liquid to the boil. Add the chopped vegetables and spread them out in the pan. Cook for 3 to 5 minutes until the vegetables are tender. Remove the pan from the heat, cover and keep warm.

6. Lift the swordfish steaks off the plate and let the excess marinade drip on to the plate. Discard the marinade. Brush the cooking grates clean. Grill the steaks over **direct medium heat** for 8 to 10 minutes, with the lid closed as much as possible but turning once, until the centre is opaque but the flesh juicy. Serve the swordfish warm with the vegetable mixture.

HOW TO MAKE SWORDFISH ESCABÈCHE

1. Swordfish steaks work well here, as would any firm-flesh fish. Remove the tough outer skin before marinating and grilling the steaks.

2. Barbecuing the tomatoes and chilli, as well as the squash and mushrooms, will add depth and complexity to the final dish.

3. Escabèche is a preparation involving fish and hot vinegar-based liquid poured over the top. Barbecued vegetables enliven the savoury liquid.

HOW TO BARBECUE FISH FILLETS IN BANANA LEAVES

As you get closer and closer to the equator, you will find more and more barbecuers in the tropics using banana leaves to wrap and steam fish, vegetables, rice and tamales. These inexpensive leaves, which are now available frozen in most Asian and Latino food shops, trap moisture and add a subtle tea-like fragrance to the food. Thaw them in the refrigerator for a few hours, or pour boiling water over them to make them pliable quickly.

1. Cut the leaves into rectangles large enough to wrap around each fish fillet. Leave the sturdy fibrous vein along one edge intact, which holds the leaves together.

2. Wipe both sides with a damp piece of kitchen paper to clean the leaves, moving in the same direction as the grain so you don't split them open.

3. Fold one side over the marinated fish, and then overlap the first side with the opposite side.

4. Fold down the top and bottom sides so that they overlap in the centre. If the leaf splits, use a second leaf to double-wrap the fish.

5. Thread a cocktail stick in and out of the overlapping leaves but not into the fish itself.

6. Brush each packet generously with water to prevent it drying out. Assemble the packets on a roasting tray and cover with damp dishtowels until ready to grill.

7. Let the charcoal burn down to a medium heat.

8. Grill the packets with the cocktail sticks on top most of the time so the wood does not burn.

9. When the fish is fully cooked, you can unwrap the leaves and use them as serving plates.

GINGER AND MISO BLACK COD IN BANANA LEAVES

SERVES: 6
PREP TIME: 20 MINUTES
MARINATING TIME: 2 HOURS

HEAT: DIRECT MEDIUM HEAT 180° TO 230°C
(350° TO 450°F)
GRILLING TIME: 8 TO 10 MINUTES

MARINADE
5 tablespoons white miso paste
4 tablespoons unsweetened coconut milk, stirred
2 teaspoons very finely chopped garlic
2 teaspoons sugar
1 teaspoon finely grated fresh root ginger

6 skinless black cod (sable fish) fillets, 150 to 175 g (5 to 6 oz)
    each and about 1 cm (½ inch) thick
6 banana leaves, each about 30 cm (12 inches) square
6 spring onions, white and light green parts, thinly sliced
1½ teaspoons low-sodium soy sauce
About 1 kg (2 lb) steamed rice, optional

1. Whisk the marinade ingredients into a smooth paste in a small bowl. Smear the paste all over the fillets. Cover with clingfilm and refrigerate for 2 hours.

2. Rinse the banana leaves under cool running water or carefully wipe them clean with damp kitchen paper.

3. Prepare the barbecue for direct cooking over a medium heat.

4. Remove the excess marinade from the fillets, then discard the marinade and place each fillet on the centre of a banana leaf. Place some spring onions on top. Fold the leaf over to completely enclose the fillet and make a packet. Secure with a cocktail stick, being careful not to pierce the fish. Brush each packet on both sides with water.

5. Brush the cooking grates clean. Grill the packets over **direct medium heat** for 8 to 10 minutes, with the lid closed as much as possible but turning the packet once, until the leaves are blackened in some parts. (If the leaves begin to burn through, move the packet[s] over indirect medium heat.) Remove one of the packets from the barbecue to check the fish for doneness. If it is opaque all the way through, the fish is done. If not, return to the barbecue for a few more minutes.

6. Carefully open each packet, remove any pin bones from the fillets, drizzle each with ¼ teaspoon of soy sauce, or more to taste, and serve with steamed rice, if desired.

HOW TO FILLET RED SNAPPER

1. Scale the fish, remove the head and make a shallow cut all along one side of the backbone.

2. Run the knife under the top fillet and over the fish bones.

3. Use your other hand to steady the fish as you slide the knife towards the tail. Remove the top fillet.

4. Turn the fish over and make a second shallow cut, this time on the other side of the backbone.

5. Use the tip of the knife to make deeper and deeper cuts along the tops of the bones.

6. Use your other hand to pull the fillet gently upwards so you can see where to cut.

7. To skin the fillets, hold the end of the skin with your fingertips and run the knife just under the flesh.

8. Cut the fillets into individual portions.

RED SNAPPER IN COCONUT BROTH

SERVES: 8

PREP TIME: 20 MINUTES

HEAT: DIRECT HIGH HEAT 230° TO 290°C (450° TO 550°F)

GRILLING TIME: 4 TO 5 MINUTES

STOCK
3 tablespoons groundnut oil
125 g (4 oz) carrot, finely diced
40 g (1½ oz) shallot, finely chopped
1 teaspoon freshly grated fresh root ginger
1 teaspoon finely grated lime rind
1 can (400 ml/14 fl oz) unsweetened coconut milk, stirred
125 ml (4 fl oz) water
3 tablespoons fresh lime juice
1 tablespoon sugar
2 teaspoons very finely chopped or thinly sliced red birds-eye chilli
1 teaspoon fish sauce

8 skinless red snapper fillets, each 125 to 175 g (4 to 6 oz) and about 1 cm (½ inch) thick
Groundnut or rapeseed oil
Sea salt
Freshly ground black pepper

1. Warm the oil in a small saucepan over a medium heat. Add the carrot, shallot, ginger and lime rind, mix well and cook for 3 to 5 minutes, until the carrots are softened, stirring often. Add the remaining stock ingredients, mix well and allow to simmer for 2 to 3 minutes.

2. Prepare the barbecue for direct cooking over a high heat. Lightly brush each fillet on both sides with oil. Season evenly with salt and pepper. Brush the cooking grates clean. Grill over **direct high heat** for 4 to 5 minutes, with the lid closed as much as

possible but turning once with a fish slice, until the fish just barely begins to flake when you poke it with the tip of a knife. Meanwhile, warm the stock over a medium heat.

3. Spoon equal portions of the stock into 8 shallow bowls. Lay a fillet in the centre of each bowl. Serve warm.

HOW TO USE A GRILL PAN FOR VEGETABLES AND FISH

1. Coat the fillets generously with the marinade on both sides.

2. Preheat the grill pan over a medium heat for about 10 minutes to prevent food from sticking.

3. Place the vegetables on the grill pan and cook until they soften and begin to brown.

4. Grill each fillet flesh side down first, turning with a fish slice only when it releases easily from the grill pan.

SOUTH-OF-THE-BORDER GRILL-PAN FISH

SERVES: 4
PREP TIME: 15 MINUTES
MARINATING TIME: 30 MINUTES

HEAT: DIRECT MEDIUM HEAT 230° TO 290°C
(450° TO 550°F)
GRILLING TIME: 16 TO 20 MINUTES
SPECIAL EQUIPMENT: PERFORATED GRILL PAN

MARINADE
4 tablespoons extra-virgin olive oil
4 teaspoons fresh lime juice
2 teaspoons pure chilli powder
1½ teaspoons sea salt
½ teaspoon ground cumin
½ teaspoon garlic granules
½ teaspoon dried Mexican oregano
½ teaspoon paprika

4 rock cod, grouper or red snapper fillets (with skin), 175 to 250 g
(6 to 8 oz) each and about 1.5 cm (¾ inch) thick
Sea salt

2 poblano chillies, stems and seeds removed, and cut into
1-cm (½-inch) rings
4 plum tomatoes, cored and cut into 1-cm (½-inch) slices
8 garlic cloves, peeled
4 large spring onions, rinsed and trimmed

1. Combine the marinade ingredients in a small bowl. Transfer 2 tablespoons of the marinade to a large bowl.

2. Arrange the fillets in a single layer on a platter, pour the marinade from the small bowl over the fillets to coat each piece evenly and season with some salt. Cover with clingfilm and marinate at room temperature for 30 minutes.

3. Place the chillies, tomatoes, garlic and spring onions in the large bowl with the reserved marinade and toss to coat them evenly.

4. Prepare the barbecue for direct cooking over a medium heat. Brush the cooking grates clean. Preheat the grill pan over **direct medium heat** for about 10 minutes. When hot, grill the vegetables on the pan for 6 to 8 minutes, with the lid closed as much as possible but turning occasionally, until the chillies and tomatoes are softened and the garlic and spring onions begin to brown. Remove the vegetables from the grill pan and set aside. Grill the fish, skin side up, on the grill pan, over **direct medium heat** for 10 to 12 minutes, with the lid closed as much as possible but carefully turning once when the fish releases easily from the grill pan, until the fish is opaque and still juicy.

5. Transfer the fish to a serving platter and arrange the vegetables all around. Serve warm.

SEAFOOD

WHOLE STRIPED BASS
IN MOROCCAN MARINADE

SERVES: 4 TO 6
PREP TIME: 10 MINUTES
MARINATING TIME: 2 TO 3 HOURS

HEAT: DIRECT MEDIUM HEAT 180° TO 230°C
    (350° TO 450°F)
GRILLING TIME: 12 TO 15 MINUTES

MARINADE
5 tablespoons extra-virgin olive oil
4 tablespoons fresh lemon juice
15 g (½ oz) flat leaf parsley, chopped
15 g (½ oz) fresh coriander, chopped
1 tablespoon very finely chopped garlic
1½ teaspoons sweet paprika
1 teaspoon ground cumin
1 teaspoon sea salt
½ teaspoon freshly ground black pepper
¼ teaspoon ground cayenne pepper

2 whole striped bass, 750 g to 2 kg (1½ to 2 lb) each, scaled,
    cleaned and fins removed

1. Combine the marinade ingredients in a bowl. Set aside
5 tablespoons to spoon over the fish after grilling.

2. Cut 3 or 4 slashes about 1 cm (½ inch) deep and 2.5 cm
(1 inch) apart on each side of the fish.

3. Place the fish on a roasting tray. Spread the marinade over the
fish, inside and out, working it into the cuts. Cover with clingfilm
and refrigerate the fish and the reserved marinade for 2 to 3 hours.

4. Prepare the barbecue for direct cooking over a medium heat.

5. Remove the fish from the refrigerator and brush with a little
more olive oil. Grill over **direct medium heat** for 12 to 15 minutes,

with the lid closed as much as possible but carefully turning once,
until the flesh is opaque near the bone but still juicy. Transfer
to a platter and spoon the reserved marinade over the top. If
desired, serve with Roasted Pepper, Lemon and Olive Relish
(see recipe below).

ROASTED PEPPER, LEMON AND OLIVE RELISH
PREP TIME: 10 MINUTES

2 roasted red peppers, peeled, deseeded and cut into 5-mm
    (¼-inch) dice
1 whole lemon, peeled, white pith removed, segmented,
    deseeded and coarsely chopped
75 g (3 oz) oil-cured black olives, stoned and coarsely chopped
5 tablespoons extra-virgin olive oil
2 tablespoons fresh lemon juice
2 tablespoons chopped fresh coriander
Sea salt
Freshly ground black pepper

1. Combine the relish ingredients, including salt and pepper to
taste, in a bowl. Keep at room temperature.

HOW TO PREP WHOLE FISH

1. Scale the fish and cut off the pectoral fins with kitchen shears.

2. Cut the spiny dorsal fins off the backbone.

3. Also cut off the fins along the belly (ventral) side of the fish.

4. Cut 3 or 4 slashes about 1 cm (½ inch) deep and 2.5 cm (1 inch) apart on each side of the fish.

HOW TO BARBECUE TROUT IN A BASKET

Whole fish can be difficult to barbecue without their skins sticking to the grate. A fish basket allows you to turn the fish easily. Just be sure to grease the basket itself so the skins of the fish pull away cleanly after they are cooked.

1. Lining the fish basket with orange slices, lettuce leaves or thick spring onions prevents the skins of the fish from sticking to the basket.

2. In this recipe, the juice of the orange also complements the sake marinade on the fish.

3. Lower the moveable section of the basket so that it rests snugly on the top layer of orange slices, preventing the ingredients from shifting.

4. You can grill the fish without the cooking grate. Just wear barbecue mitts or oven gloves and hold the basket over the coals, turning it over as needed for even cooking.

5. If flare-ups occur, move quickly to rotate the basket away from the flames.

6. The goal is to lightly char the orange and cook the fish all the way to the bone without burning the skins.

SAKE-MARINATED TROUT

SERVES: 4
PREP TIME: 25 MINUTES
MARINATING TIME: 15 TO 30 MINUTES

HEAT: DIRECT MEDIUM HEAT 180° TO 230°C
(350° TO 450°F)
GRILLING TIME: ABOUT 8 MINUTES
SPECIAL EQUIPMENT: FISH BASKET

MARINADE
5 tablespoons sake or dry sherry
4 tablespoons soy sauce
4 tablespoons mirin (sweet rice wine)
2 tablespoons peeled and finely chopped fresh root ginger
2 tablespoons unseasoned rice vinegar
2 garlic cloves, finely chopped
¼ teaspoon crushed red chilli flakes

4 whole boneless trout, each about 375 g (13 oz), cleaned
and gutted
Sunflower or other vegetable oil
4–6 oranges, cut into 32 slices, each about 5 mm (¼ inch)
thick

1. Whisk the marinade ingredients together in a bowl. Place the trout in a large, resealable plastic bag and pour in the marinade.

Press out the air and seal the bag tightly. Turn to distribute the marinade. Refrigerate for 15 to 30 minutes. Take care not to over-marinate the fish. (Although this marinade isn't highly acidic, the delicate flesh could become overwhelmed by the sake, soy sauce and mirin.)

2. Remove the trout from the bag and transfer to a roasting tray. Strain the marinade into a saucepan and bring to a boil over medium-high heat. Cook for about 10 minutes, until syrupy and reduced to about 4 tablespoons. Set aside.

3. Prepare the barbecue for direct cooking over a medium heat.

4. Lightly brush the inside of the fish basket with oil. Lay 4 orange slices in the basket and place 1 trout on top of them. Then place 4 more orange slices on top of the fish in the same manner. Repeat with the remaining trout, and then close and secure the fish basket. (If your fish basket is not large enough to hold 4 whole trout, you will need to grill the fish in 2 batches.) Grill the trout over **direct medium heat** for about 8 minutes, with the barbecue lid open, turning the basket every 2 minutes and rotating when needed for even cooking, until the flesh is opaque in the centre and the skin and oranges are lightly charred. Using a fish slice, carefully remove the trout from the fish basket and transfer each fish to a dinner plate. Serve hot with the reduced marinade on the side.

HOW TO TRIM TROUT

1. Trim off the collar bone with scissors and cut off the head.

2. Cut off the dorsal fin.

3. Cut off the fins attached to each side of the belly.

4. Cut off the fin near the tail.

5. Trim the very thin edges of the belly.

6. Remove the bit of backbone between the fillets.

HOW TO SEGMENT AN ORANGE

1. Slice off the ends of each orange and stand it upright. Following the curve of the sides, slice off the peel, leaving as much flesh as possible.

2. Cut out the individual segments by slicing as close as possible to the membrane on both sides of each segment.

3. Squeeze the remaining orange 'skeleton' to capture all the juices.

4. Use the segments for the salad and the juice for the dressing.

Heat the soaked cedar planks by themselves until they begin to smoke and char, then turn them over and set the trout on top to cook and smoke simultaneously.

CEDAR-PLANKED TROUT WITH ROCKET, FENNEL AND ORANGE

SERVES: 4 TO 6
PREP TIME: 20 TO 25 MINUTES

HEAT: DIRECT MEDIUM-HIGH HEAT 190° TO 230°C
   (375° TO 450°F)
GRILLING TIME: 11 TO 18 MINUTES
SPECIAL EQUIPMENT: 2 UNTREATED CEDAR PLANKS,
   EACH 30 TO 38 CM (12 TO 15 INCHES) LONG AND
   1 TO 1.5 CM (½ TO ¾ INCH) THICK, SOAKED IN WATER
   FOR AT LEAST 1 HOUR

2 tablespoons red wine vinegar
1 small shallot, finely chopped
2 oranges
4 tablespoons grapeseed oil
Sea salt
Freshly ground black pepper

4 whole boneless trout, each about 375 g (13 oz), cleaned
   and gutted with head, tails and fins removed
Extra-virgin olive oil

175 g (6 oz) rocket
1 fennel bulb, cored and thinly sliced

1. Combine the vinegar and shallot in a small, non-metallic bowl. Remove the rind of 1 of the oranges, then peel and segment both oranges, reserving the juice. Set aside the orange segments. Whisk the orange juice (there should be about 4 tablespoons) into the vinegar and shallot. Drizzle in the oil, whisking constantly, and then season to taste with salt and pepper.

2. Prepare the barbecue for direct cooking over a medium-high heat. Rinse the trout under cold water and pat dry with kitchen paper. Lightly brush the inside of the trout with oil and generously season with salt and pepper.

3. Place the soaked planks over **direct medium-high heat** and close the lid. After 5 to 10 minutes, when the planks begin to smoke and char, turn them over and then place 2 trout, slightly overlapping, on each plank. Grill over **direct medium-high heat** for 6 to 8 minutes, with the lid closed, until the fish are firm to the touch and cooked through.

4. Use a fish slice to carefully lift each fish on to an individual serving plate, skin side down and open like a book.

5. Put the rocket in a bowl and the orange segments and fennel in another. Season both with salt and pepper and toss with vinaigrette. Spoon some of the orange-fennel mixture over each fish, top with the dressed greens and garnish with the remaining orange and fennel mixture.

HOW TO PREP SQUID

1. Cleaning a whole squid (left) will leave you with a tube-like body and separate tentacles (right).

2. To start, pull the tentacles away from the body (tube) of each squid, then reach inside to grab the end of the hard quill.

3. Pull the plastic-like quill out of the tube and discard.

4. Squeeze the tube to push out and discard the mushy innards.

5. Scratch the surface of the brownish skin and peel it off the tubes. Discard the skin.

6. Cut the tentacles from the head just above the eyes. Discard the eyes.

7. Squeeze the hard mouth (beak) from the tentacles and discard it.

8. Slide a knife into each tube.

9. The knife inside the tube allows you to score each tube without cutting all the way through.

10. As you remove the squid from the marinade, shake off the excess liquid to help browning.

11. Grill the tubes as quickly as possible over a very high heat.

12. The tentacles will cook a little faster. Be careful not to lose them through the cooking grate.

THAI SQUID

SERVES: 4
PREP TIME: 45 MINUTES
MARINATING TIME: 20 MINUTES

HEAT: DIRECT HIGH HEAT 230° TO 290°C (450° TO 550°F)
GRILLING TIME: 2 TO 3 MINUTES

12 whole, small squid

MARINADE
15 g (½ oz) fresh coriander, finely chopped
4 tablespoons fresh lime juice
4 tablespoons fish sauce
2 tablespoons sugar
1 tablespoon very finely chopped garlic
½ teaspoon freshly ground black pepper

1. Hold each squid and gently pull to separate the tube from the tentacles. Pull out and discard any remaining contents from inside each tube, including the plastic-like quill. Peel off the brownish skin that covers the tubes. Rinse the inside of the tubes and set aside. Slice off each tentacles portion just above the eyes and discard everything except the tentacles. Squeeze out and discard the hard beak found at the base of the tentacles. Remove the gritty 'teeth' on the tentacles (you can feel them) by rubbing them between your fingers under cold running water.

2. Combine the marinade ingredients in a large bowl. Add the squid and toss to coat them evenly. Cover and refrigerate for 20 minutes. Prepare the barbecue for direct cooking over a high heat.

3. Remove the squid from the bowl and discard the marinade. Brush the cooking grates clean. Grill the squid over **direct high heat** for 2 to 3 minutes, with the lid open and turning once, until they are just turning opaque and no longer look wet. Serve warm.

HOW TO BARBECUE CALAMARI UNDER BRICKS

1. Separate the tubes from the tentacles on a roasting tray. Everything should be well coated with the marinade.

2. Line up the tubes on the barbecue in groups of 4. Immediately set a brick on top of each group, with the smooth side of the foil facing down.

3. Grill the tubes for about 2 minutes. Then carefully roll the bricks over on to their sides so you can turn the tubes over.

4. Grill the tentacles beside the bricks, turning them once and being careful not to lose them through the grate.

5. For the most flavourful, tender calamari possible, lightly char them over very high heat, then remove them from the barbecue before they overcook.

BRICKYARD CALAMARI SALAD

SERVES: 4
PREP TIME: 25 MINUTES
MARINATING TIME: 30 MINUTES

HEAT: DIRECT HIGH HEAT 230° TO 290°C (450° TO 550°F)
GRILLING TIME: ABOUT 4 MINUTES PER BATCH
SPECIAL EQUIPMENT: 2 FOIL-WRAPPED BRICKS

DRESSING
3 tablespoons fresh lemon juice
1 teaspoon very finely chopped garlic
½ teaspoon crushed red chilli flakes
½ teaspoon sea salt
¼ teaspoon freshly ground black pepper
5 tablespoons extra-virgin olive oil

12 whole, small squid, cleaned (see page 224)
¼ teaspoon sea salt
¼ teaspoon freshly ground black pepper
250 g (8 oz) small cherry tomatoes, halved
40 g (1½ oz) red onion, cut into 5-mm (¼-inch) diced
2 large ripe Haas avocados, cubed
1½ tablespoons chopped oregano

1. Combine the lemon juice, garlic, chilli flakes, salt and pepper in a bowl. Slowly whisk in the olive oil.

2. Season the calamari with the salt and pepper and place on a roasting tray with 2 tablespoons of the dressing. Toss to coat, then allow to marinate at room temperature for about 30 minutes.

3. Prepare the barbecue for direct cooking over a high heat. Brush the cooking grates clean.

4. Place about 4 calamari tubes in 2 rows over **direct high heat** so they can be weighted under the bricks. Place the bricks on top of the tubes, with the smooth side of the foil facing down, and grill for about 2 minutes, with the lid closed as much as possible, until the tubes easily lift off the cooking grate. Wearing insulated barbecue mitts or oven gloves and using tongs, carefully tilt the bricks on to their sides off of the tubes. Turn the tubes over, then set the bricks back in place over the tubes for a further 2 minutes. Transfer the tubes to a platter. Repeat with the remaining tubes, brushing the cooking grates clean after you remove the first batch. Grill the tentacles beside the bricks for about 4 minutes, turning once.

5. Put the tomatoes and onion into the bowl with the remaining dressing and toss to coat. Spoon the tomatoes and diced onion over the calamari tubes and add the avocado. Sprinkle with the oregano.

VEGETABLES

TECHNIQUES

RECIPES

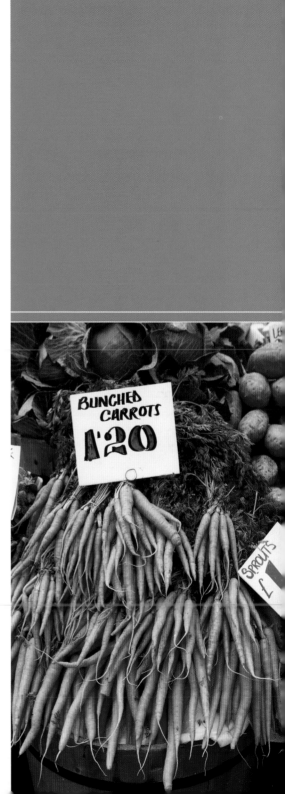

HOW TO MAKE POLENTA

1. As soon as the polenta begins to boil, turn the heat to low and stir with a wooden spoon to prevent the hot mixture from splattering out of the saucepan.

2. Cook over a low heat until the polenta is thick and no longer gritty. Continue to stir every few minutes to prevent sticking and scorching on the sides of the saucepan.

3. Scrape the hot polenta into a greased pan and smooth it out with the back of a wet spoon or spatula. Allow the mixture to cool and firm up for a couple hours, then flip it on to a board and cut it into serving pieces.

4. Tomatillos provide really nice tangy and herb-like flavours to the base of the sauce. You will find them in Mexican food shops with papery husks still attached. Peel the husks off and rinse each tomatillo under water to remove the sticky coating.

5. Grill the tomatillos over direct medium heat until their skins begin to break, turning occasionally. During this grilling time, their flavours will turn richer, sweeter and more concentrated.

6. Grill the poblano chilli and onion slices at the same time as the tomatillos. Once the pepper has been peeled and deseeded, purée the vegetables with some olive oil, fresh coriander, brown sugar and salt for a bold vegetarian sauce to serve with grilled polenta.

POLENTA WITH QUESO FRESCO AND ROASTED TOMATILLO SAUCE

SERVES: 4
PREP TIME: 40 MINUTES
COOLING TIME: 2 HOURS

HEAT: DIRECT AND INDIRECT MEDIUM HEAT 180° TO 230°C
(350° TO 450°F)
GRILLING TIME: 18 TO 22 MINUTES

POLENTA
25 g (1 oz) unsalted butter
75 g (3 oz) yellow onion, finely chopped
1 litre (1¾ pints) milk
125 g (4 oz) polenta
1 teaspoon chilli con carne seasoning
¾ teaspoon sea salt
Extra-virgin olive oil

SAUCE
2 slices yellow onion, each about 1 cm (½ inch) thick
4 tomatillos, about 250 g (8 oz) total, papery skins
   removed and rinsed
1 small poblano chilli, 7.5 to 10 cm (3 to 4 inches) long
15 g (½ oz) fresh coriander leaves
½ teaspoon brown sugar
¼ teaspoon sea salt

125 g (4 oz) queso fresco cheese, crumbled
1 ripe Haas avocado

1. Melt the butter in a large saucepan over a medium heat. Add the onion and cook for 3 to 5 minutes, stirring occasionally until lightly browned. Add the milk, polenta, chilli seasoning and salt, whisking until the mixture begins to boil. Turn the heat to very low and stir with a wooden spoon almost constantly to prevent splattering or burning. Cook and stir for 15 to 20 minutes until the polenta is very thick and no longer gritty to the bite.

2. Brush the inside of a 20-cm (8-inch) square tin with 1 tablespoon of oil. Scrape the hot polenta into the tin and spread into a smooth, even layer. Allow it to cool at room temperature for 2 hours. Prepare the barbecue for direct and indirect cooking over a medium heat.

3. Brush the onion slices, tomatillos and chilli with olive oil. Brush the cooking grates clean. Grill the vegetables over **direct medium heat**, with the lid closed as much as possible but turning as necessary, until the onions are lightly charred, the tomatillos soften and begin to collapse and the chilli is slightly softened and lightly charred. The onions will take 8 to 10 minutes, the tomatillos about 10 minutes and the chilli, 10 to 12 minutes. Remove the vegetables from the barbecue as they are done. Place the chilli in a bowl, cover with clingfilm and allow to steam for 10 to 15 minutes.

4. When the chilli is cool enough to handle, pull off and discard the skin, stem and seeds. Put the vegetables, the coriander, brown sugar and salt in a food processor or blender and whizz until evenly puréed. Add more brown sugar and salt to taste.

5. Invert the tin of polenta on to a chopping board, tapping to release the polenta, if necessary. Cut the polenta into 4 to 8 pieces of whatever size and shape you like.

6. Set the pieces of polenta, smooth and greased side down, over **indirect medium heat**. Carefully pile the crumbed cheese on top of each piece. Grill for 8 to 10 minutes, with the lid closed, until the polenta is warmed and the cheese has begun to melt. While the polenta is on the barbecue, peel and thinly slice the avocado.

7. Transfer the polenta to serving plates. Spoon the tomatillo sauce over the polenta and top with avocado slices.

HOW TO BARBECUE CORN

1. Cut off the exposed brownish silk and peel the layers of the husk until you begin to see some kernels showing through the layers. Now the charcoal flavours can penetrate the kernels.

2. Lay the ears of corn on and alongside the embers, turning them as the husks blacken in spots.

3. Let the ears of corn cool a bit and then peel off the remaining layers of the husk. Finish cooking the corn in a tin of melted lemon-curry butter.

EMBER-ROASTED CORN WITH LEMON-CURRY BUTTER

SERVES: 4
PREP TIME: 10 MINUTES

HEAT: DIRECT MEDIUM HEAT 180° TO 230°C
    (350° TO 450°F) FOR CHARCOAL BARBECUES ONLY
GRILLING TIME: 20 TO 25 MINUTES

BUTTER
50 g (2 oz) unsalted butter, softened
1 tablespoon finely chopped dill
2 teaspoons finely grated lemon rind
1 teaspoon curry powder
½ teaspoon sea salt
⅛ teaspoon freshly ground black pepper

4 ears fresh sweetcorn, in husks

1. Prepare the charcoal barbecue as seen on the left. Allow the coals burn down to medium heat.

2. Mash the butter ingredients together in a bowl with the back of a fork, mixing until the ingredients are evenly distributed.

3. Trim the pointed end of each ear of corn, cutting off and discarding the fine silk sticking out of the husk. Remove and discard a layer or two of the tough outer leaves of each husk. If you can see some kernels through the transparent leaves, that's good.

4. Carefully lay the ears of corn in a single layer on the charcoal grate, on and alongside the coals. Cook the ears of corn there for 15 to 20 minutes, with the lid closed as much as possible but swapping the positions of the ears and rolling them over a few times for even cooking, until the husks are blackened all over and the kernels are tender. If any of the kernels are exposed, keep that side away from direct exposure to the coals. If the outer leaves burn, that's okay.

5. Use long-handled tongs to carefully remove the ears of corn from the barbecue. Allow them to cool for a few minutes, or until you can safely hold them in your hands. Carefully peel off and discard the husk and silk from each ear of corn. Leave the stalk ends attached to use as handles.

6. Arrange the corn in a single layer in a tin that will fit on the barbecue. Add the butter to the tin. When ready to serve, place the tin on the cooking grate and grill over *direct medium heat* for about 5 minutes, with the lid closed as much as possible but turning occasionally, until the butter has melted and the ears of corn are warmed. If desired, keep the corn warm in the tin over indirect heat while you finish cooking other parts of the meal.

GINGER-AND-LIME-GLAZED CORN ON THE COB

SERVES: 6
PREP TIME: 15 MINUTES

HEAT: DIRECT MEDIUM HEAT 180° TO 230°C (350° TO 450°F)
GRILLING TIME: 10 TO 15 MINUTES

GLAZE
5 tablespoons chicken stock
50 g (2 oz) unsalted butter
1 tablespoon sugar
1 teaspoon finely grated lime rind
1 teaspoon sea salt
1 teaspoon grated fresh root ginger

6 ears fresh sweetcorn, in husks

1. Prepare the barbecue for direct cooking over a medium heat.

2. Stir the glaze ingredients together in a saucepan over a medium-high heat and bring to the boil. Continue to boil for 5 to 7 minutes until the glaze slightly thickens. Keep the glaze warm.

3. Cut off the top of each ear of corn just above the first row of kernels. Set aside a couple of corn husks to make long strips. Pull the corn husks back, but do not break them off the ears. Remove and discard the corn silk. Gather the husks together on each ear where they narrow towards the ends and use a strip of husk about 1 cm (½ inch) wide to tie the husks together for a handle. Mix and then brush the glaze all over the corn. Brush the cooking grates clean. Grill the corn over ***direct medium heat*** for 10 to 15 minutes, with the lid closed as much as possible and letting the husks extend over indirect heat so they do not burn, but turning several times until they are browned in spots and tender. Transfer to a platter and baste the kernels with the remaining glaze.

HOW TO PREP CORN ON THE COB

1. Pull the husks back, but leave them attached at the stalk end so you have handles. Remove and discard the corn silk.

2. Use a couple of long husks from the outer layers to cut long strips for tying up the handles.

3. Brush the exposed corn kernels with some of the glaze.

4. Grill the corn over direct medium heat, with the handles extending over indirect heat so that they do not burn.

For optimal flavour, fresh corn should be shucked just before grilling. Many of the kernels will turn golden brown and crisp-tender over direct medium heat.

GRILLED CORN AND MUSHROOM RISOTTO

SERVES: 4 TO 6
PREP TIME: 50 MINUTES

HEAT: DIRECT MEDIUM HEAT 180° TO 230°C (350° TO 450°F)
GRILLING TIME: 8 TO 10 MINUTES
SPECIAL EQUIPMENT: 30-CM (12-INCH) FRYING PAN

250 g (8 oz) button mushrooms
1 poblano chilli, about 15 cm (6 inches) long
3 ears fresh sweetcorn, husked
1 yellow onion, cut crossways into 1-cm (½-inch) slices
Extra-virgin olive oil
1.2 litres (2 pints) chicken stock
25 g (1 oz) unsalted butter
200 g (7 oz) Arborio rice
½ teaspoon sea salt
100 g (3½ oz) chile jack or Parmesan cheese, grated
65 g (2½ oz) feta cheese, crumbled
15 g (½ oz) fresh coriander leaves, chopped

1. Prepare the barbecue for direct cooking over a medium heat.

2. Wipe the mushrooms with a damp cloth or kitchen paper. Remove and discard the discoloured stalk ends. Lightly brush the mushrooms, chilli, corn and onion slices with oil.

3. Grill the vegetables over **direct medium heat** for 8 to 10 minutes, with the lid closed as much as possible but turning as

needed, until the mushrooms and onion slices are tender, the chilli is blackened and blistered all over and the corn is browned in spots and tender. Remove the vegetables from the barbecue and allow them to cool. Coarsely chop the mushrooms and cut the corn kernels off the cobs. Scrape off the loosened bits of skin from the chilli and discard along with the seeds and stem; finely chop the remaining part of the chilli. Roughly chop the onion. Combine the mushrooms, chilli and corn in a bowl. Set the onion aside. (The vegetables can sit at room temperature for 3 to 4 hours.)

4. Warm the stock until it simmers in a large saucepan over a medium heat.

5. Melt the butter in a 30-cm (12-inch) frying pan over a high heat. Add the onion and rice and cook for 2 to 3 minutes, stirring frequently, until the rice is slightly opaque. Pour in 250 ml (8 fl oz) of the hot stock and stir the mixture often until the stock is absorbed.

6. Continue to add the hot stock, 250 ml (8 fl oz) at a time, and cook at a simmer for 20 to 30 minutes, stirring frequently, until the stock is absorbed and the rice is tender. When the rice is fully cooked, the mixture should be creamy but not soupy. At this point, add the remaining grilled vegetables and the salt.

7. Remove the risotto from the heat, add the cheese and stir until melted. Spoon risotto into warm, wide bowls, and top with feta cheese and coriander.

MARINATED BABY PAK CHOI AND SHIITAKES

SERVES: 4
PREP TIME: 15 MINUTES
MARINATING TIME: 1 TO 2 HOURS

HEAT: DIRECT MEDIUM HEAT 180° TO 230°C (350° TO 450°F)
GRILLING TIME: ABOUT 5 MINUTES
SPECIAL EQUIPMENT: PERFORATED GRILL PAN

MARINADE
5 tablespoons low-sodium soy sauce
4 tablespoons dry sherry
1 tablespoon light brown sugar
1 tablespoon dark sesame oil
4 slices peeled fresh root ginger, each 8 mm (⅛ inch) thick, crushed
2 garlic cloves, crushed
¼ teaspoon crushed red chilli flakes

4 baby pak choi, larger ones cut in half
20 large shiitake mushrooms

1. Whisk the marinade ingredients together in a bowl until the sugar has dissolved.

2. Plunge the pak choi into a bowl of water and shake to clean off the dirt nestled between the leaves. Wipe the mushrooms clean with a damp cloth or kitchen paper and then remove and discard the stalks.

3. Place the vegetables into a large, resealable plastic bag and pour in the marinade. Press the air out of the bag and seal tightly. Turn the bag to distribute the marinade and let stand at room temperature for 1 to 2 hours, turning occasionally.

4. Prepare the barbecue for direct cooking over a medium heat. Preheat a grill pan over **direct medium heat** for about 10 minutes.

5. Remove the vegetables from the bag and reserve the marinade. When the grill pan is hot, place the pak choi and mushrooms on to the pan, spreading them out in a single layer. Grill over **direct medium heat** for about 5 minutes, with the lid closed as much as possible but turning once or twice and basting occasionally with the reserved marinade, until the pak choi is crisp-tender and the shiitakes are heated through. Serve hot.

HOW TO BARBECUE PAK CHOI AND SHIITAKE MUSHROOMS

1. Plunge the baby pak choi under water to remove any dirt between the leaves.

2. Remove and discard the tough stalks from the mushrooms.

3. Cut the larger pak choi in half, keeping the root ends intact.

4. Leave the smaller pak choi whole.

5. Coat the vegetables with the marinade in a large plastic bag.

6. Grill the vegetables on a preheated grill pan, basting occasionally with the marinade.

PORTABELLO MUSHROOM SANDWICHES WITH BASIL AND BALSAMIC AÏOLI

SERVES: 6
PREP TIME: 20 MINUTES
MARINATING TIME: 15 TO 20 MINUTES

HEAT: DIRECT MEDIUM HEAT 180° TO 230°C (350° TO 450°F)
GRILLING TIME: 8 TO 12 MINUTES

AÏOLI
5 tablespoons mayonnaise
2 tablespoons balsamic vinegar
1 teaspoon sea salt
½ teaspoon very finely chopped garlic

MARINADE
175 ml (6 fl oz) extra-virgin olive oil
4 tablespoons red wine vinegar
2 tablespoons very finely chopped shallot
1 teaspoon very finely chopped garlic
1 teaspoon sea salt
½ teaspoon freshly ground black pepper

6 large portabello mushrooms, cleaned, with stalks and black
    gills removed (see photos below)
Sea salt
Freshly ground black pepper

6 hamburger buns or baps, cut in half
50 g (2 oz) basil, trimmed, rinsed and dried

1. Combine the aïoli ingredients in a small bowl. Refrigerate
until ready to assemble the sandwiches.

2. Whisk the marinade ingredients together in another small
bowl. Place the mushroom caps, gill sides down, in a large dish.
Brush the mushroom caps generously with the marinade and
turn the caps over. Spoon the rest of the marinade over the gill
side. Allow the mushrooms to marinate at room temperature for
15 to 20 minutes.

3. Prepare the barbecue for direct cooking over a medium heat.

4. Remove the mushrooms from the dish and reserve the
marinade. Lightly season the mushrooms with salt and pepper.
Brush the cooking grates clean. Grill the mushrooms, gill
sides down, over **direct medium heat** for 4 to 6 minutes, with
the lid closed as much as possible, until they begin to soften.
Brush the cap sides of the mushrooms with some of the
remaining marinade from the pan. Turn the mushrooms over
and grill them for a further 4 to 6 minutes until they are tender
when pierced with a knife.

5. Grill the buns, cut sides down, over **direct medium heat** for
about 30 seconds until lightly toasted.

6. Spread aïoli on the toasted buns and top each one with a
mushroom and some basil. Serve warm.

HOW TO BARBECUE PORTABELLO MUSHROOMS

1. Cut away the stalks and any curled edges around the rims.

2. With a spoon, gently scrape away the dark gills that might be holding dirt.

3. Use a vinaigrette to marinate and baste the mushrooms.

4. Finish grilling the mushrooms with the stalk sides facing up so that the juices are held inside the caps.

MARINATED PORTABELLO MUSHROOMS WITH ASIAGO

SERVES: 6
PREP TIME: 10 MINUTES
MARINATING TIME: 15 TO 20 MINUTES

HEAT: DIRECT MEDIUM HEAT 180° TO 230°C (350° TO 450°F)
GRILLING TIME: 8 TO 12 MINUTES

MARINADE
4 tablespoons extra-virgin olive oil
3 tablespoons balsamic vinegar
1 tablespoon soy sauce
1 teaspoon chopped rosemary, or ½ teaspoon dried crushed
    rosemary
½ teaspoon freshly ground black pepper
¼ teaspoon sea salt

6 large portabello mushrooms, each 12 to 15 cm (5 to 6 inches)
    in diameter
40 g (1½ oz) fresh breadcrumbs
1 tablespoon finely chopped flat leaf parsley
150 g (5 oz) Asiago cheese, grated
Sea salt
Freshly ground black pepper

1. Whisk the marinade ingredients together in a small bowl.

2. Wipe the mushrooms clean with a damp cloth or kitchen paper. Remove and discard the stalks. Carefully scrape out and discard the black gills from the mushroom caps with a teaspoon (see photos on opposite page). Place the mushrooms, cap sides up, on a rimmed plate and brush them with the marinade. Turn the mushrooms over and brush again with the marinade. Allow them to stand for 15 to 20 minutes at room temperature. Meanwhile, Prepare the barbecue for direct cooking over a medium heat.

3. Combine the breadcrumbs with the parsley in another small bowl.

4. Brush the cooking grates clean. Grill the mushrooms, gill sides down, over **_direct medium heat_** for 4 to 6 minutes, with the lid closed, until the mushrooms begin to soften. Brush the cap sides with some of the remaining marinade from the plate, turn them over, add one-sixth of the cheese on top of each mushroom, close the lid and cook for 4 to 6 minutes until tender when pierced with a knife. During the last minute of cooking, place the breadcrumb mixture evenly on top of each mushroom. Remove from the barbecue, add salt and pepper to taste and serve immediately.

HOW TO BARBECUE PIZZA

1. A grill pan is a convenient tool for grilling small pizza toppings such as chopped mushrooms and pepper slices. Roast the garlic in a foil packet.

2. To flatten and stretch dough easily, without it springing back, it needs to be at room temperature. If you buy refrigerated dough to save time, allow it sit on a work surface for a few hours so it will warm up and relax.

3. A bit of olive oil on your hands and your board will make the dough more pliable. Finish flattening each piece of dough on a sheet of parchment paper.

4. The parchment paper will help to hold the shape of the dough as you flip it on to the barbecue. After a minute or so of grilling, peel off the paper.

5. The oil will prevent sticking and promote even browning. When the underside is crisp and toasted, transfer the crusts to a work surface, with the grilled sides facing up.

6. Arrange the toppings on the toasted sides, return the pizzas to the barbecue and cook until the bottoms of the crusts are crisp and the cheese has melted.

PIZZA WITH MUSHROOMS, PEPPERS, GARLIC AND SMOKED MOZZARELLA

SERVES: 8
PREP TIME: 25 MINUTES
RISING TIME: 1½ TO 2 HOURS

HEAT: DIRECT MEDIUM HEAT 180° TO 230°C (350° TO 450°F)
AND DIRECT MEDIUM-HIGH HEAT ABOUT 230°C (450°F)
GRILLING TIME: 29 TO 46 MINUTES
SPECIAL EQUIPMENT: ELECTRIC STAND MIXER

DOUGH
350 ml (12 fl oz) warm water (40° to 43°C/100° to 110°F)
1 sachet fast-action dried yeast
½ teaspoon sugar
625 g (1¼ lb) strong white flour
3 tablespoons extra-virgin olive oil
2 teaspoons sea salt

4 tablespoons extra-virgin olive oil
½ teaspoon sea salt
¼ teaspoon freshly ground black pepper
10 garlic cloves, peeled
1 large red pepper, cored, deseeded and cut into
     5-mm (¼-inch) strips
250 g (8 oz) brown mushrooms, cleaned, stalks removed and
     quartered
225 g (7½ oz) smoked mozzarella cheese, grated

1. Combine the water, yeast and sugar in the bowl of an electric stand mixer. Stir briefly and allow to stand for 5 minutes, or until the top surface has a thin, frothy layer. (This indicates that the yeast is active.) Add the flour, oil and salt. Fit the mixer with the dough hook and mix on low speed for about 1 minute or until the dough begins to come together. Increase the speed to medium, and continue to mix for about 10 minutes until the dough is slightly sticky, smooth and elastic. Form the dough into a ball and place in a lightly greased bowl. Turn it over to coat all sides and tightly cover the bowl with clingfilm. Allow the dough to rise in a warm place for 1½ to 2 hours until it has doubled in size.

2. Mix 4 tablespoons oil with the salt and pepper in a large bowl. Place the garlic cloves in the middle of a small sheet of aluminium foil, about 20 cm (8 inches) square, and pour 1 table-spoon of the oil mixture over the garlic. Fold up the sides to make a sealed packet, leaving a little room for the expansion of steam.

3. Add all the peppers and mushrooms to the bowl with the remaining oil mixture. Toss to coat the vegetables evenly.

4. Prepare the barbecue for direct cooking over a medium-high heat. Preheat a perforated grill pan over ***direct medium-high heat*** for about 10 minutes. While the pan is preheating, place the packet of garlic over ***direct medium-high heat*** and cook for 15 to 20 minutes until the cloves are soft and light brown. Remove the packet from the barbecue. When the grill pan is really hot, lift the mushrooms and peppers from the bowl with tongs and spread them out in a single layer on the pan. Cook for about 6 minutes, stirring once or twice, until they are nicely browned and tender. Wearing barbecue mitts, remove the pan from the barbecue and set it down on a heatproof surface.

5. Cut the dough into 8 equal-sized pieces. Lightly brush eight, 23-cm (9-inch) squares of parchment paper on one side with oil. Using your fingers, flatten each piece of dough on a sheet of parchment paper to create 8 rounds. Each round should be about 8 mm (⅓ inch) thick and 15 to 20 cm (6 to 8 inches) in diameter. Lightly brush the tops with oil. Allow the rounds to sit at room temperature for 5 to 10 minutes.

6. Lower the temperature of the barbecue to a medium heat. Brush the cooking grates clean. Working with 4 rounds at a time, place the dough on the cooking grate with the paper sides facing up. Grill over ***direct medium heat*** for 2 to 5 minutes, with the lid closed as much as possible but rotating as needed for even cooking, until the dough is well marked and firm on the underside. Peel off and discard the parchment paper. Transfer the crusts to a work surface with the grilled sides facing up. Repeat with the other 4 rounds.

7. Spread the cheese evenly over the crusts and then arrange some garlic, mushrooms and pepper slices on top. Return the pizzas to the barbecue and cook over ***direct medium heat*** for 2 to 5 minutes, with the lid closed as much as possible but rotating the pizzas occasionally for even cooking, until the cheese has melted and the bottom of the crusts are crisp. Transfer to a chopping board and cut into wedges. Serve warm.

Go ahead and burn them. Roasting chillies is one technique where it is okay to burn the food... to a degree. Charring the peppers until black (see above, left) helps to loosen the skin so you can peel it away and enjoy the sweet flesh below (see above, right).

ROASTED PEPPER AND BACON BRUSCHETTA

SERVES: 6 AS A STARTER (MAKES 18 PIECES)
PREP TIME: 15 MINUTES

HEAT: DIRECT MEDIUM HEAT 180° TO 230°C (350° TO 450°F)
GRILLING TIME: 13 TO 17 MINUTES

3 red peppers
6 bacon rashers, cooked, drained and finely chopped
2 tablespoons extra-virgin olive oil, divided
1 tablespoon red wine vinegar
Sea salt
1 loaf Italian or French bread, cut in half lengthways
2½ tablespoons freshly grated Parmigiano-Reggiano cheese
15 g (½ oz) basil, finely chopped

1. Prepare the barbecue for direct cooking over a medium heat. Brush the cooking grates clean. Grill the peppers over *direct medium heat* for 12 to 15 minutes, with the lid closed as much as possible but turning every 3 to 5 minutes, until blackened and blistered all over. Place the peppers in a bowl and cover with clingfilm. Allow them to stand for 10 to 15 minutes. Remove the peppers from the bowl and peel away and discard the charred skins. Cut off and discard the tops and seeds, and then chop the peppers. Transfer the chopped peppers to a bowl and toss with the bacon, 2 teaspoons of the oil and the vinegar. Season to taste with salt.

2. Lightly brush or spray the cut sides of the bread with the remaining 4 teaspoons of oil and grill over *direct medium heat* for 1 to 2 minutes, until toasted. Remove from the barbecue and cut the bread on the diagonal into 5-cm (2-inch) wide pieces.

3. Just before serving, add the cheese to the pepper mixture. Spoon the mixture on the toasted pieces of bread. Sprinkle the basil on top and serve at room temperature.

HOW TO BARBECUE ONIONS

1. Cut off the root and stem ends from each onion. Peel off the papery skin.

2. Cut each onion crossways into 1-cm (½-inch) slices.

3. The layers will hold together best if they are evenly sliced.

4. When turning the slices, hold the layers closest to the centre with tongs.

ROASTED PEPPERS, GRILLED ONIONS AND FETA CHEESE SALAD

SERVES: 6
PREP TIME: 15 MINUTES

HEAT: DIRECT MEDIUM HEAT 180° TO 230°C (350° TO 450°F)
GRILLING TIME: 12 TO 15 MINUTES

VINAIGRETTE
4 tablespoons extra-virgin olive oil
2 tablespoons red wine vinegar
½ tablespoon very finely chopped garlic
½ teaspoon sea salt
¼ teaspoon freshly ground black pepper

2 red onions, cut crossways into 1-cm (½-inch) slices
Extra-virgin olive oil
2 large red peppers
350 g (12 oz) rocket, rinsed and dried
65 g (2½ oz) toasted walnuts, coarsely chopped
125 g (4 oz) feta cheese, crumbled

1. Prepare the barbecue for direct cooking over a medium heat.

2. Whisk the vinaigrette ingredients together in a small bowl until emulsified.

3. Lightly brush the onion slices with oil. Brush the cooking grates clean. Grill the onions and peppers over *direct medium heat*, with the lid closed as much as possible and turning occasionally, until the onions are tender and the skins of the peppers are evenly charred and blistered. The onions will take 8 to 12 minutes and the peppers, 12 to 15 minutes. Remove the veggies from the barbecue. Place the peppers in a bowl, cover with clingfilm, and allow them to steam for 10 to 15 minutes. When the peppers are cool enough to handle, remove and discard the charred skins, stalks and seeds and cut them into strips about 1 cm (½ inch) wide.

4. Place the peppers and onions in a bowl. Add 2 tablespoons of the vinaigrette and toss to coat.

5. Toss the rocket with the remaining dressing in a salad bowl. Top with the onions and peppers and then add the walnuts and feta cheese. Serve right away.

GRILL-ROASTED TOMATO SOUP
WITH PARMESAN CROÛTONS

SERVES: 4
PREP TIME: 30 MINUTES

HEAT: DIRECT LOW HEAT 110° TO 180°C (250° TO 350°F)
GRILLING TIME: 8 TO 10 MINUTES
SPECIAL EQUIPMENT: PERFORATED GRILL PAN

1 kg (2 lb) firm but ripe plum tomatoes
1 red onion, quartered through the root end and peeled
10 garlic cloves, peeled
15 g (½ oz) thyme sprigs
4 tablespoons extra-virgin olive oil
1 litre (1¾ pints) chicken stock
1 teaspoon sugar
1 teaspoon sea salt
½ teaspoon freshly ground black pepper
25 g (1 oz) unsalted butter, softened
8 slices French bread, each about 5 mm (¼ inch) thick
50 g (2 oz) Parmigiano-Reggiano cheese, grated
2 tablespoons roughly chopped basil

1. Prepare the barbecue for direct cooking over a low heat. Preheat a grill pan over **direct low heat** for about 10 minutes.

2. Combine the tomatoes, onion, garlic, thyme and oil in a bowl and toss to coat. Using tongs, arrange all the vegetables and herbs on the grill pan and cook over **direct low heat** for 20 to 25 minutes, with the lid closed as much as possible but turning the vegetables occasionally, until the tomato skins have wrinkled and started to brown. Transfer the tomatoes to a large saucepan. Continue to cook the onions, garlic and thyme for 5 to 10 minutes until the onions and garlic are lightly charred on all sides. Add the onions and garlic to the pan. Discard the thyme.

3. Add the chicken stock to the pan and bring to the boil. Reduce the heat and simmer for 8 to 10 minutes until the tomatoes have collapsed completely. Transfer the soup to a

blender and purée until very smooth. Pour the soup through a mesh sieve to remove all the tomato seeds and skin. Season with the sugar, salt and pepper.

4. If the barbecue has an infrared burner above the warming rack, preheat the burner on high, with the barbecue lid open. Butter one side of each slice of bread. Top each buttered side with about 1 teaspoon of cheese. Use tongs to position the bread slices on the warming rack (towards the back) just in front of the burner. Cook for about 2 minutes, with the lid open, until the cheese has melted and browned. Watch carefully so the cheese doesn't burn. Remove the croûtons from the warming rack. (If your barbecue does not have an infrared burner, toast the croûtons under a conventional grill.)

5. Just before serving, reheat the soup, if necessary, and add the basil. Ladle the soup into bowls and float the croûtons on top. Garnish with any remaining cheese. Serve warm.

HOW TO BARBECUE-ROAST TOMATOES

1. Coat the tomatoes and other vegetables with oil and spread them out on a preheated grill pan.

2. Cook over direct low heat until the tomato skins are wrinkled and browned.

3. Turn the vegetables occasionally for even caramelization.

4. Don't be afraid of deep, dark colours on the vegetables. That's where the flavour is.

PANZANELLA SKEWERS
WITH SHERRY VINAIGRETTE

SERVES: 4
PREP TIME: 15 MINUTES

HEAT: DIRECT MEDIUM HEAT 180° TO 230°C (350° TO 450°F)
GRILLING TIME: ABOUT 4 MINUTES
SPECIAL EQUIPMENT: 4 BAMBOO SKEWERS,
    SOAKED IN WATER FOR AT LEAST 30 MINUTES

VINAIGRETTE
2 tablespoons sherry vinegar
1 teaspoon Dijon mustard
½ teaspoon finely chopped garlic
6 tablespoons extra-virgin olive oil
¼ teaspoon sea salt
¼ teaspoon freshly ground black pepper

1 small loaf focaccia or Italian bread, cut into 2.5-cm (1-inch)
    cubes
12 firm but ripe cherry tomatoes
250 g (8 oz) baby rocket
2 tablespoons coarsely chopped basil leaves
2 tablespoons freshly grated Parmigiano-Reggiano cheese

1. Prepare the barbecue for direct cooking over a medium heat.

2. Whisk the vinegar, mustard, and garlic together in a small
bowl. Slowly drizzle and whisk in the oil until the vinaigrette has
emulsified. Season with the salt and pepper.

3. Combine the bread cubes and tomatoes in a large bowl with
2 tablespoons of the vinaigrette and toss to coat. Thread the
bread cubes and tomatoes alternately on the skewers.

4. Brush the cooking grates clean. Grill the skewers over **direct
medium heat** for about 4 minutes, with the lid open but turning
every minute (if the bread starts to burn, move the skewer over
indirect heat for the remaining time), until the tomato skins are
browned and the bread is lightly toasted.

5. Toss the rocket and basil in a large bowl with 2 tablespoons
of the vinaigrette. Brush the skewers with the remaining
vinaigrette. To serve, divide the salad greens evenly on to
serving plates and top with a panzanella skewer. Sprinkle with
the cheese.

HOW TO PREP VINAIGRETTE

1. Whisk the vinegar, mustard and garlic first. The mustard will
help to emulsify the oil.

2. Add the extra-virgin olive oil slowly, whisking all the time for
a smooth dressing.

HOW TO PREP SKEWERS

Cut the bread cubes just a little bigger than the tomatoes so
that the cubes will toast nicely before the tomatoes collapse.

HOW TO BARBECUE ARTICHOKE HEARTS

1. Bend back the dark outer leaves of each artichoke, breaking them just above the base. Stop when you see the pale green and yellowish leaves exposed.

2. Trim the stalk of each artichoke, leaving 1.5 cm (¾ inch) or so attached.

3. Remove the pale green and yellowish leaves above the base of each artichoke with a sharp knife.

4. Use a small spoon to scrape out the fuzzy choke from each artichoke heart.

5. Cut each artichoke heart in half lengthways through its stalk.

6. Using a vegetable peeler or paring knife, trim most of the rough edges from the artichoke hearts and trim off a thin layer of the stem to expose the softer interior.

7. After blanching the artichoke hearts in boiling water to make them tender, brush them with oil, season them with salt and grill them over direct medium heat until warmed and lightly charred on all sides.

ARTICHOKE HEARTS WITH SMOKED TOMATO AND ROASTED GARLIC AÏOLI

SERVES: 4 TO 6
PREP TIME: 35 MINUTES

HEAT: INDIRECT AND DIRECT MEDIUM HEAT 180° TO 230°C (350° TO 450°F)
GRILLING TIME: 24 TO 26 MINUTES

3 plum tomatoes, about 125 g (4 oz) each, halved, cored and deseeded
Extra-virgin olive oil
3 large garlic cloves
2 handfuls oak or hickory wood chips, soaked in water for at least 30 minutes
175 g (6 oz) mayonnaise
1½ teaspoons balsamic vinegar
1 teaspoon sea salt
¼ teaspoon freshly ground black pepper

6 large artichokes, 300 to 350 g (10 to 12 oz) each
Juice of 1 lemon

1. Prepare the barbecue for indirect and direct cooking over a medium heat.

2. Lightly brush the tomatoes with oil. Cut a sheet of aluminium foil about 20 by 30 cm (8 by 12 inches). Put the garlic cloves in the centre of the foil. Drizzle ½ teaspoon of oil over the garlic cloves and fold up the sides to make a packet.

3. Drain and add the wood chips directly on to burning coals or to the smoker box of a gas barbecue, following manufacturer's instructions. Brush the cooking grates clean. As soon as the wood begins to smoke, place the tomatoes and the packet of garlic over *indirect medium heat* and cook for about 20 minutes until the tomatoes are lightly smoked and browned in spots, and the garlic is browned along the edges.

4. Purée the tomatoes and garlic in a food processor until they are smooth. Add the mayonnaise, vinegar, ½ teaspoon of the salt and the pepper. Pour the sauce into individual serving bowls. (Cover and refrigerate if you are not planning to serve the sauce within the next hour but allow it to stand at room temperature for about 30 minutes before serving.)

5. Bring a large pot of salted water to the boil.

6. Prepare the artichokes by snapping off the dark outer leaves until you expose the yellowish leaves with pale green tips. Lay each artichoke on its side. Cut off the remaining leaves just above the base. Using a small teaspoon, scoop out the fuzzy choke. Cut the base of each artichoke in half lengthways, through the stalk, and then trim the stalk, leaving about 1.5 cm (¾ inch) attached. Trim and smooth the rough and greenish

areas around the base with a vegetable peeler or small knife. Trim a very thin strip all the way around the stalk to expose the tender part of the stalk. After each artichoke heart is trimmed, place it into a large bowl mixed with lemon juice.

7. Cook the artichokes in the boiling salted water for 10 to 12 minutes until you can pierce them easily with a knife, being careful not to over-cook them. Drain the artichokes in a colander and place them in a large bowl. While still warm, add 2 tablespoons of oil and the remaining salt. Toss gently to coat the artichokes. (The artichokes may be prepared up to this point and refrigerated for up to 4 hours. Bring to room temperature before grilling.)

8. Lift the artichoke hearts from the bowl letting any excess oil drip back into the bowl. Grill the artichokes over *direct medium heat* for 4 to 6 minutes, with the lid closed as much as possible but turning them once or twice, until warmed and lightly charred. Serve warm or at room temperature with the sauce.

HOW TO BARBECUE ASPARAGUS

1. During springtime, the peak season for asparagus, look for firm spears with smooth skins and tightly closed heads.

2. Spears of medium thickness do better on the barbecue than pencil-thin spears. They are less likely to fall through the cooking grate and they usually have fuller flavours. Both purple and green spears will be green when they are cooked.

3. Coat raw, trimmed asparagus spears with a vinaigrette. The dressing will add flavour and promote even browning on the barbecue; however, the spears should not be dripping wet when you lay them on the barbecue, which would cause flare-ups.

4. So that you don't lose spears through the cooking grate, align them so that they run perpendicular to the bars. Roll the spears over every few minutes with tongs to cook them evenly.

HOW TO BARBECUE PARMA HAM

1. While the asparagus is grilling, lay thin slices of Parma ham over direct heat and grill them until crisp, turning once or twice.

2. It will take only a minute or two for most of the fat to melt, making the meat golden brown and delicious. Let the slices cool and then break them into bits and pieces for a garnish.

ASPARAGUS AND PARMA HAM WITH LEMON VINAIGRETTE

SERVES: 4
PREP TIME: 20 MINUTES

HEAT: DIRECT MEDIUM HEAT 180° TO 230°C (350° TO 450°F)
GRILL TIME: 6 TO 8 MINUTES

VINAIGRETTE
2 tablespoons cider vinegar
1 tablespoon finely chopped shallot
2 teaspoons finely grated lemon rind
1 teaspoon Dijon mustard
4 tablespoons extra-virgin olive oil
¼ teaspoon sea salt
¼ teaspoon freshly ground black pepper

750 g (1½ lb) asparagus
½ teaspoon sea salt
4 thin slices Parma ham, about 50 g (2 oz) total

1. Prepare the barbecue for direct cooking over a medium heat.

2. Whisk the vinegar, shallot, lemon rind and mustard together in a small bowl. Slowly drizzle and whisk in the oil until the vinaigrette has emulsified. Season with the salt and pepper.

3. Remove and discard the tough bottom of each asparagus spear by grasping each end and bending it gently until it snaps at its natural point of tenderness, usually two-thirds of the way down the spear. If desired, use a vegetable peeler to peel off he outer skin from the bottom half of each spear. Spread the asparagus on a large plate. Drizzle with a few tablespoons of the vinaigrette and season evenly with the salt.

4. Brush the cooking grates clean. Grill the asparagus and the Parma ham over ***direct medium heat***, with the lid closed as much as possible but turning once or twice, until the asparagus is tender and the Parma ham is crisp. The asparagus will take 6 to 8 minutes and the Parma ham will take 1 to 2 minutes.

5. Arrange the asparagus on a platter, spoon over the vinaigrette and crumble the crisp Parma ham on top.

LEMON BROCCOLI

SERVES: 4
PREP TIME: 10 MINUTES

HEAT: DIRECT MEDIUM HEAT 180° TO 230°C (350° TO 450°F)
GRILLING TIME: 4 TO 6 MINUTES
SPECIAL EQUIPMENT: PERFORATED GRILL PAN

2½ teaspoons sea salt
500 g (1 lb) broccoli florets
2 tablespoons extra-virgin olive oil
1 tablespoon finely grated lemon rind
40 g (1½ oz) Parmigiano-Reggiano cheese, grated

1. Fill a large saucepan with water to within a few centimetres (inches) of the top. Add 2 teaspoons of the salt to the water and bring to the boil over a high heat. Add the broccoli to the boiling water and cook for 3 to 5 minutes until crisp-tender. Remove the florets from the pan and plunge them into a bowl of iced water to rapidly cool them, then remove them from the water and drain.

2. Prepare the barbecue for direct cooking over a medium heat. Brush the cooking grates clean. Preheat a grill pan over **direct medium heat** for about 10 minutes.

3. Mix the broccoli, oil, lemon rind and the remaining ½ teaspoon salt together in a large bowl.

4. Spread the broccoli on the grill pan in a single layer. Grill over **direct medium heat** for 4 to 6 minutes, with the lid closed as much as possible but turning occasionally, until the broccoli is warmed and just beginning to brown.

5. Remove the broccoli from the barbecue and sprinkle with the cheese. Serve warm.

HOW TO BARBECUE BROCCOLI

1. Cut broccoli florets into even-sized pieces before blanching them.

2. For quick browning, preheat the grill pan before laying out the florets.

3. Turn the florets occasionally with tongs or shake the grill pan wearing an insulated barbecue mitt or oven gloves.

GREEN BEANS WITH LEMON OIL

SERVES: 4
PREP TIME: 20 MINUTES
COOLING TIME: 30 MINUTES TO 1 HOUR

HEAT: DIRECT MEDIUM HEAT 180° TO 230°C (350° TO 450°F)
GRILLING TIME: 5 TO 7 MINUTES
SPECIAL EQUIPMENT: PERFORATED GRILL PAN

LEMON OIL
1 lemon
4 tablespoons extra-virgin olive oil
2 large garlic cloves, thinly sliced
¼ teaspoon crushed red chilli flakes

500 g (1 lb) fresh, skinny green beans
2 tablets (500 mg each) vitamin C
Sea salt

1. Remove wide strips of yellow rind from the lemon with a vegetable peeler. Put them in a small saucepan with the oil, garlic and chilli flakes. Cook over a low heat until the oil simmers, then allow it to simmer for about 2 minutes. Remove the pan from the heat and allow the oil cool and steep for 30 minutes to 1 hour.

2. Remove and discard the stem ends from the green beans. Pile the beans into a large bowl.

3. Remove and discard the lemon rind and garlic from the oil. Using the sharp blade and the side of a knife, chop and crush the vitamin C tablets into a powder. Add the powder and ½ teaspoon salt to the oil and mix well.

4. Prepare the barbecue for direct cooking over a medium heat. Preheat the grill pan over **direct medium heat** for about 10 minutes.

5. Pour the oil mixture over the green beans and toss the beans over and over again to make sure they are well coated.

6. Lift the green beans from the bowl with tongs and shake off any excess oil, letting it fall back into the bowl. Spread the green beans on the grill pan in a single layer. Grill over **direct medium heat** for 5 to 7 minutes, with the lid closed as much as possible but turning occasionally, until browned in spots and crisp-tender.

7. Remove the green beans from the pan. Season to taste with salt and freshly squeezed lemon juice. Serve warm.

HOW TO BARBECUE GREEN BEANS

1. To infuse olive oil with more flavour, heat it with strips of lemon rind, garlic and chilli flakes.

2. Crushed vitamin C (an antioxidant) in the oil will help to keep the beans bright green as they cook.

3. Spread the beans on a preheated grill pan so they cook quickly in direct contact with the pan.

HOW TO BARBECUE CARROTS

1. I once considered carrots too crunchy to grill, then I realized that I should just boil them first to make them tender. Now they are one of my favourite side dishes, especially when I find young carrots with their tops still attached. They are so sweet and fabulous.

2. Trim off the tops and leaves 2.5 cm (1 inch) or so above the end of each carrot. Next, peel the carrots and blanch them in boiling salted water until they are barely tender.

3. Stop the cooking by plunging the carrots in a bowl of iced water. At this point, you could drain the carrots and set them aside for several hours before grilling them.

4. When you are ready to grill, coat the carrots in a bowl with melted butter, honey, orange rind and a little balsamic vinegar.

5. Arrange the carrots more or less perpendicular to the bars of the cooking grate so that you don't lose any. Grill them over direct medium heat until they develop handsome grill stripes.

6. Finally, return the carrots to the bowl with the glaze and coat them again for extra flavour.

ORANGE-GLAZED CARROTS

SERVES: 4 TO 6
PREP TIME: 8 TO 10 MINUTES

HEAT: DIRECT MEDIUM HEAT 180° TO 230°C (350° TO 450°F)
GRILLING TIME: 4 TO 6 MINUTES

2¼ teaspoons sea salt
12 carrots, each 15 to 20 cm (6 to 8 inches) long and about
    2.5 cm (1 inch) wide at the top, peeled and trimmed
3 tablespoons unsalted butter, melted
40 g (1½ oz) runny honey or maple syrup
2 teaspoons finely grated orange rind
2 teaspoons balsamic vinegar
2 tablespoons finely chopped flat leaf parsley
Orange wedges, to serve (optional)

1. Fill a large saucepan with water to within a few centimetres (inches) of the top. Add 2 teaspoons of the salt to the water and bring to the boil over a high heat. Add the carrots to the boiling water and cook for 4 to 6 minutes until tender but still crisp. Remove the carrots from the saucepan and plunge into a bowl of iced water to cool them rapidly, then remove them from the water and drain.

2. Prepare the barbecue for direct cooking over a medium heat.

3. Combine the melted butter, honey, orange rind, vinegar and the remaining ¼ teaspoon of salt in a large bowl. Add the carrots to the bowl and toss to coat them evenly.

4. Brush the cooking grates clean. Remove the carrots from the bowl and let the excess butter mixture drip back into the bowl. Set the bowl aside. Grill the carrots over **direct medium heat** for 4 to 6 minutes, with the lid closed as much as possible but turning occasionally, until lightly caramelized. Place the carrots back into the bowl with the remaining butter mixture. Toss to coat thoroughly. Sprinkle with the parsley and serve warm with orange wedges for squeezing over, if desired.

HOW TO BARBECUE TOFU

1. 'Steaks' of tofu can be a delicious alternative to meat. Buy extra-firm tofu so that it holds together well on the barbecue.

2. To give tofu some added flavour, coat the steaks in a marinade based on lemon juice, fresh root ginger and soy sauce.

3. Grilling tofu steaks on sheets of aluminium foil avoids any risk of sticking. The heat conducted through the foil browns the surfaces nicely.

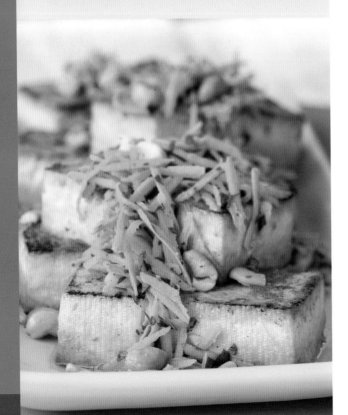

LEMON-GINGER TOFU STEAKS WITH CARROT AND CASHEW SALAD

SERVES: 4
PREP TIME: 20 MINUTES
MARINATING TIME: 3 TO 4 HOURS

HEAT: DIRECT HIGH HEAT 230° TO 290°C (450° TO 550°F)
GRILLING TIME: 6 TO 8 MINUTES

MARINADE
4 tablespoons fresh lemon juice
4 tablespoons rapeseed oil
4 tablespoons soy sauce
2 tablespoons freshly grated root ginger
2 tablespoons light brown sugar
1 teaspoon chilli-garlic sauce, such as Sriracha

2 packages (425g/14 oz each) extra-firm tofu
   (not silken-style)

SALAD
225 g (7½ oz) carrot, coarsely grated
65 g (2½ oz) cashews, roughly chopped
4 tablespoons very finely chopped spring onions, white and light green parts
2 tablespoons finely chopped fresh coriander or flat leaf parsley
2 teaspoons fresh lemon juice
1 teaspoon dark sesame oil
1 teaspoon soy sauce

1. Whisk the marinade ingredients together in a bowl. Remove the blocks of tofu from their containers, leaving the liquid behind. Cut each block lengthways into 4 slices, each about 2.5 cm (1 inch) thick. Arrange the slices in a single layer on a rimmed platter or in an ovenproof dish.

2. Pour the marinade over the tofu slices and brush the marinade on all sides. Cover with clingfilm and refrigerate for 3 to 4 hours, turning the slices over once or twice.

3. Combine the salad ingredients in a large bowl and mix well. Set aside at room temperature.

4. Prepare the barbecue for direct cooking over a high heat. Brush the cooking grates clean. Lay a large sheet of aluminium foil, about 40 by 30 cm (16 by 12 inches), directly on the cooking grate. Lift the tofu slices from the platter and arrange them in a single layer on the foil, reserving the marinade for glazing. Grill the tofu over **_direct high heat_** for 6 to 8 minutes, with the lid closed as much as possible but turning once and brushing occasionally with some of the reserved marinade, until both sides are nicely caramelized and the slices are warmed. Using a spatula or fish slice, transfer the slices of tofu to serving plates. Stack the salad on top. Serve warm or at room temperature.

VEGETABLES

When roasting, peeling and opening the chillies, be careful that you maintain enough structure in the chillies so they can hold the cheese filling.

CHILLIES RELLENOS WITH TOMATO SALSA AND GUACAMOLE

SERVES: 6
PREP TIME: 30 MINUTES

HEAT: DIRECT AND INDIRECT MEDIUM HEAT 180° TO 230°C
     (350° TO 450°F)
GRILLING TIME: 22 TO 31 MINUTES

SALSA
3 firm but ripe tomatoes, halved and cored
1 small white onion, cut crossways into 1-cm (½-inch) slices
Extra-virgin olive oil
2 tablespoons finely chopped fresh coriander leaves
1 tablespoon fresh lime juice
1 teaspoon very finely chopped serrano or jalapeño chilli
1 teaspoon sea salt

GUACAMOLE
3 large ripe Haas avocados
40 g (1½ oz) red onion, finely chopped
2 tablespoons fresh lime juice
1 teaspoon sea salt

6 large poblano chillies
100 g (3½ oz) Monterey Jack or Wensleydale cheese, grated
100 g (3½ oz) Cheddar cheese, grated
65 g (2½ oz) fresh goats' cheese, crumbled

1. Prepare the barbecue for direct and indirect cooking over a medium heat. Brush the cooking grates clean.

2. Lightly brush the tomatoes and onion slices with oil. Grill over **direct medium heat** for 6 to 8 minutes, with the lid closed as much as possible but turning once, until lightly charred all over. Remove from the barbecue, finely chop and transfer to a bowl. Stir in the remaining salsa ingredients.

3. Using a fork, coarsely mash the avocados in another bowl. Stir in the onion and lime juice, then season with the salt. Cover with clingfilm, placing the plastic directly on the surface of the guacamole to prevent it from browning, and refrigerate until about 1 hour before serving.

4. Grill the chillies over **direct medium heat** for 10 to 15 minutes, with the lid open but turning occasionally, until the skins are blackened and blistered all over. (The goal is to char the skins quickly so that you can peel them without the chillies collapsing. You will need chillies with enough structure, even when roasted, to hold the filling.) Place the chillies in a large bowl, cover with clingfilm and allow them to steam for about 10 minutes. Gently peel and discard the skin from the chillies, leaving the stems intact. Carefully cut a slit down one side of each chilli and remove and discard the seeds and veins.

5. Combine the cheeses in a bowl and mix together with a fork. Carefully stuff the mixture into the chilli cavities. Brush the chillies with olive oil.

6. Grill the stuffed chillies, seam sides up, over **indirect medium heat** for 6 to 8 minutes, with the lid closed, until the cheese has melted. Carefully remove them from the barbecue with a spatula. Serve warm with the salsa and guacamole.

HOW TO ROAST GARLIC

1. Cut off the top of a head of garlic to expose the cloves, and drizzle with some oil.

2. Wrap the head in foil and grill it over indirect heat until the cloves are soft and beginning to brown.

3. Allow the head of garlic to cool at room temperature and then squeeze out the soft, mellow-tasting garlic cloves.

HOW TO PREP AUBERGINE

1. Globe aubergines should be quite firm, with glossy, unblemished skins. Look for cylindrical shapes that feel heavy for their size.

2. A male aubergine (left) will often have fewer seeds than a female aubergine (right), making the pulp of the male sweeter and less bitter.

3. Prick the whole aubergines several times with a fork and grill them over direct high heat until the skins are charred and beginning to collapse.

4. Cut the cooled aubergines in half lengthways and scoop out the pulp for the dip, but remove and discard any clumps of seeds that could turn the dip bitter.

ROASTED AUBERGINE DIP

SERVES: 8 TO 10 AS A STARTER
PREP TIME: 10 MINUTES

HEAT: INDIRECT AND DIRECT HIGH HEAT 230° TO 290°C
  (450° TO 550°F), DIRECT MEDIUM HEAT 180° TO 230°C
  (350° TO 450°F)
GRILLING TIME: 42 TO 52 MINUTES

1 head garlic
1 teaspoon extra-virgin olive oil
2 globe aubergines, about 500 g (1 lb) total
1 tablespoon fresh lemon juice
1 teaspoon fresh oregano leaves
½ teaspoon sea salt
½ teaspoon freshly ground black pepper

BAGEL CHIPS
2 bagels
2 tablespoons extra-virgin olive oil
¼ teaspoon sea salt

1. Prepare the barbecue for indirect and direct cooking over a high heat.

2. Remove the loose, papery outer skin from the head of garlic and cut off the top to expose the cloves. Place the garlic on a large square of aluminium foil and drizzle the oil over the top of the cloves. Fold up the sides to make a sealed packet, leaving a little room for the expansion of steam. Brush the cooking grates clean. Grill over **indirect high heat** for 40 to 50 minutes, with the lid closed, until the cloves are soft.

3. Prick the aubergines several times with a fork. Grill over **direct high heat** for 15 to 20 minutes, with the lid closed as much as possible but turning occasionally, until the skins are charred and they have begun to collapse. A knife should slide in and out of the flesh without resistance.

4. Once the garlic and aubergines are cool enough to handle, squeeze out the garlic cloves into the large bowl of a food processor fitted with a metal blade. Cut the aubergines in half lengthways and, using a large spoon, scrape away the flesh from the skin. Discard the skin and any large seed pockets. Add the flesh of the aubergines to the food processor and pulse to create a thick paste. Add the lemon juice and oregano and process until the mixture is smooth. Season with the salt and pepper. Decrease the temperature of the barbecue to a medium heat.

5. Slice the bagels in half so you have two half-moons. Slice the bagel halves lengthways into 5-mm (¼-inch) thick slices.

6. Lightly brush the bagel slices with the oil. Sprinkle with salt and grill over **direct medium heat** for about 2 minutes, turning once, until the chips begin to brown and get crisp.

7. Serve the dip warm with bagel chips and fresh vegetables.

HOW TO BARBECUE SANDWICHES

1. Cut the courgettes and aubergines lengthways and evenly into 8-mm (⅓-inch) slices and grill them over direct medium heat before assembling the sandwiches.

2. Coarsely chop the fresh herbs, garlic and sun-dried tomatoes. Distribute the spread on the inside of each bread slice.

3. Brush the outside of each slice of bread with oil and grill the sandwiches until toasted on each side.

VEGETABLE SANDWICHES WITH SUN-DRIED TOMATO SPREAD

SERVES: 4
PREP TIME: 20 MINUTES

HEAT: DIRECT MEDIUM HEAT 180° TO 230°C (350° TO 450°F)
GRILLING TIME: 10 TO 14 MINUTES

SPREAD
50 g (2 oz) basil leaves
50 g (2 oz) flat leaf parsley
1 garlic clove
40 g (1½ oz) oil-packed sun-dried tomatoes, finely chopped
2 tablespoons oil from the jar of oil-packed sun-dried tomatoes
1 teaspoon finely grated lemon rind
1 teaspoon fresh lemon juice
¼ teaspoon sea salt

2 Japanese aubergines, about 500 g (1 lb) total, trimmed and cut lengthways into 8-mm (⅓-inch) slices
1–2 yellow courgettes, about 250 g (8 oz) total, trimmed and cut lengthways into 8-mm (⅓-inch) slices
Extra-virgin olive oil
½ teaspoon sea salt
¼ teaspoon freshly ground black pepper
8 slices country-style sourdough bread, each about 1 cm (½ inch) thick
4 slices provolone cheese, cut to fit the bread

1. Prepare the barbecue for direct cooking over a medium heat.

2. Finely chop the basil and parsley with the garlic. Place the herb mixture in a small bowl. Add the remaining spread ingredients and mix well to form a paste.

3. Lightly brush both sides of the aubergine and courgette slices with oil. Season with the salt and pepper. Grill the vegetable slices over ***direct medium heat*** for 8 to 10 minutes, with the lid closed as much as possible but turning once or twice, until nicely marked on both sides. The courgette will cook a little faster than the aubergine. Transfer the vegetables from the barbecue to a platter as they are done.

4. Distribute the spread on the inside of each bread slice. Arrange the cheese and grilled vegetables in layers on half of the bread slices, making sure the cheese is in the centre. Place the top slice of bread on and gently press with your hand to keep the sandwich together. Lightly brush the outsides of the bread with oil.

5. Grill over ***direct medium heat*** for 2 to 4 minutes, with the lid open but turning once, until the bread is toasted and the cheese has melted. Serve warm.

HONEY-AND-CURRY-GLAZED SQUASH

SERVES: 4 TO 6
PREP TIME: 15 MINUTES

HEAT: INDIRECT MEDIUM HEAT 180° TO 230°C
  (350° TO 450°F)
GRILLING TIME: 1 HOUR TO 1 HOUR AND 10 MINUTES

2.5 to 3 kg (5 to 6 lb) winter squashes, such as acorn and
    butternut
4 tablespoons extra-virgin olive oil
Sea salt
Freshly ground black pepper

GLAZE
50 g (2 oz) unsalted butter
75 g (3 oz) runny honey
1 tablespoon cider vinegar
2 teaspoons mild curry powder
¼ teaspoon ground chipotle chilli powder

1. Prepare the barbecue for indirect cooking over a medium
heat.

2. Wash the squashes under cold water. Cut the ends off of
each squash and then cut each squash into 4 or 6 pieces.
Using a tablespoon, scoop out and discard the seeds and pulp.
Place the squash pieces on a baking tray and brush the flesh
with the oil and season to taste with salt and pepper.

3. Brush the cooking grates clean. Grill the squash pieces, skin
sides down, over **indirect medium heat** for about 30 minutes,
with the lid closed.

4. Meanwhile, combine the glaze ingredients in a small
saucepan over a medium heat and heat for about 2 minutes,
stirring often, until the butter has melted and the glaze is
smooth. Remove the pan from the heat.

5. After the first 30 minutes of cooking, return the squash
pieces to the baking tray. Close the barbecue's lid to maintain
the heat inside. Brush the flesh with the glaze, return the
squash to the barbecue, and continue to roast over **indirect
medium heat** for 30 to 40 minutes, with the lid closed as much
as possible but glazing every 15 to 20 minutes, until the squash
pieces are soft and tender. Season with more salt, if desired.
Drizzle with the remaining glaze and serve warm.

Grill the squash pieces over indirect medium heat for about
30 minutes before glazing them. Applying a sweet glaze too
early could cause burning. During the final 30 to 40 minutes
of cooking, glaze the squash every 15 to 20 minutes, but
close the lid as quickly as possible to maintain the correct
temperature.

After roasting red and golden beetroot over indirect heat, put them in separate bowls so their colours won't run together, and cover the bowls with clingfilm to loosen their skins with steam. Wear rubber gloves to avoid staining your hands when peeling the beetroot with a paring knife.

GRILL-ROASTED BEETROOT SALAD WITH PEPITAS AND FETA

SERVES: 4
PREP TIME: 30 TO 40 MINUTES

HEAT: INDIRECT MEDIUM HEAT 180° TO 230°C
 (350° TO 450°F)
GRILLING TIME: 1 TO 1½ HOURS

4 golden or red beetroots (or a combination of both), about
 1 kg (2 lb) total
Extra-virgin olive oil

DRESSING
2 tablespoons red wine vinegar
1 teaspoon Dijon mustard
1 teaspoon runny honey
1 teaspoon ground cumin
¼ teaspoon crushed red chilli flakes
125 ml (4 fl oz) extra-virgin olive oil
½ teaspoon sea salt
¼ teaspoon freshly ground black pepper

175 g (6 oz) baby Cos lettuce leaves, whole or torn into pieces
4 tablespoons pepitas (shelled pumpkin seeds), toasted
125 g (4 oz) feta or goats' cheese, crumbled

1. Prepare the barbecue for indirect cooking over a medium heat. Brush the cooking grates clean.

2. Trim off the leafy tops and root ends from the beetroots and scrub them under cold water. Lightly brush them with oil. Grill the beetroot over **indirect medium heat** for 1 to 1½ hours, with the lid closed as much as possible but turning occasionally, until they are tender with pierced with the tip of a knife. Remove from the barbecue and place the red beetroot and golden beetroot in separate bowls. Cover the bowls with clingfilm and allow them to stand at room temperature until cool enough to handle. Cut off the ends and remove the skins. Cut the beetroots crossways into 5-mm to 1-cm (¼- to ½-inch) slices and keep the slices in their separate bowls (to keep the red beetroot from dying the golden beetroot red).

3. Whisk or pulse the vinegar, mustard, honey, cumin and chilli flakes together in a bowl or food processor. Slowly drizzle in the oil, whisking until the dressing has emulsified, then season with the salt and pepper.

4. Divide the lettuce and beetroot slices between 4 salad plates and drizzle with some dressing. Garnish each plate with pepitas and cheese. Serve warm.

FENNEL AND FONTINA

SERVES: 4 TO 6
PREP TIME: 10 MINUTES

HEAT: DIRECT MEDIUM-LOW HEAT ABOUT 180°C (350°F)
GRILLING TIME: 23 TO 28 MINUTES

3 fennel bulbs
3 tablespoons extra-virgin olive oil
1 tablespoon fresh lemon juice
½ teaspoon sea salt
⅛ teaspoon freshly ground black pepper
125 g (4 oz) fontina cheese, grated

1. Prepare the barbecue for direct cooking over a medium-low heat.

2. If the fennel stalks have the fronds attached, trim off the fronds and chop enough to make 2 tablespoons. Cut off the thick stalks above the bulbs and save the stalks for another use. Cut each fennel bulb into quarters and then remove the thick triangular-shaped core. Cut the fennel vertically into 5-mm (¼-inch) thick slices.

3. Pile the fennel off to one side of a sheet of heavy-duty aluminium foil, about 60 by 20 cm (24 by 12 inches), leaving enough foil to completely cover and envelope the fennel. Pour the oil and lemon juice over the fennel and season with the salt and pepper. Fold the foil over the fennel and seal the packet tightly so that no liquid can escape.

4. Grill the packet over ***direct medium-low heat*** for 20 to 25 minutes, with the lid closed, until the fennel is barely tender. Carefully open the packet with tongs and sprinkle the cheese over the fennel. Grill for 2 to 3 minutes, with the foil packet open, until the cheese has melted slightly. Carefully remove the packet from the barbecue and garnish with chopped fennel fronds. Serve warm.

HOW TO BARBECUE FENNEL

1. Cut off the thick stalks and the root end from each bulb, but reserve some of the fronds for garnish.

2. Cut each bulb lengthways into quarters and cut away nearly all the tough core.

3. Thinly slice the fennel, then arrange the slices on a large sheet of foil and coat them with good-quality olive oil.

4. Grill the fennel in a sealed foil packet until barely tender. Open the packet and finish cooking the fennel with grated fontina cheese. Sprinkle with the chopped fronds and serve.

Shelled pistachios and garlic are at the heart of a non-traditional but delicious pesto for coating grill-roasted potatoes.

POTATO SALAD WITH PISTACHIO PESTO

SERVES: 4 TO 6
PREP TIME: 20 MINUTES

HEAT: DIRECT MEDIUM HEAT 180° TO 230°C (350° TO 450°F)
GRILLING TIME: 10 TO 15 MINUTES
SPECIAL EQUIPMENT: PERFORATED GRILL PAN

PESTO
1 garlic clove
50 g (2 oz) basil leaves
25 g (1 oz) shelled unsalted pistachios
2½ tablespoons mayonnaise
2 teaspoons white wine vinegar
½ teaspoon sea salt
¼ teaspoon freshly ground black pepper

8 waxy potatoes, each 5 to 7.5 cm (2 to 3 inches) in diameter, about 1 kg (2 lb) total, scrubbed (do not peel)
Sea salt
2 large red or yellow (or 1 of each) peppers, cored, deseeded and chopped into 2.5- to 3.5-cm (1- to 1½-inch) pieces
2 tablespoons extra-virgin olive oil
Freshly ground black pepper
2 tablespoons torn basil leaves, optional

1. Very finely chop the garlic in a food processor. Add the basil and pistachios and pulse until they are finely chopped. Transfer the mixture to a large bowl and mix with the remaining pesto ingredients.

2. Cut each potato into eighths and put them into a large saucepan. Cover with at least 2.5 cm (1 inch) water. Add 2 teaspoons of salt to the water and bring to the boil over a high heat. Reduce the heat to a simmer and cook for 5 to 10 minutes until the potatoes are barely tender.

3. When the potatoes are barely tender, drain them in a colander and return them to the dry pan. Add the pepper pieces, oil and ½ teaspoon of salt, then toss to coat the vegetables evenly.

4. Prepare the barbecue for direct cooking over a medium heat. Preheat the grill pan over **direct medium heat** for about 10 minutes. When the pan is hot, spoon the potatoes and peppers on to the pan, spreading them out in a single layer. Grill over **direct medium heat** for 10 to 15 minutes, with the lid closed as much as possible but turning occasionally, until the potatoes are seared with golden brown marks on all sides and they are quite tender. Transfer the vegetables to the bowl with the pesto and gently toss to coat the vegetables completely. Allow the potatoes to cool for at least 5 minutes. Season to taste with salt and pepper. Garnish with basil, if desired. Serve warm or at room temperature.

COCONUT-GLAZED SWEET POTATOES

SERVES: 4 TO 6
PREP TIME: 15 MINUTES

HEAT: DIRECT MEDIUM HEAT 180° TO 230°C (350° TO 450°F)
FOR CHARCOAL BARBECUES ONLY
GRILLING TIME: ABOUT 1 HOUR
SPECIAL EQUIPMENT: 30-CM (12-INCH) CAST-IRON
    FRYING PAN

4 sweet potatoes

GLAZE
1 can (425 ml/14 fl oz) coconut milk
Finely grated rind and juice of 1 lime
2 tablespoons light brown sugar
15 g (½ oz) unsalted butter
1 jalapeño chilli, very finely chopped
½ teaspoon sea salt

30 g (1¼ oz) coconut flesh, grated

1. Wash and dry the potatoes and then wrap them individually in sheets of aluminium foil.

2. Prepare a bull's-eye fire for a medium heat (see below). When the coals are ready, place the sweet potatoes directly on the charcoal grate resting on the edge of the charcoal. Close the lid and cook for 45 to 55 minutes, turning them occasionally, until the potatoes are soft. To check for doneness, squeeze the potatoes with a pair of tongs.

3. Remove the potatoes from the barbecue and allow them to cool for about 15 minutes before unwrapping them. Slit the skins with a knife and peel off and discard the skins. Cut the flesh into 1-cm (½-inch) cubes. Set aside while you make the glaze.

4. Place a 30-cm (12-inch) cast-iron frying pan over **direct medium heat**. (You can also do this step on the hob.) Combine the glaze ingredients in the pan and bring the mixture to a simmer, stirring occasionally. Allow the mixture to simmer for 5 to 8 minutes, stirring occasionally, until reduced by half. The glaze will be slightly thick. Remove the pan from the heat and add the sweet potato cubes, gently stirring to coat with the glaze, being careful not to mash them.

5. Toast and brown the coconut for about 2 minutes in a small frying pan over a high heat.

6. Place the potatoes in a serving bowl and sprinkle the toasted coconut over the top. Serve warm.

HOW TO BARBECUE SWEET POTATOES

1. Choose cylindrical sweet potatoes of similar size and thickness so that they cook evenly.

2. Wrap them in foil and lay them against the coals, turning them occasionally.

3. Moisten and flavour the potatoes with a thick glaze based on coconut milk and brown sugar.

4. Garnish with shredded coconut that has been toasted in a frying pan.

HOW TO MAKE FLAT BREAD

1. To make sticky dough easier to handle, add a little oil to the dough and the chopping board.

2. Use a 'bench scraper' (shown here) or a large knife to cut the dough into equal-sized portions.

3. Make 12 equal-sized balls and use your hands to press and stretch each one into whatever shape you like, as long as they are about 8 mm (⅓ inch) thick.

4. Stack the flattened pieces of dough between sheets of parchment paper. Make sure every piece of dough has a coating of oil on each side to prevent it from sticking on the barbecue.

GRILLED FLAT BREAD WITH THREE TOPPINGS

SERVES: 4
PREP TIME: 15 MINUTES
RISING TIME: 1½ TO 2 HOURS

HEAT: DIRECT MEDIUM HEAT 180° TO 230°C (350° TO 450°F)
GRILLING TIME: ABOUT 6 MINUTES FOR EACH BATCH
SPECIAL EQUIPMENT: ELECTRIC STAND MIXER

DOUGH
350 ml (12 fl oz) warm water (40° to 43°C/100° to 110°F)
1 sachet fast-action dried yeast
½ teaspoon sugar
625 g (1¼ lb) strong white flour
3 tablespoons extra-virgin olive oil
2 teaspoons sea salt

1. Combine the water, yeast and sugar in the bowl of an electric stand mixer. Stir briefly and allow to stand for 5 minutes, or until the top surface has a thin, frothy layer. (This indicates that the yeast is active.) Add the flour, oil and salt. Fit the mixer with the dough hook and mix on low speed for about 1 minute or until the dough begins to come together. Increase the speed to medium. Continue to mix for about 10 minutes until the dough is slightly sticky, smooth and elastic. Form the dough into a ball and place in a lightly greased bowl. Turn it over to coat all sides and tightly cover the bowl with clingfilm. Allow the dough to rise in a warm place for 1½ to 2 hours, until it has doubled in size.

2. Prepare the barbecue for direct cooking over a medium heat.

3. Turn the dough out on to a lightly greased surface and cut it into 12 equal-sized portions, 50 to 75 g (2 to 3 oz) each. Using your fingers and the palms of your hands (oil them, too), stretch the dough to a length of about 20 cm (8 inches). The first stretch will probably shrink back, but continue to pull and stretch using gentle pressure until you achieve the proper length. Add more oil to the surface, as needed, to keep the dough moist and pliable. Stack the pieces of dough between sheets of parchment paper.

4. Brush the cooking grates clean. Carefully lay the pieces of dough, a few at a time, over **direct medium heat**. Within 1 to 2 minutes the undersides of the dough should crisp, darken and harden, and the tops will puff slightly. Turn them over and continue to cook for about 6 minutes total, turning over every minute, until both sides are dark brown. If desired, keep warm over indirect heat. Serve warm or at room temperature with the topping(s) of your choice.

WHITE BEAN PURÉE WITH ROASTED GARLIC

MAKES: 1½ TO 2 CUPS
PREP TIME: 10 MINUTES

HEAT: INDIRECT MEDIUM HEAT 180° TO 230°C
(350° TO 450°F)
GRILLING TIME: 45 MINUTES TO 1 HOUR

1 small head garlic
2 tablespoons plus 1 teaspoon extra-virgin olive oil
1 can (425 g/14 oz) cannellini beans, rinsed and drained
1 teaspoon finely grated lemon rind
2 tablespoons fresh lemon juice
1 teaspoon sea salt
¼ teaspoon freshly ground black pepper
15 g (½ oz) flat leaf parsley leaves
2–3 small fresh sage leaves

1. Prepare the barbecue for indirect cooking over a medium heat.

2. Remove the loose, papery outer skin from a head of garlic and cut off the top to expose the cloves. Place the garlic on a large square of aluminium foil and drizzle 1 teaspoon of the oil over the top of the cloves. Fold up the sides to make a sealed packet, leaving a little room for the expansion of steam. Grill over **indirect medium heat** for 45 minutes to 1 hour, with the lid closed, until the cloves are soft.

3. Squeeze the garlic into the bowl of a food processor, being careful not to add any of the papery skin, then add the beans, the remaining 2 tablespoons of oil, the lemon rind, lemon juice, salt and pepper and purée. Add the parsley and sage and process to give the purée a consistency that resembles the texture of hummus. If necessary, add additional oil to create a smoother consistency.

TOMATO TAPENADE

MAKES: 1 CUP
PREP TIME: 10 MINUTES

75 g (3 oz) stoned kalamata olives, drained
75 g (3 oz) oil-packed, sun-dried tomatoes, drained
1 small garlic clove or several roasted garlic cloves
3–4 tablespoons extra-virgin olive oil
15 g (½ oz) basil leaves
2 tablespoons capers, drained
2 teaspoons balsamic vinegar
¼ teaspoon freshly ground black pepper

1. Pulse the olives, tomatoes and garlic in a food processor several times to coarsely chop them. Add in 3 tablespoons of the oil and the rest of the ingredients. Continue to purée until the mixture is well combined. Add the remaining tablespoon of oil if the tapenade seems too chunky.

BLUE CHEESE-WALNUT SPREAD

MAKES: 1 CUP
PREP TIME: 10 MINUTES

125 g (4 oz) blue cheese, crumbled
50 g (2 oz) unsalted butter, softened
65 g (2½ oz) walnuts, lightly toasted and coarsely chopped
40 g (1½ oz) very finely chopped shallot
1 tablespoon fresh lemon juice
¼ teaspoon freshly ground black pepper
Finely chopped flat leaf parsley

1. Mix the blue cheese and butter in a blender or using a fork to form a semi-smooth spread. It's okay if there are some chunks of blue cheese. Fold in the remaining ingredients, including parsley to taste.

FRUIT

TECHNIQUES

RECIPES

HOW TO BARBECUE PINEAPPLE UPSIDE-DOWN CAKE

1. Trim about an 2.5 cm (1 inch) from both the top and bottom of a ripe pineapple.

2. Stand the pineapple upright and rotate it as you cut off the tough skin.

3. Go back around the pineapple to trim off the dark 'eyes'.

4. Cut the pineapple crossways into 1-cm (½-inch) slices.

5. Use a paring knife to cut round the core of each slice (on both sides), then remove it.

6. Brush the slices with butter and grill them over a direct medium heat.

7. Combine brown sugar, cream and cinnamon in a 30-cm (12-inch) cast-iron frying pan.

8. Melt the brown sugar mixture over direct medium heat.

9. When the mixture bubbles around the outer edge, remove the pan from the heat.

10. Very carefully arrange cut pineapple slices in the hot mixture and pour the cake mixture on top.

11. Spread the mixture evenly to the edge of the frying pan.

12. Cook over indirect heat until a skewer inserted in the centre comes out clean. Invert the cake onto a large platter and allow to cool.

PINEAPPLE UPSIDE-DOWN CAKE

SERVES: 6 TO 8
PREP TIME: 30 MINUTES

HEAT: DIRECT AND INDIRECT MEDIUM HEAT 180° TO 230°C
(350° TO 450°F) FOR GAS BARBECUES ONLY
GRILLING TIME: 46 TO 58 MINUTES
SPECIAL EQUIPMENT: 12-INCH CAST-IRON FRYING PAN

TOPPING
6 rings fresh (not canned) pineapple, each 1 cm (½ inch) thick,
    peeled and cored
25 g (1 oz) unsalted butter, melted
100 g (3½ oz) dark brown sugar
4 tablespoons double cream
½ teaspoon ground cinnamon

CAKE MIXTURE
150 g (5 oz) plain white flour
1 teaspoon baking powder
½ teaspoon sea salt
¼ teaspoon bicarbonate of soda
150 ml (5 fl oz) buttermilk
2 eggs
1 teaspoon vanilla extract
125 g (4 oz) unsalted butter, softened
150 g (5 oz) sugar

1. Prepare the barbecue for direct and indirect cooking over a
medium heat. Brush the cooking grates clean.

2. Brush the pineapple rings with the melted butter. Grill them
over ***direct medium heat*** for 4 to 6 minutes, with the lid open
and turning once, until nicely marked. Remove from the
barbecue and allow them to cool. Leave one pineapple
ring whole and cut the others in half.

3. Combine the brown sugar, cream, cinnamon and any melted
butter remaining from brushing the pineapple slices in a 30-cm
(12-inch) cast-iron frying pan over ***direct medium heat***. Cook
for about 2 minutes until the sugar has melted and the liquid
has started to bubble round the outer edge. Remove the pan
from the heat and place on a roasting tray. Place the whole
pineapple ring in the centre of the pan, then arrange the
pineapple halves around it. Set aside.

4. Mix the flour, baking powder, salt and bicarbonate of soda
together in a large bowl. Whisk the buttermilk, eggs and vanilla
in a separate bowl.

5. Cream the butter and sugar with an electric mixer on
medium-high speed for 2 to 4 minutes until light and fluffy. With
the mixer on low, add the buttermilk mixture and then gradually
add the flour mixture. Blend until smooth, scraping down the
side as necessary. Using a rubber spatula, spread the mixture
evenly over the pineapple slices in the pan.

6. Bake the cake over ***indirect medium heat*** for 40 to 50 minutes,
keeping the temperature of the barbecue as close to 180°C
(350°F) as possible, with the lid closed, until the top is golden
brown and a skewer inserted into the centre comes out clean.
Wearing insulated barbecue mitts or oven gloves, remove the
cake from the barbecue and allow it to cool at room temperature
for about 10 minutes.

7. Before removing the cake from the pan, run a palette knife
around the edge to loosen it. Place a serving platter, large enough
to hold the cake, over the top of the pan. Wearing mitts, carefully
invert both the pan and platter, and then slowly remove the pan.
Replace any pineapple that has stuck to the bottom of the pan.
Let the cake cool briefly before slicing into wedges and serving. It
is best served warm or at room temperature the day it is made.

HOW TO MAKE CRÈME FRAÎCHE

1. After 8 hours at room temperature, a bit of buttermilk turns double cream into thick crème fraîche.

2. After 24 hours, the same crème fraîche is even thicker and more delicious.

HOW TO BARBECUE APPLES

1. Apple slices coated with butter quickly turn brown and tender on the barbecue.

2. Toss them with caramel sauce before assembling the dessert.

APPLE CARAMEL ON PUFF PASTRY

SERVES: 4
PREP TIME: 20 MINUTES

HEAT: DIRECT MEDIUM HEAT 180° TO 230°C (350° TO 450°F)
GRILLING TIME: 8 TO 10 MINUTES
SPECIAL EQUIPMENT: PERFORATED GRILL PAN

1 sheet frozen puff pastry, about 23 cm (9 inches) square, thawed

SAUCE
75 g (3 oz) light brown sugar
125 ml (4 fl oz) double cream
50 g (2 oz) unsalted butter

4 Granny Smith apples, peeled, cored and cut into 1-cm (½-inch) thick wedges
50 g (2 oz) unsalted butter, melted
Coarse sea salt, optional
4 tablespoons crème fraîche (recipe follows) or whipped cream

1. Cut 4 rounds from the pastry sheet using a 10-cm (4-inch) biscuit cutter. Prick each pastry round about 12 times with a fork to prevent the dough from rising too much in the oven. Following packet instructions, bake the pastry rounds on a baking sheet until golden brown. Transfer to a wire rack to cool.

2. Combine the sauce ingredients in a small saucepan over a medium heat and cook for 4 to 5 minutes, stirring constantly until the sugar has dissolved and the butter has melted. Remove the pan from the heat and set aside.

3. Toss the apple slices with the melted butter in a large bowl to coat well.

4. Prepare the barbecue for direct cooking over a medium heat. Preheat a perforated grill pan over **direct medium heat** for about 10 minutes. Add the apple slices to the pan and grill them for 8 to 10 minutes, with the lid closed as much as possible but turning once or twice, until they are well browned

and tender. Transfer the apple slices to a bowl. Reheat the sauce over a low heat, if necessary, and spoon some of the sauce over the apple slices, gently tossing to coat.

5. To assemble, place each pastry round on a dessert plate. Arrange the apple slices on top of the pastry rounds. Spoon the remaining sauce over the apples, allowing it to run down on to the plates. Sprinkle with a little coarse sea salt, if desired. Finish with a dollop of crème fraîche or whipped cream.

CRÈME FRAÎCHE
MAKES: 275 ML (9 FL OZ)
PREP TIME: 2 MINUTES
STANDING TIME: 8 TO 24 HOURS

250 ml (8 fl oz) double cream
2 tablespoons buttermilk

1. Combine the cream and buttermilk in a small bowl. Cover and allow to stand at room temperature for 8 to 24 hours. It can be kept in the refrigerator for up to 10 days.

GINGERBREAD
WITH GRILLED APRICOTS

SERVES: 12
PREP TIME: 30 MINUTES

HEAT: INDIRECT AND DIRECT MEDIUM HEAT 180° TO 230°C
    (350° TO 450°F) FOR GAS BARBECUES ONLY
GRILLING TIME: 39 TO 41 MINUTES
SPECIAL EQUIPMENT: 23- OR 25-CM (9- OR 10-INCH)
    CAST-IRON FRYING PAN

200 g (7 oz) plain white flour
1 teaspoon ground ginger
¾ teaspoon ground cinnamon
¾ teaspoon bicarbonate of soda
¾ teaspoon sea salt
125 g (4 oz) unsalted butter, softened, plus more for the pan
100 g (3½ oz) sugar
1 egg, at room temperature
175 g (6 oz) unsulphured light molasses
125 ml (4 fl oz) hot water
3 tablespoons chopped crystallized ginger

12 firm but ripe apricots, cut in half lengthways and stoned
40 g (1½ oz) unsalted butter, melted
40 g (1½ oz) sugar
1 tablespoon dark rum, optional

12 scoops vanilla ice cream

1. Combine the flour, ginger, cinnamon, bicarbonate of soda and salt in a small bowl. In a separate bowl, beat the butter and the sugar with an electric mixer on high speed for about 3 minutes until the mixture is light and fluffy. Beat in the egg and then the molasses. With the mixer on low speed, gradually add in the flour mixture, scraping down the side of the bowl with a rubber spatula. Add the water and mix until smooth. Stir in the ginger. Lightly butter the inside of a 23- or 25-cm (9- or 10-inch) cast-iron frying pan. Evenly spread the mixture in the pan.

2. Prepare the barbecue for indirect cooking over a medium heat. Brush the cooking grates clean.

3. Grill the gingerbread over **indirect medium heat** for about 35 minutes, with the lid closed, until a cocktail stick inserted in the centre comes out clean. Keep the barbecue's temperature as close to 180°C (350°F) as possible. Wearing insulated barbecue mitts or oven gloves, carefully remove the pan from the barbecue.

4. Gently toss the apricots with the melted butter, sugar and rum in a large bowl. Lift the apricots from the butter mixture, letting the excess butter fall back into the bowl. Grill the apricots, cut sides down, over **direct medium heat** for 4 to 6 minutes, with the lid closed as much as possible but turning and brushing the apricots with the butter mixture once, until heated through. Cooking times will vary depending on the ripeness of the apricots.

5. Cut the gingerbread into wedges and serve warm with the apricots. Spoon any remaining butter mixture over the top and serve with ice cream.

HOW TO BARBECUE GINGERBREAD AND APRICOTS

1. Cook gingerbread over indirect medium heat until a cocktail stick comes out clean.

2. Cut each apricot in half and remove the stones.

3. Toss the apricots in a bowl with sugar and melted butter.

4. Grill the apricots, cut sides down first, over direct medium heat, then turn over.

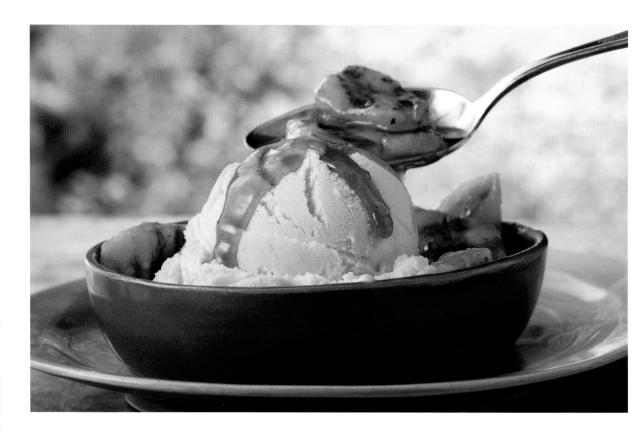

BANANAS FOSTER

SERVES: 6 TO 8
PREP TIME: 10 MINUTES

HEAT: DIRECT MEDIUM HEAT 180° TO 230°C (350° TO 450°F)
GRILLING TIME: 2 TO 3 MINUTES

4 firm but ripe bananas
25 g (1 oz) unsalted butter, melted

SAUCE
125 g (4 oz) unsalted butter
100 g (3½ oz) dark brown sugar
¼ teaspoon ground cinnamon
⅛ teaspoon ground nutmeg
125 ml (4 fl oz) dark rum
4 tablespoons banana liqueur

Vanilla ice cream

1. Prepare the barbecue for direct cooking over a medium heat.

2. Cut each banana in half lengthways and leave the skins attached (they will help the bananas hold their shape on the barbecue). Brush the cut sides with the melted butter.

Grill banana halves in their skins to hold the fruit together. Peel and cut the fruit before adding it to the rum sauce.

3. Brush the cooking grates clean. Grill the bananas over **direct medium heat** for 2 to 3 minutes, with the lid open and without turning, until warmed and well marked but not too soft. Remove from the barbecue. Peel the banana halves, cut them into quarters and set aside.

4. To make the sauce, melt the butter in a large frying pan over a medium-high heat. Add the brown sugar, cinnamon and nutmeg, and cook for about 2 minutes, stirring constantly, until it bubbles. Stir in the rum and banana liqueur. Allow the liquid to warm for a few seconds and then carefully ignite the rum with a long match or multi-purpose lighter, then allow the flames to die down. Add the banana pieces and cook over a medium heat for 2 to 3 minutes, or until the bananas curl slightly. Spoon the banana mixture over vanilla ice cream and serve immediately.

GRILLED BANANA S'MORES

SERVES: 8
PREP TIME: 15 MINUTES

HEAT: INDIRECT AND DIRECT MEDIUM HEAT
  ABOUT 200°C (400°F)
GRILLING TIME: 15 TO 21 MINUTES
SPECIAL EQUIPMENT: 20- BY 20-CM (8- BY 8-INCH) BAKING
  TIN SUITABLE FOR THE BARBECUE

CRUST
75 g (3 oz) digestive biscuits, finely crumbled
50 g (2 oz) unsalted butter, melted
1 small egg yolk

15 g (½ oz) unsalted butter, melted
1 teaspoon brown sugar
2 firm but ripe bananas
400 g (14 oz) mini marshmallows
75 g (3 oz) chocolate chips

1. Prepare the barbecue for indirect and direct cooking over a medium heat.

2. Combine the crust ingredients in a a large bowl and mix well. Firmly and evenly press the mixture into the bottom of a 20- by 20-cm (8- by 8-inch) baking tin. Grill the crust over *indirect medium heat* for 6 to 8 minutes, with the lid closed as much as possible, until firm. Remove the crust from the barbecue and set aside to cool for about 10 minutes. This will allow the crust to set.

3. Meanwhile, combine the butter and brown sugar in a small bowl. Cut each banana in half lengthways and leave the skins attached (they will help the bananas hold their shape on the barbecue). Liberally brush the cut sides of the bananas with the butter mixture.

4. Grill the bananas, cut sides down, over *direct medium heat* for 2 to 4 minutes, with the lid open and without turning, until they start to soften. Remove the bananas from the barbecue and allow them to cool briefly, then score the bananas into bite-sized pieces.

5. Fill the pan with half of the marshmallows, making sure they cover the bottom of the crust evenly. Next, scoop out and distribute the banana pieces, followed by the remaining marshmallows.

6. Grill the pie over *indirect medium heat* for 5 to 7 minutes, with the lid closed, keeping the temperature of the barbecue as close to 200°C (400°F) as possible, until the marshmallows have puffed up and started to brown. At this point carefully sprinkle the chocolate chips over the top and continue cooking for about 2 minutes until the chips appear glossy and melted. Remove the pie from the barbecue and allow to cool for 5 minutes. Spoon into small serving bowls and serve warm.

HOW TO BARBECUE BANANA S'MORES

1. Pour the crumb mixture into a pan, level it out and press it into the corners with a spatula.

2. Cook the crust until firm. Grill the buttered bananas in their skins so they hold their shapes.

3. Cut the bananas into bite-sized pieces and layer them in the pan between the marshmallows.

4. During the last couple minutes, sprinkle chocolate chips on top so they melt into the sweet, gooey marshmallows.

HOW TO PREP PANNA COTTA

1. Sprinkle gelatine over cold water to soften it.

2. Grease the ramekins to help the panna cotta slide out later.

3. Fill the ramekins and chill the panna cottas for at least 8 hours.

4. Very gently separate the chilled dessert from each ramekin with your thumb.

LEMON-BUTTERMILK PANNA COTTA WITH GRILLED FIGS

SERVES: 6
PREP TIME: 20 MINUTES
CHILLING TIME: AT LEAST 8 HOURS

HEAT: DIRECT MEDIUM HEAT 180° TO 230°C (350° TO 450°F)
GRILLING TIME: 4 MINUTES
SPECIAL EQUIPMENT: SIX 175-G (6-OZ) RAMEKINS OR
    CUSTARD CUPS

PANNA COTTA
2½ teaspoons (1 sachet) gelatine
4 tablespoons cold water
250 ml (8 fl oz) double cream
100 g (3½ oz) sugar
500 ml (17 fl oz) low-fat buttermilk, well shaken
½ teaspoon vanilla extract
1 tablespoon finely grated lemon rind

Sunflower or other vegetable oil

9 ripe figs, about 40 g (1½ oz) each, stalks removed and
    cut in half lengthways
1 tablespoon runny honey
1 bunch of mint, to decorate, optional

1. Sprinkle the gelatine over the water in a small bowl and allow to stand for about 5 minutes until the gelatine softens.

2. Bring the cream and sugar to a simmer in a saucepan over a medium-low heat, stirring to dissolve the sugar. Once the mixture is simmering, remove the pan from the heat and add the softened gelatine, stirring constantly for about 2 minutes until the gelatine has dissolved. Stir in the buttermilk and vanilla. Strain the mixture through a fine sieve into a large glass measuring cup or pitcher, and then stir in the lemon rind.

3. Use a wad of kitchen paper to completely grease the insides of 6 ramekins. Pour equal amounts of the mixture, about 150 ml (5 fl oz), into each ramekin. Place the ramekins on a roasting tray and loosely cover with clingfilm. Refrigerate the panna cottas for at least 8 hours, or up to 1 day, until chilled and set.

4. Prepare the barbecue for direct cooking over a medium heat. Lightly brush the cut sides of the figs with oil. Brush the cooking grates clean. Grill the figs over **direct medium heat** for about 4 minutes, with the lid closed as much as possible but turning once after 3 minutes, until well marked and heated through.

5. To remove the panna cotta from the ramekin, use your thumb to gently press each pudding round its circumference to pull it away from the sides of the ramekin. You may need to go around a couple of times before it totally releases. This works better than running a knife around the inside of each pudding, which could cut into the pudding. Place a dessert plate on top of a ramekin, and invert the plate and ramekin. Shake firmly, and let the pudding fall on to the plate. Repeat with the remaining ramekins.

6. For each serving, arrange 3 warm fig halves alongside the panna cotta and drizzle a little honey on the plate. Decorate with mint leaves, if desired.

Arrange ripe strawberries snugly in a pan and cook them over direct heat so that their juices bubble and thicken with butter, sugar, vanilla and orange liqueur.

FIRE-ROASTED STRAWBERRIES

SERVES: 6 TO 8
PREP TIME: 10 MINUTES

HEAT: DIRECT HIGH HEAT 230° TO 290°C (450° TO 550°F)
    FOR GAS BARBECUES ONLY
GRILLING TIME: 8 TO 12 MINUTES
SPECIAL EQUIPMENT: 20- BY 20-CM (8- BY 8-INCH) BAKING
    TIN SUITABLE FOR THE BARBECUE

20 to 24 fresh large strawberries, washed and blotted dry
4 tablespoons sugar
½ teaspoon vanilla extract
4 tablespoons orange-flavoured liqueur, or 2 tablespoons water
    and 1 tablespoon lemon juice
15 g (½ oz) unsalted butter, softened
Vanilla ice cream

1. Hull and trim the stalk end of the strawberries so that they are flat. Combine the berries, sugar, vanilla and liqueur in a bowl and toss to coat.

2. Use the softened butter to generously coat the base and sides of an 10- by 10-cm (8- by 8-inch) ovenproof baking tin or disposable aluminium tin. The tin should be just large enough to hold the berries in a single layer with their sides almost touching (this allows the berries to gently support one another as they begin to soften). Prepare the barbecue for direct cooking over a high heat.

3. Remove the berries from the bowl and line them up so that they fit snuggly, pointing up, in the prepared tin. Pour the contents from the bowl over the berries and cook over **direct high heat** for 8 to 12 minutes, with the lid closed, until they're bubbling and have begun to slump. Cooking times will vary depending on the variety, size and ripeness of the strawberries. Watch closely to catch them before they collapse.

4. Spoon the pan juices over the berries to moisten them, allow them to cool for 5 minutes and then carefully cut them into quarters or leave whole. Ladle the berries and their juices over ice cream.

The woodsy smoke of charcoal doesn't belong in fruit desserts like this one. Grill them over gas instead.

HOW TO MAKE SHORTCAKES

1. Mix the butter with the dry ingredients using the back of a fork to create a crumbly mixture. Leave some pea-sized clumps of butter for flaky shortcakes.

2. Add the cream and gently stir the mixture just until it comes together, but don't toughen the dough by overworking it.

3. Turn the dough out on to a lightly floured work surface and pat it to a thickness of about 2 cm (¾ inch).

4. Use a floured biscuit cutter to stamp out smooth rounds.

5. Gently gather the scraps into another single strip of dough.

6. Cut a couple more rounds from the strip.

HOW TO BARBECUE PEACHES

1. Fill the centres of the peach halves with brown sugar and grill until the sugar has melted and the peaches are tender.

2. Remove the peaches with a fish slice or spatula. Peel and discard the charred skins and chop the peaches, then serve them with split shortcakes and whipped cream.

PEACH SHORTCAKES

SERVES: 8
PREP TIME: 20 MINUTES

HEAT: DIRECT MEDIUM HEAT 180° TO 230°C
   (350° TO 450°F) FOR GAS BARBECUES ONLY
BAKING AND GRILLING TIME: 23 TO 30 MINUTES

300 g (10 oz) plain white flour, plus more for dusting
5 tablespoons sugar
1 tablespoon baking powder
½ teaspoons sea salt
125 g (4 oz) unsalted butter, cold, cut into small pieces
125 ml (4 fl oz) single cream, cold
15 g (½ oz) unsalted butter, melted

250 ml (8 fl oz) double cream
1 teaspoon vanilla extract
2 tablespoons icing sugar
4 large firm but ripe peaches, cut in half lengthways, stoned
40 g (1½ oz) light brown sugar
8 fresh mint sprigs, to decorate, optional

1. Preheat oven to 200°C (400°F).

2. Combine the flour, sugar, baking powder and salt in a bowl and blend well. Add the butter and mix with a fork or a pastry blender just until the mixture resembles coarse breadcrumbs. Add the cream and gently stir it in (the mixture will be crumbly), then use your hands to mix the dough quickly and gently in the bowl just until it comes together. Turn the dough out on to a lightly floured work surface. Lightly dust your hands with flour and gently pat out the dough to about 2 cm (¾ inch) thick. Dip a 6- to 7-cm (2½- to 3- inch) round biscuit cutter in flour and stamp out rounds of dough. Gather scraps of dough and pat out, using a light touch so you don't over-work the dough; cut to make a total of 8 shortcakes. Place the shortcakes about 5 cm (2 inches) apart on a baking sheet lined with parchment paper. Brush the tops with the melted butter. Bake the shortcakes for 15 to 20 minutes. Set aside to cool.

3. Combine the cream, vanilla and icing sugar in a large bowl and beat just to stiff peaks; do not over-beat. Cover and refrigerate until serving.

4. Prepare the barbecue for direct cooking over a medium heat. Brush the cooking grates clean. Sprinkle the cut sides of the peach halves with the brown sugar. Grill the peach halves, cut sides up, over **_direct medium heat_** for 8 to 10 minutes, with the lid closed, until the sugar has melted and the peaches are softened. Carefully remove from the barbecue and pour the melted brown sugar from the peaches into a medium bowl.

5. Pull the charred skin off the peaches and discard. Cut the peaches into bite-sized pieces and add them to the bowl with the melted brown sugar. Gently toss to coat. Split each short-cake horizontally and top each bottom half with equal portions of the peaches and whipped cream. Add the shortcake tops and decorate with mint sprigs, if desired.

PEAR AND PARMA HAM SALAD WITH CHAMPAGNE VINAIGRETTE

SERVES: 4
PREP TIME: 20 MINUTES

HEAT: DIRECT MEDIUM HEAT 180° TO 230°C (350° TO 450°F)
GRILLING TIME: 4 TO 6 MINUTES

VINAIGRETTE
4 tablespoons champagne or white wine vinegar
2 tablespoons very finely chopped shallot
1 teaspoon Dijon mustard
½ teaspoon sugar
¼ teaspoon sea salt
¼ teaspoon freshly ground black pepper
4 tablespoons extra-virgin olive oil
2 tablespoons toasted hazelnut oil or olive oil

8 paper-thin slices Parma ham
2 firm but ripe Bartlett pears, quartered and cored
500 g (1 lb) rocket or mesclun greens
50 g (2 oz) manchego or Parmigiano-Reggiano cheese
100 g (3½ oz) skinned hazelnuts, toasted and coarsely
    chopped
Sea salt
Freshly ground black pepper

1. Whisk the vinegar, shallot, mustard, sugar, salt and pepper together in a small bowl. Gradually drizzle in both oils, whisking constantly, until emulsified. Taste, and if the vinaigrette is too acidic, add 1 tablespoon or so of water.

2. Prepare the barbecue for direct cooking over a medium heat. Brush the cooking grates clean.

3. Wrap a slice of Parma ham around each pear wedge, pressing the loose ends of the ham down so the meat stays together. Lightly brush the outside of the wrapped pears with some vinaigrette and grill them over **direct medium heat** for 4 to 6 minutes, with the barbecue lid open and turning as necessary, until the ham is slightly crisp and golden brown and the pears are warmed through.

4. Whisk the vinaigrette again to emulsify the ingredients. Toss the rocket with enough vinaigrette to lightly coat the leaves (you may not need all the vinaigrette) and divide among 4 salad plates. Top each salad with 2 warm pear wedges and drizzle with some additional vinaigrette. Shave wide ribbons of cheese over each salad with a vegetable peeler, then sprinkle with the hazelnuts. Season to taste with salt and pepper. Serve immediately.

HOW TO PREP PEAR AND PARMA HAM

1. Quarter each pear lengthways.

2. Trim away the core and seeds.

3. Cut the Parma ham into strips for wrapping round the quarters.

4. Overlap and press each strip of ham on itself so that it stays in place during cooking.

FRUIT

276

HOW TO WRAP BRIE IN VINE LEAVES

1. Overlap rinsed and dried vine leaves, vein-side up, and place the cheese in the centre.

2. Pull the edges over the cheese, overlapping them on top.

3. Create an X with 2 long pieces of butcher's string and put the cheese bundle on top.

4. Wrap the string around the cheese bundle a couple of times, knotting in the centre each time.

VINE LEAF-WRAPPED BRIE WITH GRAPE SALSA

SERVES: 4 TO 6 AS A STARTER
PREP TIME: 15 MINUTES

HEAT: DIRECT MEDIUM HEAT 180° TO 230°C (350° TO 450°F)
GRILLING TIME: 4 TO 5 MINUTES
SPECIAL EQUIPMENT: BUTCHER'S STRING

SALSA
1 tablespoon balsamic vinegar
½ teaspoon sugar
150 g (5 oz) seedless red and/or purple grapes, coarsely chopped
1 tablespoon chopped mint

6 large vine leaves
1 wheel triple-cream Brie cheese, about 250 g (8 oz)
1 baguette, about 250 g (8 oz), cut diagonally into 1-cm (½-inch) slices
1 tablespoon grapeseed oil or olive oil

1. Combine the vinegar and sugar in a small sauté pan over a medium heat. Add the grapes and cook for about 2 minutes, stirring occasionally, to soften them. Transfer them to a small bowl and cover to keep warm. Add the mint just before serving.

2. Prepare the barbecue for direct cooking over a medium heat.

3. Unroll and rinse the vine leaves. Spread out the leaves on a work surface and pat dry with kitchen paper. Cut off and discard the tough stalks. Overlap 4 vine leaves, vein-side up, into a 23- or 25-cm (11- or 12-inch) circle. Put another leaf in the centre, and then put the cheese on top. Cover the cheese with another vine leaf. Wrap the leaves around the cheese, overlapping them to prevent the cheese from ultimately leaking out. Knot together two 90-cm (3-feet) pieces of butcher's string in the centre. Lay on a work surface in the shape of an 'X'. Set the cheese bundle on top. Bring the string to the top and tie snugly. Wrap the string round the cheese 1 or 2 more times like spokes on a wheel, knotting snugly in the centre each time. Tuck in any loose leaf edges. Trim the ends of the string.

4. Lightly brush the cheese bundle and bread slices all over with oil. Brush the cooking grates clean. Grill the cheese over **direct medium heat** for 3 to 4 minutes, with the lid closed as much as possible but turning once, until each side is soft when gently pressed. Carefully remove the cheese and allow it to rest for about 2 minutes. Meanwhile, grill the bread slices over **direct medium heat** for about 1 minute until they are lightly toasted on one side only. By grilling only one side of the bread it ensures a nice sturdy base for the melted cheese and salsa.

5. Arrange the cheese and grilled bread on a serving plate or tray. Cut the string and discard it. Pull the vine leaves open to reveal the cheese inside. Be sure to do this just before serving as the cheese begins to ooze out as soon as you remove the vine leaves. Top the cheese with some of the grape salsa or serve it alongside in a bowl. Use spoons to scoop up cheese and salsa, and place on slices of grilled bread.

RESOURCES

BARBECUING GUIDES AND TIPS

RECIPES

RUBS

A rub is a mixture of spices, herbs and other seasonings (often including sugar) that can quickly give a boost of flavours to foods before barbecuing. The following pages provide some mighty good examples, along with recommendations for which foods they complement, but dare to be different. One of the steps towards developing your own style at the barbecue is to concoct a signature rub recipe or two. Only you will know exactly what ingredients are blended in your special jar of 'magic dust'.

A word about freshness: ground spices lose their aromas in a matter of months (8 to 10 months maximum). If you have been holding on to a little jar of coriander for years, waiting to blend the world's finest version of curry powder, forget about it. Dump the old, tired coriander and buy some freshly ground. Better yet, buy whole coriander seeds and grind them yourself. Whatever you do, store your spices and spice rubs in airtight containers away from light and heat, to give them a long, aromatic life.

HOW LONG?

If you leave a rub on for a long time, the seasonings intermingle with the juices in the meat and produce more pronounced flavours, as well as a crust. This is good to a point, but a rub with a lot of salt and sugar will draw moisture out of the meat over time, making the meat tastier, yes, but also drier. So how long should you use a rub? Here are some guidelines.

1 TO 15 MINUTES	Small foods, such as shellfish, cubed meat for kebabs and vegetables
15 TO 30 MINUTES	Thin cuts of boneless meat, such as chicken breasts, fish fillets, pork fillet, chops and steaks
30 TO 90 MINUTES	Thicker cuts of boneless or bone-in meat, such as leg of lamb, whole chickens and beef joints
2 TO 8 HOURS	Big or tough cuts of meat, such as racks of ribs, whole gammons, pork shoulders and turkeys

CLASSIC BARBECUE SPICE RUB

MAKES: ABOUT 5 TABLESPOONS

4 teaspoons sea salt
2 teaspoons pure chilli powder
2 teaspoons light brown sugar
2 teaspoons garlic granules
2 teaspoons paprika
1 teaspoon celery seeds
1 teaspoon ground cumin
½ teaspoon freshly ground black pepper

CHICKEN AND SEAFOOD RUB

MAKES: ABOUT 4½ TABLESPOONS

4 teaspoons onion granules
4 teaspoons garlic granules
1 tablespoon sea salt
2 teaspoons chilli con carne seasoning
2 teaspoons freshly ground black pepper

CRACKED PEPPER RUB

MAKES: ABOUT 1½ TABLESPOONS

1 teaspoon whole black peppercorns
1 teaspoon mustard seeds
1 teaspoon paprika
½ teaspoon garlic granules
½ teaspoon sea salt
½ teaspoon light brown sugar
⅛ teaspoon ground cayenne pepper

Crush the black peppercorns and mustard seed in a
spice mill or using a mortar and pestle. Transfer to a
small bowl and combine with the remaining ingredients.

CAJUN RUB

MAKES: ABOUT 3 TABLESPOONS

2 teaspoons finely chopped thyme
1½ teaspoons sea salt
1 teaspoon garlic granules
1 teaspoon onion granules
1 teaspoon paprika
1 teaspoon light brown sugar
¾ teaspoon freshly ground black pepper
¼ teaspoon ground cayenne pepper

PORK RUB

MAKES: ABOUT 2½ TABLESPOONS

2 teaspoons pure chilli powder
2 teaspoons freshly ground black pepper
2 teaspoons sea salt
2 teaspoons ground cumin
2 teaspoons dried oregano
1 teaspoon garlic granules

BEEF RUB

MAKES: ABOUT 4 TABLESPOONS

4 teaspoons sea salt
1 tablespoon pure chilli powder
1 tablespoon onion granules
1½ teaspoons garlic granules
1 teaspoon paprika
1 teaspoon dried marjoram
½ teaspoon ground cumin
½ teaspoon freshly ground black pepper
¼ teaspoon ground cinnamon

FENNEL RUB

MAKES: ABOUT 4 TABLESPOONS

3 teaspoons ground fennel seeds
3 teaspoons sea salt
3 teaspoons pure chilli powder
1½ teaspoons celery seeds
1½ teaspoons freshly ground black pepper

KEY	
	RED MEAT
	PORK
	POULTRY
	SEAFOOD
	VEGETABLES

MORE RUBS

SOUTH-WEST RUB

MAKES: ABOUT 3½ TABLESPOONS

2 teaspoons pure chilli powder
2 teaspoons garlic granules
2 teaspoons paprika
2 teaspoons sea salt
1 teaspoon ground coriander
1 teaspoon ground cumin
1 teaspoon freshly ground black pepper

CARIBBEAN RUB

MAKES: ABOUT 6 TABLESPOONS

1 tablespoon light brown sugar
1 tablespoon garlic granules
1 tablespoon dried thyme
2¼ teaspoons sea salt
¾ teaspoon freshly ground black pepper
¾ teaspoon ground allspice

TARRAGON RUB

MAKES: ABOUT 5½ TABLESPOONS

1½ tablespoons dried tarragon
2½ teaspoons sea salt
2 teaspoons freshly ground black pepper
1½ teaspoons dried thyme
1 teaspoon rubbed dried sage, packed

MAGIC RUB

MAKES: 2 TABLESPOONS

1 teaspoon dry mustard
1 teaspoon onion granules
1 teaspoon paprika
1 teaspoon sea salt
½ teaspoon garlic granules
½ teaspoon ground coriander
½ teaspoon ground cumin
½ teaspoon freshly ground black pepper

ESPRESSO-CHILLI RUB

MAKES: ABOUT 4 TABLESPOONS

2 tablespoons dark-roast coffee or espresso beans
2 teaspoons cumin seeds, toasted
1 tablespoon ground ancho chilli powder
1 teaspoon sweet paprika
1 teaspoon sea salt
1 teaspoon freshly ground black pepper

Pulse the coffee beans and cumin seed together in a spice mill until finely ground. Transfer to a small bowl, add the remaining ingredients and stir to combine.

ASIAN RUB

MAKES: ABOUT 5 TABLESPOONS

2 tablespoons paprika
2 teaspoons sea salt
2 teaspoons ground coriander
2 teaspoons Chinese five-spice powder
1 teaspoon ground ginger
½ teaspoon ground allspice
½ teaspoon ground cayenne pepper

KEY	
	RED MEAT
	PORK
	POULTRY
	SEAFOOD
	VEGETABLES

RESOURCES

BABY BACK RIBS RUB

MAKES: ABOUT 8 TABLESPOONS

2 tablespoons sea salt
2 tablespoons paprika
4 teaspoons garlic granules
4 teaspoons pure chilli powder
2 teaspoons dry mustard
2 teaspoons freshly ground black pepper

BAJA FISH RUB

MAKES: 4 TEASPOONS

1 teaspoon pure chilli powder
1 teaspoon ground cumin
1 teaspoon sea salt
½ teaspoon ground cayenne pepper
½ teaspoon ground cinnamon

MEXICAN RUB

MAKES: ABOUT 3½ TABLESPOONS

1 tablespoon ground cumin
1 tablespoon light brown sugar
2 teaspoons sea salt
1 teaspoon pasilla or pure chilli powder
1 teaspoon ground coriander
1 teaspoon dried oregano

NEW WORLD RUB

MAKES: ABOUT 2 TABLESPOONS

1 teaspoon garlic granules
1 teaspoon onion granules
1 teaspoon paprika
½ teaspoon cumin
½ teaspoon dried lemongrass
½ teaspoon dried basil
½ teaspoon dried thyme
½ teaspoon sea salt
¼ teaspoon freshly ground black pepper
⅛ teaspoon ground cayenne pepper

BARBECUE CHICKEN RUB

MAKES: ABOUT 3 TABLESPOONS

1 tablespoon smoked paprika
2 teaspoons dry mustard
1 teaspoon sea salt
½ teaspoon garlic granules
½ teaspoon onion granules
¼ teaspoon ground chipotle chilli

LEMON-PAPRIKA RUB

MAKES: ABOUT 2 TABLESPOONS

2 teaspoons smoked paprika
2 teaspoons sea salt
Finely grated rind of 1 lemon
½ teaspoon garlic granules
½ teaspoon freshly ground black pepper

ALL-PURPOSE RUB

MAKES: ABOUT 2 TABLESPOONS

1 teaspoon pure chilli powder
1 teaspoon garlic granules
1 teaspoon paprika
1 teaspoon sea salt
½ teaspoon ground coriander
½ teaspoon ground cumin
½ teaspoon freshly ground black pepper

PULLED PORK RUB

MAKES: ABOUT 6 TABLESPOONS

2 tablespoons pure chilli powder
2 tablespoons sea salt
4 teaspoons garlic granules
2 teaspoons freshly ground black pepper
1 teaspoon dry mustard

MARINADES

Marinades work more slowly than rubs, but they can seep in a little deeper. Typically, a marinade is made with some acidic liquid, some oil and some combination of herbs and spices. These ingredients can 'fill in the gaps' when a particular meat, fish or vegetable (yes, vegetable) lacks enough taste or richness. They can also give food characteristics that reflect regional/ethnic cooking styles.

If indeed your marinade includes some acidic liquid, be sure to use a non-metallic container. This is a dish or bowl made of glass, plastic, stainless steel or ceramic. A container made of aluminium, or some other metals, will react with acids and add a metallic flavour to food.

HOW LONG?

The right times vary depending on the strength of the marinade and the food you are marinating. If your marinade includes intense ingredients, such as soy sauce, a spirit or hot chillies and spices, don't overdo it. A fish fillet should still taste like fish, not a burning-hot, salt-soaked piece of protein. Also, if an acidic marinade is left too long on meat or fish, it can make the surface mushy or dry. Here are some general guidelines to get you going.

15 TO 30 MINUTES	Small foods, such as shellfish, fish fillets, cubed meat for kebabs and tender vegetables
1 TO 3 HOURS	Thin cuts of boneless meat, such as chicken breasts, pork fillet, chops and steaks, as well as sturdy vegetables
2 TO 6 HOURS	Thicker cuts of boneless or bone-in meat, such as leg of lamb, whole chickens and beef joints
6 TO 12 HOURS	Big or tough cuts of meat, such as racks of ribs, whole hams, pork shoulders and turkeys

BEER MARINADE

MAKES: ABOUT 300 ML (½ PINT)

250 ml (8 fl oz) dark Mexican beer
2 tablespoons dark sesame oil
1 tablespoon finely chopped garlic
1 teaspoon dried oregano
1 teaspoon sea salt
½ teaspoon freshly ground black pepper
¼ teaspoon ground cayenne pepper

JERK MARINADE

MAKES: ABOUT 250 ML (8 FL OZ)

75 g (3 oz) yellow onion, roughly chopped
1 jalapeño chilli pepper, roughly chopped
3 tablespoons white wine vinegar
2 tablespoons soy sauce
2 tablespoons rapeseed oil
½ teaspoon ground allspice
¼ teaspoon garlic granules
¼ teaspoon ground cinnamon
¼ teaspoon sea salt
¼ teaspoon freshly ground black pepper
⅛ teaspoon ground nutmeg

PACIFIC RIM MARINADE

MAKES: ABOUT 500 ML (17 FL OZ)

1 small yellow onion, roughly chopped
   (about 150 g/5 oz)
5 tablespoons soy sauce
4 tablespoons fresh lemon juice
4 tablespoons rapeseed or other vegetable oil
2 tablespoons dark brown sugar
2 tablespoons very finely chopped garlic
½ teaspoon ground allspice

MOJO MARINADE

MAKES: ABOUT 175 ML (6 FL OZ)

4 tablespoons fresh orange juice
3 tablespoons fresh lime juice
3 tablespoons extra-virgin olive oil
2 tablespoons finely chopped fresh coriander
1 tablespoon finely chopped jalapeño chilli,
   including seeds
1 tablespoon very finely chopped garlic
¾ teaspoon ground cumin
½ teaspoon sea salt

LEMON-SAGE MARINADE

MAKES: ABOUT 250 ML (8 FL OZ)

1 tablespoon finely grated lemon rind
4 tablespoons fresh lemon juice
4 tablespoons extra-virgin olive oil
3 tablespoons finely chopped sage
2 tablespoons very finely chopped shallot
2 tablespoons wholegrain mustard
1 tablespoon finely chopped garlic
1 tablespoon freshly cracked black peppercorns

TERIYAKI MARINADE

MAKES: ABOUT 600 ML (1 PINT)

250 ml (8 fl oz) pineapple juice
125 ml (4 fl oz) low-sodium soy sauce
75 g (3 oz) yellow onion, finely chopped
1 tablespoon dark sesame oil
1 tablespoon grated fresh root ginger
1 tablespoon very finely chopped garlic
1 tablespoon dark brown sugar
1 tablespoon fresh lemon juice

GREEK MARINADE

MAKES: ABOUT 125 ML (4 FL OZ)

6 tablespoons extra-virgin olive oil
3 tablespoons red wine vinegar
½ teaspoon very finely chopped garlic
½ teaspoon sea salt
½ teaspoon dried oregano
¼ teaspoon crushed red chilli flakes

MORE MARINADES

MEDITERRANEAN MARINADE

MAKES: ABOUT 125 ML (4 FL OZ)

2 tablespoons extra-virgin olive oil
2 teaspoons paprika
1 teaspoon ground coriander
1 teaspoon ground cumin
1 teaspoon garlic granules
1 teaspoon sea salt
¼ teaspoon freshly ground black pepper

SOUTH-WEST MARINADE

MAKES: ABOUT 250 ML (8 FL OZ)

125 ml (4 fl oz) fresh orange juice
3 tablespoons extra-virgin olive oil
2 tablespoons red wine vinegar
1 tablespoon very finely chopped garlic
2 teaspoons pure chilli powder
1½ teaspoons dried oregano
1 teaspoon sea salt
½ teaspoon freshly ground black pepper
½ teaspoon ground cinnamon

TEQUILA MARINADE

MAKES: ABOUT 450 ML (¾ PINT)

250 ml (8 fl oz) fresh orange juice
125 ml (4 fl oz) tequila
2 tablespoons fresh lime juice
2 tablespoons light brown sugar
2 teaspoons ground cumin
1 jalapeño chilli, cut into 8-mm (⅓-inch) slices

BOURBON MARINADE

MAKES: ABOUT 250 ML (8 FL OZ)

125 ml (4 fl oz) bourbon
4 tablespoons ketchup
2 tablespoons extra-virgin olive oil
2 tablespoons soy sauce
1 tablespoon white wine vinegar
2 teaspoons very finely chopped garlic
½ teaspoon hot sauce, or to taste
½ teaspoon freshly ground black pepper

HONEY-MUSTARD MARINADE

MAKES: ABOUT 250 ML (8 FL OZ)

125 g (4 oz) Dijon mustard
75 g (3 oz) honey
2 tablespoons extra-virgin olive oil
2 teaspoons curry powder
1 teaspoon freshly grated lemon rind
½ teaspoon garlic granules
½ teaspoon sea salt
¼ teaspoon ground cayenne pepper
¼ teaspoon freshly ground black pepper

TARRAGON-CITRUS MARINADE

MAKES: ABOUT 250 ML (8 FL OZ)

4 tablespoons extra-virgin olive oil
4 tablespoons roughly chopped tarragon
Rind and juice of 1 orange
Rind and juice of 1 lemon
2 tablespoons sherry vinegar
2 teaspoons sea salt
1 teaspoon very finely chopped garlic
1 teaspoon grated fresh root ginger
½ teaspoon chilli con carne seasoning
½ teaspoon freshly ground black pepper

KEY

RED MEAT
PORK
POULTRY
SEAFOOD
VEGETABLES

MONGOLIAN MARINADE

MAKES: ABOUT 300 ML (½ PINT)

125 ml (4 fl oz) hoisin sauce
2 tablespoons oyster sauce
2 tablespoons soy sauce
2 tablespoons dry sherry
2 tablespoons rice vinegar
2 tablespoons rapeseed oil
1 tablespoon honey
1 tablespoon very finely chopped ginger
1 tablespoon very finely chopped garlic
½ teaspoon crushed red chilli flakes (optional)

SPICY CAYENNE MARINADE

MAKES: ABOUT 125 ML (4 FL OZ)

4 tablespoons extra-virgin olive oil
2 tablespoons fresh lemon juice
1 tablespoon very finely chopped garlic
2 teaspoons dried oregano
2 teaspoons paprika
1½ teaspoons sea salt
1 teaspoon celery seeds
1 teaspoon ground cayenne pepper

CUBAN MARINADE

MAKES: ABOUT 500 ML (17 FL OZ)

125 ml (4 fl oz) fresh orange juice
125 ml (4 fl oz) fresh lemonade
65 g (2½ oz) yellow onion, finely chopped
4 tablespoons extra-virgin olive oil
2 tablespoons very finely chopped garlic
2 tablespoons dried oregano
2 tablespoons fresh lime juice

CHINESE HOISIN MARINADE

MAKES: ABOUT 175 ML (6 FL OZ)

125 ml (4 fl oz) hoisin sauce
2 tablespoons red wine vinegar
1 tablespoon rapeseed oil
2 teaspoons very finely chopped garlic
1 teaspoon very finely chopped fresh root ginger
1 teaspoon hot sauce, or to taste
1 teaspoon dark sesame oil

TANDOORI MARINADE

MAKES: ABOUT 300 ML (½ PINT)

250 g (8 oz) plain yogurt
1 tablespoon grated fresh root ginger
1 tablespoon paprika
1 tablespoon sunflower or other vegetable oil
2 teaspoons very finely chopped garlic
2 teaspoons sea salt
1½ teaspoons ground cumin
1 teaspoon ground turmeric
½ teaspoon ground cayenne pepper

BARCELONA MARINADE

MAKES: ABOUT 175 ML (6 FL OZ)

5 spring onions, cut into 2.5-cm (1-inch) pieces
50 g (2 oz) basil leaves
3 large garlic cloves
2 serrano chilli peppers, roughly chopped
4 tablespoons extra-virgin olive oil
2 tablespoons sherry vinegar
1 teaspoon sea salt
½ teaspoon freshly ground black pepper

Process the ingredients in a food processor or blender for 1 to 2 minutes until a smooth paste forms.

CORIANDER PESTO MARINADE

MAKES: ABOUT 250 ML (8 FL OZ)

2 tablespoons coarsely chopped walnuts
2 garlic cloves
75 g (3 oz) fresh coriander leaves and tender stalks
25 g (1 oz) flat leaf parsley and tender stalks
½ teaspoon sea salt
¼ teaspoon freshly ground black pepper
4 tablespoons extra-virgin olive oil

Finely chop the walnuts and garlic in a food processor. Scrape down the sides of the bowl. Add the coriander, parsley, salt and pepper and process until finely chopped. With the motor running, slowly add the oil to create a smooth purée.

SAUCES

Sauces open up a world of flavours for barbecuers. They offer us almost limitless ways for distinguishing our food and making it more interesting. Once you have learnt some of the fundamentals about balancing flavours and some of the techniques for holding sauces together, you are ready to develop your own. I've included several styles of sauces on the following pages, some of them featuring a barbecued ingredient or two for greater depth. Find the sauces that suit you and the kind of food you like to barbecue. Return to them a couple times so that you understand how and why they work, then start pushing the parameters. A little more of this. A little less of that. Maybe a few more minutes simmering over the fire. Sauces are playgrounds for discovery. Learn the basics and build from there.

PASILLA BARBECUE SAUCE

MAKES: ABOUT 500 ML (17 FL OZ)

2 tablespoons extra-virgin olive oil
6 garlic cloves, peeled
100 g (3½ oz) red onion, finely chopped
2 dried pasilla chillies, stemmed, deseeded and cut into strips
250 g (8 oz) canned tomatoes with juice, diced
250 ml (8 fl oz) amber Mexican beer
1 tablespoon cider vinegar
1 teaspoon sea salt
½ teaspoon dried oregano
¼ teaspoon freshly ground black pepper

Heat the oil in a small, heavy-based saucepan over a medium heat. Add the garlic and cook for 4 to 5 minutes, turning occasionally, until lightly browned. Add the onion and chillies, cook for about 3 minutes, stirring occasionally. Add the remaining ingredients and bring to the boil, then simmer for 15 minutes. Remove the pan from the heat and allow the mixture to stand for 15 minutes to soften the chillies and blend the flavours. Purée in a blender.

CLASSIC RED BARBECUE SAUCE

MAKES: ABOUT 350 ML (12 FL OZ)

175 ml (6 fl oz) apple juice
137 g (4½ oz) ketchup
3 tablespoons cider vinegar
2 teaspoons soy sauce
1 teaspoon Worcestershire sauce
1 teaspoon molasses
½ teaspoon pure chilli powder
½ teaspoon garlic granules
¼ teaspoon freshly ground black pepper

Mix the ingredients together in a small saucepan. Simmer for a few minutes over a medium heat, and then remove the pan from the heat.

RED CHILLI BARBECUE SAUCE

MAKES: ABOUT 500 ML (17 FL OZ)

4 dried pasilla chillies, about 20 g (¾ oz) total
2 tablespoons rapeseed oil
137 g (4½ oz) ketchup
3 tablespoons soy sauce
2 tablespoons balsamic vinegar
3 garlic cloves, crushed
1 teaspoon ground cumin
½ teaspoon dried oregano
¼ teaspoon sea salt
¼ teaspoon freshly ground black pepper

Remove the stalks and cut the chillies crossways into sections about 5 cm (2 inches) long. Remove most of the seeds. Warm the oil in a frying pan over a high heat. Add the chillies and toast them for 2 to 3 minutes, turning once, until they puff up and begin to change colour. Transfer the chillies and oil to a small bowl, cover with 250 ml (8 fl oz) of hot water and allow the chillies to soak for 30 minutes. Pour the chillies, along with the oil and water, into a blender or food processor. Add the remaining ingredients and process until very smooth.

SASSY BARBECUE SAUCE

MAKES: ABOUT 250 ML (8 FL OZ)

125 ml (4 fl oz) water
137 g (4½ oz) ketchup
2 tablespoons molasses
1 tablespoon white wine vinegar
1 tablespoon Dijon mustard
1 tablespoon light brown sugar
2 teaspoons Worcestershire sauce
½ teaspoon sea salt
¼ teaspoon hot sauce, or to taste
¼ teaspoon garlic granules
¼ teaspoon freshly ground black pepper

Whisk the ingredients together in a small, heavy-based saucepan. Bring to the boil over a medium heat, then reduce the heat and simmer for 10 minutes, stirring occasionally.

ANCHO BARBECUE SAUCE

MAKES: ABOUT 250 ML (8 FL OZ)

40 g (1½ oz) flaked almonds
2 dried ancho chillies, about 15 g (½ oz) total
6 tablespoons fresh orange juice
40 g (1½ oz) roasted red peppers from a jar, roughly chopped
3 tablespoons ketchup
2 tablespoons extra-virgin olive oil
1 tablespoon red wine vinegar
½ teaspoon garlic granules
¼ teaspoon sea salt
¼ teaspoon freshly ground black pepper

Toast the almonds in a frying pan over a medium heat for 3 to 5 minutes, stirring occasionally, until golden brown. Transfer the almonds to a food processor. Remove the stalks from the chillies, make a slit down the side of each one with scissors and remove the veins and seeds. Flatten the chillies and place them in the pan over a medium heat. Use a spatula to hold the chillies flat for 5 seconds, then turn them over and repeat for another 5 seconds. Transfer the chillies to a bowl and allow the chillies to soak in hot water for 15 minutes. Remove the chillies, squeeze out the excess water and then roughly chop. (You should have about 4 tablespoons.) Place the chillies and the remaining ingredients in the food processor with the almonds. Process to create a coarse purée.

MORE SAUCES

CREAMY HORSERADISH SAUCE

MAKES: ABOUT 250 ML (8 FL OZ)

175 ml (6 fl oz) soured cream
2 tablespoons prepared horseradish
2 tablespoons finely chopped flat leaf parsley
2 teaspoons Dijon mustard
2 teaspoons Worcestershire sauce
½ teaspoon sea salt
¼ teaspoon freshly ground black pepper

Thoroughly mix the ingredients together in a bowl. Cover and refrigerate until about 30 minutes before serving.

CHIMICHURRI SAUCE

MAKES: ABOUT 350 ML (12 FL OZ)

4 large garlic cloves
50 g (2 oz) flat leaf parsley
50 g (2 oz) fresh coriander leaves
25 g (1 oz) basil leaves
175 ml (6 fl oz) extra-virgin olive oil
4 tablespoons rice vinegar
1 teaspoon sea salt
½ teaspoon freshly ground black pepper
½ teaspoon hot sauce, or to taste

Very finely chop the garlic in a food processor with the motor running. Add the parsley, coriander and basil and pulse to finely chop the herbs. With the motor still running, slowly add the oil in a thin stream and then add the remaining ingredients.

ROMESCO SAUCE

MAKES: ABOUT 175 ML (6 FL OZ)

2 red peppers
1 garlic clove
25 g (1 oz) whole almonds, toasted
25 g (1 oz) flat leaf parsley
2 teaspoons sherry wine vinegar
½ teaspoon sea salt
⅛ teaspoon ground cayenne pepper
4 tablespoons extra-virgin olive oil

Grill the peppers over **direct medium heat** (180° to 230°C/350° to 450°F) for 12 to 15 minutes, with the lid closed as much as possible but turning occasionally, until they are blackened and blistered all over. Place the peppers in a small bowl, cover with clingfilm and set aside for about 10 minutes, then remove and discard the skins, stalks and seeds. Finely chop the garlic in a food processor. Add the almonds and process until finely chopped. Add the peppers, parsley, vinegar, salt and cayenne and process to create a coarse paste. With the motor running, slowly add the oil and process until you have a fairly smooth sauce.

GARLIC AND RED PEPPER SAUCE

MAKES: ABOUT 150 ML (5 FL OZ)

1 large red pepper
4 tablespoons mayonnaise
2½ tablespoons soured cream
1 tablespoon finely chopped basil
2 teaspoons very finely chopped garlic
2 teaspoons balsamic vinegar
¼ teaspoon sea salt

Grill the peppers over **direct medium heat** (180° to 230°C/350° to 450°F) for 12 to 15 minutes, with the lid closed as much as possible but turning occasionally, until they are blackened and blistered all over. Place the peppers in a small bowl and cover with clingfilm to trap the steam. Set aside for at least 10 minutes, then remove the pepper from the bowl and peel away the charred skin. Cut off the top, remove the seeds and roughly chop the pepper. Place the pepper in a food processor along with the remaining ingredients and process until smooth. Cover and refrigerate until about 20 minutes before serving.

KEY	
	RED MEAT
	PORK
	POULTRY
	SEAFOOD
	VEGETABLES

COOL GREEN CHILLI SAUCE

MAKES: ABOUT 350 ML (12 FL OZ)

3 long Anaheim chillies
3 spring onions, root ends discarded, all the rest
    roughly chopped
15 g (½ oz) fresh coriander leaves and tender stalks
1 small garlic clove
125 g (4 oz) soured cream
125 g (4 oz) mayonnaise
Finely grated rind and juice of 1 lime
¼ teaspoon sea salt

Grill the chillies over **direct high heat** (230° to 290°C/
450° to 550°F) for 3 to 5 minutes, with the lid open
and turning occasionally, until they are blackened and
blistered in spots all over. Remove the chillies from the
barbecue. When cool enough to handle, remove and
discard the stalk ends. Use a sharp knife to scrape off
and discard nearly all the blackened skins. Roughly
chop the remaining parts of the chillies and drop them
into a food processor or blender. Add the spring onions,
coriander and garlic and process to make a coarse
paste, scraping down the side once or twice. Add the
remaining ingredients and process for 1 to 2 minutes to
create a smooth sauce. If it seems too thick, add a little
water. Adjust the seasonings. Cover and refrigerate until
about 30 minutes before serving.

TOMATILLO SALSA

MAKES: ABOUT 500 ML (17 FL OZ)

1 yellow onion, cut into 1-cm (½-inch) slices
Extra-virgin olive oil
10 tomatillos, husked and rinsed, about 250 g
    (8 oz) total
1 small jalapeño chilli, stalk removed
15 g (½ oz) fresh coriander leaves and tender stalks
1 garlic clove
½ teaspoon dark brown sugar
½ teaspoon sea salt

Lightly brush the onion slices on both sides with oil.
Brush the cooking grate clean. Grill the onion slices,
tomatillos and jalapeño over **direct high heat** (230°
to 290°C/450° to 550°F) for 6 to 8 minutes, with the
lid closed as much as possible but turning once or
twice and swapping their positions as needed for even
cooking, until lightly charred. Be sure the tomatillos
are completely soft as you remove them from the
barbecue. Combine the onion slices, tomatillos and
jalapeño in a food processor, along with the remaining
ingredients, and process until fairly smooth. Taste and
adjust the seasonings.

RÉMOULADE

MAKES: ABOUT 175 ML (6 FL OZ)

125 g (4 oz) mayonnaise
1 tablespoon capers, drained and very finely chopped
1 tablespoon sweet pickle relish
1 tablespoon finely chopped tarragon
2 teaspoons very finely chopped shallot
1 teaspoon tarragon vinegar
1 teaspoon very finely chopped garlic
½ teaspoon Dijon mustard
¼ teaspoon paprika
⅛ teaspoon sea salt

Whisk the ingredients together in a bowl. If not using right
away, cover and refrigerate for as long as 24 hours.

BALINESE PEANUT SAUCE

MAKES: ABOUT 300 ML (½ PINT)

175 g (6 oz) smooth peanut butter
125 ml (4 fl oz) stirred coconut milk
2 tablespoons fresh lime juice
2 teaspoons garlic-chilli sauce, such as Sriracha
2 teaspoons fish sauce

Combine the ingredients in a small saucepan over a
very low heat and cook for 3 to 5 minutes, whisking
occasionally, but do not let the sauce simmer, until the
sauce is very smooth. If the sauce seems too thick, whisk
in 1 to 2 tablespoons of water.

TOMATO SALSA

MAKES: ABOUT 500 ML (17 FL OZ)

275 g (9 oz) ripe tomatoes, finely diced
65 g (2½ oz) white onion, finely diced and rinsed in a
    sieve under cold water
2 tablespoons finely chopped fresh coriander
1 tablespoon extra-virgin olive oil
2 teaspoons fresh lime juice
1 teaspoon very finely chopped jalapeño chilli (with seeds)
¼ teaspoon dried oregano
¼ teaspoon sea salt
¼ teaspoon freshly ground black pepper

Mix the ingredients together in a bowl. Allow the salsa to
stand at room temperature for about 1 hour. Drain in a
sieve just before serving.

RED MEAT

WHAT YOU NEED TO KNOW

TASTE AND TENDERNESS ARE TRADE-OFFS

When you pay more for steak, usually you are paying for tenderness. That's why a fillet steak is more expensive than a flank steak, even though the flank steak has more flavour. The pricey and tender steaks, like the porterhouse, the T-bone, the fillet and the sirloin, come from the loin area of a cow, which gets very little exercise while the cow lumbers around. Other steaks, like the flank and the rump, come from parts of the cow that get more of a workout.

FEED MATTERS

It's natural for cows to eat grass. But feeding them grass their whole lives is expensive. It requires moving the animals from pasture to pasture as the seasons change. It's cheaper to herd them in one place and feed them a grain-based diet, which fattens them up faster than grass too, and makes them more tender. Grass-fed cattle are usually leaner and free of the added hormones and antibiotics that grain-fed animals often receive, but the meat is a little tougher and stronger in flavour.

BE A SMART SHOPPER

Whether you shop at a butcher's or a supermarket, it is up to you to know what to look for when buying meat. Be selective and choose the cuts with a coarse marbling or milky white fat. The flesh should be a rich pink or light cherry colour. If you see any with a deep red or brown colour, it could mean those steaks came from older, tougher animals. And the surface should be moist, but not wet or sticky. When you get your purchase home, immediately refrigerate at the bottom of the refrigerator, where there isn't any chance of it cross-contaminating cooked or ready-to-eat foods.

BROWN IS BETTER

Whichever cut of meat you choose, and whatever its quality might be, you'll get the most flavour from it when the surface is cooked to a deep brown colour. When sugars and proteins in the meat are heated by the barbecue, they produce literally hundreds of flavours and aromas. That's why so many recipes in this book involve searing over direct heat. A lot of people will tell you that searing seals in moisture, but that theory has been debunked. Instead, searing develops a layer of incredible flavour and also some nice texture.

Wet meat doesn't sear, it steams, so be sure to pat the surface dry with kitchen paper before cooking. Salt can also affect searing. I recommend waiting to salt red meat until 20 to 30 minutes before cooking, because, over a longer period of time, salt pulls blood and juices from inside the meat, making the surface wet. Salt does, however, need to go on before cooking. Salt added afterwards doesn't penetrate very well.

CUTS OF STEAK

RIB-EYE
A rib-eye steak's abundant internal fat melting into the meat creates one the juiciest steak-eating experiences imaginable. Do yourself a favour: before barbecueing, trim the fat around the perimeter to about 5 mm (¼ inch). That will reduce the chance of flare-ups.

SIRLOIN
Also known in America as a New York strip, a Kansas City strip, a strip loin, a top loin, a shell steak, a club steak, an ambassador steak…it all depends on where you are and who's talking. Regardless of the name, sirloin's a relatively lean cut with a firmer texture than a rib-eye or fillet, but the flavour is great.

FILLET
Pricey and velvety soft, fillets make a nice splurge for special guests, though it's really the tenderness you are buying. The flavour can be a little underwhelming unless you lightly char the outside with a blazing hot barbecue.

PORTERHOUSE
This is the classic American steakhouse steak that features both a sirloin steak and a fillet, separated by a bone. Start these steaks over high heat and finish them on a cooler section of the barbecue so you don't blacken the bone or the meat beside it.

T-BONE
It's just like a porterhouse except the piece of fillet is not as big, because this steak is cut a little further forwards on the animal.

RUMP
These flat, firmly grained steaks bring kebabs quickly to mind because it's so easy to cut them into solid cubes. Pick out the rump steaks with visible marbling and don't take them beyond medium rare.

TRI-TIP
Not widely available, a tri-tip is taken from the sirloin area. It's not so much a steak as it is a skinny roast, but you can cook it like a thick steak. The meat is affordable and very flavourful. Just don't overcook it.

FLANK
You can quickly spot this steak by its flat oval shape and its long, clearly defined grain. It used to be the steak of choice for London broil. Now the flank steak stars in all kinds of barbecue recipes. Minimize the chewy effect of the grain by slicing across it.

SKIRT
Like the flank steak, the coarsely grained skirt steak is cut from the chest area of the animal, so chewiness is an issue. Even so, after barbecueing, it tends to be juicier and richer in flavour than flank steak, especially if you marinate it first.

FEATHER
Normally you would expect a steak cut from the shoulder to be tough, but the flatiron, a.k.a. a top blade steak, is nestled into a tender pocket of the shoulder area, so it's a surprisingly soft exception to the rule. In some cases you'll need to remove a thin vein of gristle running down the centre of a feather.

TYPES OF RED MEAT FOR THE BARBECUE

Tender cuts for barbecuing	Moderately tender cuts for barbecuing	Bigger cuts for searing and grill-roasting	Tougher cuts for barbecuing
Beef fillet (filet mignon steak)	Beef rump steak	Beef whole fillet	Brisket
Beef rib steak/rib-eye steak	Beef flank steak	Beef tri-tip roast	Beef ribs
Beef porterhouse steak	Beef hanger steak	Beef rib roast (prime rib)	
Beef T-bone steak	Beef skirt steak	Rack of veal	
Sirloin steak	Beef feather steak	Rack of lamb	
Lamb loin chop	Veal shoulder blade chop	Leg of lamb	
Veal loin chop	Lamb shoulder blade chop		
	Lamb sirloin chop		

HOW TO FREEZE STEAKS

Cutting steaks from a big piece of meat like a sirloin or a boneless rib roast allows you to make steaks just the right thickness. Barbecue some of the steaks now and freeze the remaining ones for another day. Here's how: the key to freezing a steak properly is to prevent air from touching the surface of the meat. Wrap each steak individually with clingfilm, not butcher paper or aluminium foil, and seal it as tightly as possible. Place the wrapped steaks in a resealable freezer bag and set the freezer as close to -18°C (0°F) as it will go. The colder, the better. Steaks packaged this way will keep very well for about three months. Label them so that you don't forget when to cook them!

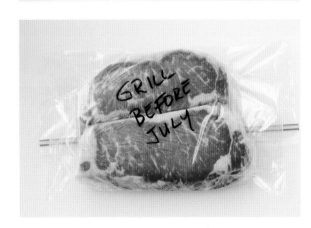

WHEN IS IT DONE?

Recognizing the moment when a big piece of red meat has reached the degree of doneness you want is actually quite simple. Stick the probe of an instant-read thermometer into the thickest part of the meat. When the internal temperature is 5 to 10 degrees below what you ultimately want to eat, take the meat off the barbecue. That's because larger pieces of meat retain quite a bit of heat as they 'rest' at room temperature and they continue to cook.

The Food Standards Agency (FSA) approves eating rare steaks and other whole cuts of beef (and lamb), as long as the outsides have been properly sealed. For other beef products, such as burgers, kebabs, sausages and pork, however, the FSA recommends they should be cooked all the way through with an internal temperature of 70°C (160°F) for more than 2 minutes at their thickest part. Rolled joints made from several pieces of any meat, however, should also not be eaten rare, according the FSA guidelines. Most chefs today tend to cook their meats to a lower internal temperature. The chart below gives you some indication of what professional cooks consider the optimum internal temperatures. Ultimately, it is up to you what degree of doneness you choose.

Checking for the doneness of steaks and chops is a little more difficult with an instant-read thermometer because you need to position the sensing 'dimple' of the probe right in the centre of the meat. It's easy to miss the centre and get an inaccurate reading, so I recommend learning to use the 'touch test.' Most raw steaks are as soft as the fleshiest part of your thumb when your hand is relaxed. As they cook, the steaks get firmer and firmer. If you press your index finger and thumb together and press the fleshiest part of your thumb again, the firmness is very close to that of a rare steak. If you press your middle finger and thumb together, the firmness on your thumb is very close to that of a medium-rare steak.

If you are still not sure of the doneness, take the steak off the barbecue and put the best-looking side (presentation side) facing down on a chopping board. With the tip of a sharp knife, make a little cut in the middle so you can see the colour of the meat inside. If the colour is still too red, put it back on the barbecue. Otherwise, get the rest of the meat off the barbecue.

DONENESS	CHEF STANDARDS
Rare	49° to 52°C (120° to 125°F)
Medium rare	52° to 57°C (125° to 135°F)
Medium	57° to 63°C (135° to 145°F)
Medium well	63° to 68°C (145° to 155°F)
Well done	68°C (155°F) +

BEEF BARBECUING GUIDE

The following cuts, thicknesses, weights and cooking times are meant to be guidelines rather than hard and fast rules. Cooking times are affected by such factors as altitude, wind, outside temperature and desired doneness. Two rules of thumb: cook steaks and kebabs using the direct method for the time given on the chart or to your desired doneness, turning once. Barbecue joints and thicker cuts using the indirect method for the time given on the chart, or until an instant-read thermometer reaches the desired internal temperature. Let joints, larger cuts of meat and thick steaks rest for 5 to 10 minutes before carving. The internal temperature of the meat will rise during this time.

BEEF	THICKNESS/ WEIGHT	APPROXIMATE TIME
Steak: sirloin, porterhouse, rib-eye, T-bone and fillet	1.5 cm (¾ inch) thick	**4 to 6 minutes** direct high heat
	2.5 cm (1 inch) thick	**5 to 8 minutes:** sear 4 to 6 minutes direct high heat, grill 1 to 2 minutes indirect high heat
	3 cm (1¼ inches) thick	**8 to 10 minutes:** sear 6 minutes direct high heat, grill 2 to 4 minutes indirect high heat
	3.5 cm (1½ inches) thick	**10 to 14 minutes:** sear 6 to 8 minutes direct high heat, grill 4 to 6 minutes indirect high heat
	5 cm (2 inches) thick	**14 to 18 minutes:** sear 6 to 8 minutes direct high heat, grill 8 to 10 minutes indirect high heat
Skirt steak	5 mm to 1 cm (¼ to ½ inch) thick	**4 to 6 minutes** direct high heat
Flank steak	750 g to 1 kg (1½ to 2 pounds), 1.5 cm (¾ inch) thick	**8 to 10 minutes** direct high heat
Kebab	2.5 to 3.5 cm (1 to 1½ inch) cubes	**4 to 6 minutes** direct high heat
Fillet, whole	1.75 to 2 kg (3½ to 4 lb)	**35 to 45 minutes:** sear 15 minutes direct medium heat, grill 20 to 30 minutes indirect medium heat
Minced beef burger	1.5 cm (¾ inch) thick	**8 to 10 minutes** direct high heat
Rib roast (prime rib), boneless	2.5 to 3 kg (5 to 6 lb)	**1¼ to 1¾ hours** indirect medium heat
Rib roast (prime rib), with bone	4 kg (8 lb)	**2½ to 3 hours:** sear 10 minutes direct medium heat, grill 2⅓ to 3 hours indirect low heat
Strip loin roast, boneless	2 to 2.5 kg (4 to 5 lb)	**50 to 60 minutes:** sear 10 minutes direct medium heat, grill 40 to 50 minutes indirect medium heat
Tri-tip roast	900 g to 1.25 kg (2 to 2½ lb)	**30 to 40 minutes:** sear 10 minutes direct medium heat, grill 20 to 30 minutes indirect medium heat
Veal loin chop	2. cm (1 inch) thick	**5 to 8 minutes:** sear 4 to 6 minutes direct high heat, grill 1 to 2 minutes indirect high heat

Note: All cooking times are for medium-rare doneness, except minced beef (medium)

LAMB: THE OTHER RED MEAT

When buying lamb, look for meat that is light red (not too dark) and finely grained (not coarse). The fat should be white (not yellow). Lamb chops cut from the rack are quite flavourful and tender. Be sure to trim the fat close to the meat so you don't face flare-ups. The lamb loin also produces very nice chops, with a little bone in the middle of each one, just like a miniature T-bone steak. Even chops from the sirloin and shoulder areas are tender enough for barbecuing, because the animals are almost always younger than one-year-old when they are brought to market. A leg of lamb opens up lots of possibilities, too, including grill-roasting it over indirect heat or cutting the meat into cubes for kebabs.

LAMB BARBECUING GUIDE

The following cuts, thicknesses, weights and cooking times are meant to be guidelines rather than hard and fast rules. Cooking times are affected by such factors as altitude, wind, outside temperature and desired doneness. Two rules of thumb: cook chops using the direct method for the time given on the chart or to your desired doneness, turning once.

Barbecue joints and thicker cuts using the indirect method for the time given on the chart, or until an instant-read thermometer reaches the desired internal temperature. Let joints, larger cuts of meat and thick chops rest for 5 to 10 minutes before carving. The internal temperature of the meat will rise during this time.

LAMB	THICKNESS/ WEIGHT	APPROXIMATE TIME
Chop: loin, rib or shoulder	1.5 to 3 cm (¾ to 1½ inches) thick	**8 to 12 minutes** direct medium heat
Leg of lamb, boneless, rolled	1.25 to 1.5 kg (2½ to 3 lb)	**30 to 45 minutes:** sear 10 to 15 minutes direct medium heat, grill 20 to 30 minutes indirect medium heat
Leg of lamb, butterflied	1.5 to 1.75 kg (3 to 3½ lb)	**30 to 45 minutes:** sear 10 to 15 minutes direct medium heat, grill 20 to 30 minutes indirect medium heat
Rib crown roast	1.5 to 2 kg (3 to 4 lb)	**1 to 1¼ hours** indirect medium heat
Minced lamb burger	1.5 cm (¾ inch) thick	**8 to 10 minutes** direct medium heat
Rack of lamb	500 to 750 g (1 to 1½ lb)	**15 to 20 minutes:** sear 5 minutes direct medium heat, grill 10 to 15 minutes indirect medium heat

Note: All cooking times are for medium-rare doneness, except minced lamb (medium).

PORK

PORK BARBECUING GUIDE

The following cuts, thicknesses, weights and cooking times are meant to be guidelines rather than hard and fast rules. Cooking times are affected by such factors as altitude, wind, outside temperature and desired doneness. Two rules of thumb: cook chops and bratwursts using the direct method for the time given on the chart or to your desired doneness, turning once. Barbecue joints and thicker cuts using the indirect method for the time given on the chart, or until an instant-read thermometer reaches the desired internal temperature. Let joints, larger cuts of meat and thick chops rest for 5 to 10 minutes before carving. The internal temperature of the meat will rise during this time.

PORK	THICKNESS/ WEIGHT	APPROXIMATE TIME
Bratwurst, fresh		**20 to 25 minutes** direct medium heat
Bratwurst, pre-cooked		**10 to 12 minutes** direct medium heat
Pork chop, boneless or bone-in	1 cm (½ inch) thick	**5 to 7 minutes** direct high heat
	1.5 cm (¾ inch) thick	**6 to 8 minutes** direct high heat
	2.5 cm (1 inch) thick	**8 to 10 minutes** direct medium heat
	3 to 3.5 cm (1¼ to 1½ inches) thick	**10 to 12 minutes:** sear 6 minutes direct high heat, grill 4 to 6 minutes indirect high heat
Fillet	500 g (1 lb)	**15 to 20 minutes** direct medium heat
Loin roast, boneless	1.25 kg (2½ lb)	**40 to 50 minutes** direct medium heat
Loin roast, bone-in	1.5 to 2.5 kg (3 to 5 lb)	**1¼ to 1¾ hours** indirect medium heat
Pork shoulder, boneless	2.5 to 3 kg (5 to 6 lb)	**5 to 7 hours** indirect low heat
Minced pork burger	1 cm (½ inch) thick	**8 to 10 minutes** direct medium heat
Ribs, baby back	750 g to 1 kg (1½ to 2 lb)	**3 to 4 hours** indirect low heat
Ribs, spareribs	1.25 to 1.75 kg (2½ to 3½ lb)	**3 to 4 hours** indirect low heat
Ribs, country-style, boneless	750 g to 1 kg (1½ to 2 lb)	**12 to 15 minutes** direct medium heat
Ribs, country-style, bone-in	1.5 to 2 kg (3 to 4 lb)	**1½ to 2 hours** indirect medium heat

WHEN IS IT DONE?

The Food Standards Agency recommends that pork should be cooked to an internal temperature of 70°C (160°F), but most chefs today cook it to 65° to 67°C (150° to 160°F), when it still has some pink in the centre and all the juices haven't been driven out. Of course, the doneness you choose is entirely up to you.

The pork chop on the left, with raw meat in the centre, is clearly undercooked. The chop on the right, with a dry, grey appearance, is overcooked. The chop in the middle, with a little bit of pink in the centre, is cooked to 65°C (150°F), which is just right in my opinion. See how the meat gives a little under pressure.

BABY BACK RIBS VERSUS SPARERIBS

Despite the big differences in the size of baby back ribs and spareribs, they are really just two pieces of the same slab of meat. Baby back ribs (bottom of photo) are cut from the top of the ribcage, near the backbone. Spareribs (top of photo) are cut from the bottom of the ribcage, and sometimes they include the brisket, which is a bony piece of meat that hangs from the bottom. The further down the ribcage you go, the meatier the ribs get. That is essentially why spareribs take longer to cook.

WHAT IS A SHINER?

A shiner is an exposed bone on a rack of ribs. It is what unfortunately happens when a butcher cuts too close to the bone. Ribs should be meaty all over, so if you see a rack with shiners at the market, look for something better. Also avoid all ribs with dry edges or yellowish fat. And know that fresh ribs will almost always yield better results than previously frozen ribs.

TYPES OF PORK FOR THE BARBECUE

Tender cuts for barbecuing	Moderately tender cuts for barbecuing	Bigger cuts for searing and grill-roasting	Tougher cuts for barbecuing
Rib chop Loin chop Centre-cut chop Fillet (whole or in medallions)	Sirloin chop Shoulder blade steak Gammon steak	Rack of pork Centre rib roast Centre loin roast Cured gammon Country-style ribs	Baby back ribs Spareribs Shoulder

POULTRY

WHAT TO LOOK FOR IN CHICKEN

Chicken is chicken, right? Not exactly. Most supermarkets carry big national brands, or sometimes supermarkets put their own brands on these mass-produced birds raised in cages. They are low in fat, they cook quickly and they are pretty tender, however their flavour is pretty darn bland. Fortunately, the barbecue provides just what they need. With a little oil, some seasonings and maybe a sauce, they are very good on the barbecue.

Today we are seeing more and more premium chickens available, and usually they are worth their higher price, though not always. Typically, these chickens are from old-fashioned breeds known more for their flavour than their plump breasts and perfectly even shape. Often called 'free-range' chickens, they have access to the outdoors, or at least the freedom to wander indoors. The exercise contributes to firmer, more flavourful meat. Check them out. Any chickens you buy should have skins that fit their bodies well, not spotty or shrivelled or too far overlapping. The colour of the skin says little

about quality, but the smell of a chicken will tell you everything you need to know about freshness. If it smells funny, don't buy it.

How chickens are processed can also affect the quality. Some producers submerge their chickens in chlorinated iced water, which works quickly, but often the process means that the chickens absorb some water to chill them. Another process involves spraying the chickens with chlorinated water and then sending them though long tunnels filled with cold air. The air-chilled chickens absorb less water, which is good. Who wants to pay extra for iced water?

Some chickens, even when they have been properly chilled, carry upsetting bacteria like salmonella. There is no sense in rinsing raw chickens prior to cooking. That would only raise the chances of spreading bacteria around your kitchen. Simply cook your chickens properly and all the dangerous bacteria will be killed.

WHEN IS IT DONE?

The Food Standards Agency recommends cooking poultry until the internal temperature reaches 70°C (160°F), however my recipes give you an internal temperature of 74°C (165°F) with tender, succulent results. Keep in mind that in whole birds the internal temperature will rise 5 to 10 degrees during resting.

Check the thigh meat by inserting the probe of a thermometer into the thickest part (but not touching the bone). If you don't have a thermometer, cut into the centre of the meat. The juices should run clear and the meat should no longer be pink at the bone.

POULTRY BARBECUING GUIDE

The following cuts, weights and cooking times are meant to be guidelines rather than hard and fast rules. Cooking times are affected by such factors as altitude, wind and outside temperature. Two rules of thumb: cook boneless poultry pieces using the direct method for the time given on the chart, turning once. Barbecue whole poultry and bone-in poultry pieces using the indirect method for the time given on the chart or until an instant-read thermometer reaches the desired doneness. Cooking times are for an internal temperature of 74°C (165°F). Let whole poultry rest for 5 to 10 minutes before carving. The internal temperature of the meat will rise by 5 to 10 degrees during this time.

POULTRY	WEIGHT	APPROXIMATE TIME
Chicken breast, boneless, skinless	175 to 250 g (6 to 8 oz)	**8 to 12 minutes** direct medium heat
Chicken thigh, boneless, skinless	125 g (4 oz)	**8 to 10 minutes** direct high heat
Chicken breast, bone-in	300 to 375 g (10 to 12 oz)	**30 to 40 minutes** indirect medium heat
Chicken pieces, bone-in leg/thigh		**30 to 40 minutes** indirect medium heat
Chicken wing	50 to 75 g (2 to 3 oz)	**18 to 20 minutes** direct medium heat
Chicken, whole	1.75 to 2.2 kg (3½ to 4½ lb)	**1 to 1½ hours** indirect medium heat
Cornish game hen	750 g to 1 kg (1½ to 2 lb)	**50 to 60 minutes** indirect high heat
Turkey breast, boneless	1.25 kg (2½ lb)	**1 to 1¼ hours** indirect medium heat
Turkey, whole, unstuffed	5 to 6 kg (10 to 12 lb)	**2½ to 3½ hours** indirect low heat
	6.5 to 7.5 kg (13 to 15 lb)	**3½ to 4½ hours** indirect low heat
Duck breast, boneless	300 to 350 g (10 to 12 oz)	**9 to 12 minutes:** grill 3 to 4 minutes direct low heat, grill 6 to 8 minutes indirect high heat
Duck, whole	2.5 to 3 kg (5½ to 6 lb)	**40 minutes** indirect high heat

SEAFOOD

TIPS TO PREVENT STICKING

CLEAN COOKING GRATES
Use a stainless-steel bristle brush to get the grates really clean.

A LITTLE OIL
Coat the fish on all sides with a thin layer of oil, but don't grease the grates.

HIGH HEAT
Fish comes off the grate after a delicate crust of caramelization develops between the flesh and grate. That requires heat, usually high heat.

A LOT OF PATIENCE
Leave the fish alone. Caramelization happens faster when the fish stays in place on the hot grate. Keep the lid down as much as possible and turn the fish only once.

GOOD TIMING
The first side down on the grates will be the side that eventually faces you on the plate. Cook it a few minutes longer than the second side and it will release more easily and look fabulous on the plate, with picture-perfect grill marks.

HOW TO REMOVE FISH FROM THE COOKING GRATES
If the fillets have skin attached, cook the skin side last. When each fillet is ready to serve, slide a fish slice or spatula between the skin and flesh and then lift each fillet, leaving the skin behind.

WHAT TO LOOK FOR IN FISH

The first thing to know is that firm fish and seafood are easiest to barbecue. The meatier they are, the better they hold together as they cook and as you turn them over. Many tender fish work nicely, too. Though they require a little more care. The chart below features many of your widely available choices. Feel free to substitute within the categories. If you find two fish with similar sizes and textures, just replace one for the other.

TYPES OF FISH FOR THE BARBECUE

Firm fillets and steaks	Medium-firm fillets and steaks	Tender fillets	Whole fish	Shellfish
Swordfish	Monkfish	Striped bass	Red snapper	Prawns
Tuna	Halibut	Bluefish	Striped bass	Scallops
Salmon	Mahi-mahi	Trout	Grouper	Lobster
Grouper	Mackerel		Bluefish	Oysters
Squid	Sea bass		Mackerel	Mussels
	Red snapper		Trout	Clams

WHEN IS IT DONE?

Overcooking fish is a crime. With almost every kind of fish, you should get it off the barbecue before it flakes by itself. You are looking for an internal temperature of 52° to 55°C (125° to 130°F), but that's tough to measure with fillets or steaks, so rely on the internal appearance (the whitish colour of the fish should be opaque all the way to the centre), as well as the times given in the recipes and in the chart below.

SEAFOOD BARBECUING GUIDE

The following types, thicknesses, weights, and cooking times are meant to be guidelines rather than hard and fast rules. Cooking times are affected by such factors as altitude, wind, outside temperature and desired doneness. The general rule of thumb for barbecuing fish: 4 to 5 minutes per 1 cm (½ inch) thickness; 8 to 10 minutes per 2.5 cm (1 inch) thickness.

FISH	THICKNESS/ WEIGHT	APPROXIMATE TIME
Fish, fillet or steak Includes halibut, red snapper, salmon, sea bass, swordfish and tuna	5 mm to 1 cm (¼ to ½ inch) thick	**3 to 5 minutes** direct high heat
	1 to 2.5 cm (½ to 1 inch) thick	**5 to 10 minutes** direct high heat
	2.5 to 3 cm (1 to 1¼ inches) thick	**10 to 12 minutes** direct high heat
Fish, whole	500 g (1 lb)	**15 to 20 minutes** indirect medium heat
	1 to 1.2 kg (2 to 2½ lb)	**20 to 30 minutes** indirect medium heat
	1.5 kg (3 lb)	**30 to 45 minutes** indirect medium heat
Prawn	40 g (1½ oz)	**2 to 4 minutes** direct high heat
Scallop	40 g (1½ oz)	**4 to 6 minutes** direct high heat
Mussel (discard any that do not open)		**5 to 6 minutes** direct high heat
Clam (discard any that do not open)		**6 to 8 minutes** direct high heat
Oyster		**2 to 4 minutes** direct high heat
Lobster tail		**7 to 11 minutes** direct medium heat

VEGETABLES

COOK WHAT'S GROWING AT THE TIME
Vegetables in season locally have big advantages over whatever has been shipped from across the world. They are riper, so they taste better. That means you can cook them simply with great results.

EXPOSE AS MUCH SURFACE AREA AS POSSIBLE
Cut each vegetable to give you the biggest area to put in direct contact with the cooking grates. The more direct contact, the better the flavours will be. For example, choose peppers with flat sides that you can easily slice off the core. The flatter the sides, the more surface area will caramelize on the hot cooking grates.

USE THE GOOD OIL
Vegetables need oil to prevent sticking and burning. Neutral oils like rapeseed oil will do the job fine, but an extra-virgin olive oil provides the added benefit of improving the flavour of virtually every vegetable. Brush on just enough to coat each side thoroughly but not so much that the vegetables would drip oil and cause flare-ups. Season the vegetables generously with salt and pepper (some of it will fall off). For more flavours, marinate the vegetables at room temperature for 20 minutes to an hour in olive oil, vinegar, garlic, herbs and spices.

WHEN IS IT DONE?
I like firm vegetables, such as onions and fennel, to be somewhere between crisp and tender. If you want them softer, cook them a few minutes longer, although watch them carefully for burning. The barbecue intensifies the sweetness of vegetables quickly and that can lead to burning. Cut the vegetables as evenly as you can. A 1 cm (½ inch) thickness is right for most of them.

VEGETABLE BARBECUING GUIDE

Just about everything from artichokes to tomatoes tends to cook best over direct medium heat. The temperature should be somewhere between 180° and 230°C (350° and 450°F). If any parts get a little too dark, turn the vegetables over. Otherwise turn them as few times as possible.

VEGETABLES	THICKNESS/SIZE	APPROXIMATE TIME
Artichoke (300 to 375 g/10 to 12 oz)	whole	**14 to 18 minutes:** boil 10 to 12 minutes; cut in half and grill 4 to 6 minutes direct medium heat
Asparagus	1-cm (½-inch) diameter	**4 to 6 minutes** direct medium heat
Aubergine	1-cm (½-inch) slices	**8 to 10 minutes** direct medium heat
Beetroot (175 g/6 oz)		**1 to 1½ hours** indirect medium heat
Carrot	2.5 cm (1-inch) diameter	**7 to 11 minutes:** boil 4 to 6 minutes, grill 3 to 5 minutes direct high heat
Chilli, sweet	5-mm (¼-inch) slices	**6 to 8 minutes** direct medium heat
Courgette	1-cm (½-inch) slices	**3 to 5 minutes** direct medium heat
	halved	**4 to 6 minutes** direct medium heat
Fennel	5-mm (¼-inch) slices	**10 to 12 minutes** direct medium heat
Garlic	whole	**45 to 60 minutes** indirect medium heat
Mushroom, portabello		**10 to 15 minutes** direct medium heat
Mushroom, shiitake or button		**8 to 10 minutes** direct medium heat
Onion	halved	**35 to 40 minutes** indirect medium heat
	1-cm (½-inch) slices	**8 to 12 minutes** direct medium heat
Pepper	whole	**10 to 15 minutes** direct medium heat
Potato	whole	**45 to 60 minutes** indirect medium heat
	1-cm (½-inch) slices	**14 to 16 minutes** direct medium heat
Potato, new	halved	**15 to 20 minutes** direct medium heat
Spring onion	whole	**3 to 4 minutes** direct medium heat
Squash, acorn (750 g/1½ lb)	halved	**40 to 60 minutes** indirect medium heat
Sweetcorn, husked		**10 to 15 minutes** direct medium heat
Sweetcorn, in husk		**25 to 30 minutes** direct medium heat
Sweet potato	whole	**50 to 60 minutes** indirect medium heat
	5-mm (¼-inch) slices	**8 to 10 minutes** direct medium heat
Tomato, garden or plum	halved	**6 to 8 minutes** direct medium heat
	whole	**8 to 10 minutes** direct medium heat

FRUIT

Barbecuing fruit is much like barbecuing vegetables. Select fruit that's ripe (or almost ripe) and firm, because it will soften on the barbecue. Also, because of its texture, it's a good idea to watch fruit carefully while barbecuing and to turn it occasionally. The sweet succulence of most fruits turns golden brown and delicious on the barbecue, but if left too long in one place, golden brown can turn to black and bitter. To check the colour and doneness, slide a thin spatula or fish slice gently under the fruit and slightly lift.

Warm fruit off the barbecue needs only a scoop of ice cream or frozen yogurt to seal a meal with style. Or use the barbecued fruit to accompany a shortbread biscuit, a wedge of gingerbread or a slice of Madeira cake. Fruit served like this shows all your guests that you've developed the techniques to barbecue almost anything, from starters to desserts.

FRUIT BARBECUING GUIDE

The following types, thicknesses and cooking times are meant to be guidelines rather than hard and fast rules. Cooking times are affected by such factors as altitude, wind and outside temperature. Barbecuing times for fruit will depend on the ripeness of the fruit.

FRUIT	THICKNESS/SIZE	APPROXIMATE TIME
Apple	whole	**35 to 40 minutes** indirect medium heat
	1-cm (½-inch) slices	**4 to 6 minutes** direct medium heat
Apricot	halved, stone removed	**6 to 8 minutes** direct medium heat
Banana	halved lengthways	**6 to 8 minutes** direct medium heat
Nectarine	halved lengthways, stone removed	**8 to 10 minutes** direct medium heat
Peach	halved lengthways, stone removed	**8 to 10 minutes** direct medium heat
Pear	halved lengthways	**10 to 12 minutes** direct medium heat
Pineapple	peeled and cored, 1-cm (½-inch)	**5 to 10 minutes** direct medium heat
Strawberry		**4 to 5 minutes** direct medium heat

BARBECUE MAINTENANCE

A little TLC is all it takes to ensure that you get years of use from your barbecue. Maintenance is the key (consult the owner's manual that came with your barbecue). Each time you use the barbecue, remember to clean the cooking grates. With the barbecue on high (either right before cooking or right after), brush the cooking grates with a long-handled, stainless-steel brush. Be sure to get in between the grates with your brush, too.

MONTHLY MAINTENANCE PLAN FOR GAS BARBECUES

1. When your barbecue is warm, but not hot, use a wet, soapy sponge or cloth to wipe the inside of the lid. This will help keep natural carbon build-up from accumulating inside the lid.

2. Remove the grates and brush the metal bars that shield the burners. A good brush, like the one you use to brush the cooking grates, will work well. This will help to eliminate flare-ups. (If you barbecue often, like I do, you may need to do this a little more frequently than once a month.)

3. Gently clean the burner tubes with a steel brush. Brush side-to-side along the burner tubes and take care not to damage the openings themselves by brushing too hard.

4. Use a plastic putty knife or spatula to scrape the grease from the bottom of the barbecue. If your barbecue has a collection tray, scrape the bits into it, then dispose of the contents of the collection tray.

5. Wash the inside of the barbecue with warm, soapy water. Take care not to get water in the burner tubes.

6. Reassemble, wait a month, and repeat.

MONTHLY MAINTENANCE PLAN FOR CHARCOAL BARBECUES

1. When the barbecue is cold, remove the ash from the bowl. Because the ash naturally contains a small amount of moisture, it is important to get the ash out of the bowl each time you use it and before storing your barbecue. If your barbecue has an ash catcher, empty after each use.

2. Wipe the inside of the bowl with a warm, wet sponge. This will help to keep natural carbon build-up from accumulating inside your barbecue.

MONTHLY MAINTENANCE PLAN FOR ELECTRIC BARBECUES

1. When your barbecue is warm, but not hot, use a wet, soapy sponge or cloth to wipe the inside of the lid. This will help to keep natural carbon build-up from accumulating inside the lid of the barbecue.

2. Remove the grates. Use a plastic putty knife or spatula to scrape the grease from the bottom of the barbecue. If your barbecue has a collection tray, scrape the bits into it, then dispose of the contents of the collection tray.

3. Wipe the inside of the barbecue with a warm, damp sponge, being very careful not to get the heating element wet.

SELECTING YOUR BARBECUE

One of the most valuable skills a good cook learns is the art of substitution. Tuna fillets, for instance, can substitute for mahi-mahi in a pinch, and a T-bone steak will work nicely in place of a porterhouse. When it comes to barbecues, however, there simply is no substitute for quality. After all, the one thing every meal you prepare from this book will have in common is your barbecue.

WHAT TO LOOK FOR IN A GAS BARBECUE

1. Check out the construction and durability. A barbecue is an important purchase and you will own it for years to come. Since most barbecues are kept outside and exposed to the elements, they need to be well made and durable. If you choose a stainless-steel barbecue, look for heavy-gauge construction that will ensure the barbecue will last more than a season or two. A porcelain-enamel finish will also hold up well. Carefully check out the corners to make sure there are no sharp edges. Size up the fit and finish. If a barbecue's doors or frame are misaligned, it may be a reflection of poor design.

2. Lift the lid and kick the tyres. The inner workings and construction of a barbecue are more important than how the barbecue looks on the outside. Lift the lid and see how the barbecue opens and closes. It should have a tight fit and the barbecue shouldn't feel wobbly when you open it. Look for heavy-duty cooking grates that will hold up to years of use.

3. Look at burner placement. Uneven heat is a barbecuer's worst nightmare. A well-designed gas barbecue will have burners placed evenly across the cooking box. Angled metal bars will cover the burners, directing drippings away from the flames and minimizing flare-ups. These bars also serve to distribute the heat evenly across the entire cooking surface.

4. Give yourself room. The cooking grate needs to be big enough to handle the amount food you like to cook, and remember, many recipes call for both direct and indirect heat. Be sure you have the room to move your food from direct to indirect heat any time.

5. Don't be blinded by BTUs. It's a common belief that more is better when it comes to BTUs. Not necessarily so. BTU stands for British Thermal Unit. It's a measure of how much heat it takes to raise one pound of water by one degree Fahrenheit. A gas barbecue burning 35,000 BTUs per hour should reach a searing temperature of around 290°C (550°F), no problem. Unless your cooking area is large, you should be fine with a barbecue with a BTU rating of 35,000 to 40,000 BTUs. More than that and you may be wasting energy.

6. Don't overlook the basics. One of the most important things you should consider when buying a gas barbecue is where the grease and debris will go. Grease is combustible and if it is not channelled away from the inside of your barbecue it could lead to some serious flare-ups. A well-designed system should include a removable grease tray that is accessible from the front of the barbecue. The drip pan itself should be at least a couple of centimetres (inches) deep and should come with disposable liners to make clean-up easier.

7. Be critical of the bells and whistles. These days, many barbecues come with nice added features, such as a side burner or a rotisserie. These options can improve your barbecuing experience, if they are done well. Make sure the side burner has adequate power to do the job or it may be a waste of money. It should also have a hinged cover so that you don't lose valuable cooking space when the burner is not in use. An added benefit of a hinged cover is that it can act as a windshield, improving the burner's performance. If you are buying a barbecue with a rotisserie, check out the motor. A wimpy motor will lead to wimpy performance. You will need a heavy-duty motor to turn larger items like turkey and leg of lamb. And check out the heft of the spit. Again, it needs to be strong enough to hold larger items and should have strong forks to hold the meat in place. Finally, look at the position of the rotisserie. Is the motor or the spit over the side burner? If so, you'll limit your ability to use it when you are rotisserie cooking.

WHAT TO LOOK FOR IN A CHARCOAL BARBECUE

1. Go for one with a lid. Open barbecues, such as hibachis, are fun to use but the design limits your flexibility. Buying a barbecue with a lid broadens your options. When you buy a charcoal barbecue, make sure it has a well-fitting lid, with top and bottom vents for airflow. The lid effectively turns the barbecue into an outdoor oven capable of both direct and indirect cooking. The vents allow you to control the temperature inside.

2. Make sure it's built to last. A good charcoal barbecue should last for years. Look for solid construction and a durable porcelain-enamel finish over thick-gauge metal.

3. Look for great grates. Your charcoal barbecue should have thick, durable grates. Either heavy wire or stainless steel work well. For the serious barbecuer, I recommend a hinged cooking grate that allows you to add more coals while cooking. My favourite way to prepare the Thanksgiving turkey is on my charcoal barbecue, and a hinged cooking grate allows me to easily add coals each hour to maintain even heat.

4. Make sure clean-up is easy. Charcoal is going to produce ash, which can be a mess to clean-up. Therefore I recommend you choose a charcoal barbecue that is designed with a system to push ash from the bottom of your barbecue into a removable ash catcher. After all, the easier it is to clean your barbecue, the more you're going to use it.

ELECTRIC BARBECUES

Until recently, if you lived in a flat that didn't allow propane or charcoal barbecues, your only option was a less-than-stellar electric patio barbecue – or an indoor work surface barbecue. I'm happy to report that technology has improved and now there are new options with much improved performance. Like their gas and charcoal counterparts, electric barbecues should be solid, stable and built to last.

SAFETY

GENERAL NOTES

1. Always read your owner's manual prior to use.

2. Barbecues radiate a lot of heat, so always keep the barbecue at least 1.5 m (5 feet) away from any combustible materials, including the house, garage, deck rails and so on. Combustible materials include, but are not limited to, wood or treated wood decks, wood patios or wood porches. Never use a barbecue indoors or under a covered patio.

3. Keep the barbecue in a level position at all times.

4. Use proper tools with long, heat-resistant handles.

5. Don't wear loose or highly flammable clothing when barbecuing.

6. Do not leave infants, children or pets unattended near a hot barbecue.

7. Use insulated barbecue mitts or oven gloves to protect hands while cooking or adjusting the vents.

GAS BARBECUE SAFETY

1. Always keep the bottom tray and grease catch pan of your gas barbecue clean and free of debris. This not only prevents dangerous grease fires, it deters visits from unwanted animals. (A sprinkle of cayenne pepper is another safe way to discourage animals.)

2. If a flare-up does occur, turn off all burners and move food to another area of the cooking grate. Any flames will quickly subside. Then light the barbecue again. Never use water to extinguish flames on a gas barbecue.

3. Do not line the funnel-shaped bottom tray with foil. This could prevent grease from flowing into the grease catch pan. Grease is also likely to catch in the tiny creases of the foil and start a fire.

4. Never store propane tanks or spares indoors (that means the garage, too).

Keep a fire extinguisher handy in case of a mishap.

5. For the first few uses, the temperature of a new gas barbecue may run hotter than normal. Once your barbecue is seasoned and the inside of the cooking box is less reflective, the temperature will return to normal.

CHARCOAL BARBECUE SAFETY

1. Charcoal barbecues are designed for outdoor use only. If used indoors, toxic fumes will accumulate and cause serious bodily injury or death.

2. Do not add charcoal starter fluid or charcoal impregnated with charcoal starter fluid to hot or warm charcoal.

3. Do not use gasoline, alcohol or other highly volatile fluids to ignite charcoal. If using charcoal starter fluid, remove any fluid that may have drained through the bottom vents before lighting the charcoal.

4. Do not use a barbecue unless all parts are in place. Make sure the ash catcher is properly attached to the legs underneath the bowl of the barbecue.

5. Remove the lid from the barbecue while lighting and getting the charcoal started.

6. Always put charcoal on top of the charcoal grate and not directly into the bottom of the bowl.

7. Do not place a chimney starter on or near any combustible surface.

8. Never touch the cooking or charcoal grate or the barbecue to see if they are hot.

9. Use the hook on the inside of the lid to hang the lid on the side of the bowl of the barbecue. Avoid placing a hot lid on carpet or grass. Do not hang the lid on the bowl handle.

10. To extinguish the coals, place the lid on the bowl and close all of the vents (dampers). Make sure that the vents/dampers on the lid and the bowl are completely closed. Do not use water as it will damage the porcelain finish.

11. To control flare-ups, place the lid on the barbecue and close the top vent about halfway. Do not use water.

12. Handle and store hot electric starters carefully. Do not place starters on or near any combustible surfaces.

13. Keep electrical cords away from the hot surfaces of the barbecue.

FOOD SAFETY TIPS

1. Wash your hands thoroughly with hot, soapy water before starting any meal preparation and after handling fresh meat, fish and poultry.

2. Do not thaw meat, fish or poultry at room temperature. Thaw them in the refrigerator.

3. Use different utensils and preparation surfaces for raw and cooked foods.

4. Wash all plates and cooking utensils that have come into contact with raw meats or fish with hot, soapy water and rinse well with hot water.

5. When resting meats at room temperature before barbecuing, note that room temperature is 18° to 20°C (65° to 70°F). Do not place raw food in direct sunlight or near any heat source.

6. Always barbecue minced meats and poultry to at least 70°C (160°F), the internal temperature recommended by the Food Standards Agency.

7. If a sauce will be brushed on meat during barbecuing, divide the sauce, using one part for brushing and the other for serving at the table. Vigorously boil marinades that were used for raw meat, fish or poultry for at least 30 seconds before using as a baste or sauce.

PROPER BARBECUING FORM

1. Trim excess fat from steaks and chops, leaving only a scant 5-mm (¼-inch) of fat, which is sufficient to flavour the meat. Less fat is a virtual guarantee against flare-ups and makes clean-up easier.

2. A light coating of oil will help brown your food evenly and keep it from sticking to the cooking grates. Always brush or spray oil on your food, not the cooking grates.

3. Keep a lid on it! A Weber® barbecue is designed to cook foods with the lid down. Keeping the lid on allows heat to circulate, cooking food evenly and without flare-ups. Every time you lift/open the lid, except when instructed to in a recipe, you add extra cooking time.

4. Take the guesswork out of barbecuing. Use a thermometer and a timer to let you know when it's time to take food off the barbecue. Checking meats for internal temperatures is the best way to determine when food is properly cooked or when done is about to become overdone.

5. Use the right utensils. Long-handled tools and long insulated barbecue mitts or oven gloves protect you from the heat. Use forks only to lift fully cooked foods from the barbecue and tongs or turners to turn them (forks pierce food and flavourful juices are lost).

6. Remember that cooking times in charts and recipes are approximate and based on 20°C (70°F) weather with little or no wind. Allow more cooking time on cold or windy days, or at higher altitudes, and less in extremely hot weather.

INDEX

TECHNIQUES

INDEX

RECIPES